Praise for *LinkedIn Marketing: An Hour a Day*

"Viveka is an exceptionally knowledgeable LinkedIn and social media trainer. I've had the great pleasure of featuring Viveka several times on my various classes and she always delivers. Not only does she have tremendous expertise on LinkedIn in particular, her teaching style is extremely effective. She has the ability to chunk down and sequence everything you need to know to really optimize and succeed using LinkedIn. In her new book, she is able to bring her skills and voice to the written page. Apply Viveka's teachings in this book and you will get measurable results! Two thumbs way up."

—MARI SMITH, Social Media Thought Leader, author of *The New Relationship Marketing*, and coauthor of *Facebook Marketing: An Hour A Day)*

"In her great new book, Viveka von Rosen, a very well-respected entrepreneur and LinkedIn authority, provides all the information needed to make LinkedIn a valued and highly-profitable part of one's business. Really, this is a complete and thorough, 'soup-to-nuts' guide on how to effectively utilize what is perhaps the world's most well-known online business medium; one with a huge potential that most people are still not tapping. Read this book, follow Ms. von Rosen's sage teachings and watch the quality of your connections, and your income take a sharp turn upwards."

—BOB BURG, coauthor of *The Go-Giver* and author of *Endless Referrals*

"Viveka von Rosen is my absolute go-to person for LinkedIn knowledge. She knows it inside, out, backwards, and forwards and even better, she knows how to explain LinkedIn in simple, easy-to-follow language. Her book is an absolute must for marketers, business owners, consultants, sales professionals, and anyone looking to use LinkedIn to grow their business. I know I learn something amazing every single time I talk to her and now you can get it all in one handy book!"

—ANDREA VAHL, Social Media Consultant, Strategist and Speaker, Co-author of *Facebook Marketing All-in-One for Dummies*

"Studies show that more women than men use social media to do what they do best...connect, network and collaborate. If you're a woman with a message that you want to the world to hear, with a business you want to grow or a movement you want to launch, social media is THE ticket to getting you there. But ladies...Don't limit yourself to Facebook and Twitter. LinkedIn is just as important a platform to get your word out. In her book *LinkedIn Marketing: An Hour A Day*, Viveka von Rosen meets you wherever you are on your journey, bringing you an invaluable roadmap for learning and leveraging LinkedIn in just one hour a day, so you can do what you came her to do...deliver value, make a difference and make your passion profitable! Don't wait another minute...go get *LinkedIn Marketing: An Hour A Day* today!"

—LIORA MENDELOFF, President & Founder, Women Speakers Association

"You can spend an hour a day thinking about your next marketing move or you can spend an hour a day reading this book and make many more trips to the bank to make deposits! I've known Viveka for many years, and her LinkedIn advice never fails to be anything but relevant and practical. By employing even a few of the suggestions in her book you can have a big positive impact in the results you achieve from your social marketing."

—AL LAUTENSLAGER, Author, Guerrilla Marketing in 30 Days

"LinkedIn is a phenomenal resource for business people to connect with each other. And Viveka von Rosen is a phenomenal guide to that central B2B hub. She knows LinkedIn through and through - and has kicked its tires more than a few times. If you have wanted to get up to speed quickly in the most 'connected' space for business people to gather, read this book!"

—LAURIE MACOMBER, CEO, Blue Skies Marketing

Wow! I thought I was using LinkedIn effectively, but after reading Viveka von Rosen's book, I'm really ready to rock it in a much bigger way! LinkedIn Marketing: An Hour A Day not only provides strategy, but it provides actionable tactics to get the most out of the time you invest in LinkedIn. Whether you're new to LinkedIn, or have been using it for a long time, you'll find ways to power up your results. Viveka makes it easy.

—AVA DIAMOND, Keynote Speaker, Author, Founder of Big Impact Speaking.com

If there was ever an authority on getting heard, read, and remembered on LinkedIn, Viveka von Rosen would be that authority. As a Professional LinkedIn Strategist and social media phenom, Viveka does something that not many in her industry do... Listen. Whether you're consuming her in-book brilliance or simply chatting in person, Viveka's love of learning and bringing value to others is second to none!

—BRETT FAIRALL, Creator of WOWsume

"Like many, strategically participating in LinkedIn was on my "learn how to-do" list for way too long. I was on pause simply because I wasn't sure how to move forward. Then I read Linked-In Marketing-An Hour a Day. BAM! I was on track. This book is an unbelievable resource that provides the tangible tools and step by step instructions you need to easily make participation in LinkedIn a strategic business habit. This book has been absolutely essential to my business success, making it one of my top ten resources for reaching potential clients."

—KRIS BOESCH, CEO, Choose People

"Viveka's book is a well structured, pragmatic, do-it-now, get results, piece of art. I'm amazed at the different ways to get value from LinkedIn, ways I would have never imagined."

—ALAN MARTIN, Sr. Account Executive at Oracle Telecoms North America

"When it comes to using LinkedIn, there are only a handful of people who are truly experts and Viveka von Rosen is at the top of the list. Not only is Viveka extremely smart, she knows how to teach and write about using LinkedIn so it's easy to understand and more importantly, easy to implement her tips and tactics so you get the results you want. Viveka is my go-to gal when I need to learn the latest about how to use LinkedIn to boost my visibility and my business."

—DENISE WAKEMAN, Online Visibility Mentor, http://DeniseWakeman.com

LinkedIn®
Marketing
An Hour A Day

LinkedIn®
Marketing

An Hour A Day

Viveka von Rosen

WILEY

John Wiley & Sons, Inc.

Senior Acquisitions Editor: WILLEM KNIBBE
Development Editor: ALEXA MURPHY
Technical Editor: STACY DONOVAN ZAPAR
Production Editor: REBECCA ANDERSON
Copy Editor: ELIZABETH WELCH
Editorial Manager: PETE GAUGHAN
Production Manager: TIM TATE
Vice President and Executive Group Publisher: RICHARD SWADLEY
Vice President and Publisher: NEIL EDDE
Book Designer: FRANZ BAUMHACKL
Compositor: CODY GATES, HAPPENSTANCE TYPE-O-RAMA
Proofreader: SCOTT KLEMP, WORD ONE NEW YORK
Indexer: TED LAUX
Project Coordinator, Cover: KATHERINE CROCKER
Cover Designer: RYAN SNEED
Cover Image: © ROBERT CHURCHILL / iStockPhoto

Dear Reader,

Thank you for choosing *LinkedIn Marketing: An Hour A Day*. This book is part of a family of premium-quality Sybex books, all of which are written by outstanding authors who combine practical experience with a gift for teaching.

Sybex was founded in 1976. More than 30 years later, we're still committed to producing consistently exceptional books. With each of our titles, we're working hard to set a new standard for the industry. From the paper we print on, to the authors we work with, our goal is to bring you the best books available.

I hope you see all that reflected in these pages. I'd be very interested to hear your comments and get your feedback on how we're doing. Feel free to let me know what you think about this or any other Sybex book by sending me an email at nedde@wiley.com. If you think you've found a technical error in this book, please visit http://sybex .custhelp.com. Customer feedback is critical to our efforts at Sybex.

Best regards,

Neil Edde
Vice President and Publisher
Sybex, an Imprint of Wiley

To my parents, who are the ultimate role models. I owe it all to you, Mom and Dad.

To Alan, the SIRI of my soul. And to my tribe: thank you for your support.

Acknowledgments

I have the best parents in the world. Thanks, Mom, for correcting my grammar (still) and never doubting my abilities to achieve any of my goals. Thanks, Dad, for living a life with no boundaries—showing me I could do the same.

Thanks to Alan for preventing me from throwing my Mac through the window. Many times.

Deep appreciation for Laurie Macomber, who educated me on Google and introduced me to LinkedIn. And who is the best besty.

More thank-yous go out:

To Mari Smith, who is the ultimate role model for many of us. Because of you, I knew I could create a career in this crazy industry. And you are part Canadian like me! Coolio!

To Bob Burg, I still see that first interview with you as being the beginning of my true career. You have been an amazing support to me. I am blessed to have you as a friend.

To Miles Austin, Jason Alba, Neal Schaffer, and Joseph Olewitz, who have been amazing mentors and role models. You guys are the most generous people I know!

To Laurie, Ava, Kris, Yael, and Natalie, who have seen me through so much. Every girl needs her pack. Thanks for being mine.

To Steve Cassady, if it weren't for you, the #LinkedInChat would not be around today. Thanks for being such a marvelous co-moderator.

To Willem Knibbe, Alexa Murphy, Pete Gaughan, and Becca Anderson— excellent editors.

To John Hellerman and my amazing PR team at Hellerman Baretz Communications.

And a very special thanks to my most magnificent and wonderful tech editor, Stacy Donovan Zapar, who really should be getting co-author credit on this book. I could not have done this without her knowledge, generosity, time, and general amazingness.

Finally, thanks again to my tribe; my Twitter followers especially, who have been very supportive.

Thank you!

About the Author

Viveka von Rosen is known internationally as the "LinkedIn Expert" and speaks to business owners, corporations, legal firms, and associations on the benefits of marketing with social media, and in particular, LinkedIn.

Her website, LinkedIntoBusiness.com, was a LinkedIn resource blog before LinkedIn even had its own blog. She is also a regular source on LinkedIn for prestigious news outlets such as Mashable.com, TheSocialMediaExaminer.com, Bloomberg Law, and The Miami Herald. She is the host of the biggest LinkedIn chat on Twitter: #LinkedInChat (recently quoted by Mashable as one of the top 10 business blogs) and co-moderator of LinkedStrategies, the largest strategy group on LinkedIn.

Viveka has 26,000-plus first-level connections and a network of over 24 million people on LinkedIn, as well as 45,000-plus followers on Twitter. Her seminars, webinars, and workshops have taught and trained well over 10,000 people.

She was also recently listed as:

- Forbes 10 Most Influential Women in Social Media
- Forbes 50 Most Influential People in Social Media
- TopRank's 25 Women Who Rock Social Media in 2011

Contents

Foreword   *xxiii*

Introduction   *xxv*

Chapter 1   **Get LinkedIn**   **1**

Social Marketing Is Marketing 2
The Theory of Inbound Marketing   3

Understanding LinkedIn 4
The History of LinkedIn   5
Why People Think LinkedIn Isn't a Social Network   7
The Rise of LinkedIn   8

Using LinkedIn 10
How Your Network and Advanced Search Come Together   11
What You Can Do on LinkedIn   11
Types of Profiles   11
Businesses on LinkedIn   17

The Future of LinkedIn 19
Customer Relationship Management   20
Third-Party Apps   21
The LinkedIn Profile   22
Analytics   22

Chapter 2   **Weeks 1–2: Get Started on LinkedIn**   **25**

Week 1: Prepare Your LinkedIn Presence 26
Monday: Find Your Résumé   26
Tuesday: Gather Your Existing Business Documents   26
Wednesday: Compile Your Existing Marketing Materials   27
Thursday: Google Yourself and Create a List of Web References   27
Friday: Review the Executive LinkedIn Profile Questionnaire   28

Week 2: Define Goals and Join LinkedIn 29
Monday: Create Your LinkedIn Account   29
Tuesday: Understand LinkedIn's Features   33
Wednesday: Establish Initial Settings   44
Thursday: Define and Create Goals for Your LinkedIn Presence   55
Friday: Establish Success Metrics for Your Goals   58

Chapter 3   **Weeks 3–6: Ready, Set, Profile**   **67**

Week 3: Nifty Tools and Ninja Tricks for
Creating Your Keyword List 68
Monday: Use LinkedIn's Related Skills   68
Tuesday: Discover Keywords through Google Ads   70
Wednesday: Use LinkedIn's People Search   71
Thursday: Use Thesaurus.com and Dictionary.com   72
Friday: Make Your List   72

Week 4: Optimize Your Profile and Be Findable 73

Monday: Optimizing Your Professional Headline 73

Tuesday: Optimize Your Title Fields 75

Wednesday: Optimize Your Summary Section – Specialties 81

Thursday: Optimize Your Summary – Professional Experience
and Goals 81

Friday: Optimizing Your Interests 83

Week 5: Customize Your Profile to Stand
Out in the Crowd 84

Monday: Personalize Your Public Profile
and Customize Your Websites 84

Tuesday: Customizing Education 85

Wednesday: Customize Groups and Associations 88

Thursday: Customizing Awards 89

Friday: Add Sections: Publications, Licenses, Patents,
Languages, Courses, Volunteer Work 90

Week 6: Utilizing Extra Real Estate 92

Monday: Customize Contact Me 92

Tuesday: Create Rules of Engagement 94

Wednesday: Add LinkedIn Skills & Expertise 95

Thursday: Moving Things Around 96

Friday: Back It Up 98

**Chapter 4   Weeks 7–9: Use Your Company Profile
for Branding and Positioning   101**

Week 7: Creating a Company Profile 102

Monday: Get Started on Your Company Profile 102

Tuesday: Name Your Company 103

Wednesday: Add a Company Description 104

Thursday: Designate Company Administrators 108

Friday: Edit and Revise 109

Week 8: Adding Products and Services 109

Monday: Add Photos, Descriptions, and Specialties 110

Tuesday: Create Offers 111

Wednesday: Add Disclaimers and Employee Promotion 112

Thursday: Add Video and Recommendations 113

Friday: Use Targeted Product and Service Pages 115

Week 9: Company Updates, Analytics, and
Job Postings—Yours and Others...................... 118

Monday: Create Your Own (Targeted) Updates 118

Tuesday: View Your Company Analytics 121

Wednesday: Create Job Postings 123

Thursday: Follow a Company 125

Friday: Explore Other Company Analytics 126

Chapter 5   Weeks 10–15: Creating and Managing a Network That Works   129

Week 10: Using LinkedIn's Add Connections Tool 130

Monday: Decide on a LION or LamB Network 130

Tuesday: Clean Up Your Email List   132
Wednesday: Import Your Outlook, iContacts, or CSV Email List   133
Thursday: Connecting with Email   134
Friday: Send Individual Email Invitations   136

Week 11: Connecting to Strategic Contacts 138
Monday: Create a List of Strategic Connections   141
Tuesday: Identify Potential Connections   142
Wednesday: Write Proper Messages and Invitations   143
Thursday: Contact People You Don't Know   146
Friday: Get Introduced   146

Week 12: Using LinkedIn's People
You May Know Feature 148
Monday: Invite People Using Home Page Suggestions   148
Tuesday: Invite People Using Inbox Suggestions   151
Wednesday: Invite Colleagues and Classmates   151
Thursday: Understand InMail Etiquette   153
Friday: Get TopLinked—People You Don't Know but Should   154

Week 13: Managing Your Network 155
Monday: Tag Your Connections   155
Tuesday: Use the Profile Organizer   158
Wednesday: Manually Organize by PDF   160
Thursday: Use the Outlook Social Connector Or Xobni   161
Friday: Explore Paid Management Tools—
JibberJobber and Salesforce   162

Week 14: Monitoring Your Network 163
Monday: Use Network Statistics   164
Tuesday: Use Your Home Page   165
Wednesday: Monitor Your Connections   167
Thursday: Getting Reports on LinkedIn   168
Friday: Monitor Your Competition   170

Week 15: Giving and Getting Recommendations
from Your Network 172
Monday: Find Recommendations   172
Tuesday: Ask for Recommendations   172
Wednesday: Give Recommendations   174
Thursday: Manage LinkedIn Recommendations   176
Friday: Leverage Non-LinkedIn Testimonials   177

Chapter 6   **Weeks 16–18: Getting Strategic with Groups**   **179**

Week 16: Building Your Network with Strategic Groups . . . 180
Monday: Learn Why Groups Are Important to You   180
Tuesday: Find Groups   182
Wednesday: Decide Which Groups to Join   186
Thursday: Explore Discussions, Polls,
Promotions, Jobs, and More   187
Friday: Consider "Big" Groups   191

Week 17: Creating Relationships with Groups 192
Monday: Understand Group Rules   193

Tuesday: Learn What to Do (and Not Do) in Your Group   195
Wednesday: Manage Your Groups   196
Thursday: Search for Strategic Contacts   198
Friday: Employ Reverse Engineering   201

Week 18: Creating Your Own Group 202
Monday: Name and Set Up Your Group   202
Tuesday: Select a Management Team and Create Group Rules   206
Wednesday: Learn Best Practices for Inviting Members   210
Thursday: Use Templates, RSS Feeds, and Announcements   211
Friday: Group Statistics   216

Chapter 7   Weeks 19–22: Get Strategic with LinkedIn's "Other" Options   219

Week 19: Using LinkedIn Answers 220
Monday: Understand Answers   221
Tuesday: Use Answers to Build Relationships   222
Wednesday: Use Answers to Repurpose SME Materials   224
Thursday: Use Answers for Blog Fodder   225
Friday: Identify Experts on LinkedIn   226

Week 20: Using LinkedIn Events 227
Monday: Learn Best Practices for Event Setup   227
Tuesday: Share Events Through Events App and Updates   231
Wednesday: Use Messages to Share Your Event with Key People   231
Thursday: Use Share Profile to Highlight Your
Speaker and Sharing with LinkedIn Ads   233
Friday: Connect Through Other's Events   234

Week 21: Sharing with Applications 235
Monday: Learn More about Applications   235
Tuesday: Use Box.net   237
Wednesday: Showcase Your Business with SlideShare   240
Thursday: Share with Projects and Teamspaces   242
Friday: Get WordPress or Blog Link   243

Week 22: Exploring Industry-Based and LinkedIn Apps . . . 244
Monday: Explore Apps for Legal, Business,
and Creative Professionals   245
Tuesday: Create an Amazon Reading List   248
Wednesday: Engage Your Audience with Polls   249
Thursday: Organize Your Travel with My Travel   251
Friday: Use Skills   253

Chapter 8   Week 23: Putting It All Together   255

Monday: Use Updates for Inbound Marketing 256
Planning Status Updates Related to Your LinkedIn Goals   256
Planning Campaign-Specific Status Updates   257

Tuesday: Use LinkedIn Signal 259
Creating Your Lists   260
Monitoring Your List   260
Responding to Your Searches   260

Wednesday: Create a Powerful Inbound Marketing
Connections Strategy 263
Create Your Message Worksheet   264
Craft Your Message   264
Sending Your Message   265

Thursday: Showcase Your Skills in Answers 267
Marketing via Best Answers   267
Scheduling Your Blog Using Answers   268

Friday: Understand 3 and 3. 268

Chapter 9   **Optimizing Your Time Using LinkedIn**   **271**

Getting Started on Your Checklist 272

Monthly, Daily, and Weekly Checklists 272

Checklists for Each Day of the Week 278

Chapter 10   **LinkedIn Ads, Labs, Apps, and Tools**   **283**

LinkedIn Ads. 284
Where Are LinkedIn Ads?   285
What Can You Advertise on LinkedIn?   287
How Much Will You Need to Invest?   288
Is It Worth It? (Case Studies)   288

LinkedIn Labs. 289
What Is an API and Why Should You Care?   290
Labs   290

LinkedIn Mobile 292
LinkedIn for Your iPad   292
LinkedIn on Your Smart Phone: iPhone, Blackberry,
Android, and Palm   294

LinkedIn Tools 294
Email Signature   294
Mac Search Widget   296
Outlook Social Connector   296
LinkedIn Widget for Lotus Notes   296
Sharing Bookmarklet   296

LinkedIn Third-Party Applications. 297
CardMunch   297
Here on Biz   297
Connected HQ   298
Rapportive   299
JibberJobber   299
Hachi   299
Cloze   300
Hootsuite   300
BufferApp   300
Grading Tools: Klout, Kred, and PeerIndex   301

Chapter 11 LinkedIn and You: Getting Specific   **303**

LinkedIn and Job Seekers 304
Jason Alba's Tips for Connecting and Engaging   304
Brett Fairall's Tips for Getting Noticed   307

LinkedIn for Entrepreneurs 310
Find High-Traffic, Low-Competition Keywords
Using Google's Keyword Tool   310
Create Subgroups   312
Amazon Reading List   312
Subscribe to SlideShare   313
Consider a Paid Account   314
Other Tools Miles Recommends   314
Final Words of Advice   315

Recruiters, HR Personnel, and Hiring Managers 316
Share Your Contact Information Clearly on Your Profile   316
LinkedIn Recruiter Alternatives   316
"Mine" the Knowledge from Your Own Company   317
Join Local and Big Groups   317
Use Templates   318
Do's and Don'ts for Recruiters   320

Legal Professionals 321
Mistakes to Avoid   322
Ethical Considerations for LinkedIn   324

Women on LinkedIn 326
Get Over the "Little Ol' Me" Syndrome   326
Get a Good Photo   327
Get Video   328
Give Yourself Credit   329
Get Recommendations   330
Final Words   330

Real Estate Professionals. 331
Participate   331
Participate in Groups   331
Brand Yourself   332
Make Use of LinkedIn's Features   332
Share Valuable Content   332
Limit Your Time   332

Nonprofits and LinkedIn. 333
Groups to Join   333
LinkedIn and Nonprofit Tools   333
You Might Want to Pay for LinkedIn   336
Wrapping Up   336

Some Final Tips on LinkedIn for Marketing. 336

Index   *339*

Foreword

"Relationships Matter" is the LinkedIn slogan.

I didn't realize how much relationships mattered until I started my business during the summer of 2006. I depended on relationships to find the core team to build my product, and then relied heavily on finding and nurturing relationships to help spread the word about my products and services.

I didn't use LinkedIn much back then; the tool I had at my disposal was Google. I could find people, but it wasn't until I started using LinkedIn that I could research them and figure out how to best communicate with them. LinkedIn let me learn about a prospect's background and identify talking points, including where they worked, what they did, and what industry they were in.

Such information is difficult to glean from a Google search. LinkedIn had it all in one place!

I started telling my readers to use LinkedIn shortly after I got on LinkedIn. Many said, "Okay, I'm there, now what do I do?" Years later, people ask the same question! That's probably why you bought this book, right?

If you mistakenly thought you could get on LinkedIn and set up a profile, and then you'd get business, you've probably been as disappointed. LinkedIn is a great tool, but it's as useless as a tool left in a closet unless you do certain things.

Viveka's ideas will help you get more out of LinkedIn. She'll take you from beginner through advanced tactics. Following her processes and techniques with consistency will help you find new contacts, be found, have meaningful conversations, develop and nurture professional relationships, and grow your pipeline.

Read this book with a highlighter, and more importantly, put her tactics, techniques, and tips into practice. Then you can join the ranks of people who have increased sales and improved their professional standing through relationships found on LinkedIn.

Good luck!

Jason Alba

Founder of the popular job search organizer, JibberJobber.com

Author of I'm on LinkedIn—Now What???

Introduction

I can't remember a world without social networking. Whatever did we do without Facebook and LinkedIn and Twitter? How did we connect? Set up meetings? Reach our audience? Connect with employees and investors? Oh, right. The phone. And email. And face-to-face meetings. And coffees and networking events. How much, and how little, our world has changed.

I remember the first time I heard about LinkedIn. It was at a networking event I had set up for the members of my business center. I had invited Laurie Macomber, a Web 2.0 expert, to come talk to our entrepreneurs about this crazy new world of interactive web communication. At the very end of the presentation Laurie mentioned an online business-networking site called LinkedIn.

This was early 2006, when Facebook was still a newfangled site for college students, MySpace was scaring the pants of parents, and the only social networking people knew about was Match.com. So the idea of a business-focused social networking site was fascinating to me.

I had managed to double our business in a year with face-to-face networking events (which I still strongly espouse) and thought, "If I can do that in a town of 100,000 people, what can I do with 7 million (the number of LinkedIn members at the time)?" Apparently I was not the only person having these thoughts.

A year later when I joined Twitter and got the username @LinkedInExpert, I realized I better start living up to the name. Eventually I was training and consulting so much on LinkedIn that I had to quit my day job. And I have never looked back.

Every strategy I share with you in this book I have used myself and with clients. There's no magical mystery solution. There's no sophisticated secret formula. This book is here to guide you through the ever-changing landscape of LinkedIn and give you the tools and strategies you need to succeed. I am so excited to be on this journey with you! Together we create a cohesive and powerful strategy you can use to create greater success in your business and personal life. No matter what your business, or reason for being on LinkedIn, it can definitely help move you forward. So, are you ready? Then…ready, set… get LinkedIn!

Who Should Read This Book

Raise your hand if you have been told you *must* be on LinkedIn but are not sure how to get started. Raise your hand if you have a LinkedIn account but have gained little, if any, business from it. Raise your hand if you need to grow your organization—your business, association, church, practice, or nonprofit. This book is for you. It is intended for both LinkedIn newbies and experienced LinkedIn users:

- Salespeople wanting to expand their network and visibility and increase sales, whether for business-to-business or business-to-consumer
- Marketing professionals looking to establish their company's brand
- Job seekers looking for connections to increase their likelihood of gaining employment
- Entrepreneurs hoping to position themselves as experts and gain new clients
- Churches and religious organizations hoping to increase membership
- Artists, authors, and creators hoping to expose their work
- Nonprofit directors and volunteers hoping to increase donations and visibility
- Project managers looking for a way to find and coordinate team members
- Recruiters, HR professionals, and hiring managers looking to find new candidates and employees
- Legal professionals hoping to retain and attract new clients
- Event planners looking for vendors and strategic partners

If you fall into any of these categories, you will find this book useful.

What You Will Learn

Success on LinkedIn requires that you be clear on the reason you are using LinkedIn in the first place, a manageable LinkedIn strategy and diligence. I am not here to create your brand for you or design your marketing strategy (although many of the exercises will help with that as well), but I am going to share with you the tools and strategies I have learned and developed over the years.

In fact, I include the LinkedIn checklists and schedulers I use with my clients as an added bonus to help ensure your success. (Did I mention I sell them for $250 each?) I can't do the work for you, but I can give you the steps you need to take and the tools to get you there.

Note: Throughout this book I will include tips, examples, and exercises that will help you hone your skills and improve your LinkedIn experience and presence.

What You Need

What do you need to get started on mastering LinkedIn marketing?

- A basic understanding of social media and social media marketing

- A clear idea of who you are and what you have to offer the world
- A defined goal for beginning this process
- Access to a computer and the Internet
- The willingness to devote an hour a day to yourself and your business

What Is Covered in This Book

LinkedIn Marketing: An Hour a Day is organized to walk you through every aspect of the LinkedIn platform while showing you how to optimize LinkedIn to increase your exposure, and develop, implement, and optimize a winning LinkedIn marketing strategy.

Chapter 1: Get LinkedIn This chapter introduces the idea of social marketing and LinkedIn:

- Introduces the idea that social marketing is still marketing and that you probably already have the skills you need to succeed with LinkedIn
- Gives you the history of LinkedIn, some useful statistics, and describes where LinkedIn might be heading in the future
- Shares some basic definitions you might need to use LinkedIn more effectively

Chapter 2: Weeks 1–2: Get Started on LinkedIn This chapter is a must for a user new to LinkedIn, but it's also recommended for more experienced users because it covers the basics most people miss when establishing their LinkedIn presence:

- Before getting started, there are some necessary but often ignored steps people should take to prepare them for their journey into LinkedIn.
- One part of the preparation is defining your goals, and this chapter will take you step by step through the process, as well as provide a very useful LinkedIn questionnaire you can use to make your journey easier.

Chapter 3: Weeks 3–6: Ready, Set, Profile This is the chapter to read for creating an optimized, findable, and powerful profile on LinkedIn:

- Getting your keywords so that your profile can get found
- Optimizing your profile with those keywords
- Customizing your profile so you stand out in a crowd
- Using the extra real estate LinkedIn has to offer that most people are unaware of and you can use

Chapter 4: Weeks 7–9: Use Your Company Profile for Branding and Positioning This chapter is all about LinkedIn company profiles: how you can create your own, optimize your existing profile, and strategically follow and analyze other company profiles:

- A closer look at what a company profile can and can't do on LinkedIn so that you can use or create an effective one (and don't make any inadvertent mistakes)
- Instructions for adding your products and services to your company profile

- Information on company updates, analytics, and job postings so that you can begin to work them into your strategy

Chapter 5: Weeks 10–15: Creating and Managing a Network That Works This chapter will guide you through how to find the people you need to connect to, what to do once you find them, when you should connect and when you shouldn't, and what to say when you do reach out.

- Using LinkedIn's Add Connections tool so you don't get in trouble and render LinkedIn useless
- Using the Advanced People search to connect effectively with strategic contacts
- Using LinkedIn's People You May Know feature to safely grow your network
- Monitoring your network to make sure it is growing how and where you want it to grow
- Managing your network so that you can communicate more effectively
- Giving and getting recommendations from your network

Chapter 6: Weeks 16–18: Getting Strategic with Groups In this chapter we will take a look at best practices for both interacting in groups you join as well as the specific step-by-step process for creating and setting up a viable, interesting, and engaging group:

- Building your network with strategic groups to increase visibility and connectability
- Creating relationships with groups through reversed engineering and search features
- Creating your own group for better communications and thought leader positioning

Chapter 7: Weeks 19–22: Get Strategic with LinkedIn's "Other" Options LinkedIn has several tools and applications found on the More tab. In this chapter we'll take a look at:

- LinkedIn Answers
- LinkedIn polls
- LinkedIn skills
- LinkedIn events
- LinkedIn applications
- Third-party applications

Chapter 8: Week 23: Putting It All Together In this chapter we'll look at some of these daily, weekly, and monthly practices producing powerful connections and dramatic increases in business resulting from those relationships:

- Using your updates every day as an inbound marketing tool
- Monitoring your brand and your competition, and creating relationships with LinkedIn Signal

- Creating a powerful inbound marketing connection strategy
- Marketing subject matter expertise through Answers
- Using the "3 and 3 technique"

Chapter 9: Optimizing Your Time Using LinkedIn This chapter will provide you with the checklists I use with my clients.

Chapter 10: LinkedIn Ads, Labs, Apps, and Tools There are several other features that LinkedIn offers that aren't really a part of the user interface. In this chapter you'll learn about:

- LinkedIn Ads
- LinkedIn labs
- LinkedIn third-party applications
- LinkedIn Mobile

Chapter 11: LinkedIn and You: Getting Specific This chapter gives you tips for specific areas:

- Job seekers
- Recruiters
- Legal professionals
- Women
- Entrepreneurs
- Real estate professionals
- Nonprofits

How to Contact the Author

I welcome feedback from you about this book or about books you'd like to see from me in the future. You can reach me by writing to viveka@LinkedIntoBusiness.com. For more information about my work, please visit my website at www.linkedintobusiness.com.

Sybex strives to keep you supplied with the latest tools and information you need for your work. Please check their website at www.sybex.com/go/linkedinhour, where we'll post additional content and updates that supplement this book if the need arises.

Get LinkedIn

Welcome to LinkedIn Marketing: An Hour a Day. It is my intention to share with you not only the features of LinkedIn, but also actionable strategies you can use to create greater business success using this amazing social media platform.

In Chapter 1 you'll look at the origins, not only of LinkedIn, but also of social or inbound marketing. I'll explain why I think LinkedIn has grown into the largest and most influential of business social networks and where it might be going in the future. I'll clarify the different accounts available on LinkedIn as well as the various kinds of businesses that can use it.

Understanding LinkedIn and its features and uses will help you to be more effective in your marketing, in your networking, and in your business.

1

Chapter Contents

Social Marketing Is Marketing
Understanding LinkedIn
Using LinkedIn
The Future of LinkedIn

Social Marketing Is Marketing

Here's the good news. When it comes to marketing with LinkedIn, you do not have to throw the baby out with the bathwater. In fact, many of the skills, tools, and strategies you have developed as a businessperson will not only be applicable to your LinkedIn social media marketing strategy but will be absolutely essential. There may be times when reading this book that you think, "Well, that's not social media marketing, that's commonsense marketing!" And you would be absolutely right. Social media is just another tool that you can add to your business toolbox. It might be the Swiss Army knife of your arsenal, providing many different tools in one, but it is still just a tool you can use. I think people get overwhelmed with the social media platforms themselves, forgetting the most crucial elements of marketing: communication and engagement; listening and sharing (notice which I put first). LinkedIn, like Facebook and Twitter, just gives you a different, sometimes better, sometimes more informed way to communicate with your business audience.

Do you remember your world before social networking? Those ancient days before Facebook, LinkedIn, Pinterest and Twitter? Whatever did we do before social networking? How did we connect? How did we set up meetings? Reach our audience? Connect with employees and investors? How did we communicate before texting, tweets, and status updates? I vaguely remember a piece of ancient technology I used to use before Skype: it was called the phone. And there was that other text-based communications channel called email…as well as those practically prehistoric practices of face-to-face meetings, including coffees and networking events.

I'm being a little sarcastic here to make a point. With the "new" technology and platforms available today, many people forget to use the traditional communication platforms from which they originally built their businesses. Perhaps one of the biggest mistakes people make is only adopting social media to the exclusion of more traditional forms of communication. I'm here to tell you that even though this book is about communicating and marketing with LinkedIn, those traditional tools of the trade—your phone, your email service, your favorite coffee house, trade shows and conferences—will remain an integral part of your business marketing success. When it comes to business communication and marketing, it is amazing to me how much, and how little, our world has changed.

Do you remember the first time you heard about LinkedIn? I remember it clearly. I was the general manager of the Executive Center where we rented office space, full and part time, as well as business services and equipment to solopreneurs, entrepreneurs, and small business owners. I was sitting in one of our conference rooms overlooking beautiful old-town Fort Collins, Colorado, listening to an Internet marketing and copywriting expert, Laurie Macomber of Blue Skies Marketing, speak about Web 2.0 and how the interactivity of the Internet was affecting how we were doing business. Even though the Executive Center had a website and we did some basic brochure type marketing on the Web, I had no idea of the power of web marketing. I learned many things from Laurie that day. Near the end of her presentation, Laurie mentioned this online business networking site called LinkedIn and how she had used it in her move from Manhattan to Fort Collins to find the office space, realtors, vendors, and business contacts she would need in a new city.

> ## Web 2.0
>
> Wikipedia describes Web 2.0 as a "loosely defined intersection of web application features that facilitate participatory information sharing, interoperability, user-centered design and collaboration on the World Wide Web. A Web 2.0 site allows users to interact and collaborate with others in…dialogue as creators of user-generated content in a virtual community, in contrast to websites where users are limited to the passive viewing of content that was created for them. Examples of Web 2.0 are social networking sites, blogs, wikis, video-sharing sites, hosted services, web applications, and mashups."

This was early 2006 when Facebook was still a newfangled site for college students, MySpace was scaring the pants off parents and the only social networking sites that "normal" people knew about was Classsmates.com and Match.com. So the idea of a business-focused social networking site was intriguing to me. Since I had doubled our office business center membership in a year with face-to-face networking events (which I still strongly advocate), I thought, "If I can do that in a town of 100,000 people, what can I do with 7 million people using LinkedIn?" Our business was an interesting combination of business-to-business (B2B), business-to-consumer (B2C), virtual, and brick-and-mortar, so there really were no limits. Apparently I was not the only person having these thoughts. In 2006, LinkedIn soared to 20 million users and it became apparent that this was a social networking site that wasn't going away.

The Theory of Inbound Marketing

There are all kinds of descriptions and theories of inbound marketing. In fact, we have a whole book on it, *Inbound Marketing: Get Found Using Google, Social Media, and Blogs*, co-authored by the "Father" of inbound marketing, Brian Halligan and Dharmesh Shaw (John Wiley & Sons, October 2009). To put it simply, take everything you know about traditional marketing and turn it on its head.

Traditional outbound or push marketing is about sending out (blasting) your message to your potential customers and clients and "interrupting" them in their homes, places of work, and so forth. Traditional marketing tools are TV and radio ads, direct mail, newsletters, coupons, and just about any other form of marketing you and your ancestors experienced up until about 2004. Traditional marketing takes a lot of money, research, and time. Traditional marketing worked in the past because people had to interact with the marketing medium. They had to watch the commercials on TV and listen to ads on the radio. The ads were in our newspapers, in our newsletters, and in our mailboxes.

But then we, as the consumer, started making our own choices. We recorded TV shows and fast-forwarded through commercials. Later the adoption of TIVO and DVR technologies allowed us to skip commercials altogether. We subscribed to XM Radio. We downloaded our own music and created our own playlists. We decided what we wanted to absorb, and in most cases it wasn't the commercials and advertising of products and services we had no interest in.

So began the shift.

Another huge shift was Web 2.0 enabling communities' ability to comment on products or services in a very public manner. We trusted our peers, what they liked or disliked, much more than the advertisements landing on our TV screen that we were no longer even looking at.

In order to grab the attention of their consumers, marketers had to start producing content that was valuable, useful, and interesting to them. They had to start building *relationships* with their consumers. And relationship marketing took on a whole new meaning. Beyond the more traditional definition of relationship marketing as getting to know your prospect on a lunch date or via referral, relationship marketing became about engaging a tribe of like-minded individuals, people who knew, liked, and trusted you enough to buy your product or service.

There's one very positive result of this inversion of the marketing pyramid: Not only is more useful content being shared, but engaging in inbound marketing is markedly less expensive than traditional marketing. Anyone with time, knowledge, passion, and a computer can play!

What does this have to do with LinkedIn? As I mentioned earlier, LinkedIn was built on a platform of relationships. Its mission statement is to "Connect the world's professionals to make them more productive and successful."

Many of the techniques you'll learn in this book have to do with creating and sharing content that your connections and network will find interesting and valuable. I'll share step-by-step techniques, whether you are a beginner or an advanced user, that will help you to more easily engage with the exact people you need to in order to be "more productive and successful."

Understanding LinkedIn

Very simply: LinkedIn is a social networking platform that allows you to connect, engage, and do business with other professionals by making the relationships of your business network visible and by giving you the tools you need to connect with them.

As of this printing, there are almost 200 million business members on LinkedIn and over 2 million company profiles.

LinkedIn is growing by about 100 percent per year. While it will never reach Facebook's or even Twitter's numbers, one has to concede that LinkedIn is a force to be reckoned with. As a business professional, no matter what industry you work within, whether you are a jobseeker, employee or an owner, LinkedIn will probably become an integral part to your business communications, positioning, marketing, and lead generation. Even those not in marketing, PR, sales, and similar fields will find some uses for LinkedIn. (More on that in the final chapter of this book, Chapter 11, "LinkedIn and You: Getting Specific.")

The relationships you build on LinkedIn open the way to new customers and clients, business and referral partners, affiliates and vendors, mentors, advisers and coaches, hiring managers, recruiters, employers and employees. LinkedIn is a channel to increase, not a tool to replace, your networking efforts, and it is an excellent vehicle to facilitate some facets of your marketing and business strategies.

I want to make it clear from the onset that while I think LinkedIn is one of the most powerful tools a business professional can utilize, nothing replaces business referrals and face-to-face meetings. Throughout this book I will share many strategies that you can use to increase your business relationships "the old-fashioned way." Of course, today business is online and immediate, so I will also show you ways of using LinkedIn with recent social marketing strategies.

The History of LinkedIn

According to LinkedIn's "About Us" section (`http://press.linkedin.com/about`), LinkedIn was created in the living room of co-founder Reid Hoffman in December 2002 and was officially launched on May 5, 2003. Hoffman, who is now executive chairman, remained CEO of LinkedIn until 2009.

Hoffman was working at PayPal and conceived the idea with four others, two of whom he had worked with previously to create SocialNet.com (a dating site).

Allen Blue was a Stanford buddy and executive at SocialNet.com, as was Jean-Luc Vaillant. Also in the founder's circle were Eric Ly and Konstantin Guericke. According to LinkedIn legend, on its May 5, 2003 launch date (known to the company as "Cinco de LinkedIn"), Hoffman, Blue, Vaillant, Ly, and Guericke invited 350 of their friends to connect. By the end of May, LinkedIn had a total of 4,500 members in the network. Their "rapid" growth, as well as a focus on recruiting, earned $4.7 million in financing from the well-known Silicon Valley venture capital firm Sequoia Capital. By the end of 2003, LinkedIn's membership had grown to over 81,000 members and they had a staff of 14 employees.

A little different than that other social network created by some college kids in a dorm room... The business minds that conceived LinkedIn were shaped in places like eBay and PayPal, Logitech, IBM, Sun, and Fujitsu. The five men who created LinkedIn all had rich experience in Silicon Valley and had already been fairly successful in their previous business ventures. The foundation of LinkedIn was formed on their business practices and experience.

In December 2008 LinkedIn hired Jeff Weiner, and in June 2009 Weiner changed his title from interim president of LinkedIn to CEO. Weiner had been running the day-to-day operations for about 6 months, during that time achieving record operating and financial results. Prior to LinkedIn, Weiner was an executive in residence at venture capital firms Accel Partners and Greylock Partners. He had also spent over seven years in key leadership roles at Yahoo!.

Reid Hoffman wrote in the blog announcing Jeff's new position: "Jeff's experience building multiple products on a global scale is highly relevant to LinkedIn and will be critical as we continue to grow the LinkedIn professional network around the world." See the announcement here:

http://blog.linkedin.com/2009/06/24/new-linkedin-ceo-jeff-weiner-has-updated-his-profile/

Although never confirmed by LinkedIn Corporate, many people believe Weiner was brought in to take LinkedIn public, and on May 19, 2011—almost 8 years to the date that the company was first launched—LinkedIn executed its initial public offering (IPO).

Today LinkedIn operates the world's largest professional network on the Internet with members in over 200 countries and territories. Sixty percent of LinkedIn members are currently located outside of the United States, and LinkedIn is available in 16 languages: English, Czech, Dutch, French, German, Indonesian, Italian, Japanese, Korean, Malay, Portuguese, Romanian, Russian, Spanish, Swedish, and Turkish.

Some of the latest Worldwide Membership Statistics show LinkedIn has:

- 161m professionals around the world as of March 31, 2012
- 44m+ members in the EMEA region (Europe, Middle East and Africa) as of February 17, 2012
- 34m+ members in Europe as of February 17, 2012
- 9m+ members in the UK as of April 2, 2012
- 3m+ members in France as of November 29, 2011
- 3m+ members in the Netherlands as of December 6, 2011
- 2m+ members in Italy
- 2m+ members in the DACH region (Germany, Austria and Switzerland)
- 3m+ members in Spain as of March 27, 2012
- 1m+ members in Belgium as of September 22, 2011
- 1m+ members in Sweden as of June 20, 2012
- 1m+ members in Turkey as of February 10, 2012

- 25m+ members in Asia and the Pacific as of January 29, 2012
- 15m+ members in India as of May 29, 2012
- 4m+ members in Southeast Asia as of January 29, 2012
- 1m+ members in Indonesia as of February 21, 2012
- 1m+ members in the Philippines as of March 12, 2012
- 5m+ members in Canada as of January 19, 2012
- 8m+ members in Brazil as of May 3, 2012
- 3m+ members in Australia as of March 12, 2012
- As of March 31, 2012, students and recent college graduates are the fastest-growing demographic on LinkedIn.

LinkedIn counts executives from *all* 2012 Fortune 500 companies as members, and its corporate hiring solutions are used by 75 of the Fortune 100 companies. More than 2 million companies have LinkedIn company pages, and there are more than 1 million LinkedIn groups. That's a lot of networking!

Despite these numbers, there are still millions of businesspeople *not* using LinkedIn in their businesses. If you are one of those people, keep reading!

Why People Think LinkedIn Isn't a Social Network

You say "social network" or "social media" and people think Facebook, Twitter, YouTube, Pinterest, and Google+ (usually in that order). Most people associate social media with the sharing of piano-playing cat videos, unfortunate photos of your cousin's last vacation, and narcissistic updates about every move your ex-roommate makes. Despite reams of case studies, research, white papers, and proof to the contrary, there are still people who think social media is a monumental waste of time, with no business or marketing value whatsoever.

If you think social networking has no place in your business world, I encourage you to read Dave Evans' *Social Media Marketing: An Hour a Day* (Sybex, 2008) or any of the social media *For Dummies* books. What I would like to convince you of is LinkedIn's place in the world of social networking and its invaluable place in your business.

In my opinion (whether you asked for it or not) LinkedIn is *the* social network. It was built, after all, on the precepts of professional networking—people connecting with people they know, and using those connections to facilitate other connections and business relationships.

As LinkedIn continues to evolve, it has embraced most of the same applications as Facebook and Twitter. LinkedIn's status updates are almost identical to Facebook status updates—down to the "share, comment, and like" capabilities. And with LinkedIn Signal, the update stream is searchable and much more manageable, in many ways resembling Twitter. You can read more about LinkedIn Signal in Chapter 8, "Week 23: Putting It All Together."

While prolific personal photo and video uploading is not a part of LinkedIn (thank goodness), the sharing of news with LinkedIn Today brings an informational and business-oriented social aspect to the platform.

So while LinkedIn still carries a stigma of being a recruiter or job seeker's network, please take a second look. Whether you are an engineer or a massage therapist, a business owner or a lifelong employee, LinkedIn is a tool you can use in your business.

The Rise of LinkedIn

LinkedIn was not the first business networking site. A UK-based site called Ecademy was founded in 1998, a good five years before LinkedIn. It is one of the longest-standing online business networking sites, with millions of users worldwide. So why did LinkedIn become the biggest business social networking site in the world? There are four reasons:

- LinkedIn doesn't pretend to be anything other than a business networking site.
- LinkedIn's basic (free) account is still very functional.
- LinkedIn has exponential network growth and visibility.
- LinkedIn has a multifield search engine that works.

Let's take a closer look at LinkedIn's advantages now.

Exclusively Business Focused

While Facebook certainly has a strong business presence with more than 37 million "pages" (according to this filing: www.sec.gov/Archives/edgar/data/1326801/000119312512034517/d287954ds1.htm#toc287954_3a) and has made a stab at usurping business social marketing with apps like BranchOut and BeKnown, it is not solely a business-networking site. Even though almost one billion people have a Facebook profile, many business individuals are still wary of Facebook.

Twitter is utilized for both business and personal use. But early on it earned a reputation for being too noisy and having users who shared overly irrelevant information. So while it is a great marketing and PR tool, many businesspeople avoid the platform.

On the other hand, LinkedIn is clearly a business network. There are really no other uses for it. When you start to use LinkedIn you can expect that the people you interact with are also businesspeople, whether you are looking for a vendor, employee, customer, or client. Are there people who abuse the network? Of course. But your chances of finding the right business contact on LinkedIn are much higher than finding them easily and accurately on Pinterest, Twitter, or Facebook.

Functional Free Account

LinkedIn has both a free and several paid memberships (from its basic Business Account at $24.95 to its Recruiter Account that can run in the thousands). What I like about LinkedIn's free account is that it is completely "usable" once you implement a few of the strategies shared in this book. Having a paid account makes searching and communicating on LinkedIn easier, but you don't have to have a paid account to use LinkedIn effectively.

Besides LinkedIn, there are probably hundreds of thousands, if not millions, of online business applications available that you can use to engage your customer base, build relationships, and communicate pertinent information. However, LinkedIn has done a great job of combining numerous business applications and functions into one relatively cohesive platform. LinkedIn becomes the landing site for your résumé, Rolodex, networking, news, and communications platforms.

While there are now many online business social networking platforms (Ryze, Plaxo, Ecademy, Quora, etc.), LinkedIn still offers the most options and interactivity. Even with the recent decreased functionality of the free account, LinkedIn offers its users a more comprehensive, business-focused, and interactive platform than many of the other paid and free networking-based sites.

Exponential Network Growth and Visibility Potential

Nothing compares with LinkedIn when it comes to growing your business network. The reason LinkedIn is so much more than a Rolodex is the very clear path of connection. Whether you upload your contact list, upload business cards from a tradeshow, use the CardMunch app, find someone to connect with in a search, or use one of LinkedIn connection suggestions, LinkedIn will show you the degree to which you are connected (first, second, or third) and who you share a group with. You can even jump into your first-level connections profiles and see whom they are connected to (if they have not turned off that option in Settings). Some third-party applications allow you to see the depth of connection on Twitter and Facebook, but on LinkedIn the level of connection and visibility of connection is built right into the system and is extremely accurate!

Why is this important? Imagine you are looking for the executive director of a local not-for-profit that you wish to offer your vendor services to. When you do a search, you find out that your neighbor is directly connected to the person you wish to contact. Now you can either use LinkedIn's tools or walk across the street and ask for the introduction. Without LinkedIn you might have never "seen" that connection and could still be trying to get past the volunteer at the front desk!

You can read more about finding and growing your network in Chapter 5, "Weeks 10–15: Creating and Managing a Network That Works."

Effective Multifield Search Engine

LinkedIn's search algorithm works. Period. Even with the free account, LinkedIn's advanced search gives you numerous fields to search in:

- Keyword
- First Name
- Last Name
- Location
- Country
- Postal Code
- Title
- Company Name
- School
- Industry
- Relationship
- Language

The basic business paid account includes these additional search fields:

- Company Size
- Seniority Level
- Interested In
- Fortune 1000 Level
- OpenLink

Note: The Premium and Premium+ accounts add even more search fields, but most users find the free or basic business account sufficient.

When you get your search results, you can see exactly how you are connected to the individual you searched for and what you need to do in order to make contact and engage with them. LinkedIn puts its connection tools (Connect, Get Introduced, Send InMail, Send a Message) right there in the LinkedIn member's profile for you to see and use.

You'll learn more about doing an effective search on LinkedIn in Chapter 11.

Using LinkedIn

Before we get into the meat of LinkedIn, let's take a look at why it works and who can use it.

How Your Network and Advanced Search Come Together

One thing I have said from the beginning is "You are only as visible as the size of your network on LinkedIn." (I should probably trademark that!) One of the biggest complaints I get from clients is that LinkedIn just doesn't work. And they are absolutely correct! If your network is too small, then LinkedIn won't work: every time you do a search for a potential employee, client, or vendor, you get a "LinkedIn Member" result and an invitation from LinkedIn to upgrade to a paid account. But there is a way around that: strategically and systematically grow a network that makes you visible, and that makes your connections visible to you. You'll learn more about this strategy in Chapter 5.

What You Can Do on LinkedIn

Almost anything you do in marketing your existing business can be done on LinkedIn. Use LinkedIn to:

- Increase your ability to be known. There are many ways to participate on LinkedIn that will help define your personal and corporate brand. By contributing, giving, and sharing in a positive way, you can develop a good reputation in your target communities.
- Find others. With a big enough network, you can develop the reach you need to search for and find the employees, potential customers, clients, vendors, partners, donors, sponsors, and strategic connections you need to excel at your business.
- Learn and share your knowledge. LinkedIn Answers, Status Updates, and groups are excellent tools to showcase expert advice, position yourself as a thought leader, and learn from other subject matter experts in your industry.
- Connect with LinkedIn group members. There are many exclusive groups that give you access to other members, people who share commonalities.
- Demonstrate your social marketing "savvy." Show you are plugged into current technology. Active participation in LinkedIn tells others you are serious and competent about networking and new technology.

Types of Profiles

LinkedIn is similar to Facebook in that you have to create a personal account (on LinkedIn known as a "professional" account) before you can create a company account or a business account. One question I am always getting asked is: Can or should I create more than one account on LinkedIn?

The short answer is no, mainly because it goes against LinkedIn's end-user agreement (EUA). LinkedIn itself doesn't seem to be monitoring for duplicate accounts, but if another user reports your duplicate profile, LinkedIn will suspend both accounts and, if they are feeling generous that day, ask you to choose the account that you want to keep.

That means all the time and effort you put into creating your "second" account—all the people you invited, all the recommendations you received, all the work you did on writing your profile—will be deleted. I know this for a fact because I created a second account strictly for training purposes (LinkedIn should have known this because the headline said: "This account is for training purposes only") and it was closed down. At the time that account had over 500 connections and 10 recommendations. A lot of effort down the drain.

Some reasons people feel the need to have more than one account are:

- They are a C-level executive at a company but also have their own small venture.
- They might be working for a company but also be considering new options and looking for a job on LinkedIn.
- They might be an entrepreneur with three viable businesses and one start-up.
- They might be a Mom-preneur with a successful day job and a hobby that pays—in a different industry.
- They might be a student with vastly different interests.
- They might be both a professional musician and a teacher.
- They might be both an artist and an attorney.
- They might want a profile to reflect them as a person and a profile to reflect their company (a big no-no in the EUA—they have company profiles for that: www.linkedin.com/company/add/show).

In each of these cases, having more than one account or several different accounts might seem viable. And although some solutions are allowed on LinkedIn (professional profile and company profile, for example), there are many times when people break LinkedIn's EUA without even knowing it.

Some LinkedIn users will knowingly break the EUA:

- They might be a LinkedIn trainer and want a free account so they don't teach their clients how to do something only available on a paid account.
- They might have reached the connection limit and have created a second account to keep growing their network.
- They might be a recruiter seeking confidentiality so they created a secondary bogus account to keep from revealing any telling information about their employer or client.
- They might be a spammer who is knowingly abusing LinkedIn policies and doesn't want to risk getting their "real" account shut down.

Whether you create more than one account knowingly or unknowingly, the result is the same: LinkedIn will suspend both accounts and you will have to delete one. In some extreme cases, LinkedIn might delete both accounts for you.

So let's look at the different types of profiles and accounts on LinkedIn to see which accounts will work best for you and your business.

Professional Profile

Your professional profile is the personal profile you first create when you sign up for LinkedIn. It is from your professional profile that most of your interactions take place. Your professional profile on LinkedIn is "you." It is autonomous. It is the initiator of all other profiles. You can't have another profile on LinkedIn without your professional profile. When I mention "profile" from now on in this book, this is the one I am talking about. See Figure 1.1 for an example.

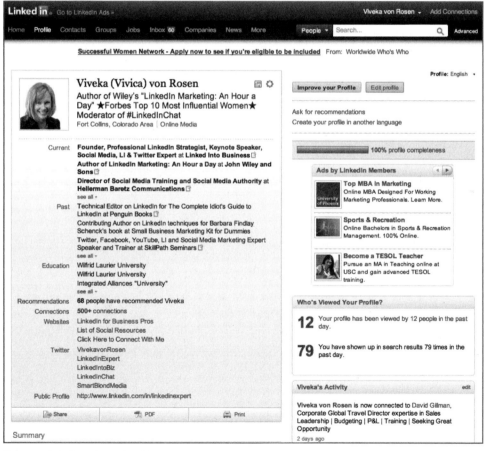

Figure 1.1 LinkedIn professional profile

Your LinkedIn professional profile is discoverable through searches on Google, Bing, and Yahoo! (and any other search engine you might use) as well as through LinkedIn's own search algorithm. You are in complete control over what others see on your profile. Leveraging this profile to showcase your skills and talents ensures the right people and opportunities will find you.

A few ways to differentiate your personal and public profiles:

- Status Update feature
- Links for websites, connections, and Twitter
- "See All" link for experience and education
- Public profile URL

To read more about optimizing and leveraging your profile, read Chapter 3, "Weeks 3–6: Ready, Set, Profile."

Public Profile

When you create your professional profile, LinkedIn automatically creates a more limited public profile that can be seen by anyone who has access to the Internet. Be aware that LinkedIn's default setting is to make everything you add to your profile visible to the general public. While I am very thorough in creating a professional profile full of business and company details, I do recommend limiting your public profile to information you don't mind sharing with the entire world.

When you Google yourself, it is your LinkedIn public profile that shows up. You might want to see what the rest of the world is seeing, and if you are overly exposed, jump into LinkedIn's Public Profile settings and reduce your visibility, as shown in Figure 1.2.

You can make your profile completely private, which will make it unfindable in a web search, or you can turn it on to full view. I recommend customizing the display of individual elements. By checking or unchecking the boxes in this section, you control the parts of your profile you desire to be visible in a web search.

You can tell you are in your public profile (see Figure 1.3) because less information will be visible, you lose hyperlinks, and most obviously, you will be invited to view (*Name*'s) full profile.

For more on LinkedIn settings, read Chapter 2, "Weeks 1–2: Get Started on LinkedIn."

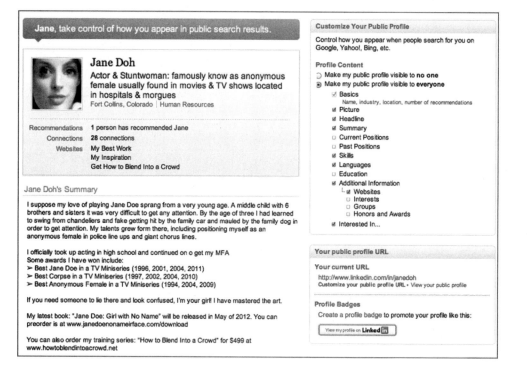

Figure 1.2 Editing Public Profile settings

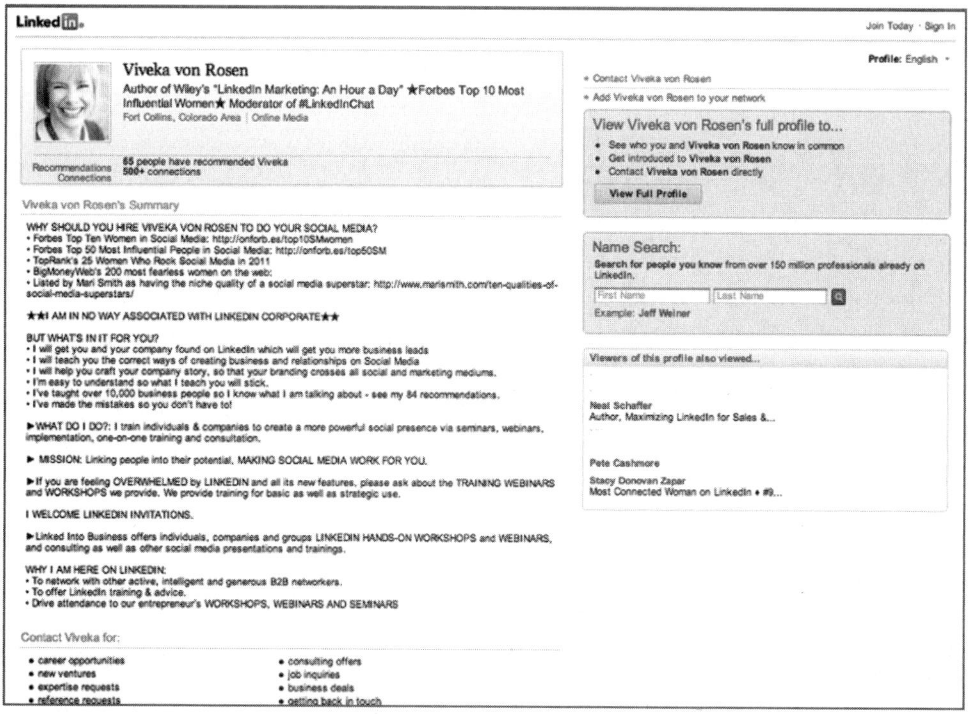

Figure 1.3 LinkedIn public profile

Business Profile

LinkedIn recently added a business profile, which is an account that you have to create in order for you and other people in your company to manage ads on LinkedIn. I only mention it here because it is brand-new and LinkedIn might do something with this administrative account in the future.

> ## Your Professional Profile Is Not a Business Profile
>
> People often mistake a professional profile for a business profile, thinking a division must exist between the person who does the job and the job itself. Your professional profile is where you list your businesses and business expertise for *all* your businesses, past and present.
>
> Some people will use a personal profile to create a business presence, using a logo instead of their picture and a company name instead of their first and last name. This goes against LinkedIn's EUA and I recommend that you don't do it.
>
> Creating a business profile is a common and often innocent error, but much like creating a duplicate account, it is likely that someone will report this profile as inappropriate and LinkedIn will freeze it or even delete it.

Company Profile

A company profile is a profile either you or another company employee can create. Your company profile will be linked to the company name you entered in the Experience section. Only one company profile is allowed per domain name. For instance, if you worked for PepsiCo, you could not create a company profile for Pepsi because the PepsiCo company page has already been created and "attached" to the name@pepsico.com domain. However, if you have your own business and your own name@domainname.com email address, you can certainly create your own company profile. If you have five businesses and five domain names with emails attached, you could create five company profiles.

There is no way, at this time, to create a unique URL in LinkedIn for your company profile, but LinkedIn is pretty good about creating a profile URL that will read www.LinkedIn.com/company/your-company-name.

Unlike Facebook, the company profile is *not* autonomous. However, you can:

- Tell your company's story
- Highlight your products and services
- Share career opportunities
- Share company status updates to targeted followers

For millions of professionals, a company page is a place to:

- Explore companies of interest
- Get the latest company updates and industry news
- Get stock market information
- Research products and services
- Learn about job opportunities

Clear as mud? The differences between professional, public, and company profiles will become clearer as you read through this book. But think of it this way: Your professional profile is you as the person who goes to work in the morning, with all your business knowledge and experience integral to who you are. Your public profile is the business clothes you put on and the business persona that you show the world. And your company profile represents your place of employment and holds within it all the other people who work there, the products and services you sell, and jobs that might be available, as well as the business newsletter.

Businesses on LinkedIn

I want to cover, very briefly, the different types of businesses and business professionals that can use LinkedIn. We will dive much deeper into how you can use LinkedIn as a B2B, B2C, not-for-profit, big business, small business, virtual business, and brick-and-mortar business in each chapter of this book. Just in case you thought LinkedIn is not for you because you are:

- An entrepreneurial service-based businessperson with no storefront
- A massage therapist working out of your home
- A lawyer in a big law firm
- A retailer
- A holistic practitioner
- A business consultant
- The executive director of a not-for-profit
- A student
- A job seeker
- Age 16
- Age 86

Let me try to convince you differently!

B2B and LinkedIn

When speaking to audiences, I'll often ask the folks in the room to raise their hands if they think LinkedIn is just a business-to-business (B2B) networking site, and most of the hands in the room will go up. LinkedIn certainly can be a B2B networking site. When LinkedIn was launched, it was primarily created for and used by the B2B market. But every day more and more B2C companies and businesspeople are using LinkedIn to find and connect to vendors, employees, prospects, and partners.

B2C and LinkedIn

One of the fastest-growing industries on LinkedIn is the "service" industry. I realize this is an awfully broad generalization, but let's look at some numbers.

I recently searched on the following keywords and these were the results:

- Massage therapist: 67,745 members
- Magician: 131,000 members
- School teacher: 60,662 members
- Garbage collector: 496 members
- Dive instructor: 6,900 members
- Virtual or administrative assistant: 641,245 members

There is a place for B2Cs because the "professionals" using LinkedIn need your services. With the strategies and tools I will share with you in this book, you will learn how to attract new clients and customers, build referral and affiliate relationships, find vendors, and position yourself as the very best service-based professional in your industry!

LinkedIn for Large or Small Corporations

Size doesn't matter. Whether you are a solopreneur or the CEO of a Fortune 500, there is a place on LinkedIn for you. You might use it a little differently, but you can still use it to facilitate numerous business transactions such as:

- Promoting new products
- Hosting an event
- Running a poll
- Connecting with old colleagues
- Finding employees
- Attracting new clients

The biggest difference is likely to be the budget you have in using LinkedIn ads, and whether you choose to use the free account or purchase the business or corporate account. And even with the different accounts, much of the functionality stays the same.

LinkedIn for Brick-and-Mortar Businesses

When I started using LinkedIn, I had a brick-and-mortar business—a physical space where people came to do business. If you have a retail store, a law office, a business office, or a salon, you have a brick-and-mortar business. And that is a very exciting thing!

First of all, there is certain legitimacy with a storefront that purely virtual businesses might have a harder time establishing. Let's face it; today it is easy to create a business out of thin air with a Facebook page and an idea. But for those of you who have invested great time, money, and resources into creating a "real" business, you have an edge over those of us without that physical marker.

Why I love LinkedIn for brick and mortar is that you have an even better chance of creating and developing relationships with local businesspeople. People can come to you...get a feel for you and your business. Catch the vibe, as it were. If you have the right kind of physical presence, you can engender a sense of calm and trustworthiness before you even begin your business communications and negotiations.

I'll get into the actual strategies later in the book, but to give you a taste, you can use LinkedIn's Advanced Search to find "local influencers" and then use LinkedIn's tools to contact them and invite them to meet up with you. You can create a local group and establish yourself and your business in LinkedIn's virtual world. You can create amazing referral partnerships with other local businesses. The sky is the limit when you are a brick-and-mortar business using LinkedIn.

The Future of LinkedIn

While I have a few of my own ideas, I decided to ask other LinkedIn members where they saw LinkedIn going. It turns out most people had the same predictions for LinkedIn's future, as well as a similar wish list.

Beyond the inevitability of yearly facelifts (one of the reasons I appreciate LinkedIn is that its designers don't feel the need to change its look and functions every few months), most of the people who responded to my LinkedIn Poll, LinkedIn Question, and #LinkedInChat were hopeful that LinkedIn would focus on making valid connectability among its members easier and more effective.

Note: The #LinkedInChat is a Tweetchat held every Tuesday night on Twitter. Anyone (with a Twitter account) who has questions about LinkedIn, LinkedIn Best Practices, or LinkedIn and Social Media Strategies they would like to share may participate. To learn more about the #LinkedInChat or Tweetchats in general, go to www.linkedintobusiness.com/linkedinchats.

Most of the people who responded hoped LinkedIn would move in the following four directions:

- Increased customer relationship management (CRM) tools
- More open application programming interface (API), resulting in more and better third-party applications
- More visually attractive LinkedIn profile
- Better analytics

Customer Relationship Management

Many of the respondents stated a desire for an interactive scheduling program turning LinkedIn into a true CRM system. While the LinkedIn for Salesforce app is already available to Salesforce users, there was a strong desire by the respondents for a CRM system integrated into the Contacts tab that would help connections to interact more strategically.

```
http://static02.linkedin.com/scds/common/u/pdf/salesforce_overview_
sheet_v1.pdf
```

LinkedIn obtained CardMunch.com in January 2011, so an initial step has been taken. See

```
http://techcrunch.com/2011/01/26/linkedin-buys-business-card-converter-
cardmunch-will-offer-its-services-for-free/
```

Note: CardMunch is a free iPhone app that allows the user to take a photo of a business card, which is then transcribed into an address book. From the CardMunch iPhone interface you can not only see to what degree you are connected to the contact, but also see a "snapshot" of their profile and invite them to connect with a default invitation with a single click. CardMunch just updated its app and now you can sort your contacts alphabetically or by company. I anticipate the ability to make notes or schedule follow-ups, although these features are not available at this time. Nonetheless, it's a great first step toward a more functional LinkedIn CRM system.

LinkedIn also recently purchased ConnectedHQ and is now making it available to the public for free. (It used to have a $9.95/mos price tag.) A truly usable CRM system will help to organize your network, make notations, and connect with and schedule communications with your entire network. At this time both CardMunch and ConnectedHQ only work with your first-level connections, but they are great CRMs to start off with. And did I mention they were both free? As of this printing, ConnectedHQ has *not* been integrated into LinkedIn's actual user interface (UI), but remains a viable third-party application.

Many of the necessary elements are already available with LinkedIn's paid and free memberships:

- You can make notes about your contacts on their profiles. (In case you were wondering, they cannot see your notes.)
- You can export your contacts into a comma-separated values (CSV) file and then into your own CRM system (like ConnectedHQ).
- Connection tagging allows you to classify your network into groupings of people according to a "tag" you assign. (In case you were wondering, they cannot see how you tag them.)
- The Profile Organizer is available with a paid account and allows you to organize your entire network into different folders and make notes on those contacts. The more you pay for a membership, the more folders you get.

So the elements are there. LinkedIn just has to pull them together and provide them, most likely as a paid service, to their membership.

> **Note:** The LinkedIn Recruiter, which can cost thousands of dollars a month, has a very solid CRM system. A "light" version of that would be a great offer for free and lower priced membership users. Nothing like that is offered at this time within the LinkedIn UI.

Third-Party Apps

According to LinkedIn, there are more than 60,000 developers using LinkedIn APIs to create innovative tools and services for professionals, averaging over 2 billion API calls per month. Despite the huge number of developers creating tools that use LinkedIn data, there remain a limited number of "approved" LinkedIn applications found within the platform itself. I foresee greater application utilization and interactivity in LinkedIn's future. In December 2011 LinkedIn launched its Certified Developer's Program—a "best-in-class network of developers to help marketers, agencies and companies leverage the LinkedIn platform to drive engagement with their audiences" (http://press.linkedin.com/node/895). At that time, launch partners included AKQA, Buddy Media, HootSuite Media Inc., and Wildfire, bringing with them a range of social media marketing capabilities, including campaign management, social promotions, enhanced analytics, custom applications, and more.

There is a division of opinions when it comes to more open APIs. While I would love to see more applications available, and I certainly have some thoughts about existing and new applications I would like to see using LinkedIn's API, I also appreciate the tighter security resulting from LinkedIn's more restrictive API. The apps they do have are easy to find and relatively easy to use. You'll find more on these apps and how to use them in Chapter 7, "Weeks 19–22: Get Strategic with LinkedIn's 'Other' Options."

The LinkedIn Profile

With the recent changes to Facebook (Timelines) and due to the massive appeal of Pinterest, I believe a more visually appealing LinkedIn user profile might be on its way. A few more photo opportunities (as long as they are business oriented) would not be amiss.

There seems to be a consensus that LinkedIn must do more with video, perhaps creating a new video application for limited but easier video upload. However, LinkedIn seems to have gone the other way, getting rid of Google Presentations. Now you can only use SlideShare to upload video, but the process is a bit tricky and very buggy. LinkedIn already has the technology on its company pages, allowing the uploading of YouTube video URLs that play on your company page's Products & Services tab. So a similar application within the LinkedIn profile is not out of the question.

Many people expressed (with either desire or distaste) the likelihood that LinkedIn might integrate other social platforms like Facebook and Google+. In some ways social integration seems inevitable—although LinkedIn seems to be heading in the opposite direction as they just dropped the Tweets application. (You can still link your Twitter account to LinkedIn and import your tweets.) While LinkedIn has adopted many social networking conventions—status updates, a better update search using LinkedIn Signal (more about that in Chapter 8), automatic URL shortening, link uploading, commenting, and "liking"—LinkedIn isn't doing much at this time to further integrate with other social platforms. The imported Tweetstream is misused by many people and will probably result in tighter regulations, not more open relationships between platforms.

I hope that LinkedIn will make use of one of Facebook's inventions: the autonomous business page. They are definitely moving in that direction with the company page status update and targeted update feature. I love the customized banner ads and some of the other features, including analytics that LinkedIn has recently added. You'll learn more about company pages in Chapter 4, "Weeks 7–9: Use Your Company Profile for Branding and Positioning."

Note: There seems to be a consensus that LinkedIn must do more with video, perhaps creating a new video application for limited but easier video upload.

Analytics

As businesspeople, we need to know the return on our time and financial investments. If we are spending an hour a day on LinkedIn, is it paying off? If we are paying our assistants to message our connections, is it paying off? Is our time and money paying off? If there is no way to monitor, measure, or analyze our LinkedIn presence and activity, then there is no way of knowing if LinkedIn is worth the investment. Not only are analytics important in business, but also there is a huge trend toward social analytics, and I expect LinkedIn will amp up aspects of its analytics.

Some possibilities are more in-depth analytics on our personal profiles beyond who has viewed us, joined our network, and where they are from. Personal update analytics similar to company update analytics would be a great start since they already have the technology in place. More information about *when* our network is active would be useful (and could be embedded in a robust CRM system). More statistics about the LinkedIn users in our own networks might be nice as well. For more on what you can monitor, measure, and analyze on LinkedIn, read Chapter 2.

With LinkedIn's recent IPO, we can be sure of two things: LinkedIn will change and the site is not going away. It will continue to morph and grow, but at a more stately and reserved rate than Facebook and Twitter. As trends shift the current of the social landscape, LinkedIn will inevitably adjust and integrate. The social hotspots of video, analytics, monitoring, and social CRM will hopefully find a more permanent place within the LinkedIn platform as LinkedIn becomes an even more integral part of its users' social marketing strategies.

Now that you understand the LinkedIn landscape, let's start crafting your winning presence on LinkedIn. So are you ready? Then…ready, set…LinkedIn!

Weeks 1–2: Get Started on LinkedIn

This chapter covers both the initial setup for your LinkedIn professional profile as well as best practice LinkedIn settings for your profile. Even if you have been on LinkedIn for a while, it will be worth your time to read this chapter because LinkedIn has recently made changes and added tools and applications you might not know about.

Specifically, I'll talk about defining your goals for using LinkedIn and getting started by optimizing your LinkedIn presence. I'll walk you through defining and creating your SMART (specific, measurable, attainable, realistic, and timely) goals, establishing metrics, and creating your professional account, and I'll take you on a tour of the home page. LinkedIn's Settings section can be intimidating, so I'll show you what I think are your best options. Finally, I'll share the resources you should have on hand to get started on LinkedIn.

Chapter Contents
Week 1: Prepare Your LinkedIn Presence
Week 2: Define Goals and Join LinkedIn

Week 1: Prepare Your LinkedIn Presence

As a new user, you'll want to collect some information before embarking on creating a LinkedIn profile. If you've been on LinkedIn for some time, it won't hurt to read this section and gather together the information and documents that can help you optimize your existing profile.

Monday: Find Your Résumé

Those of you with an "incomplete profile" (according to LinkedIn) may have noticed a link on the right side of the Edit Profile page that gives you the option to import your résumé. Don't do it! I have worked one on one with hundreds of people and not a single person had any luck uploading their résumé using this tool.

You still will need your résumé. Even if you're not looking for a job and you've been in the same position for 10 years, I recommend digging up that battered old résumé (or a newly polished one) to make your life easier when you begin optimizing your profile on LinkedIn.

I know that many experts recommend that you have a unique résumé for each position that you're applying for. Unfortunately, LinkedIn just isn't set up for that. That's the bad news. The good news is you have full editability on your LinkedIn profile. So if you ever want to change a title or add a position to target a specific employer or niche client, you can easily do so. (Just remember to turn off your activity broadcasts and activity feed first!)

Another thing to consider is that your LinkedIn profile is like your résumé on steroids. You get to put on your LinkedIn profile all that stuff you always wanted to tell people about your job but never had the room for on your old résumé.

I'll talk a lot more about this in Chapter 3, "Weeks 3–6: Ready, Set, Profile." Your résumé is merely a starting point—a seed from which you can grow your LinkedIn profile and presence.

If you have an electronic version of your résumé, I recommend saving it as "*YourName* LinkedIn Résumé." Doing so will allow you to make any necessary changes without destroying the original résumé document.

If the only résumé you have is a hard copy, open a new document, call it "*YourName* LinkedIn résumé," and transcribe the pertinent information. Don't transcribe your entire résumé just yet. But know that this will be a worksheet for your future efforts.

Tuesday: Gather Your Existing Business Documents

You may be pleased to know that I'm not going to ask you to create your LinkedIn presence from scratch. Obviously those of you who've been on LinkedIn for a while will be using this book to polish up your existing profile. But even those of you just starting out on LinkedIn have business documents that you can use to create a better, more well-rounded profile.

I recommend creating a folder on your desktop specifically for the documents you'll be using as you improve and enhance your LinkedIn presence. Mine lives on my desktop and is called "Stuff for LinkedIn Profile." Really.

Browse your desktop, check your filing cabinets (physical and electronic), and scan or copy any business-related documents into this folder. What kind of documents might these be? Any docs that you might want a future client, donor, employee candidate, partner, or employer to see.

You might have brochures, logos, photos, whitepapers, portfolios, testimonials, recommendations, or newsletters. All of these items can be used to create a bigger, better, and more impressive LinkedIn profile.

Make an effort to pull some of that information together right now. And as you come across it in the weeks to come, copy any pertinent files over to this new LinkedIn folder.

Wednesday: Compile Your Existing Marketing Materials

Graphic designers will be familiar with the term *style sheet*. (Style sheets are the way that standards-compliant web designers define the layout, look and feel, and design of their pages.) I want you to create a LinkedIn style sheet. You'll go through all your previous marketing efforts: print ads, brochures, newsletters, ad copy, logos, pictures of your business, and so forth—anything that you (or your marketing team) might have in your marketing file, scan or copy into your "Stuff for LinkedIn" folder. Any traditional media or new media is game for this folder.

While you might not use all of this content, refreshing yourself on previous marketing attempts will set you up to be more successful for your social marketing on LinkedIn.

Do you know the ROI on your previous marketing efforts? Do you have your numbers? What you spent and the results of those expenses and efforts? You'll be starting from a position of power if you know the numbers for your current and previous marketing efforts.

Spend some time reviewing your previous and current marketing materials and spreadsheets.

Thursday: Google Yourself and Create a List of Web References

When was the last time you Googled yourself? Are there some forgotten interviews? Some wonderful references to your business or to you personally? Google yourself and make a comprehensive list of every positive web presence that you can find. And when I say Google yourself, I mean go to Yahoo! and Bing as well.

I created a Microsoft Excel spreadsheet for an easy web presence reference. My spreadsheet has the following:

- The date of the event or mention
- A description
- The URL (linked)
- Miscellaneous information
- Contact information

Now take a look at your own website. If you are an executive or marketing director of a large corporation, make note of every important landing page on your website(s). Large corporations have an edge when it comes to LinkedIn: You can have your many employees highlight different pages of your website when adding websites to their profile. So instead of three websites, you can have as many landing pages as you have employees on LinkedIn.

As a solopreneur, you are it! You'll choose the top three pages of your website or web references to highlight in the My Websites section that will most help "define and shine" your company.

Friday: Review the Executive LinkedIn Profile Questionnaire

You have almost everything you need in place. Now it's time to review your Executive LinkedIn Profile Questionnaire. To download a copy of the questionnaire, go to www.sybex.com/go/linkedinhour.

Once you have downloaded the form, keep a clean copy and then Save As a copy (maybe with the date or your name). I recommend doing the actual writing of your LinkedIn profile in this document. You just never know when LinkedIn might erroneously delete some of your content, you might mistakenly overwrite some of your information, or LinkedIn might even close down your account. If you have this LinkedIn questionnaire already filled out with your pertinent profile information, you are 10 steps ahead of the poor soul who is left with nothing.

Another reason to use the Executive LinkedIn Profile Questionnaire is that you can do a small amount of formatting in a Microsoft Word or Pages document that you can't do in the plain text on your LinkedIn profile page. Once you have formatted a section with bullets and spacing, you can copy and paste that section to your LinkedIn profile.

LinkedIn does not have a grammar or spell check. And even if your browser does have spell check, it won't catch as many errors as your word processing program will. Also, the fields LinkedIn gives you to work within are miniscule. This questionnaire will tell you how many characters you have in each field, which will allow you to fully optimize each section.

Take some time to look over the Executive LinkedIn Profile Questionnaire and fill in what you can. Most of the areas will be extensively covered in the next few chapters.

Week 2: Define Goals and Join LinkedIn

When creating any marketing campaign, you should know why you are doing it. And yet I find many people cobbling a LinkedIn profile together for no other reason than someone told them they should. But you have a huge opportunity here to create a marketing tool that might seriously contribute to the success of your business. So take a few minutes to think about why you are using LinkedIn and come up with some goals and metrics you can measure.

Monday: Create Your LinkedIn Account

For those of you who are brand-new to LinkedIn, now it's time to get started. Even if you have been on LinkedIn for some time, I recommend following along to make sure you have your basics in place.

If you have not yet done so, go to www.LinkedIn.com. You'll be prompted for your name, email address, and password, as Figure 2.1 shows.

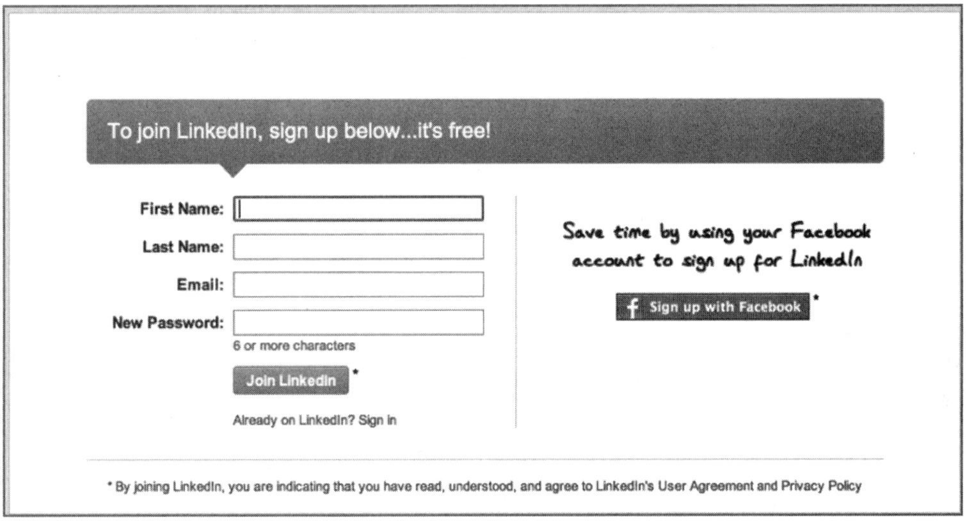

Figure 2.1 Creating your account for the first time

Interestingly, LinkedIn now allows you to create your LinkedIn account by signing in with Facebook. So perhaps LinkedIn is already moving towards integration. I just have to wonder what kind of information LinkedIn could possibly grab from a Facebook profile beyond your name and email address! Yikes!

Understanding Email and Password Best Practices

Many people use their business email addresses when creating their LinkedIn account because it's a business-networking site. But this might not be the best practice for a few reasons.

First, what happens if you lose or change jobs or something happens to your hosting site and you lose your domain name? If you lose access to your business email address and you forget your password, you are out of luck. You could ask LinkedIn's customer support at customerservice@LinkedIn.com to give you access to your account, but you are not assured of a response or positive outcome.

Another reason is that social media sites get hacked. While LinkedIn is very safe compared to Facebook and Twitter, LinkedIn *was* just hacked in June of 2012 compromising over 6.5 million accounts. So I always recommend to my clients and students that they create an email account just for their social media platforms.

As you can imagine, social media will generate increased email volume. On LinkedIn alone you might receive email for notifications, group messages, invitations, and direct messages. Creating a social media account will keep your "real" email account from getting overwhelmed.

If the worst happened and LinkedIn was hacked and someone used my email address to spam my contacts, I could just delete that email account and start over. If you've had to delete and change your company email address or the email address you've had for the past 15 years, you know what a hassle it is to let everyone know about the changes. And even then you'll lose communication with those folks. Avoid all those issues by creating an account just for your social media.

Eventually, you'll want to add all your email accounts. You'll learn more about that later in this chapter when we discuss settings.

When it comes to creating a password, please don't use the same one you use on your bank account for obvious reasons. Also don't use your dog's name (Mom!) or your daughter's birthday. Pick a series of numbers you can remember and then add a word to it (like LinkedIn). That way, you are more likely to remember your password if you get on a new computer, but your cubicle mate won't guess it in three tries. Or to create revolving passwords nearly impossible to hack, use a tool like RoboForm at http://Roboform.com or 1Password at https://agilebits.com/onepassword.

Setting Up Name, Company, and Location

When setting up your account for the first time, as shown in Figure 2.2, use the name most people know you by. If your name is Roberta but everyone calls you Bobbi, then go with Bobbi. (You will be able to use the Maiden Name field later on for your real name, your nickname, a common misspelling of your name—or, of course, your maiden name. You can only choose one.) Be aware that LinkedIn is smart enough to know the difference between Bob and Robert, but not Richard and Dick. So when first setting up your profile, choose the name most people know you by.

Don't worry too much about your company name when you are filling out this section. You'll have plenty of opportunity to add, edit, and change your company name when we get into setting up your profile.

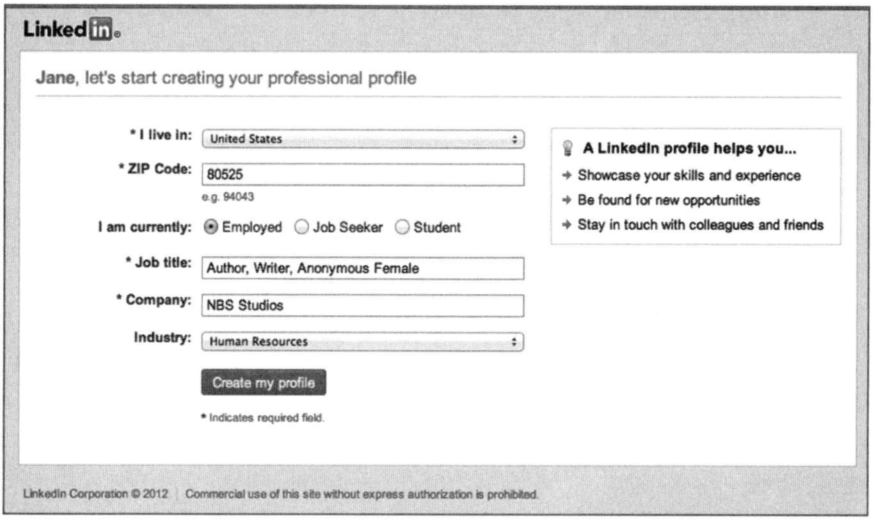

Figure 2.2 Creating your professional profile

If you are a job seeker and don't have a company name, you can always add a company you are doing volunteer work with. Greig Wells of BeFoundJobs suggests you create a group on LinkedIn and put your experience as Moderator of that group. I think this is a brilliant idea.

More on how job seekers can use LinkedIn in Chapter 11, "LinkedIn and You: Getting Specific."

Location used to be an issue with LinkedIn because it simply did not recognize the postal codes for some cities. For instance, if you lived in Greeley or Loveland, Colorado, you would have to choose either Fort Collins or Greater Denver Area. But they changed that about a year ago. If you haven't visited your "location" in your LinkedIn profile lately, it might be worth looking at again.

Once you have created an account, you can edit all you name and location information by clicking on edit next to your name on the profile page. This is also where you can add your nickname, misspelling of your name, proper name, etc. I've found it extremely useful to put the most common misspelling of my name, "Vivica," in this field. I noticed almost immediately that more people were able to find and message me with that misspelling of my name. The real spelling of my name, "Viveka," is not intuitive, which made me harder to find.

Using the Initial Connections Setup Screen

When you first sign into LinkedIn, it will try and gather names from your email address as shown in shown in Figure 2.3. I like it because it uploads the contacts from my email account (I need to supply the email address and password for the email account that has my contact list) and will tell me who in my contact list is on LinkedIn and who is not. So it can save me an immense amount of time.

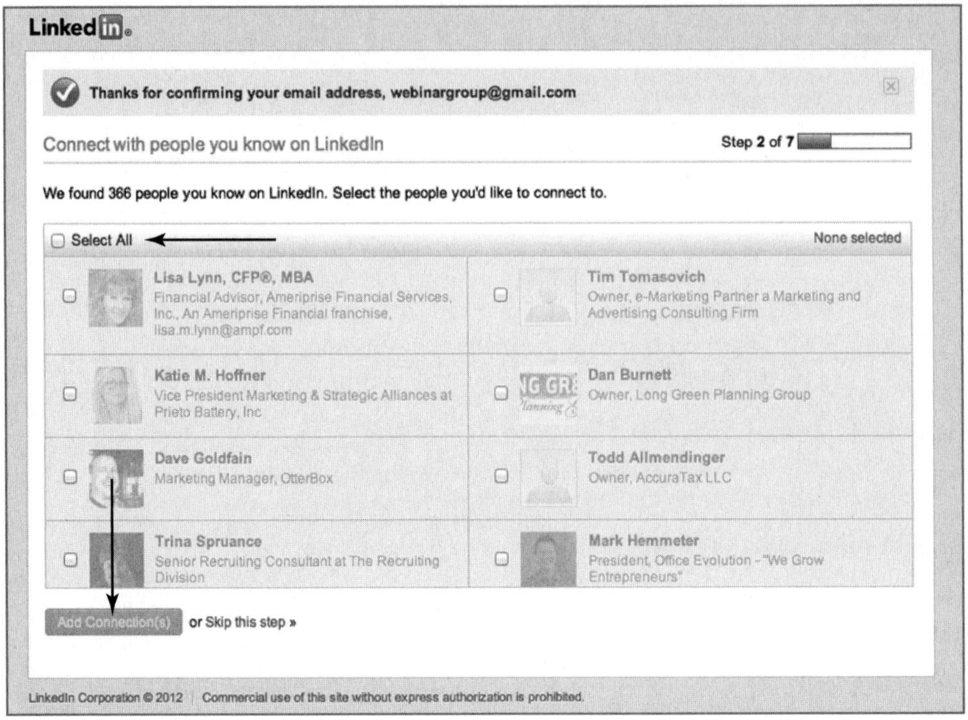

Figure 2.3 See who you know

I don't like it for a couple of reasons:

- Many people are nervous that LinkedIn is going to abuse their contacts (LinkedIn promises us they won't).

- LinkedIn fails to mention *anywhere* that you can only invite 3,000 people in a lifetime. This is a problem for many of my clients, whose contacts lists are 3,000-plus.

LinkedIn makes it too easy to click the Select All and Add Connections buttons, which might lead to you inviting your ex-fiancé, customer service at AT&T, and your ex-wife's attorney to connect! In fact, if you deselect the Select All check box, LinkedIn grays out your connections, which in most cases means "you can't click here." In fact, you *can* click on the people you want to connect to, but it is not obvious. If you do not want to add any connections at this time, click Skip This Step. (In fact, you will want to click on "skip this step" until you get to your profile. We'll cover all the steps you'll be skipping through the rest of the book.)

About 10 percent of your profile completeness depends on your connections, so you will definitely want to use this tool later. After you have done the initial set up of your LinkedIn account, LinkedIn will add a "Welcome [YourName]! See who you already know on LinkedIn" feature to your home page. This will bring you back to the same screen as above. I do recommend using this tool, but hold off until Chapter 5,

"Weeks 10–15: Creating and Managing a Network That Works." I'll walk you through best practices so you can feel secure as you reach out and connect with your network.

Tuesday: Understand LinkedIn's Features

Let's take a look at LinkedIn's landscape. We'll take a quick tour of the home page and settings so you have a better idea of where everything is.

A Review of the Home Page

There is so much good stuff on the home page. Figure 2.4 shows a typical home page on LinkedIn. Let's take a look at where everything is located.

Logo On the top-left side of your screen, you'll see the LinkedIn logo. Any time you want to return to your home screen, no matter what page you are on, just click on that LinkedIn logo.

Account Type Just to the right of the logo, you'll see a blue link that says what account type you have. You can click this link to see what other (paid) accounts are offered on LinkedIn. Miles Austin talks about paid accounts and if they are necessary (yes) in Chapter 11.

Name and Settings At the top right of the screen you'll see your name next to a link that says Add Connections. If you hover your cursor over your name, a drop-down menu will appear with the options Settings and Sign Out.

I'll talk about LinkedIn's settings and what might work best for you in the next few pages.

> **Note:** If you are using a public or work computer, always remember to sign out of LinkedIn. One thing you might have noticed after using LinkedIn for a while is that any time you go back to this Settings section or leave LinkedIn idle for a few moments, LinkedIn makes you sign back into your account. And that's a useful (albeit somewhat annoying) security measure. But even better is remembering to sign out.

Add Connections I'll talk a lot more about the Add Connections link in Chapter 5. This is the link you go to in order to upload your mailing list or add connections one at a time by email address.

Menu Bar I'll cover the menu bar in the next section.

Search To the right of the menu bar you'll see the People drop-down menu and a search box. Hover your cursor over People and you'll get access to:

- People
- Updates
- Jobs
- Companies

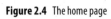

Figure 2.4 The home page

- Answers
- Inbox
- Groups
- Turn Off Suggestions

Just be aware that LinkedIn automatically changes the name in the drop-down search box depending on what page you're on. I still get frustrated looking for People when I'm on a company page, not even realizing that the search box has the wrong designation—or more accurately, LinkedIn has the right search box and I'm on the wrong page.

Advanced Search Although I might use the basic search box to do a quick search, I always recommend using the Advanced search link just to the right of the search box. Advanced search is available to everybody whether you have a free or a paid account. Make sure your cursor is on People in the drop-down menu in order to pull up the Advanced link. Clicking the link will take you to a whole new search screen. You'll learn more about how to use the Advanced search in Chapter 5.

Note: Newer users will see a screen that says "Welcome *YourName*. See who you already know on LinkedIn." That's just LinkedIn's way of helping you find people to connect with. After a while, that screen disappears. As mentioned earlier, you can also get to this screen to upload your contact list by clicking Add Connections.

Share an Update This status update will look a lot like a Facebook status update or a tweet on Twitter. Just remember that LinkedIn is a business social network. Be friendly, but keep your updates business focused.

LinkedIn Today LinkedIn shares its top news. Move over, MSN! This section is customizable and intuitive. The more you customize and use it, the more accurate LinkedIn Today will be.

LinkedIn All Updates This section shows some (or all) of the status updates and activity of some (or all) of your network. Later in this chapter we'll talk about how to limit the noise using the Settings section.

Just Joined LinkedIn Heading back over to the left side of your screen, underneath Updates By Your Network you'll see Just Joined LinkedIn. This section pulls information from places you've worked and the education institutes you've attended. When you click the link, LinkedIn shows you any new LinkedIn members who are either colleagues or fellow alumni. This section is a fantastic place to find new connections.

People You May Know If you have taken the time to fill out your profile and have been connecting to a few folks, then on the right side of your screen you'll see a box that says People You May Know. If you're new to LinkedIn, you won't have this option yet because LinkedIn doesn't have enough information to figure out who you might know. But the more people you connect to, the sooner LinkedIn will give you this option.

LinkedIn just updated People You May Know, as you can see in Figure 2.5.

Now you can click on either the school or company where you know people and connect to them all or individually. What I like about this new feature is that you don't have to classify how you know the person in order to send them an invitation and personal note.

When it comes to reaching out to people, I always recommend sending a personal note if at all possible. More about this in Chapter 5.

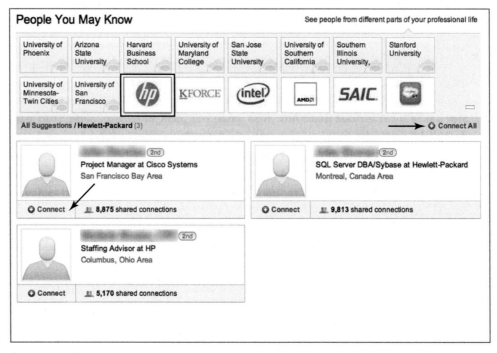

Figure 2.5 People You May Know

Ads by LinkedIn Members Right under the People You May Know box are paid ads by LinkedIn members. We'll talk more about how to create ads in Chapter 11.

Who's Viewed Your Profile Underneath the ad is a box that says Who's Viewed Your Profile. This becomes one of those very powerful metrics I talked about earlier. You want to keep an eye on how many people are viewing your profile daily and how many times you're showing up in search results.

Your LinkedIn Network Underneath Who's Viewed Your Profile is the Your LinkedIn Network box. Keep an eye on how many connections you have and how many new people you have added to your network. Did you notice the Add Connections button beneath this box? It will take you to the same screen as the Add Connections green link at in the top-right corner of your profile.

Jobs You Might Be Interested In If you've been on LinkedIn for a while, especially if you are a job seeker, underneath the Your LinkedIn Network you'll also see Jobs You Might Be Interested In. This feature is in beta mode as of this writing, but it is still extremely effective!

Groups You May Like Underneath Jobs You Might Be Interested In is the box Groups You May Like, a handy tool that uses your previous connections and interests, work history, and education to make group suggestions. While I recommend using the Groups Directory link in the Groups tab in the menu bar, also take a quick look at the groups LinkedIn thinks you might be interested in. I highly recommend to my new users that they join a few groups based on these recommendations.

Companies You May Want To Follow Below Groups You May Like is Companies You May Want To Follow. I'm going to talk a lot more about following companies in Chapter 4, "Weeks 7–9: Use Your Company Profile for Branding and Positioning." But it's definitely worth clicking on some of these companies to see what opportunities might be available.

(Not Shown) Applications You have the option in the Applications section to show your applications on your home screen, as Figure 2.6 shows. If you are using LinkedIn's applications, this section is where you control whether they will show up on your home page.

Figure 2.6 Applications screen

Don't be discouraged if your screen doesn't look exactly like the one in Figure 2.6. It's going to reflect who you are connected to, what you've done on LinkedIn, and how long you've been using LinkedIn.

A Review of the Menu Bar

I've already pointed you in the direction of LinkedIn's menu bar, but let's look at the tabs in detail as shown in Figure 2.7. (This might be a good section to dog-ear if you are new to LinkedIn.)

Figure 2.7 LinkedIn menu bar

One thing you'll notice about LinkedIn is that there are often many ways to get to the same screen. So choose the path that you find easiest to remember.

LinkedIn Home Tab

When you hover over the Home link on the menu bar, you'll see the options LinkedIn Home and Advertise On LinkedIn. I always just click on the LinkedIn logo at the top left of any page to get to the home page, but this is another option. (We'll talk a lot more about LinkedIn Ads in Chapter 10, "LinkedIn Ads, Labs, Apps, and Tools.")

Profile Tab

The next item on the menu is the Profile tab. This is where I usually edit and view my profile. I also go here to get and manage my recommendations and to access the Profile Organizer.

Any time you want to edit your LinkedIn profile, from experience to education to additional information, you'll click Edit Profile. Any changes you want to make to sections you add to LinkedIn like Applications and Skills also can be done in the Edit Profile section.

Note: Just be aware that it is easy to accidentally click View Profile instead of Edit Profile. So if you're having a hard time finding the Edit button on your profile to make those changes, check under Profile and make sure you are in Edit Profile mode and not View Profile.

Once you've made a change to your profile, I recommend clicking the View Profile link to see what your profile will look like to other people. Sometimes the spacing gets a little wacky and your content might not translate the way you want it to. Other sections of LinkedIn turn into linked searches (Interests, Groups, and Associations), so you want to make sure those sections are formatted in such a way to make the search work more efficiently.

The third link under the Profile tab is Recommendations. This is where you'll go to ask for recommendations as well as manage your recommendations. We're going talk a lot more about recommendations in Chapter 5.

The last option under the Profile tab is Profile Organizer. You have to have at least the minimum paid account on LinkedIn in order to use the Profile Organizer. This tool allows you to organize your network's profiles into folders you create.

Contacts Tab

The next menu bar item is Contacts. This is where you'll find your Connections, Add Connections, and Network Statistics, as well a list of links to businesses you've added to the experience sections and links to the schools you have added to your profile, as shown in Figure 2.8.

Connections are your first-level contacts—people you've invited or who have invited you to connect. The invitation has to be accepted for those people to show up under your Connections.

When we talk about creating and managing a network in Chapter 5, much of the work will be done in the Connections section.

On the Contacts page next to the Connections tab you'll see Imported Contacts. Be careful with this one. If you have used the LinkedIn Add Connections tool to upload your contacts, make sure you don't invite all the people you upload (like your ex-wife and her lawyer!). It's tempting, especially when you want to grow your network to just click on Select All and Invite selected contacts, but be very discerning with who you invite to connect. You can always go back and invite these people later if you decide to add more contacts.

The next link is the Profile Organizer that I've already mentioned. To the right of the Profile Organizer is Your Network Statistics. This tool tells you how many first-level connections you have, who they are connected to (your second-level connections), and their connections (your third-level connections). A few strategic first-level connections can add up to a very large network overall.

You'll also see a Remove Connections link on the right side. When you click Remove Connections, a list of everyone you are connected to appears. Feel free to remove anyone who is annoying you here. LinkedIn won't inform them that you have removed them as connections, although they might notice you are no longer first-level connections when they try to send you a message!

Groups Tab

The next tab on the menu bar is Groups. This menu tab will show you who your groups are, groups you might like, a Groups directory (so you can find groups), and a link that will allow you to create your own group, as shown in Figure 2.9.

Your groups are just that—groups that you've joined or are in the process of joining. We'll talk a lot more about groups in Chapter 6, "Weeks 16–18: Getting Strategic with Groups."

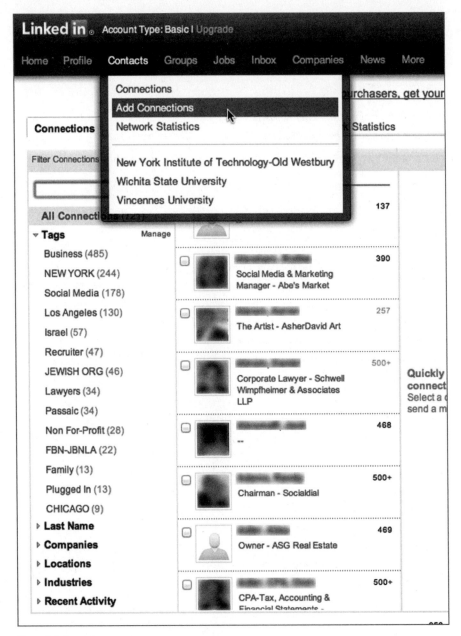

Figure 2.8 Connections

When you click Your Groups, you might notice the ability to reorder your groups. This will allow you to prioritize the groups that are more important to you, rather than having to always search your groups by alphabetical order. This does not reorder your groups on your profile.

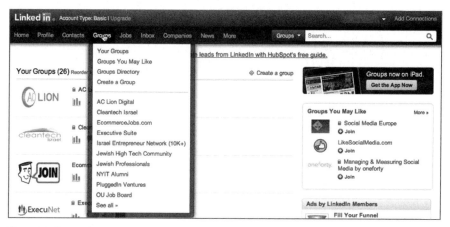

Figure 2.9 Groups tab

Also on this page are icons indicating which groups are currently having discussions and which groups have jobs posted.

The Groups You May Like link will show up once you've joined a few groups. LinkedIn uses its own analytics to go through your profile and your interests to define groups you might like, just like on your home page. You can also search for groups according to keywords, categories, and languages. It is also from this section that you can search for groups by keyword.

Or you can simply go to the Groups directory, which allows you to search for groups. You'll get the same results.

Jobs Tab

Next you'll find the Jobs tab. Here you'll see the links Find Jobs, the Job Seeker Premium account details, and Post A Job (which is a paid tool). Other paid options on this tab are Manage Your Jobs, Find Talent, and Hiring Solutions.

The Find Jobs link is one of the most useful tools LinkedIn offers a job seeker—more on that in Chapter 10. As shown in Figure 2.10, you can search for jobs by job title, keyword, or company name. If you choose the Advanced Search option for Find Jobs (which I recommend), you can also search by location (within 10–100 miles of a postal code) as well as by functions, experience, industries, and the date the job was posted. With the Job Seeker Premium account, you can also search by salary.

The Jobs tab allows you to apply for jobs from right within LinkedIn. It also enables you to see not only the company profile of the company posting the jobs but also who you know at that company. In addition, you can save the job for future review.

If you are using LinkedIn to find and hire candidates, then you should be using the job posting tools, which are very affordable starting at $99 a month. If you do post jobs on LinkedIn, you'll manage those jobs and candidates in this section as well. You'll learn more about posting jobs in Chapter 4.

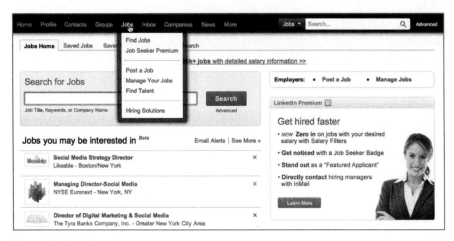

Figure 2.10 Jobs tab

Inbox Tab

The next tab is Inbox. When you hover over your Inbox, a pop-up screen appears with your pending invitations and messages. I hope this particular tab gets a lot of action for you!

Job Seeker Premium

The Job Seeker Premium account has great offers for a job seeker and might be worth the $29-a-month investment. You can do the following:

- Contact anyone directly with InMail
- Get the full list of who has viewed your profile
- Zero in on $100K plus jobs with detailed salary
- Move to the top of the list as a Featured Applicant
- Enjoy exclusive access to LinkedIn's job seeker community
- Get noticed by recruiters and hiring managers with a Job Seeker Badge
- Get introduced to the companies you're targeting
- Let recruiters message you for free with OpenLink
- Get Priority Customer Service

I recommend clicking the Invitations tab because you have a few more options (such as Report Profile). It also provides a better snapshot of your pending invitations, as you can see in Figure 2.11.

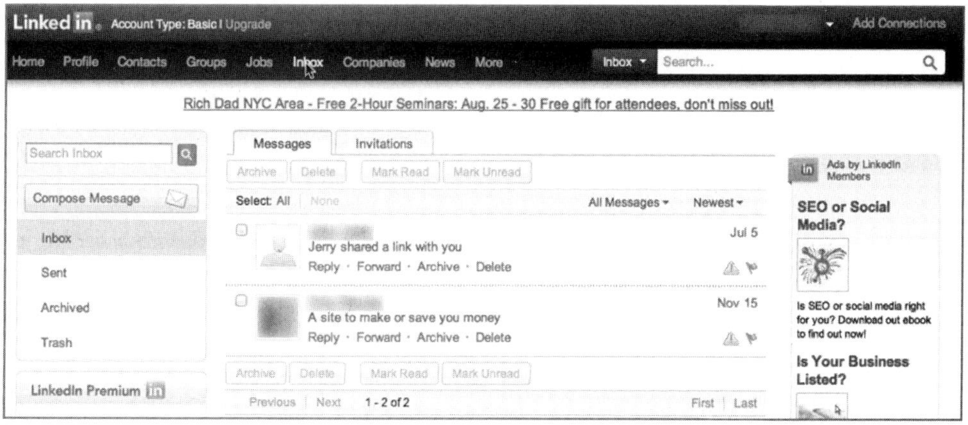

Figure 2.11 Inbox tab

Your Messages tab contains messages and replies to messages from your first-level connections as well as invitations, introductions and introduction requests, profile forwards, group invitations, InMails (LinkedIn's paid messaging service), job notifications, and questions from your network.

Companies Tab

The next tab, Companies, allows you to search for companies by keyword, company name, and industry. This is also where you'll go to see the companies that you are following and any updates from those you are following.

If you want to create a company, this is where you can add a company as well (more in this in Chapter 4).

When you click the Company tab, you might notice on the right side of this page a similar box to what you saw on the home page—Companies You May Want To Follow. If you have already created a company page on LinkedIn, you'll also be able to view some information about your company page, as well as edit the information on that page. I usually just go to my company page, which shows up as a link, and edit from there.

News Tab

Next to Companies is the News tab. Here you'll see LinkedIn Today articles you've saved as well as LinkedIn Signal.

LinkedIn Today pulls the top articles from across the blogosphere into your LinkedIn profile. You can choose what industries and topics you want to read about. The articles that show up on your home page are chosen according to categories you select and are based on how many LinkedIn users share them. LinkedIn Today is also intuitive and will make suggestions according to your selections.

Beneath the LinkedIn Today link is Saved Articles. You have to start organizing your reading list before you can save any headlines. But this is a great place to keep information that you might want to use as a resource later.

Beneath saved articles is LinkedIn Signal, one of my absolute favorite tools for monitoring my brand as well as finding, connecting to, and building relationships with potential clients, customers, vendors, employees or employers, or partners. You'll learn more about LinkedIn Signal in Chapter 8, "Week 23: Putting It All Together."

More Tab

Finally you'll see the More tab. I always say this is where LinkedIn puts everything that couldn't fit on the menu bar. You'll find the following options:

- Answers
- LinkedIn's Learning Center
- Skills
- Upgrade Your Account
- Get More Applications

We'll spend a lot of time talking about applications in Chapter 7, "Weeks 19–22: Get Strategic with LinkedIn's 'Other' Options."

Answers is where you can go to ask and answer questions on LinkedIn. I talked earlier about getting an expertise ranking from LinkedIn Answers. Well, this is where you get it. Chapter 7 discusses this topic in greater depth.

The Learning Center is just that: a place where LinkedIn has collected all their blogs, training webinars, and videos. The Learning Center is a great source of information.

I love the Skills link; learn more in Chapter 3.

And finally, the More tab includes a Get More Applications link. You might notice that some applications are already a part of your LinkedIn profile: Reading List by Amazon, LinkedIn Events, and LinkedIn Polls.

Wednesday: Establish Initial Settings

It's time to establish your initial settings on LinkedIn. We'll talk about creating profile settings; setting email preferences; using groups, companies, and applications; and identifying paid accounts and settings that are right for your situation.

Using Profile Settings: Activity Broadcasts, Activity Feed, Visibility, Twitter, and Public Profile

To get to your settings, hover your cursor over your name on the top-right side of your LinkedIn screen and select Settings from the drop-down menu, as shown in Figure 2.12. LinkedIn usually makes you sign in again with your email and password. Don't worry—this is a security measure. You haven't done anything wrong.

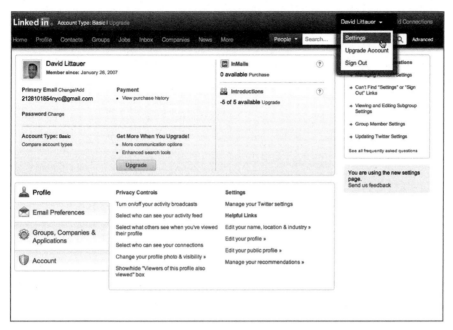

Figure 2.12 Settings

The top section of Settings gives you a quick snapshot of your account:

- Your name

- Your Member Since date

- Your primary email address (which you can always change)

- Your payments (if you bought ads or have a paid account)

- A place to change your password

- The type of account you have

- InMails

- Introductions (used and available)

You'll also notice on the right side frequently asked questions about LinkedIn. Beneath your account settings are the tabs you'll use the most in this section:

- Profile

- Email Preferences

- Groups, Companies & Applications

- Account

By default, the Profile tab will be highlighted (black). This is not the same as the Profile tab in your menu bar. Profile gives you access to Privacy Controls, Settings, and Helpful Links.

Privacy Controls

The first link under Privacy Controls is Turn On/Off Your Activity Broadcasts. I recommend *turning off* your activity broadcasts. By default, every time you make a change to the static content of your profile, it will get blasted to your network unless you choose to turn this section off. Some people think it's good to leave this option on because they want their network to know when they've made a change in their business or career. If that applies to you, then I recommend you turn it off while you read this book, make the suggested changes, and turn it back on when you feel your profile is complete. Personally I leave this section off as most folks don't like getting blasted with every change people make on their profile.

The second link allows you to select who can see your activity feed. Your *activity feed* is any communication action you perform on LinkedIn: questions you've asked or answered; responses to discussions or updates you've posted, liked, or commented on; companies and groups you've followed; and topics you've followed on LinkedIn Today. The activity feed is all the activity that you have performed and shows up on your professional profile. You can let other people see it (or not) when they go to your professional profile page.

I often get asked about security on LinkedIn. The next section allows you to Select What Others See When *You* View *Their* Profile (emphasis mine). If you do not want people to know you've been looking at their profile, you can change these settings. The default is that your name, your photo, and your professional headline and location will show up when you view another person's profile. If you choose to be partially anonymous (your Industry or Title will show up) or completely anonymous, be aware those options will disable your ability to view your profile statistics if you have the free account. And profile statistics are some of those metrics you definitely want to keep an eye on to measure your success on LinkedIn. You can certainly turn on and off your anonymity.

The next link is Select Who Can See Your Connections. Many people are uncomfortable with the idea that first-level connections or contacts might be visible to their entire network—especially if you have a small network and a large majority of your contacts are also clients. One of the reasons I encourage a larger network is to hide your key contacts within it! To limit visibility, choose Only Me. (Even if you limit who can see your connections, your network will be able to see your shared connections. There is no way to turn that off.)

Some people feel they may be discriminated against because of age, sex, or race. The next link allows you to change your profile photo and visibility. I don't recommend hiding your photo. I've read statistics that you have a 60 percent better chance of someone contacting you if you have a photo uploaded on your LinkedIn profile. I question people who don't show their photo, at least to their network, on LinkedIn. I know some people are concerned about identity theft, so again, it is your choice to whom you make your photo visible. I recommend a smiling close-up. Do not use a logo in this section—doing so goes against the end-user agreement.

There is an option that will show or hide the Viewers Of This Profile Also Viewed box in a search. You may want to turn off that option if you don't want to be compared to your competitors. Or you might want to leave it on to keep an eye on your competitors. It is completely up to you. By default, LinkedIn will display the Viewers Of This Profile Also Viewed box on your profile page.

> **Note:** Recruiter Stacy Donovan Zapar says, "There's a very compelling reason to leave it turned on. Makes it very easy for you to be found by others who are seeking out your competition. As a recruiter, I loved this feature and would find great candidates this way."

Settings

The next section is called Settings (not to be confused with the Settings section currently being discussed!). I'm guessing that in the future LinkedIn might add more links to this section. Currently, the only "Setting" is Manage Your Twitter Settings. You'll learn more about Twitter settings during Week 4 in Chapter 3.

Helpful Links

Next comes the Helpful Links section. I'm going to skip the Edit Your Name, Location And Industry and Edit Your Profile links because I cover them in Chapter 3.

The next link, Edit Your Public Profile, is very important. Remember in Chapter 1 that I mentioned the public profile that's based completely on the information you add to your professional LinkedIn profile? Well, here you choose what the general public can see of your professional LinkedIn profile, as well as edit your LinkedIn public profile URL.

If you are brand-new to LinkedIn, when you click Customize Your Public Profile, you won't get many options to show or make fields invisible. As you add your photo, a headline summary, positions, skills, education, and additional information, you'll have more fields whose visibility you can turn on and off, as shown in Figure 2.13.

By default, your public profile will be made visible to everyone on the Web, not just LinkedIn members. Your picture, your skills, additional information, websites, and Interested In data will be visible. You'll have to turn on visibility for any other section you want the public to be able to view. I do not recommend showing your current and past positions, or your education. While I tend to trust my LinkedIn network with my information, I do not trust the 6+ billion people who have access to the Internet. If someone abused your relationship on LinkedIn, you could always report them, but you'd have little recourse on the Web.

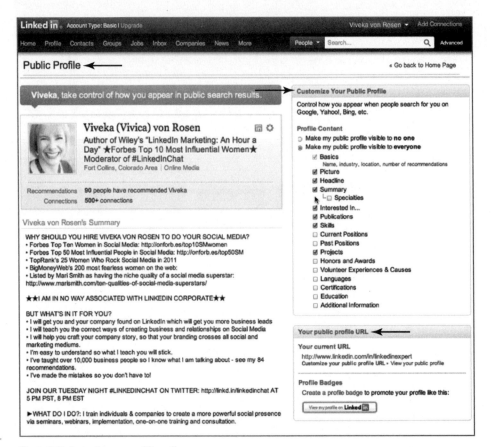

Figure 2.13 Customizing your public profile

Beneath Customize Your Public Profile you'll see Your Public Profile URL. Click that link to access the edit screen. Add your "FirstNameLastName" with no spaces or special characters, as shown in Figure 2.14.

LinkedIn will let you know if that URL is available by giving you a green check mark or providing suggestions if the URL you chose is already in use. If you have a common name like Jane Doe, you might have to put in the middle initial. Rather than www.LinkedIn.com/pub/firstname_lastname56994388245, you get something simple to remember: www.linkedin.com/in/JaneWDoh.

You can also put your company name in this section so that it reads something like www.LinkedIn.com/in/LinkedIntoBusiness, or include your area of expertise: www.linkedin.com/in/linkedinexpert.

Note: The box that lets you customize the URL appears *above* the Customize Your Public Profile box for users who have not yet created a customized URL. Once you've created one, the box jumps *below* the Customize Your Public Profile box.

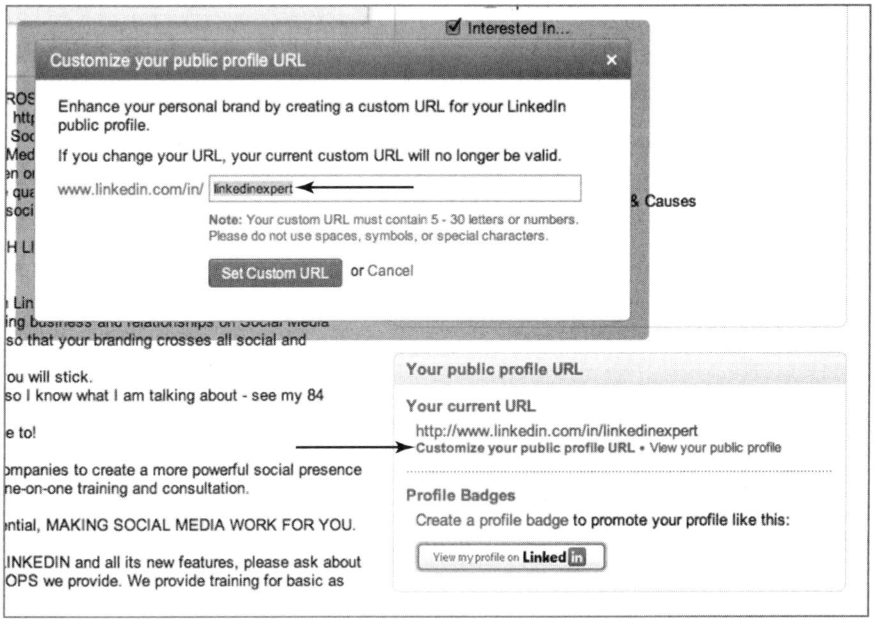

Figure 2.14 Customizing your public profile URL

Beneath the area for customizing your LinkedIn public profile URL is Create A Profile Badge. Walk through these easy steps to get a piece of code you can then use in your email signature, on your website, or in your blog.

The final link is Manage Your Recommendations. We'll be spending a lot more time talking about your recommendations and how to ask for them, give them, and manage them during Week 15 in Chapter 5.

Setting Email Preferences

The next tab in the Settings section is Email Preferences. Options include Select The Types Of Messages You're Willing To Receive, Set The Frequency Of Emails, Select Who Can Send You Invitations, and Select The Frequency Of Group Digest Emails.

You also can set your LinkedIn Communications with Turning On/Off LinkedIn Announcements, Turning On/Off Invitations To Participate In Research, and Turning On/Off Partner InMail.

I am okay with receiving LinkedIn announcements and participating in market research, but Partner InMail is advertising: LinkedIn Partner InMails are messages from our partners with informational or promotional content that is part of a marketing or hiring campaign. Partner InMails are sent to LinkedIn users based on such information as the title of your current position, your primary industry, or your region, and are not from individual recruiters using LinkedIn. Your name and email address aren't disclosed to LinkedIn's marketing partners.

You can adjust your email preference settings, as you can see in Figure 2.15.

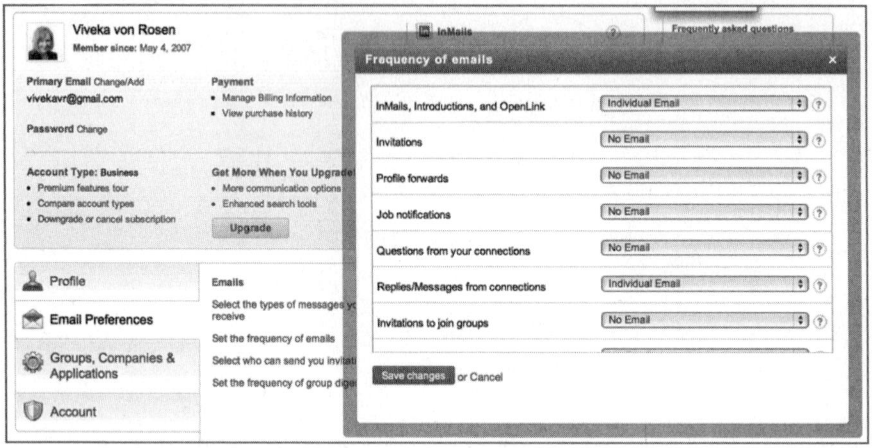

Figure 2.15 Email preferences

If you've been on LinkedIn for a while, you'll recognize the types of messages you're willing to receive from the bottom section of your LinkedIn profile, which also reads Contact *YourName* At. This is where you can specify the type of communications you're willing to receive:

- Career opportunities
- Expertise requests
- Consulting offers
- Business deals
- New ventures
- Personal reference request
- Job inquiries
- Requests to reconnect

I recommend checking them all because any one of them might lead to a new client, donor, employee, or job.

With the free account, you have the option of accepting introductions and InMail. This option is recommended by LinkedIn and I also recommend you choose it. If someone wants to send me an InMail, then I want to receive it!

Because of the price of InMails (LinkedIn prices them at $10 each), it is much less likely that someone will spam you through an InMail. If you do not want to receive messages from people you don't know, you can choose to receive introductions only.

Set The Frequency Of Emails allows you to choose what messages you are willing to receive *in your email*, in addition to LinkedIn's inbox:

- InMail
- Introductions

- OpenLink Messages
- Invitations
- Profile Forwards
- Job Notifications
- Questions And Replies
- Messages
- Network Updates
- Activity Notifications
- Referral Suggestions
- Actionable Emails
- Connections Suggestions
- LinkedIn Today

You can also choose how often you'll receive these emails. Some of this content will be noise, but depending on your reason for being on LinkedIn, you might even choose Individual emails (as they happen) and no email or weekly digests (my default in most cases).

You can select who can send you invitations. I highly recommend choosing Anyone On LinkedIn to avoid missing out on an invitation from someone important to your business or career.

You can also click set the frequency of group digest emails from this section; you'll have access to this option in the following section as well.

Using Groups, Companies, and Applications

Now click Groups, Companies, And Applications. Some of these options will look familiar to you.

You can select your group display order in View Your Groups as well as set the frequency of group digest emails and turn on or off group invitations.

I will talk about what types of groups you'll want to join, why you might want to join them, and how often you're going to listen to them in Chapter 6.

Turn on group invitations if you want people to send you these invitations. As my network grew, I changed this option to off. If you are new to LinkedIn, however, you might want to leave this option on just in case one of your connections suggests a group that would be beneficial for you to join.

In the section Set The Frequency Of Group Digest Emails, you can change the amount of email (in the form of daily or weekly digests) you receive from your groups. If the group is getting too noisy, you can use this section to choose, in each group, whether you want a daily, weekly, or no group digest email.

Beneath Groups you'll see Companies. This is exactly the same page that you saw earlier when you clicked the View Companies You're Following link. I prefer to edit my company settings from the top menu bar.

Next to Companies is Applications. This is where you can view LinkedIn applications. You can view the various applications you've authorized to display on your profile and/or have given access to your LinkedIn profile and network data. Not only can you view and access LinkedIn applications in this section, but you can also control which external websites have access to your account.

In addition, this section lets you turn on and off your privacy controls. By default, LinkedIn can share your data with third-party applications. So I turn the section off.

The setting Manage Settings For LinkedIn Plugins On Third Party Sites lets you control your offsite privacy management. According to LinkedIn: "If you're signed in to LinkedIn when you view any page that uses LinkedIn's professional plugins, we receive information that you've visited that page. This allows us to improve your LinkedIn experience and provide you with insights from your professional network, like how many of your connections have shared an article into LinkedIn using the Share on LinkedIn plugin."

Managing Your Account

If you click on the Account tab, you'll see Privacy Controls, Settings, Email & Password, as well as Helpful Links. You might notice things start to get a little repetitious in this tab.

In Manage Advertising Preferences, LinkedIn provides more information on Ads By LinkedIn (ads shown to LinkedIn users on LinkedIn and third-party websites) and Ad Selection (ads shown to you are selected based on non-personally identifiable information.) For example advertisers may choose to target ads to LinkedIn members in a particular industry, location or a LinkedIn group. LinkedIn shares its privacy policy under Protecting Your Personal Information. You can also choose whether or not you want LinkedIn to show you ads on third-party websites.

You'll recognize Change Your Profile Photo And Visibility, an option that also lives on the Profile tab.

If you are a recruiter or hiring manager, you might want to click Show Profile Photos Of Other Members. This is a useful section for people who don't want to be accused of hiring or not hiring someone because of age, sex, or race.

One of the links I recommend spending some time on is Customize The Updates You See On Your Home Page. As shown in Figure 2.16, as you grow your network and begin to be connected to more people, this feature helps you cut down on the noise.

When you are starting out, it might be a good idea to keep an eye on new connections in your network, updates from your extended network, status updates from your connections, and posts from your connections. From your home page you can easily send a message welcoming your new connections to your network or respond to posts and status updates. When it gets overwhelming, turn off some of these features.

I turn off all the options in Profile And Recommendation, but again, the choice is yours. One reason to leave them on is to congratulate people on their promotions and recommendations, allowing you to initiate or build a relationship with them.

I leave the Questions & Answers option on in case I want to participate in a discussion. It's easier to glance at them here rather than go into Questions. You'll learn more about this topic in Chapter 7.

There are also updates for Jobs, Events, Polls, Groups, Applications, Company Pages, and News. Just because you turn off an update from your home page does not mean you'll no longer get access to these services. You can always get access to them from the menu bar tabs.

You'll also see a Hidden tab. These are the folks whose updates you have hidden from your home page. If you want to unhide their updates, just click here to Show Updates.

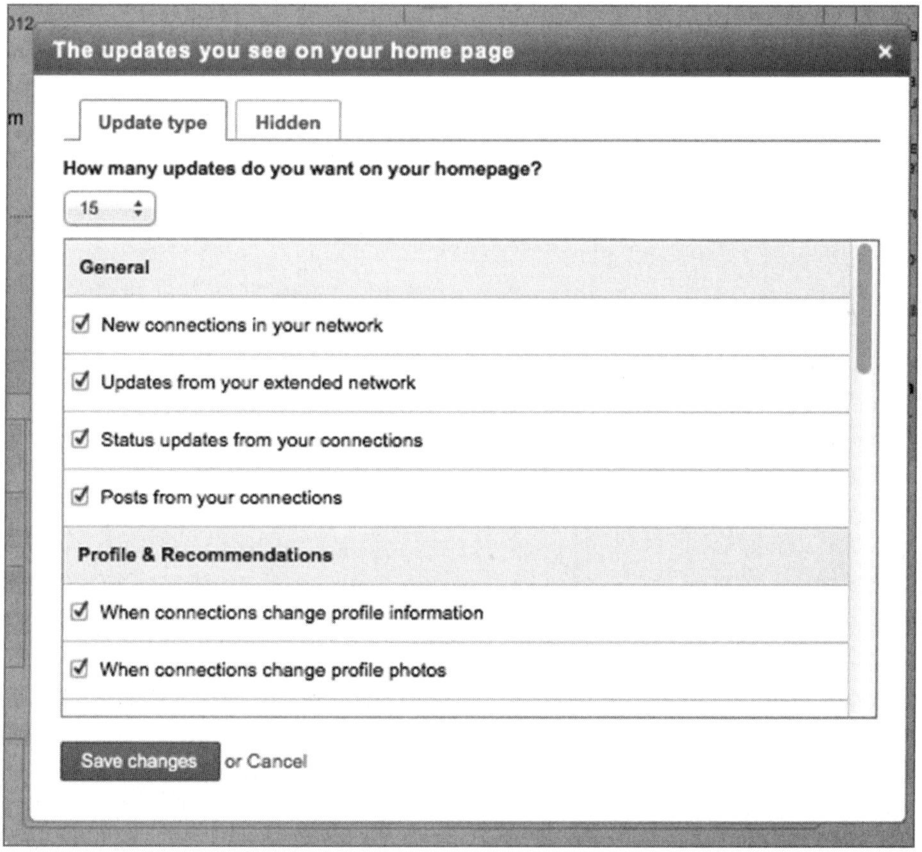

Figure 2.16 Updates You See On Your Home Page

The last two links are Select Your Language and Manage Security Settings. Select Your Language will affect the way you see some profiles, and it will affect how LinkedIn communicates with you. Manage Security Settings lets you use secure connections such as HTTPS when available, which seems like a good idea until you realize it prevents you from using some of LinkedIn apps.

The next option is Email And Password. Your first link is Add And Change Email Addresses. You'll want to put all your email addresses into this section. Only your primary email address will be visible to your network. If you fail to put an email address associated with you into this section and someone uses that email address to invite you to connect with them on LinkedIn, then LinkedIn will try to create a new account for you. In most cases, when people end up with two accounts it is because they inadvertently created a new account due to an invitation to an email address not listed in their existing account's "Email Vault." (This is my name for it, not LinkedIn's.) As far as I know, no one has ever hacked into this section.

Beneath that is an option that lets you change your password. If you feel your profile has been hacked, this is your first line of defense. Change your password!

Other Helpful Links include Upgrade Your Account and Close Your Account.

If you have more than one account, and you can remember the email address and password you used to create your "bad" account, then this is where you'll go to delete it.

You have to sign into your "bad" account, and then LinkedIn will ask you why you want to close your account (choose Duplicate Accounts), verify that this is the account you want to close, and allow you to delete the account.

You can now merge accounts on LinkedIn too, although you'll have to do this through customerservice@LinkedIn.com.

If you close your account, you'll lose that profile's contacts and connections. If you merge, you'll keep your connections intact (although you'll still lose your recommendations).

The last link on this page is Get LinkedIn Content In An RSS Feed. It's also an interesting feature, offering both public feeds as well as personal feeds (which contain private information from your network). It's worth noting that there are security concerns if you choose to publish your personal network updates in a web-based feed reader, which could make all of your LinkedIn updates available to search engines and the world at large. You can also subscribe to an RSS feed of LinkedIn Answers. Each category (and there are dozens of them) has its own public RSS feed.

What Settings Are Right for Your Situation?

The most important thing is that you choose settings you are comfortable with. I have made my suggestions based on what has worked for my clients and me, but in the end this is your account and you get to decide how visible and how open to communication you want to be.

While social media tends to encourage open communication, full visibility, and transparency, as a business owner you may have some legitimate concerns regarding privacy and customer interaction. Choose what is right for you. You can change the settings anytime you want.

Finally, keep an eye on your Settings section as well as the LinkedIn Blog at www.blog.linkedin.com. LinkedIn occasionally adds new links, options, and opportunities but rarely shares them with the members in an email before implementation. They just show up on your screen! However, the LinkedIn Blog is pretty good about sharing new features with its readers.

Thursday: Define and Create Goals for Your LinkedIn Presence

There are two types of goals you'll want to think about when considering your LinkedIn presence: umbrella goals and campaign goals. Your umbrella goal is your main purpose for being on LinkedIn. Your LinkedIn campaigns are shorter-term marketing efforts and will change according to your more immediate marketing efforts.

First, what is your umbrella goal, your purpose, for being on LinkedIn? Is it to attract new clients? Position yourself as a thought leader? Connect with influencers in your industry? Find and hire employees for your corporation? Connect with potential donors and sponsors?

Second, what are the goals you have set for individual LinkedIn marketing campaigns? Any good marketing campaign starts with knowing your goals, and your social marketing campaign is no different. Have you considered LinkedIn to position your new product or service? Increase the awareness about your new book? Find affiliates for a new online offer? Invite potential consumers to an event? While these goals will shift and change over time, you should at the very least have a sense of what they are and why you are using LinkedIn.

Take a minute to jot down 10 reasons for being on LinkedIn, and then prioritize those reasons.

Now that you have a list of prioritized goals, it's time to refine them even further. I like the acronym SMART: specific, measurable, attainable, realistic, and timely. (The acronym SMART can be attributed to George Doran, who originated the acronym back in 1981 in his article "There's a S.M.A.R.T. Way to Write Management Goals and Objectives.")

Looking through the list of goals you created for yourself, can you qualify them as being SMART?

Action Item: Your LinkedIn Goals

Take a few minutes right now to write down the reasons you are using LinkedIn.

Are you using LinkedIn to:

- Attract new clients and customers
- Create new referral partner relationships
- Attract affiliates
- Position yourself as a thought leader or subject matter expert
- Share information about your product or service
- Enhance your customer service relationship
- Attract donors and sponsors for your charity
- Position your Internet marketing business
- Sell your book
- Share information about an event
- Other

What are your goals for being on LinkedIn that are not on the above list? Write those down.

Now prioritize your goals.

Although your priorities for using LinkedIn might shift, it's always good to be clear on what they are right now.

Is Your Goal Specific?

I'm going to ask you to get specific about your goals. Why? Because the more focused you are on creating your goals, the more likely you'll be to achieve them. If you don't have a targeted audience or message, then your communications will be diluted. If you don't have a "By When" date, you might never achieve your goals.

Who? When thinking about your goals on LinkedIn, decide with whom specifically you want to connect. Is there an individual, or a specific type of person? If you do business consulting, who are you interested in connecting with? What is their business, their position, their title, their industry? By being specific about *who* you want to connect to, you have a much better chance of finding and engaging with them.

What or Why? What is your purpose in wanting to connect with these individuals? Is it simply to grow your network in case you need to communicate with them in the future, or are you looking for a specific person to do business with right now? (Both answers are correct.)

You probably already have the *whats* of your goals written down. Now go a step further and think about the *whys*. You might get more clarity and depth.

Where? Where do you do your work? Are you a virtual business? A location-based business? Both? Knowing where you want to do work will help you create a more strategic experience on LinkedIn. Just because you are a virtual business and can work with anyone in the world, that doesn't mean you necessarily should. Consider using LinkedIn to establish relationships in specific areas: your hometown, a town you visit often, a location overseas where you might want to retire to at some point.

One of the driving factors when I started my speaking career was the ability to speak to audiences all around the world. After traveling 20 days a month for the past few years, I decided that even though I can work anywhere, I might want to focus on cities a little closer to home.

Is Your Goal Measurable?

What are the measurable criteria or metrics you'll monitor to make sure you are on track? Establish concrete criteria for measuring the progress toward the attainment of each goal you set:

- How many people will you connect with?
- How many industries will your network represent?
- How often will you check your inbox and what kind of interaction are you expecting?
- How many groups will you join?
- How often will you monitor your search terms with LinkedIn Signal?
- How many messages will you send each week and to whom?
- How many companies will you follow?

Measuring your progress will help you stay on track and reach your goals. LinkedIn can be an elephant—and we all know the only way to eat an elephant is one bite at a time. Are you measuring those bites? We will go much more in depth on metrics you can measure on Tuesday.

Is Your Goal Attainable?

Spend some time on this one. Don't set goals that are impossible to achieve, but don't aim too small either. You are probably not going to connect with *all* the CEOs of the Fortune 500 this week. But maybe you can connect with someone on the executive team who can give you access to two or three of them. Wouldn't that still be useful? If you don't *try* to connect, it's unlikely you'll be able to engage with them.

If you have in your mind that a goal is unattainable, then it probably is. But if you truly believe you can achieve your goal, you might very well start to exhibit the attitude, abilities, skills, and financial capacity you need in order to reach that goal.

Is Your Goal Realistic?

For your goal to be realistic, you must be both willing and able to achieve it. There are some folks reading this book who might very well be able to engage with all the C-level executives of the Fortune 500 but might not be willing to disturb them or "call in that favor." Some people will not be able to get past the gatekeepers. One of the benefits of LinkedIn is the ability to see the path leading to your target connection. You might suddenly "see" that your neighbor is a first-level connection of someone you are desperate to contact. You know and trust your neighbor and they trust and like you. Now you are both able and willing! Suddenly the unattainable becomes a realistic goal.

Is Your Goal Timely?

Have you set up "by when" dates? This is one of the most important specifics to consider. If you don't have a "by when" date, then your project or campaign or goal for being on LinkedIn might never come to pass. By setting a time or schedule for your engagement, as well as a date when you'll have accomplished your goals, you are much more likely to achieve success.

How many of you reading this book have created vision boards? And how many of you have reached the goals or attained the things you have pictured or listed on your vision board? If you answered yes, you probably had a very clear date in mind that you want these visions manifested. Most people answer no, and the reason most of these dreams never materialize is because there is no set date for completion. For those of you who thought, "What the heck is a vision board?" it's like Pinterest—a poster board covered with images of things you wish to achieve.

Friday: Establish Success Metrics for Your Goals

I mentioned earlier in this chapter that you have to measure your progress on LinkedIn. There are two types of metrics you can measure: qualitative measurements and quantitative measurements.

Quantitative:

- Total connections
- New invitations
- LinkedIn profile views
- LinkedIn search results
- Business followers
- Article shares on LinkedIn Today
- Click-throughs to your website from LinkedIn

Qualitative:

- Inbox activity and sentiment
- Requests for business
- LinkedIn Signal keyword mentions
- Likes and comments on updates
- Group growth and interaction
- "Expert" designation in Answers
- Google SEO
- Recommendations
- Industry representation and Location representation

In Week 13 of Chapter 5, you'll dive even deeper into monitoring, measuring, and aligning your LinkedIn presence with your goals. But let's take a closer look right now at some of these qualitative and quantitative measurements and what they mean.

Quantitative Measurements

Quantitative measurements are usually associated with numbers you can measure. They tend to indicate the growth and impact of your social presence.

Total Connections

You can find your total connections in a few places. As shown in Figure 2.17, on the Contacts tab you'll see Network Statistics and your total connections will be your first-, second-, and third-level connections as well as the total number of users you can contact through an introduction, including people with whom you share a group. There are a few other places to find your network statistics that we'll look at later in this chapter.

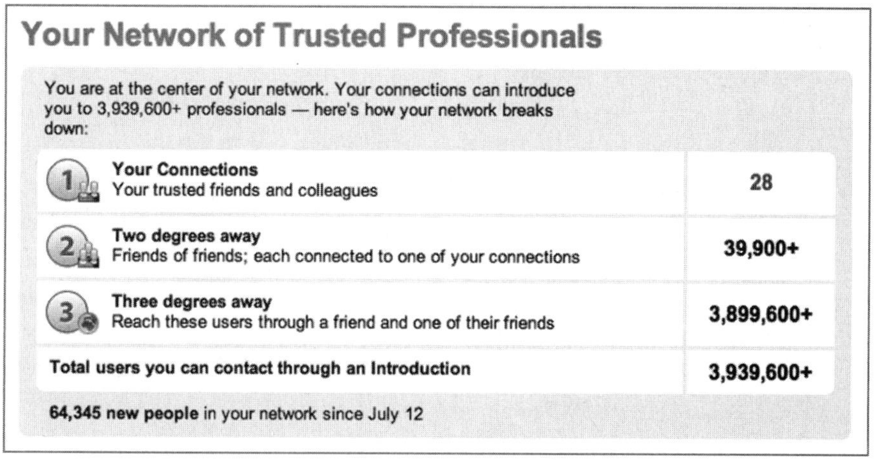

Your Network of Trusted Professionals

You are at the center of your network. Your connections can introduce you to 3,939,600+ professionals — here's how your network breaks down:

① **Your Connections** Your trusted friends and colleagues	**28**
② **Two degrees away** Friends of friends; each connected to one of your connections	**39,900+**
③ **Three degrees away** Reach these users through a friend and one of their friends	**3,899,600+**
Total users you can contact through an Introduction	**3,939,600+**

64,345 new people in your network since July 12

Figure 2.17 Network Statistics

As I mentioned in Chapter 1, *you are only as visible as the size of your network*, so it's a good idea to know how you are positioned right now. In the space provided in the sidebar "Know Your Network," write down your first-, second-, and third-level connections, as well as the number of your total connections. I'll go into greater depth as to what these levels mean in Chapter 5.

Action Item: Know Your Network

On the Connections tab, click Network Statistics and jot down your numbers for:

First-Level Connections _____

Second-Level Connections _____

Third-Level Connections _____

Total users you can contact through an introduction _____

New Connections

On your home page in Your LinkedIn Network, click the New People link and then uncheck 2nd Connections and Group Members to see a thumbnail of your 1st level connections as seen in Figure 2.18 below.

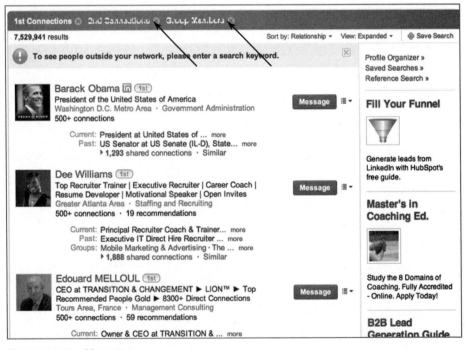

Figure 2.18 1st Level Connections

You'll want to keep an eye on these numbers to make sure they do not get stagnant. A little strategic growth every week can make all the difference to your success on LinkedIn.

LinkedIn Profile Views

Just above Your LinkedIn Network is Who's Viewed Your Profile, as shown in Figure 2.19. I find great value in this section. You'll see a blue link that reads "Your profile has been viewed by X people in the past X days." Click on this link and you'll be guided to a new page that identifies how many visitors have viewed your profile in the last X days, and that identifies these visitors by name, title, location, and/or industry. These people are known as *leads*.

If you aren't getting at least 10 views a week, then chances are you are not getting as much business as you could out of LinkedIn.

Figure 2.19 Who's Viewed Your Profile

LinkedIn Search Results

If you haven't done so yet, type the keyword or keyword phrase that best describes what you do into the People search field at the top right of your profile. How many pages do you have to scroll through until your profile shows up? Again, it's good to get the number now so you can see how much you improve later! In Chapter 3, we will focus on keyword searching and profile optimization on LinkedIn search results.

> ## Action Item: Do a People Search on Your Primary Keyword
>
> Do a People search on your name, your company name, your industry, your specialty, your product, and/or your service. Get the baselines for each.
>
> What page do you have to scroll to in order to see your LinkedIn Profile?
>
> Name: Page _____
>
> Company Name: Page _____
>
> Industry: Page _____
>
> Specialty: Page _____
>
> Product: Page _____
>
> Service: Page _____

Company Page Follows

If you have a company page on LinkedIn, keep an eye on your following. Get that baseline now and watch those numbers grow as you move through Chapter 4.

Article Shares on LinkedIn Today

If you do content marketing, keep an eye on LinkedIn Today. Nothing could be better than getting your article shared, re-shared, and commented on in this LinkedIn news feature. You'll notice it's usually the better-known blogs and newsfeeds that get shared. But once in a while a relatively unknown blog will get a lot of attention. When setting up LinkedIn Today, make sure you put in the various metrics and interests important to you and/or your network.

Website Click-Throughs

If you have the ability to create a unique link back to your website, you can add that unique link to your profile and track how many times people click on it and through to your website. I recommend using a tool like bitly to create unique links you can track.

 Note: Bit.ly is a free resource that allows you to create customized and trackable URLs for any website, including your own website and landing pages.

Qualitative Measurements

Qualitative measurement has more to do with the quality and sentiment of your engagement. You want to track this to measure your influence in your social community.

Inbox Activity and Sentiment

Are you getting any inbox activity? Some of it will definitely be spammy in nature, but it's good to keep an eye on your messages. Some people will want to build a relationship with you.

Now, evaluate the sentiment of your interactions with people. Are people thanking you for connecting? Genuinely interacting with you? Sending blanket newsletters? You'll get a bit of each, so I highly recommend nurturing the "real" communications. Feed what you want more of; ignore or delete what you want less of.

When you accept a person's invitation on LinkedIn, you are implicitly agreeing to be open to their communications. You might receive unsolicited newsletter-like communications, and while these can be annoying, they are not really spam. On the other hand, if someone tries to solicit your hand in marriage for a green card or your social security number with promises of great riches in Zambia, then hit that Report Spam button.

Requests for Business

How about requests for business? I knew there was something wrong with my LinkedIn visibility when I went from ten or more requests for consultations a week to less than three. This is probably one of the most important metrics to measure—and one of the main goals for being on LinkedIn: to get more business!

> **Note:** To avoid getting "blacklisted" by LinkedIn, don't break their end-user agreement. I put "LinkedIn Expert" in the last name field, which specifically broke the agreement to "not publish inaccurate information in the designated fields on the profile form (e.g., do not include a link or an email address in the name field)."

LinkedIn Signal Keyword Mentions

Have you checked LinkedIn Signal to see how many times your keyword search terms (company name, your name, username, industry, product, or service) are being mentioned? Once you set your metrics on LinkedIn Signal, all you have to do is click on your saved searches to see what new mentions you are getting. Learn more about LinkedIn Signal in Chapter 8.

> ### Action Item: Do a Signal Search
>
> Sign in to LinkedIn and go to www.linkedin.com/signal and type in your industry. See how many people are talking about it. Results will show both LinkedIn updates and tweets.

Likes and Comments on Updates

Many people don't even realize you can monitor your own updates to see how often people liked or commented on them.

1. Click on Profile.
2. Go to View Profile.
3. In your latest update, click See All Activity.

Now you can see exactly what you have posted and how people have responded. If you are not getting many responses, consider adjusting what you post. And do not, whatever you do, automatically post all your tweets to LinkedIn. Your LinkedIn network might be a completely different culture than your Twitter following, so the sheer quantity of tweets landing on your network's home pages might be incredibly annoying.

Group Growth and Interaction

If you manage a group, you'll want to keep an eye on your group growth and interaction. Check out how many members you have right now and make note of the number here: _____. If you have been ignoring your group, check on the content in your discussions. Is the group thriving without you, or has it been killed by spam-like postings? Learn how to build and manage your groups in Chapter 6.

"Expert" Designation in Answers

LinkedIn Answers is LinkedIn's member-driven Q&A and is one of my favorite tools for thought leader positioning on LinkedIn. One of the features is the "Best Answer" ranking given by the person who posted the question to the answer they thought most useful. Get enough best answers and you are listed as an expert on the Answers home page. Learn more about Answers in Chapter 8.

Google SEO

Have you Googled yourself lately? Where does your LinkedIn profile show up? Is your LinkedIn company profile showing up? How about your LinkedIn events or LinkedIn group? One thing I like about LinkedIn is that, because Google seems to like it so darn much, you can use your LinkedIn profile, events, groups, company pages, and even Answers to manage your reputation and push down some less optimal Google results. Learn how to optimize your profile for better Google search engine optimization (SEO) in Chapter 3.

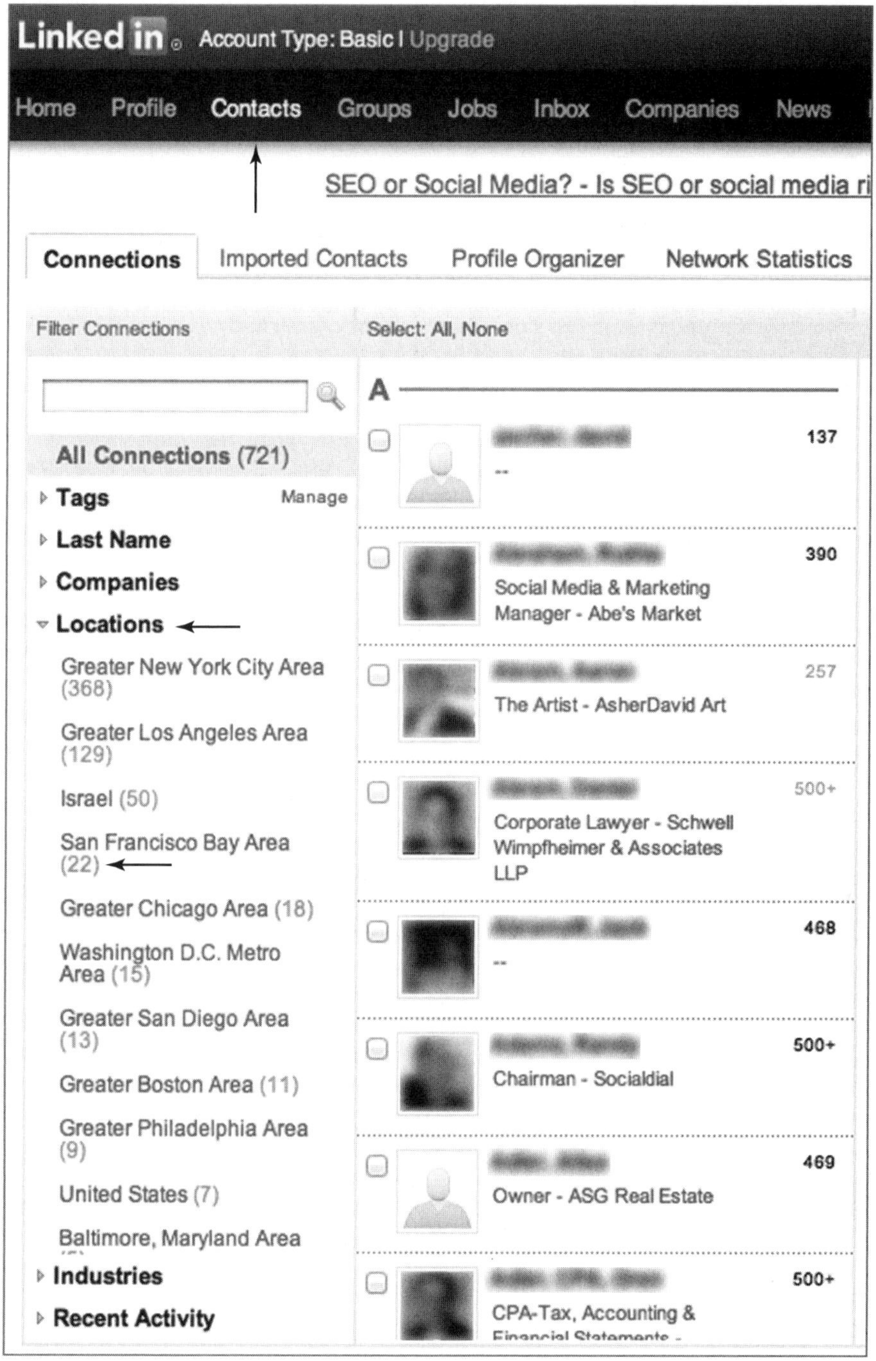

Figure 2.20 Locations and industries

Recommendations

Are you getting recommendations? Are they thorough? Descriptive? From good people? Sometimes you have to give to get. Or at least ask for them! When requesting recommendations:

- Only request recommendations from people you know.

- Remind them how you know them (change the default subject line).

- Give them some speaking points.

- If you know the person well and you think they won't mind, consider providing a few details and/or lines to get them started.

LinkedIn recommendations used to account for 15 percent of your Profile Completeness on LinkedIn, but that recently changed. (Now it doesn't contribute to completeness at all.) Nonetheless, I recommend you get 10–15 recommendations for your profile.

Week 15 in Chapter 5 focuses on giving and getting recommendations from your network.

Industry and Location Representation

When you look at your connections, what is the industry representation and location representation of your network? Are you connecting to people in the right industries and locations?

To check this out, go to the Contacts tab and the Connections drop-down, as shown in Figure 2.20. On the bottom-left side of the screen, click Locations and Industries, and you can see what industries and locations are best represented by your first-level connections. Do you need to connect with more people in more targeted companies, industries, or locations?

Well, that's it for Chapter 2. If you have completed your daily tasks then not only do you have the foundation and materials you need to create a powerful profile and marketing campaign on LinkedIn, but you've dipped your toe in and gotten started. If you're an experienced user of LinkedIn, maybe you've learned some new things and been introduced to a few of LinkedIn's new tools.

Next up: optimizing your profile!

Weeks 3–6: Ready, Set, Profile

In this chapter you'll learn how to optimize and customize your LinkedIn presence. I'll share some of the nifty "ninja tricks" I've picked up over the years, and show you, step by step, how to create a profile that will get you found and get you more business.

Chapter Contents

Week 3: Nifty Tools and Ninja Tricks for Creating Your Keyword List
Week 4: Optimize Your Profile and Be Findable
Week 5: Customize Your Profile to Stand Out in the Crowd
Week 6: Utilizing Extra Real Estate

Week 3: Nifty Tools and Ninja Tricks for Creating Your Keyword List

In a recent Tweetchat, one of the participants tweeted, "Thank you for telling us about keywords in LinkedIn. A recruiter found me and I was hired because she found my profile first."

Whether you are a job seeker, entrepreneur, sales professional, or the executive director for a nonprofit organization, having the right keywords in the right places can help you get found by whomever you want to get found by on LinkedIn.

If you have a website, you (or your web guru) might already have a good idea of what keywords are being used in your website to get your company, your product, or your service found on the Web. Keywords are simply words or phrases people use to find websites, businesses, places, or products on the Web.

Don't worry if you don't currently use, or have access to, those keywords. I'll show you some tricks that will help you gather all the keywords you will ever need for your social presence.

I want to be clear that keywording your social profiles on LinkedIn, Twitter, and Facebook is much easier than performing search engine optimization (SEO) on your website. While the keywords you gather over the next week can be used to optimize your website, those strategies are more sophisticated than the keyword techniques you'll explore in this chapter.

For more on search marketing and social publishing strategies, read Rob Garner's *Search and Social: The Complete Guide to Real-Time Marketing* (John Wiley & Sons, 2012).

Monday: Use LinkedIn's Related Skills

Do you remember seeing the Skills & Experience link on the More tab? Not only is it a great place to add skills (which is replacing the Specialties section in new LinkedIn profiles) to your profile, but also it is a great place to find keywords for your profile. Since this search originates within LinkedIn itself, it is by far my favorite keyword-finding tool.

Click on the Skills & Experience link and type in any skill that is relevant to your position, your education, your skill set, or your industry. For instance, you could start typing **Turnaround** if you do corporate turnaround or renewal consulting or management. As you begin to type, a drop-down menu should appear. If it doesn't, choose a synonym of your skill set. From the Skills page, you cannot create your own skill (but I'll show you how to do that later on), so choose the most pertinent one. For instance, you might choose from Turnaround Management, Turnaround, and Company Turnaround. Select the skill most relevant to your abilities—you can always come back to this page and other skills later.

Once you select a skill from the drop-down list, LinkedIn will take you to a new page. By clicking the blue Add Skill button, you will add your skill to your profile. Check out Figure 3.1 to see what the Skills page looks like.

Figure 3.1 Using skills to find keywords

The section of this page relevant to finding keywords is on the left side under Related Skills. Are there any of those related skills you might want to add to your profile as keywords?

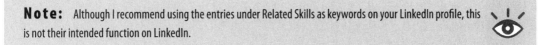

Note: Although I recommend using the entries under Related Skills as keywords on your LinkedIn profile, this is not their intended function on LinkedIn.

When the list of Related Skills is in alignment with your skill set (meaning you could indeed offer all those skills or services in your business), you can copy and paste the entire list into a Microsoft Word document, Notepad, or Microsoft Excel spreadsheet.

Note: When pasting the list into the new document, choose the option Save As Text Only if it's available. The links—which only mess up the formatting—are not copied. Most versions of Microsoft Word and Apple's Pages app offer this save option. Or you can simply use the Notepad (or similar) program many operating systems offer now.

Once you have the list in a document, just delete the skills that don't apply to you or wouldn't work as keywords. You will be creating a master list at the end of the week, so you can either save this list to your LinkedIn Executive Profile Questionnaire or create a new document. I named mine LinkedIn Keyword List and put it in my Stuff for LinkedIn folder on my desktop. If you have not done so already, you can download the LinkedIn questionnaire at www.sybex.com/go/linkedinhour.

Once you're done with one list, return to the More tab, click Skills, and add another skill to your profile. Or you can simply search using the Search Skills & Expertise field (right above Related Skills on the left side of the page). Keep diving down the rabbit hole until you have exhausted the skills you can offer. Copy and paste the list, delete unsuitable words, rinse and repeat.

We'll look at skills again later in this chapter as well as in Chapter 7, "Weeks 19–22: Get Strategic with LinkedIn's 'Other' Options."

You can add up to 50 skills to your profile. Later in this chapter I'll show you where to place your keywords for best optimization in "Week 4: Optimize Your Profile and Be Findable."

Tuesday: Discover Keywords through Google Ads

Another great tool for finding keywords is the Google AdWords Keyword Tool. It's free! You don't have to have an account or place an ad to use it. To find this tool, go to https://adwords.google.com/o/Targeting/Explorer?ideaRequestType=KEYWORD_IDEAS&__u=1657613616&__c=1078816536 or simply do an Internet search for **Google Keyword tool**. Google says this about its Keyword Tool: "You can search for keyword ideas by entering a keyword related to your business or service or a URL to a page containing content related to your business or service." What works for Google also works for LinkedIn.

If you have an AdWords account, go ahead and sign in. If you don't, ignore the request to sign in (you can still use the tool) and select the Tools And Analysis tab. On the Tools And Analysis page, you will see a Keyword Tool link on the left side. Click this link to access the Keyword Tool. Figure 3.2 shows what the Google Keyword Tool looks like and how to use it.

Since you are not optimizing your website but are looking for the most powerful search terms associated with your industry or profession, use the Word Or Phrase box. Don't worry about filling in the Website or Category section since doing so might limit the results.

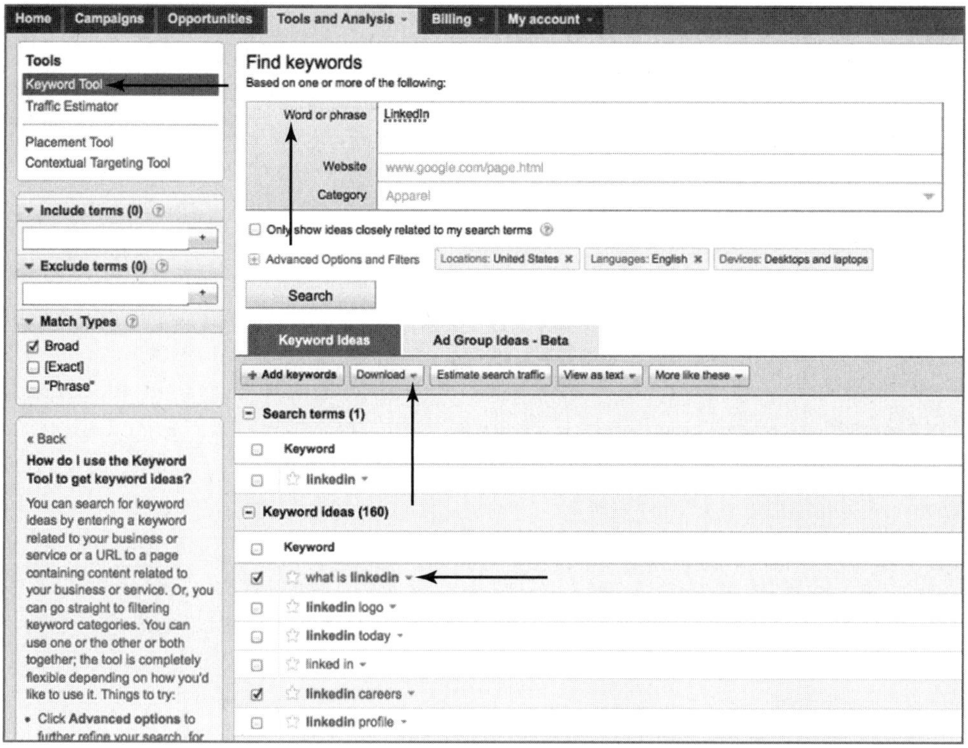

Figure 3.2 Google AdWords Keyword Tool

Choose Advanced Options and then specify your location and language. (The defaults are United States for location and English for language.) Click Show Ideas And Statistics For - Desktop And Laptop Devices. Then click Search and your new keyword results will appear.

Select the keywords you wish to download and then choose Download Selected. You can export your list to a text or a comma-separated value (CSV) file. I usually choose the text option because I do most of my work in Word, but if you are an Excel genius, then by all means choose the CSV option.

Wednesday: Use LinkedIn's People Search

If you know someone influential in your industry who has a LinkedIn profile, then look them up and check out their profile. To do so, enter their name in the simple People search field at the top right of your LinkedIn page and click on the blue magnifying glass to search. (Make sure the drop-down box reads People.)

What keywords and search terms have they used? Where have they used them? If they have been on LinkedIn for a while, they will have a Specialties section in their Summary. Often you will see keywords listed there, as well as in the Interests section.

Read through their profile and record relevant keywords. This exercise might also give you ideas about how to keyword and format your own profile. Feel free to take a look at my profile at www.linkedin.com/in/linkedinexpert.

Did you know you could download the profiles of your network's members as a PDF? When you are on a profile, you will see a link that says Download As A PDF. When you find a profile you like, download it and save it in your Stuff for LinkedIn folder for later reference.

After you have viewed all the Influencers you are interested in (or if you don't know an Influencer, or they are not on LinkedIn), search for a "type" of person: Accountant, CPA, Speaker, Trainer, IT Consultant, Attorney, and so forth.

This is one of the few times I'll tell you not to bother with the advanced search. The simple People search field will do fine:

1. Type your search term in the People search field.

2. Click on a profile.

3. Read through the profile, focusing on Specialties and Interests.

4. Add any keywords or search terms you might not have considered to your keyword list.

5. Save the profile as a PDF.

Thursday: Use Thesaurus.com and Dictionary.com

Dictionary.com and Thesaurus.com will also have some great keyword suggestions for you.

Open your keyword list document. If you go to www.dictionary.com first, put your keyword in the top search field. I like using this tool, because sometimes I choose keywords I think are appropriate to my skill set and services, but after checking Dictionary.com, I realize they are incorrect.

Once you find your word in Dictionary.com, beneath the definition of your searched word, you will see a link that says View More Related Words. When you click that link, it will take you to www.thesaurus.com. Add the related words or keywords that are relevant to your list.

Don't skip this step. It will help you create a more refined and accurate keyword list. Be sure to delete the keywords you find to be inappropriate for your skill set, service, product, or business.

Friday: Make Your List

Looking through your revised keyword list, make sure that you have the verb, noun, acronym (if applicable), and synonym for each word. (Thesauraus.com will get you your synonyms, Dictionary.com your verbs, nouns, and acronyms.) Are you a CPA? An accountant? Do you use QuickBooks? Business books? Prepare taxes? Make sure all your bases are covered!

Now you have a comprehensive (and possibly a very long) list in either a Word document or an Excel spreadsheet. Go through your list and prioritize your keywords, or number your keyword phrases from 1 to 20. If you have more keywords, great. You might be able to use them later. But most important right now is listing them 1 to 20. You'll be using these keywords in your title fields.

Now choose your top three keywords. You'll be using these top three keywords later in your professional headline.

Separate your keywords with a comma. Don't worry if there is some duplication, such as *business executive coach, executive business consultant*.

You'll be using up to 500 characters of this keyword list in Specialties (if you have access to it), and you'll be using up to 1,000 characters of this keyword list in Interests.

Every few months come back to your keyword list. Are the top three still your priority? Do some keywords need to be added or deleted? Keep your list up-to-date.

Before we move on to the next step, if you have not already done so add those top 20 keywords to your LinkedIn Executive Profile Questionnaire under the Keywords heading.

Week 4: Optimize Your Profile and Be Findable

This is one of my favorite things to do with clients: I love transforming a drab LinkedIn profile into a dynamic, findable, and effective representation of the person.

When I talk about optimizing profiles in LinkedIn, I don't just mean keyword-stuffing the section fields. I am also referring to the original meaning for the word *optimize*: to make as effective, perfect, or useful as possible.

That's what you want to accomplish in this next section—make your LinkedIn profile as effective, perfect, and useful as possible, while adding key search terms to fields heavily weighted by the LinkedIn search analytic.

Let's start with your professional headline.

Monday: Optimizing Your Professional Headline

One of the most underutilized sections on LinkedIn is Professional Headline. This is the section found right under your name, and it shows up everywhere: in searches, in your contact listing, when you start a discussion in a group or answer questions in Answers, and in company profiles. In any or all of these examples, LinkedIn will display a snapshot of your profile, including your name, your picture, and your professional headline.

Unfortunately, many people just go with the default "Title at Company" from their latest job. In fact, every time you add a position to Experience on LinkedIn, unless you *deselect* the box that says Update My Headline To, LinkedIn will overwrite whatever you have in your Professional Headline field. This is one of the reasons you should use the questionnaire—so that when LinkedIn overwrites your professional headline (and it will!), you have a record of the headline you so carefully crafted.

You have some real possibilities here. Take a look at the example professional headline in Figure 3.3.

Jane Doh

Actor & Stuntwoman: famously known as anonymous female usually found in movies & TV shows located in hospitals & morgues

Fort Collins, Colorado │ Human Resources

Figure 3.3 An example of a professional headline

Create your 120-character professional headline and add it to your questionnaire right now. This will allow you to:

- See what you are writing
- Check for spelling errors
- Add special characters like | or ★ or ✔ or •
- Do a character count
- Continue to customize as your life and work situation changes

To get to your professional headline on LinkedIn, make sure you click Edit Profile on the Profile tab. At the top of your profile, in the Header field (which has your picture, name, location, and so forth) click Edit next to your name.

About halfway down the next screen you will see the Professional Headline field. Notice how small the field is. You would never know you had 120 characters (including spaces and special characters) to write your headline. Use this section to share your areas of expertise and interest, to speak to your niche markets, and to add your tagline.

Your professional headline is a very important part of your LinkedIn presence and personal brand and it is completely editable. Take some time to create several versions of your professional headline. Ask your friends which they like best. Choose the one most appropriate for you at this time. Change it up every few months or so. Use your top three keywords if you can.

Tuesday: Optimize Your Title Fields

The Title field of your current and past positions is the most heavily weighted field by LinkedIn's search analytic. Most people only put their title in this section. But you actually have 100 characters (including spaces and special characters) to share *everything* you do at your company or business.

As I mentioned in Chapter 2, LinkedIn gives you the opportunity to upload your résumé but you shouldn't do it. You can certainly cut and paste data over from your résumé, but the Import Your Resume tool on LinkedIn can mess up your Experience and Education sections by uploading inaccurate information, uploading information into inaccurate fields, or replicating Experience and Education sections entirely. It will take you longer to fix the errors than to cut and paste the information into the appropriate fields.

Let's take a look at all the fields in the Experience section so you know what you can optimize with keywords:

- Adding A Position
- Company
- Website
- Industry
- Title

- Location
- Dates Of Employment
- Description

Figure 3.4 shows the Add Position page. Notice all the blank fields just waiting for you to fill them with keywords!

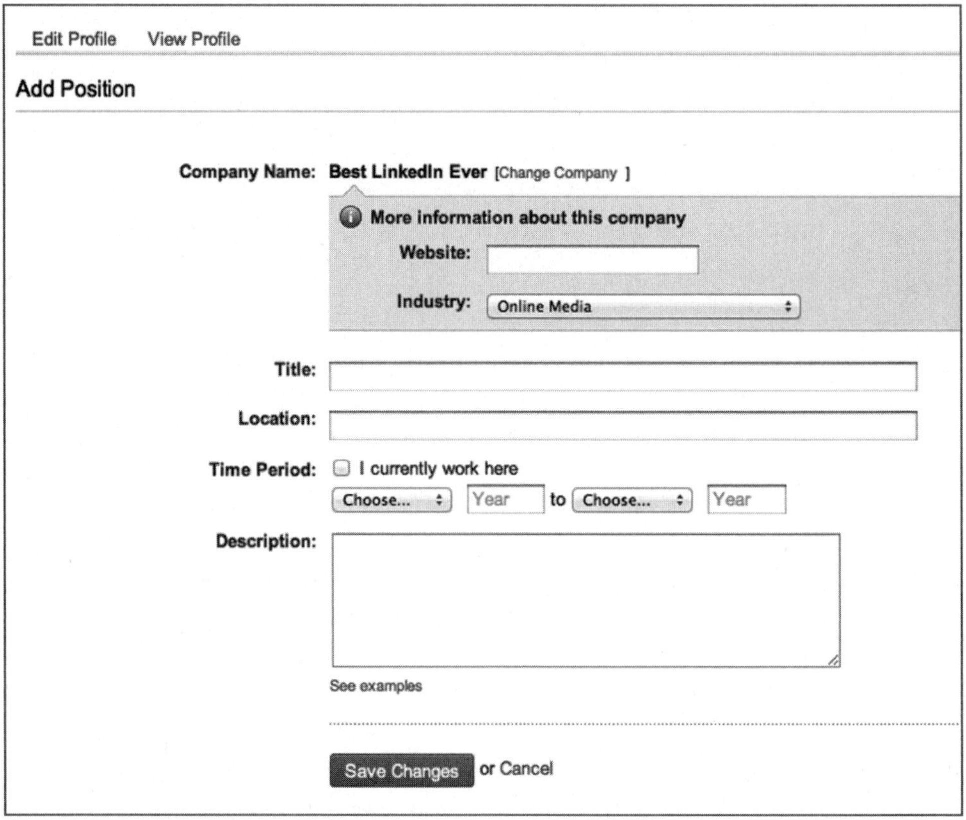

Edit Profile   View Profile

Add Position

Company Name: **Best LinkedIn Ever** [Change Company]

   ⓘ **More information about this company**

Website:

Industry: Online Media

Title:

Location:

Time Period: ☐ I currently work here

Choose... ⬍ Year to Choose... ⬍ Year

Description:

See examples

Save Changes or Cancel

Figure 3.4 Adding a current position

Adding a Position

To add a job or experience to your LinkedIn profile, whether current or past, click the link Add A Current Position. There is no Add A Past Position. To add a past position, click the current position link and make sure the I Currently Work Here box is unchecked.

Clicking Add A Current Position will take you to a field where you can add your company name, your industry, your location, your title, when you worked at the company, and a description of your business. (If you are a job seeker and don't currently work for a company, you'll find solutions in Chapter 11, "LinkedIn and You: Getting Specific.")

Company Name

As you start to type in your company name, a drop-down box will appear. If your company has already been added to LinkedIn, you can just click on the name as it appears. If it hasn't, just ignore the suggestions in the drop-down box and add your company name.

In order for you to show up as an employee in a LinkedIn company profile, your company name must match the name listed in the company profile exactly. If there is a company profile for XYZ, Inc. and you just added XYZ, you will not show up as an employee. If you have not yet created a company profile, LinkedIn might prompt you to create one. Just skip this step. We'll come back to it in Chapter 4, "Weeks 7–9: Use Your Company Profile for Branding and Positioning."

Website

After adding your company name, you can add the URL to your website if you have one. The link used to show up as a link to your website, but now your Company Title field link simply launches the LinkedIn company profile created by your company (or yourself). If there is no company profile for your company on LinkedIn, then LinkedIn will do a People search on your company name when someone clicks the link. As far as I can tell, at this time there is no reason to put your website URL in the Experience section. That being said, I still do it just in case there are some hidden benefits not apparent on the LinkedIn profile.

The website link you (may or may not) add here *is not* the websites section you see a little further down in your LinkedIn profile. I will cover how to add your websites to your LinkedIn profile a little later in this chapter.

Industry

In the LinkedIn header you were asked to add your industry. As you've probably seen, it's a rather limited list. You can add in this section whichever industry applies to you, either your own field of employment or the industry you work within. The industry does not have to be the same for each Experience section. For example, I have everything from Online Media Industry, to Publishing Industry, to Professional Speaking and Training Industry, to Marketing Industry in my various Experience sections. All are applicable, so I choose the one that is most relevant to the Experience (job) I have listed.

Location

Add the location of your business. Remember that *location* is also a keyword, especially if you are a location-based business. Many people ignore this field, but it is crucial to getting found in a LinkedIn search if people are looking for a company like yours in a specific location—Executive Business Coach in Atlanta, for example. You can add the city or town where your business is located as well as those cities you serve. If you are not location based, you can enter something like "Located in Ashland, NC, serving small business throughout the United States." You can use up to 100 characters. LinkedIn will also give you a location drop-down box as you start to type in your city, and you can choose from that as well. Be sure to separate cities or locations with a comma.

Title

Remember, this is the most critical field for LinkedIn's search analytic. I recommend putting the title that you have on your résumé first in the Title field. Then add all your job titles, your services, or your skills into this section.

If you are the CMO of a company, you might write something like this:

CMO, Chief Marketing Officer, Outbound and Inbound/Social Media Marketing Authority

Notice how you have the acronym for Chief Marketing Officer as well as the official title and the keywords Outbound, Inbound, and Social Media Marketing Authority. That way, whenever someone is looking for marketing, social media, or authority on LinkedIn, your profile will show up in the search.

On LinkedIn, the more you say something about yourself, the more findable you become! This being said, you also have to weigh the professional appearance of your profile. Just because your profile shows up doesn't mean people will read it.

If you are in a highly competitive field, it might be worth giving up a first-page LinkedIn search appearance to have a profile that is more professional.

Some people "keyword-stuff" their title fields, making up companies, in order to get found:

CEO/ Marketing Specialist/Sales and Advertising/Social Media Marketing Expert at A Company

CEO/ Marketing Specialist/Sales and Advertising/Social Media Marketing Expert at B Company

CEO/ Marketing Specialist/Sales and Advertising/Social Media Marketing Expert at C Company

CEO/ Marketing Specialist/Sales and Advertising/Social Media Marketing Expert at D Company

CEO/ Marketing Specialist/Sales and Advertising/Social Media Marketing Expert at E Company

CEO/ Marketing Specialist/Sales and Advertising/Social Media Marketing Expert at F Company

CEO/ Marketing Specialist/Sales and Advertising/Social Media Marketing Expert at G Company

CEO/ Marketing Specialist/Sales and Advertising/Social Media Marketing Expert at H Company

CEO/ Marketing Specialist/Sales and Advertising/Social Media Marketing Expert at I Company

CEO/ Marketing Specialist/Sales and Advertising/Social Media Marketing Expert at J Company

CEO/ Marketing Specialist/Sales and Advertising/Social Media Marketing Expert at K Company

Don't do that. It looks bad. Yeah, you might show up on the first page of a LinkedIn search, but no one will take your profile, or you, seriously. It might even deter business rather than attract it.

On the other hand, if you do consulting work in a highly competitive field, you might add your own business first in Experience, but then add the companies you consult with (with their permission) as other Experience instances.

If you do this, add the name of the company you consult with. Then fill out the Website, Industry, and Location fields. When adding your title, put Consultant down first and then add the various skills you bring to the table:

Consultant, Financial Forensics, Certified Financial Forensic Analysis (at Financial Forensics Company)

> **Note:** You can edit your current experience in the top gray box section of your LinkedIn profile (in Edit mode). To edit past positions, you will need to scroll down to the body of your profile.

Description

In the Description section you can use up to 1,000 characters to describe your business or what you do for it. Tell people why they should hire you or your company. Share your USP (Unique Selling Proposition). Give them the WIIFM (What's in It for Me). Most people ignore this section or copy a few lines from their résumé. But you have a real opportunity to engage prospective clients, customers, donors, partners, employees, or employers. Use CTAs (calls to action). Make the most of the 1,000 characters you are allocated.

I often recommend that people copy the About Us section from their company website into a Word document and then make it their own by customizing it to reflect their contribution to the company. Use the About Us section as a seed and customize it to reflect you and what you do for your company in your Experience section, as seen here:

> As General Manager and Marketing Director for the Executive Center, through the use of social media and networking I was able to double the business memberships at TEC in one year.
>
> At the Executive Center we consider ourselves to be an entrepreneurial incubator and training center as well as business center. We don't just provide professional, affordable suites for business owners, but we also offer training workshops, classes, networks and services our clients need to survive and excel in today's business environment. With private executive and life coaching, LinkedIn Training workshops, a Google-friendly prestigious address and so much more, we are the best bet for those professionals ready and willing to take the next step!

Your homework is to add relevant businesses you have owned, worked for, or worked with, and then go through all your listed experience, current and past, and add any relevant keywords to your Title field.

Once you have added keywords and businesses, do a quick keyword check in the People search to see where your profile shows up. (Sort by Relevance.) Continue to manipulate your Title fields until you show somewhere between the first and third pages of search results. The less competition you have on LinkedIn, the easier it is to achieve good search results.

You might have a friend look for you as well. Sometimes their results will differ, so you want to make sure you show up no matter who is looking for you!

Wednesday: Optimize Your Summary Section – Specialties

LinkedIn recently did away with the Specialties field in the Summary section. For those of you new to LinkedIn, you'll have to make do with the Skills and Expertise sections. But if you have been using LinkedIn for a while, you can still fully utilize the Specialties section.

You have 500 characters. I recommend copying and pasting your first 20 (or 30) keywords or keyword phrases into this section. Separate the words or phrases with a comma or make a bulleted list.

This section used to be highly weighted in the LinkedIn search, but with the introduction of the Skills section, I'm not sure how much longer this section will be viable—or even available.

Thursday: Optimize Your Summary – Professional Experience and Goals

The Summary section is often ignored, and yet it's very, very powerful. You can use up to 2,000 characters to write about who you are, what you want, and why someone should hire you.

Summary is similar to the Description field in the Experience section, but it's much more visible because it shows up higher in your profile.

I recommend that you create the Summary's Professional Experience and Goals first in your questionnaire so that you can:

- See how much space you actually have
- Format with bullets and special characters
- Utilize whitespace
- Catch spelling and grammatical errors
- Manipulate your compelling content

The field LinkedIn gives you to work within would make you think you had a paragraph at most to share your Experience and Goals. But 2,000 characters are closer to a page of text. Make the most of them!

In a Word document you can add bullets and special characters that will make your Summary stand out from the rest. By all means, make use of bullets and special characters, although you shouldn't go nuts with this. Using one or two special characters to draw the eye is okay, but a whole headline-full might look silly.

Note: Check your profile in different browsers. Some versions of Microsoft Internet Explorer, for example, may not translate special characters correctly.

Since you can't bold, italicize, or highlight your text, I recommend CAPITALIZING WHAT YOU WANT THE HUMAN EYE DRAWN TO. Within reason, of course. You don't want the entire paragraph to be a shouting match (many people consider capitalization shouting).

Use your whitespace. We have grown distracted as a culture, and we need to digest our information in bite-sized pieces. Breaking up your text with whitespace makes it more palatable.

Fix grammar and spelling issues. One of my clients is a well-known Internet marketing maven, and her profile was rife with spelling errors. This is a professional representation of you. Errors look bad.

You can add compelling content to this section. Why you rather than someone else? What do you bring to the table? Focus on the benefits of hiring you rather than just the features you offer.

Tell people why you are on LinkedIn and with whom you are willing to communicate. Are you an open networker who accepts most invitations? Tell people. Do you only connect to people you know? Let them know that too. Are you a recruiter? What kind of candidates are you looking for? Are you an Internet marketer? Who would make a good affiliate? Are you a job seeker? What do you bring to the table, and what kind of job or company are you looking for? Are you a service professional? Then who is your target market and what can you do for them that no one else can?

I've included a snapshot of my LinkedIn Summary in Figure 3.5.

Elements to Consider Adding to Your Summary

You might consider adding these elements to your summary. This is your opportunity to separate yourself from someone else. These are all ways to speak to and compel your audience:

- Differentiating factors: Why you?
- The WIIFM: What's in It for Me?
- USP: Unique Selling Proposition
- Mission statement
- POP: Point of Pain for your target market
- Brief list of features
- Who you'll connect with
- Why you are on LinkedIn
- CTAs: Calls to action

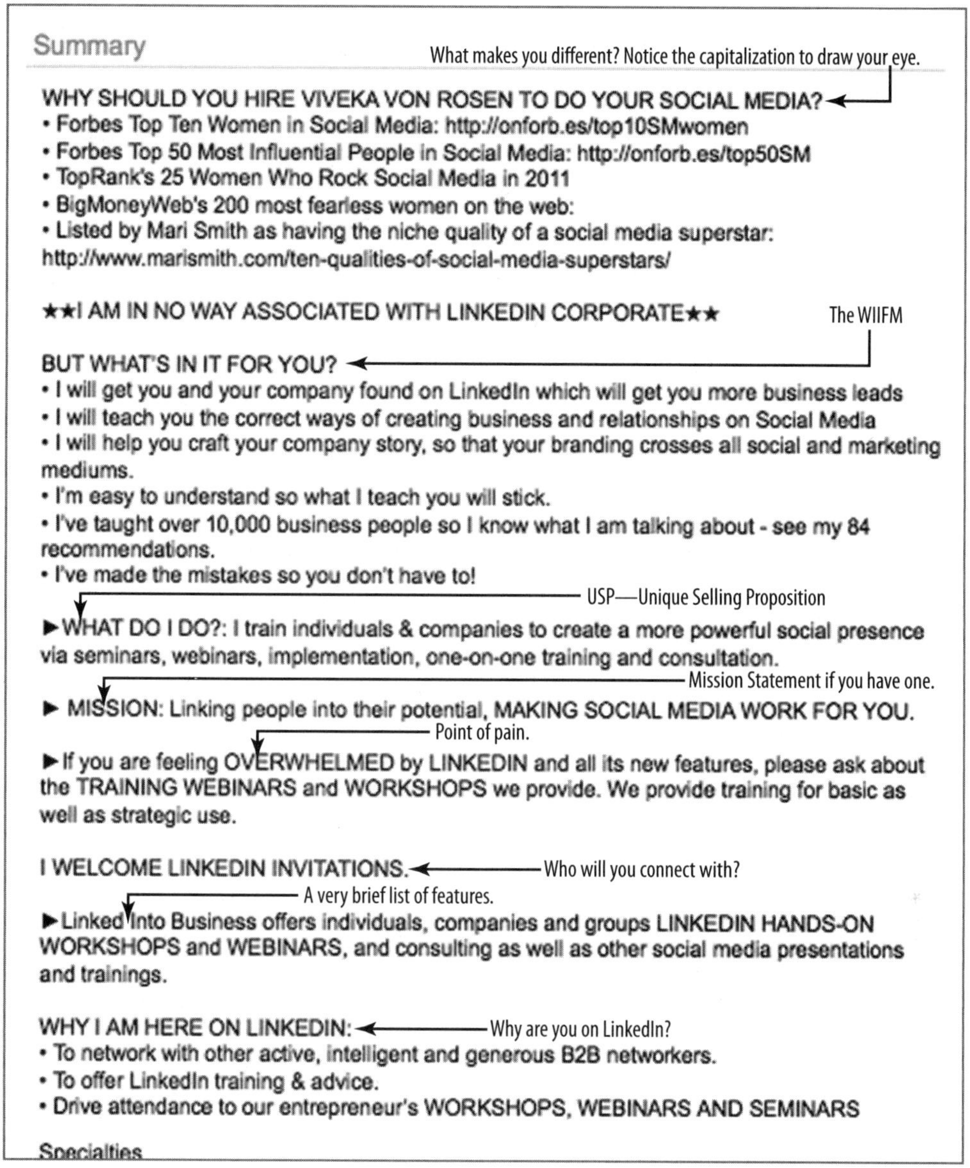

Summary   What makes you different? Notice the capitalization to draw your eye.

WHY SHOULD YOU HIRE VIVEKA VON ROSEN TO DO YOUR SOCIAL MEDIA? ◄
• Forbes Top Ten Women in Social Media: http://onforb.es/top10SMwomen
• Forbes Top 50 Most Influential People in Social Media: http://onforb.es/top50SM
• TopRank's 25 Women Who Rock Social Media in 2011
• BigMoneyWeb's 200 most fearless women on the web:
• Listed by Mari Smith as having the niche quality of a social media superstar:
http://www.marismith.com/ten-qualities-of-social-media-superstars/

★★I AM IN NO WAY ASSOCIATED WITH LINKEDIN CORPORATE★★   The WIIFM

BUT WHAT'S IN IT FOR YOU? ◄
• I will get you and your company found on LinkedIn which will get you more business leads
• I will teach you the correct ways of creating business and relationships on Social Media
• I will help you craft your company story, so that your branding crosses all social and marketing
mediums.
• I'm easy to understand so what I teach you will stick.
• I've taught over 10,000 business people so I know what I am talking about - see my 84
recommendations.
• I've made the mistakes so you don't have to!
                                              USP—Unique Selling Proposition
►WHAT DO I DO?: I train individuals & companies to create a more powerful social presence
via seminars, webinars, implementation, one-on-one training and consultation.
                                              Mission Statement if you have one.
► MISSION: Linking people into their potential, MAKING SOCIAL MEDIA WORK FOR YOU.
                                        Point of pain.
►If you are feeling OVERWHELMED by LINKEDIN and all its new features, please ask about
the TRAINING WEBINARS and WORKSHOPS we provide. We provide training for basic as
well as strategic use.

I WELCOME LINKEDIN INVITATIONS. ◄   Who will you connect with?
                                  A very brief list of features.
►Linked Into Business offers individuals, companies and groups LINKEDIN HANDS-ON
WORKSHOPS and WEBINARS, and consulting as well as other social media presentations
and trainings.

WHY I AM HERE ON LINKEDIN: ◄   Why are you on LinkedIn?
• To network with other active, intelligent and generous B2B networkers.
• To offer LinkedIn training & advice.
• Drive attendance to our entrepreneur's WORKSHOPS, WEBINARS AND SEMINARS

Specialties

Figure 3.5 Summary section

Friday: Optimizing Your Interests

It's Friday and you have better things to do, so I'm making it easy for you! Scroll
down to the bottom of your profile where it says Additional Information. Click in the
Interests field and cut and paste up to 1,000 characters' worth of your keywords into
this section. Done!

Week 5: Customize Your Profile to Stand Out in the Crowd

You can easily make a few adjustments to your LinkedIn profile that will make it more professional looking and more attractive to readers. Customizing your website links and public profile URL is a good start!

Monday: Personalize Your Public Profile and Customize Your Websites

As you learned in the previous chapter, LinkedIn allows you to create a unique URL for your LinkedIn public profile. If you missed it, here are the steps:

1. Scroll to the Public Profile link.
2. Click Edit next to the public profile URL. This will take you to a new page.
3. Click Customize Your Public Profile URL.
4. Choose FirstNameLastName with no spaces or special characters. LinkedIn will let you know if that URL is available by displaying a green check mark. If it's not available, LinkedIn will give you suggestions, or you can choose another URL. If you have a common name like Jane Doe, you might have to include your middle initial. You can also put your company name in this section so that it reads something like www.LinkedIn.com/in/LinkedIntoBusiness or include your area of expertise, as in www.linkedin.com/in/linkedinexpert.

The reasons you want to change your URL are:

- It will be easier for you to remember.
- It looks better in an email signature.
- It looks better on your résumé.
- It looks better on your business card.
- It looks more professional on your LinkedIn profile.

The other URL you can change is in the Website section. Figure 3.6 shows how I customized my website. Choose the Other option.

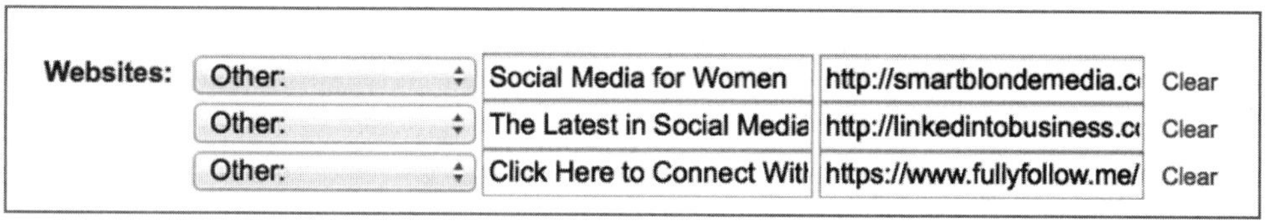

Websites:	Other:	Social Media for Women	http://smartblondemedia.c	Clear
	Other:	The Latest in Social Media	http://linkedintobusiness.c	Clear
	Other:	Click Here to Connect With	https://www.fullyfollow.me/	Clear

Figure 3.6 Customizing websites

The default for the Website option on LinkedIn is Personal Website. You also have the options Company Website, Blog, RSS Feed, Portfolio, or Other. The magic link is *Other*.

Remember when I asked you to choose your top three websites or landing pages in Chapter 2? Well, this is where you get to enter your results. Choose your top three websites or landing pages you have listed in your questionnaire and then click Other to open a new middle field. In this field you can:

- Type your URL (www.mycompany.com).
- Add your company name (Company XYZ).
- Add a call to action ("Click here for more info").
- Describe the landing page ("See testimonials here").
- Add an article ("Interview with New York Times").

If you own your business, you must choose the top three websites you want to represent yourself or your business. You can change these at any time. If you own or work for a large company, you can ask that all the websites you choose be divided up between employees. For instance, if you have three websites with 15 pages each (45 links in total) and you have 15 employees, you could assign each of them three different landing pages relevant to their position in the company, thus giving your business websites more coverage.

> **Note:** Be aware that you cannot demand that your employees add your URLs to their profiles, since legally they own their LinkedIn profile. But you can certainly request it of them, or host a training session where you walk them through this step.

Tuesday: Customizing Education

If this is the first time you are adding education to your profile, you can just click the Add A School link. It'll be in the top gray box section of your profile. But once you have added even a single school to your profile, the only place to add or edit your education is in the main body of your profile. Scroll down until you see the school you want to edit, or use the Add A School link.

You will want to add your accredited education to this section. I recommend creating a new instance for each degree. The good news is, you don't have to add the years that you attended your college or university. So those of you who attended college in 1826, no worries!

You can also add any kind of "additional" education you might have, such as professional certification or professional development activities. Did you get licensed or certified in your industry? Add that training. Did you take a weekend workshop to learn the latest and the greatest? Add that education. As long as the education is relevant to your business, you can add it to this section. See Figure 3.7 for the various fields available to you.

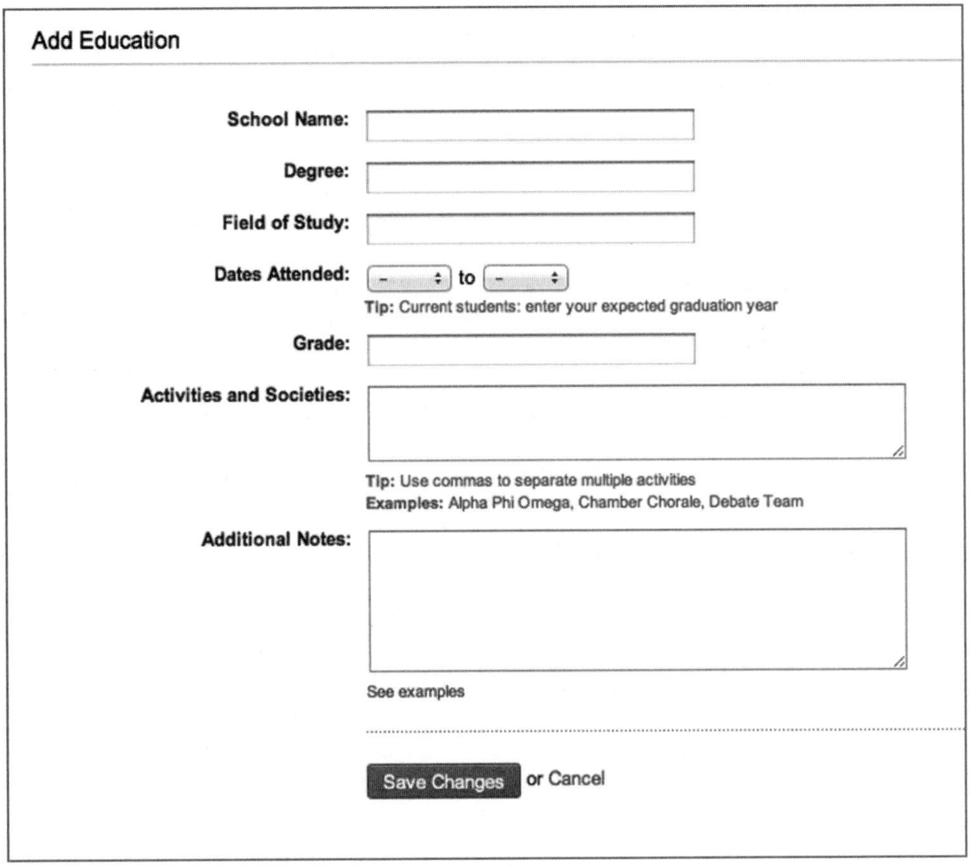

Add Education

School Name:	
Degree:	
Field of Study:	
Dates Attended:	– to –

Tip: Current students: enter your expected graduation year

Grade:	
Activities and Societies:	

Tip: Use commas to separate multiple activities
Examples: Alpha Phi Omega, Chamber Chorale, Debate Team

Additional Notes:	

See examples

 Save Changes or Cancel

Figure 3.7 Add Education

The fields you'll be working with are:

- School Name

- Degree
- Field Of Study
- Dates Attended
- Grade
- Activities And Societies
- Additional Notes

Adding a School

Make sure you are in Edit Profile mode. The first thing you are going to want to do is click Add A School (either in the top gray box section or in the body of your profile).

School Name

The first field asks for your school name. If it's an accredited institution, just add the school. If it is a certification or license, add the certifying or licensing body. If it's a weekend workshop, add the name of the workshop, seminar, or trade show. For instance, if I took a Social Media certification from The Social Media Summit, I would add **The Social Media Summit** in the School Name field.

Degree

The next field is for your degree. I recommend spelling it out (Bachelor of Science) since "Science" might be a keyword. If you attended a workshop, just add what you learned while you were there. For instance, I might add **Social Media Marketing Certification**.

Field Of Study

Under Field Of Study, describe your degree. Did you concentrate on a specific focus or topic? If you are adding the workshop, you might briefly describe what you learned, such as LinkedIn, Twitter, Facebook, Google+, and Pinterest Marketing. Often your field of study will contain keywords.

Dates Attended

As mentioned earlier, the date you attended school is now optional. In fact, once you have added all your schools and education, you can move each instance around by dragging and dropping the school, putting the most important education first. (I'll show you how to move the sections of your profile around later in this chapter.)

Harvard should probably show up before your certification in astrology.

Activities and Societies

Your activities and societies go in the next field. These are linked and can be found by the LinkedIn search algorithm. So this is a good area for keywords, although please don't add any keywords that are not relevant to your actual education.

Additional Notes

The Additional Notes section is similar to the Description field in your Experience section. You have 2,000 characters to describe what you learned and who you learned it from. You can add special projects you participated in—anything that differentiates you from everybody else.

You can also go to the school's or workshop's website (if they have one) and cut and paste information from the school or event into this section. Personalize this section a bit to describe what *you* loved and learned.

I recommend creating your Additional Notes section in a Word document first so you can format and personalize it. As with every field in LinkedIn, you can edit education whenever you want.

Remember to save your changes.

I highly recommend you take a look at your résumé right now. Add any education, schools, workshops, certifications, and licenses you might not have considered, and then edit your existing education and fill out those Activities And Societies and Additional Notes sections. Over the next few days as you begin to remember workshops you've taken, or licenses and certifications that you've earned, add those to these sections as well. Remember, you have to go into the body of the text to include additional or edit existing education.

Wednesday: Customize Groups and Associations

Another ignored area is the Groups And Associations section. If people add anything at all, it's usually a very brief mention of an association they are currently a member of. However, this 1,000-character field not only is visible to LinkedIn's search analytic, but it also helps to support your influence and authority in an industry, school, business, or location. Figure 3.8 shows an example of how I customized my Groups And Associations field.

Groups And Association is located under Additional Information and is not to be confused with Groups, found under the Groups tab in the main toolbar that we were looking at earlier.

You can add any group and/or association that you are a member of now, that you have been a member of in the past, or that you have volunteered for (unless of course that group is adversative to your business—conspiracy theorists who work for the government should probably not add their associations in this section). Use caution when adding religious or political affiliations.

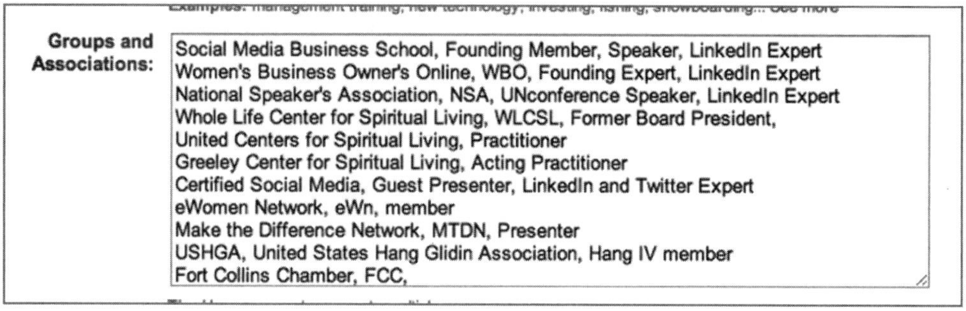

Groups and Associations:	Social Media Business School, Founding Member, Speaker, LinkedIn Expert Women's Business Owner's Online, WBO, Founding Expert, LinkedIn Expert National Speaker's Association, NSA, UNconference Speaker, LinkedIn Expert Whole Life Center for Spiritual Living, WLCSL, Former Board President, United Centers for Spiritual Living, Practitioner Greeley Center for Spiritual Living, Acting Practitioner Certified Social Media, Guest Presenter, LinkedIn and Twitter Expert eWomen Network, eWn, member Make the Difference Network, MTDN, Presenter USHGA, United States Hang Glidin Association, Hang IV member Fort Collins Chamber, FCC,

Figure 3.8 Customizing Groups And Associations

Click on Edit next to Additional Information at the bottom of your profile. I recommend adding:

- The name of the group and/or association
- The acronym for the group or association
- Your position in that group or association

You can add these in bullet form, or separate the groups or associations by commas.

Some groups or associations to consider:

- Professional groups or associations
- Corporate or scholastic alumni associations
- Networking groups
- Industry associations
- Volunteer and charitable organizations

Take a few minutes to add to this section new groups and associations you might not have considered. Also edit existing instances to include your position.

> **Note:** Remember to add groups and associations you have volunteered for, even if you were not a member. While I travel too much right now to join my local Denver NSA (National Speakers Association), I often speak at their conferences. In my Groups And Associations field I wrote "NSA, National Speakers Association, Speaker and Break Out Session lecturer." (Note the keywords.)

Thursday: Customizing Awards

Under Groups And Associations is the Awards field. This is where you will add every award you've ever achieved that is in any way, shape, or form relevant to you business or industry.

Professional awards you received will weigh more heavily than an award you won in college, so add your professional awards first. But do add anything that is relevant to your business or industry. Consider including mentions in important publications and nominations. Ask your friends and family what honors and awards they remember you getting. Over time you will slowly fill out this section.

Friday: Add Sections: Publications, Licenses, Patents, Languages, Courses, Volunteer Work

Recently LinkedIn added a new Add Sections option, shown in Figure 3.9.

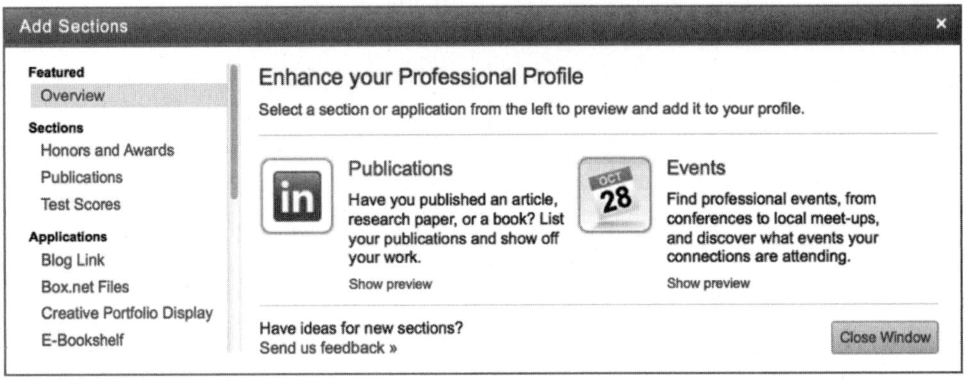

Figure 3.9 Add Sections

You can find this option right under the top gray box section under the snapshot of your profile. Click this link and add the following sections:

- Certifications
- Courses
- Honors And Awards
- Languages
- Organizations
- Projects
- Patents
- Publications
- Test Scores
- Volunteer Experience & Causes
- Applications (these are the same as those under the More tab)

Certifications Even if you added your certifications to the Education section, add them here as well. To add a certification, simply click Certification, then Add To Profile. LinkedIn will ask for your certification name, the certifying authority, your license number, and the dates of validity for your certificate. Once you have completed these fields, click Add Certification.

Courses The Courses section is pertinent to those people who are still in school, who took just a few courses to round out their experience, or who didn't finish school but still want credit for the courses taken. It might also help with keyword searchability too. You simply add the course name, course number, and the occupation associated with the course. Once you have completed these fields, click Add Course.

Honors And Awards If you want to share more information about the honor or award you received that you mentioned in the Additional Information section, then click on this additional section. You will add the name of the award, who issued it, what your occupation was at the time and when you received it, as well as up to 2,000 characters describing the award and why you received it.

Languages If you are bilingual, trilingual, or more, this section is for you. Being multilingual is a valuable skill in the business world. Obviously you want people to know which languages you are familiar and proficient with in addition to English. Click Add Language and choose your proficiency with the language. Be sure to click Save Changes.

Organizations Organizations are similar to what you added in the Groups And Associations field, but go ahead and add your organizations again. It helps with keywords and you can give a bit more detail about your activities in the organization. When you click Add Organization, LinkedIn will ask for the organization's name, your position(s), when you participated, and your occupation while you had held that position as well as a description of your position in the organization. I recommend going to the organization's website (if there is one) and copying the About Us section, customizing it to reflect your position.

Projects The Projects section allows you to include any past or current project you have worked on. It lets you fill in the name of the project, add your occupation during the project, and include other project team members to this section. You can add a URL, the timeframe (current or past), and a description. This is an incredibly powerful tool for job seekers.

Patents Do you have, or are you working on, a patent? Then you absolutely want to add this section. Click Add Patents. LinkedIn will ask for the following:

- Patent office
- Whether the patent has been issued or is pending
- Patent/application number
- Patent title
- Issue/filing date
- URL if applicable
- Other inventors (as long as you're connected to them on LinkedIn)
- Summary of the patent

Don't miss this section if you do have a patent. It goes a long way in sanctioning your expertise.

Publications Did you know you could add publications to your profile? If you are a published author, write a blog, or have created an eBook, add your publications to this section. As of this writing, LinkedIn will post your publications in the order you enter them (first entered shows up first on your profile), so make sure you add your most important publications first.

Test Scores If you are currently a student, or a recent graduate who is job seeking, you will want to add test scores. Let your future employer or clients know if you received high grades on your SATs, GREs, LSATS, and so forth. You can also share test scores for technical certifications, highlighting your proficiency in your industry.

Volunteer Experience & Causes You also want to add any volunteer experience you have or causes you support, consider adding this section to your profile. This will not only showcase your altruistic nature, but it's another opportunity to add keywords. To add Volunteer Experience & Causes, click the link and then the Add To Profile button.

Now you can choose which cause you are interested in and what organizations you support and also which ones you have volunteered for.

For Volunteer Experience, add the Organization, Role, Cause, Time Period, and a Description.

Applications We'll talk a lot more about applications in Chapter 7, "Weeks 19–22: Get Strategic with LinkedIn's 'Other' Options."

So that pretty much covers the Additional Sections tool on LinkedIn. Be sure to take the time to add these sections to your profile. They can make your profile shine in comparison to the profiles of your competitors on LinkedIn and gives you an opportunity to add lots of useful keywords to your profile.

Week 6: Utilizing Extra Real Estate

You have a lot of extra real estate on LinkedIn that gets underutilized. So let's take a look at some of the things you can do with these sections and tools on LinkedIn.

Monday: Customize Contact Me

The Contact Me section (which shows up as Contact [Your Name] For) is found at the bottom of your profile. This section is often completely ignored by LinkedIn users. But you can add up to 2,000 characters of additional information to your profile in this section. Next to Contact (Your Name), click the Change Contact Preferences link to edit this field.

As you can see in Figure 3.10, the first part of this section will be familiar to you.

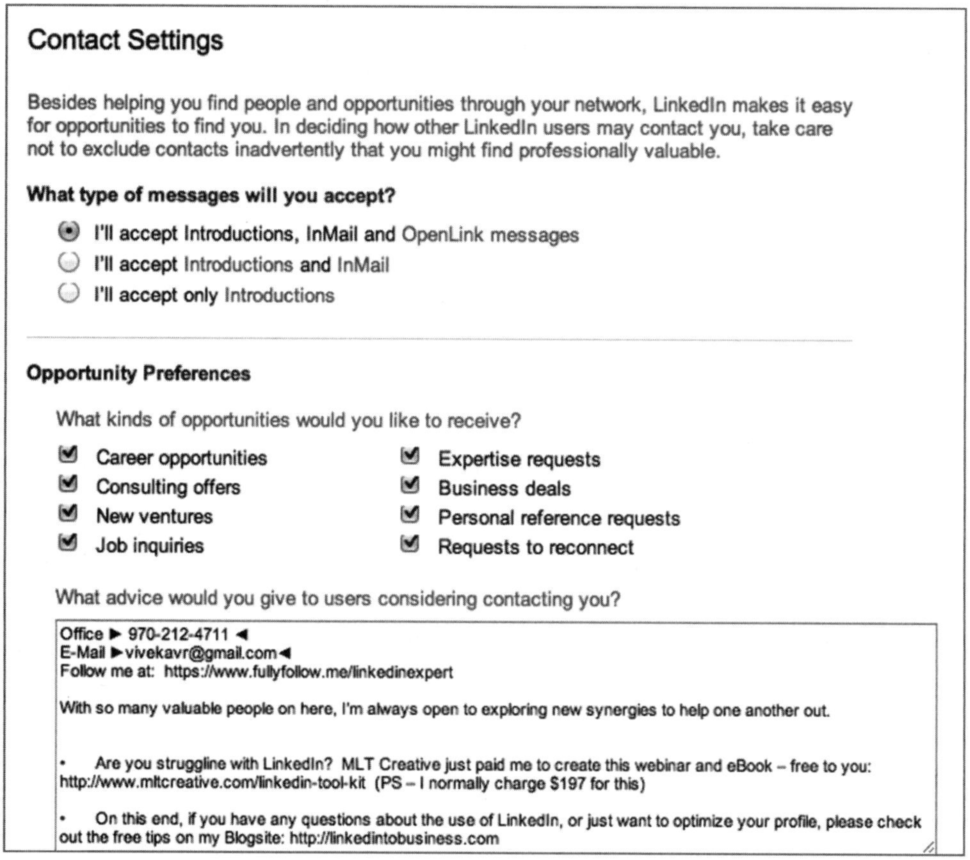

Contact Settings

Besides helping you find people and opportunities through your network, LinkedIn makes it easy for opportunities to find you. In deciding how other LinkedIn users may contact you, take care not to exclude contacts inadvertently that you might find professionally valuable.

What type of messages will you accept?

- ⦿ I'll accept Introductions, InMail and OpenLink messages
- ○ I'll accept Introductions and InMail
- ○ I'll accept only Introductions

Opportunity Preferences

What kinds of opportunities would you like to receive?

- ☑ Career opportunities
- ☑ Consulting offers
- ☑ New ventures
- ☑ Job inquiries
- ☑ Expertise requests
- ☑ Business deals
- ☑ Personal reference requests
- ☑ Requests to reconnect

What advice would you give to users considering contacting you?

> Office ▶ 970-212-4711 ◀
> E-Mail ▶ vivekavr@gmail.com ◀
> Follow me at: https://www.fullyfollow.me/linkedinexpert
>
> With so many valuable people on here, I'm always open to exploring new synergies to help one another out.
>
> •   Are you struggline with LinkedIn? MLT Creative just paid me to create this webinar and eBook – free to you: http://www.mltcreative.com/linkedin-tool-kit (PS – I normally charge $197 for this)
>
> •   On this end, if you have any questions about the use of LinkedIn, or just want to optimize your profile, please check out the free tips on my Blogsite: http://linkedintobusiness.com

Figure 3.10 Customizing Contact Settings

For types of messages you'll accept, choose I'll Accept Introductions And InMail.

Under Opportunity Preferences, I recommend checking all of the boxes. (The only exception for this might be for currently employed job seekers who don't want their boss to know they are seeking employment. In that case, leave Job Inquiries unchecked.)

Now we come to the good part. In the field that asks "What advice would you like to give users considering contacting you?" you can write just about anything you want. You would never know it by looking at this teeny tiny field, but you have 2,000 characters of real estate to work with.

Some uses for this section:

- Add more contact information like phone numbers, email addresses, and any website addresses you couldn't add to the Websites section (unfortunately, they will not be linked).

- Add recommendations or testimonials from people not on LinkedIn.

- Add additional information about yourself or your business.

- Create what I call Rules of Engagement to let people know what you are, and what you are not willing to share and do on LinkedIn (I'll discuss this in a moment).

A great example of this is Kenneth Weinberg's LinkedIn profile at www.linkedin .com/in/kennethweinberg (more on Rules of Engagement in the next section).

If there is something you want to add to your LinkedIn profile and you've run out of space in another field, this is the place to put it. (This area is not keyword searchable, so you don't have to keyword-stuff it!)

Definitely create this first in a Word document.

Tuesday: Create Rules of Engagement

There is no official section called Rules of Engagement. Nonetheless, you might want to create your own set of communication rules and share them with your network in the Contact section mentioned earlier.

Rules to consider:

- Who are you willing to connect to? Only people you know? Friends of friends? Anyone?

- Who are you willing to write a recommendation for? Will you write recommendations only for colleagues? Employees? Peers? For people you don't know? Do you want people to give you some hints about what to write? Do you want a recommendation in return?

- Who are you willing to make an introduction for? Anyone in your network? Only people you know? Who are you willing to send an introduction on to? Anyone in your network? Only people you know? What do you want from your contact in order to pass along an introduction? An explanation of why they want to be introduced?

- Who are you willing to receive messages and InMails from? Potential clients and customers, people wanting to get reacquainted, potential vendors?

- What will cause you to disconnect from someone? Spam in your message box? Spam via InMail? Getting added to newsletters without permission? Being added to a giant LinkedIn letter without BCC? Sexual solicitations or requests for your social security number because there is money waiting for you in another country?

Writing your Rules of Engagement doesn't guarantee that people will actually follow them, but it's a good first step. A great example of this is Kenneth's profile, as you can see in Figure 3.11.

```
Contact Kenneth for:

Feel free to contact me!!!
I prefer contacts through e-mail...If you drop me one I will respond.


I am a strong believer in networking and meeting new people. Sharing different ideas and ways
of accomplishing the goals that are ahead of us is what develops us and makes us constantly
more efficient.

When you will ask me to forward a request understand that I will review and consider in order
to keep my Connections free of Spam.

Requests:

I am approachable to all, and I will try and answer you all, BUT when you will ask me to
forward a request you will find me much more selective, for all the good reasons of not wanting
to spam my friends.

Be sure to give me the information that lets me know why I should endorse this person, idea,
introduction.

For example:

1) Do you know/work(ed) with/respect the person you are referring to/through me?

2) Is the idea/proposal/plan/information the person is seeking to send to/through me something
you know about and can vouch for (the quality)?

3) "Other" reason you think it is worth your/my time and credibility to support this request.
```

Figure 3.11 Rules of Engagement

Wednesday: Add LinkedIn Skills & Expertise

The Skills section allows you to add your own unique skills to your LinkedIn profile. Earlier we looked at Skills (found under More in the main toolbar at the top of the page) to find the Related Skills you can use as keywords. But how can you add and edit your Skills section once you have added it?

To edit your Skills section, scroll down into the body of your profile when you are in Edit Profile mode. As of this writing, both Edit and Add A skill will take you to the page shown in Figure 3.12.

Once on this page, you can add any skill you have, even underwater basket weaving if you want! (You cannot do this under the More tab.) You can delete any skill that is not relevant to your skill set, and you can shift your skills around to list your most pertinent skills first by dragging and dropping them.

You can even move this whole section up higher in your profile, as you will see in the next section.

Take a few minutes to cull your skills list, add skills unique to you and your abilities, and prioritize what you have. You can add up to 50 skills, although I think a happy medium of about 25 skills looks best.

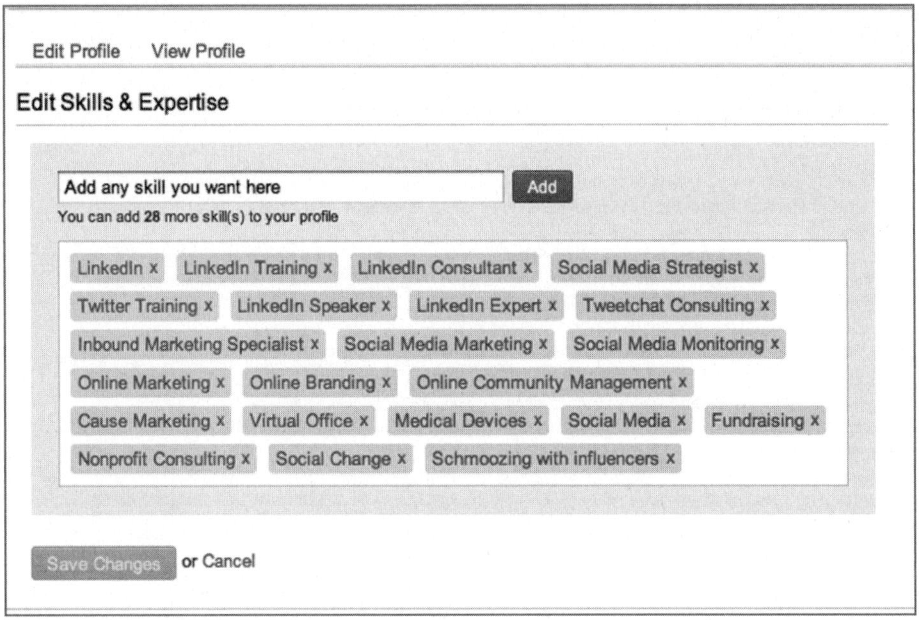

Figure 3.12 Editing Skills & Expertise

Thursday: Moving Things Around

I've already mentioned that you can move some of LinkedIn's sections around.

To do this, you must be in Edit Profile mode. Shift your cursor over the heading of the section you want to move. Your cursor will change, which will allow you to grab your section by clicking on it while holding your mouse button down. (On some computers, it's a right-click.) Shift your section to the area you want and then drop it in by releasing your mouse or tracking pad.

You can see how to do this in Figure 3.13.

Some areas you can shift:

- The entire Experience section.
- Individual current Experience sections within the greater Experience section. (Past experience will remain in chronological order.)
- The entire Education section.
- Individual schools within the Education section.
- Your entire Summary section, including Specialties if appropriate.
- All of your added sections.
- The whole Recommendations section.
- Individual Recommendations according to Experience.
- The entire Additional Information section.
- The entire Contact section.

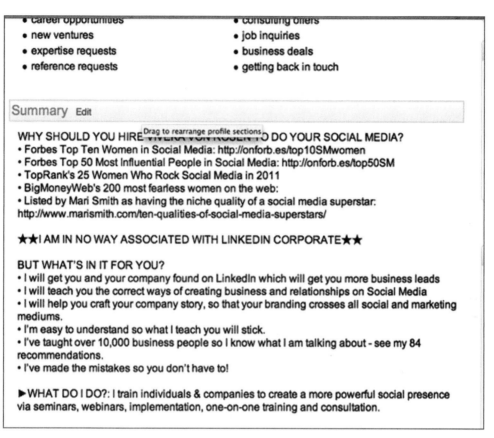

Within the image:

- career opportunities
- new ventures
- expertise requests
- reference requests

- consulting offers
- job inquiries
- business deals
- getting back in touch

Summary Edit

WHY SHOULD YOU HIRE [Drag to rearrange profile sections] TO DO YOUR SOCIAL MEDIA?
• Forbes Top Ten Women in Social Media: http://onforb.es/top10SMwomen
• Forbes Top 50 Most Influential People in Social Media: http://onforb.es/top50SM
• TopRank's 25 Women Who Rock Social Media in 2011
• BigMoneyWeb's 200 most fearless women on the web:
• Listed by Mari Smith as having the niche quality of a social media superstar:
http://www.marismith.com/ten-qualities-of-social-media-superstars/

★★I AM IN NO WAY ASSOCIATED WITH LINKEDIN CORPORATE★★

BUT WHAT'S IN IT FOR YOU?
• I will get you and your company found on LinkedIn which will get you more business leads
• I will teach you the correct ways of creating business and relationships on Social Media
• I will help you craft your company story, so that your branding crosses all social and marketing mediums.
• I'm easy to understand so what I teach you will stick.
• I've taught over 10,000 business people so I know what I am talking about - see my 84 recommendations.
• I've made the mistakes so you don't have to!

▶WHAT DO I DO?: I train individuals & companies to create a more powerful social presence via seminars, webinars, implementation, one-on-one training and consultation.

Figure 3.13 Moving things around

This is how I set up my profile and why.

I left the Summary And Specialties section right where it was. It's the first thing that shows up below the fold and is still often read by the people who find my profile. Since it includes the WIIFM (what's in it for them), it becomes an important sales tool for me.

I then pulled my Contact section up underneath Summary because I had more information I wanted to share. I added several valuable free resources (in the form of URLs) as well as descriptions of what those resources were and what they could do for the reader.

Because I think what others say is more important than what I say, I pulled my Recommendations up underneath the Contact Me section. As of this writing, you cannot shift the recommendations by Experience, but at least you can shift the recommendations *within* the Experience listing.

After Recommendations I added Skills, Publications, and then Applications to give people a better sense of my abilities and what I bring to the table (as well as examples of my writing and a video).

Then I added my Experience and Education and finished up with my Additional Information.

List your sections in order of importance to you—or more importantly, list your sections according to what is important to you potential clients, employees, employers, donors, vendors, or partners.

Friday: Back It Up

So once again it's Friday, and I'm going to make it easy on you. All I want you to do is back up your LinkedIn profile. There are a few different ways to do that.

The old-fashioned way: The first thing you can do is open your profile on LinkedIn. Make sure you are in View Profile mode (this option appears on the Profile tab).

Most browsers have an edit function, so under Edit on your browser, click Select All and then Copy. Open a new word processing page (Word, Pages, Google Docs, OpenOffice) and click Paste. I recommend that you choose Save As Text Only because otherwise you're going to have a lot of graphics and wonky formatting to deal with.

This is just a backup. You probably won't be showing this to anyone, although you might use it in the future to cut and paste information into your LinkedIn profile if for some reason yours get corrupted. (I'm a big fan of repurposing content, as you already know.) It's always good to have your LinkedIn profile backed up in case something happens. Once you have your profile in a document, save it as **LinkedIn backup** and add the date so you can differentiate between backups. Put it into your Stuff for LinkedIn folder.

For a nicer backup of your profile, save it as a PDF. This is less editable, but much nicer to share. I've shown you the PDF link in Figure 3.14.

From View Profile, you'll scroll down until you see the PDF icon. Click that icon and a PDF will open up. (If you don't have a PDF reader, I recommend Adobe Reader. You can download Adobe Reader at www.adobe.com/products/reader.html.)

Once the PDF opens, go to the File tab and click Save As. You save it as a PDF or text file, or to Word or Excel online.

> **Note:** The PDF version of your LinkedIn profile is a nice-looking document you can now share with prospective clients, vendors, employers, donors, and so forth *whether they are on LinkedIn or not*. It's better than sharing your public profile URL because you can still share the information you might have hidden from view on your public profile.

Of course, if you want a hard copy of your profile you can simply print it in that same section. Or you can save as a PDF from your printer as well.

And by the way, you can do this with other people's profiles as well as long as they are in your network. (For out-of-network folks, you can only share or print—there's no option to save as a PDF.)

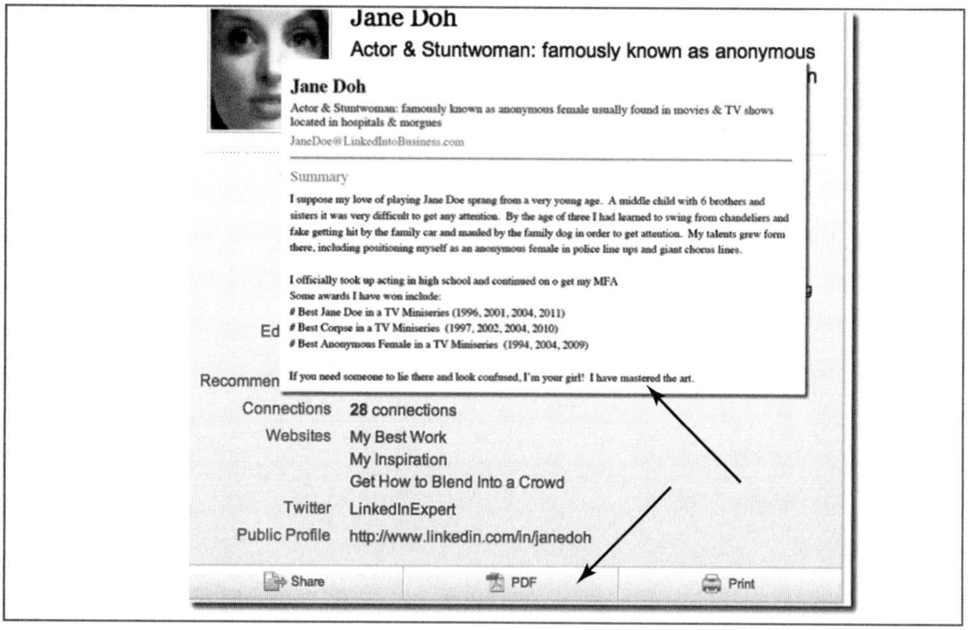

Figure 3.14 Backing up your profile

So go on! Go back up your LinkedIn profile right now. And we will see you next week for Chapter 4, "Weeks 7–9: Use Your Company Profile for Branding and Positioning."

Weeks 7–9: Use Your Company Profile for Branding and Positioning

This chapter is all about LinkedIn company profiles—how you can create your own, optimize your existing profile, and strategically follow and analyze other company profiles. We'll show you what you can and can't do with a company profile, how to get started on creating a company profile, and how to add products and services. We'll take a look at posting updates and jobs, researching analytics, and following other companies and reading their analytics.

Chapter Contents

Creating a Company Profile
Adding Products and Services
Company Updates, Analytics, and Job Postings—Yours and Others

Week 7: Creating a Company Profile

In Week 7, I'll take you step by step through creating your own company profile on LinkedIn. Even if you already have a company profile, do a quick read through this section to make sure your profile is fully optimized. LinkedIn has made a lot of changes within the past year, such as adding targeted product and service pages and company status updates. Make sure you are making the most of what LinkedIn has to offer.

Monday: Get Started on Your Company Profile

It's Monday morning and a great time to get started on creating your company profile. Before you do, it's a good idea to see if your company already has a profile on LinkedIn. Many people are surprised to discover that a company profile already exists. The reason for this is, for a while, LinkedIn was prompting everyone who added a company to their experience section to create a company. There were a lot of company profiles created by people who didn't know what they were doing. So first step first, check to see if your company already has a profile on LinkedIn.

You can search for your company's LinkedIn profile by going to the Company tab and clicking Search Companies. Or on the right-hand side of your page, in the general search area, click the Company option in the drop-down box. Both options will take you to the same page. In Search Companies, simply type in your company name and click Search.

If your company does in fact have a profile, check to see if you're in a position to edit it. If you see a small blue box on the right side of your page that says Admin Tools (as shown in Figure 4.1), then you are in good shape.

If there is *no* such box, check the Overview, Careers And Products And Services menu. There should be a linked message that reads, "To edit company pages please contact an admin," and then under that is a See Admin List link. Those are the people who are currently administering the page and they can give you administrative rights.

If you see your company profile but do not have the option of seeing the admin list, then contact customer service at CS@linkedin.com. You will have to meet LinkedIn's requirements for adding or editing company pages. These requirements are as follows:

- You must be a current company employee and your position must appear on your profile.

- You must have a company email address and it must be confirmed in the email addresses on your LinkedIn account in the Settings section.

- Your profile must be associated with the right company. You have to click on a name in the Company Name drop-down list and then edit or add your position in your profile in your Experience section in order to be associated with the right company.

- Your company's email domain must be unique to the company.

- Your profile must be more than 50 percent complete.

- You must have more than 10 connections.

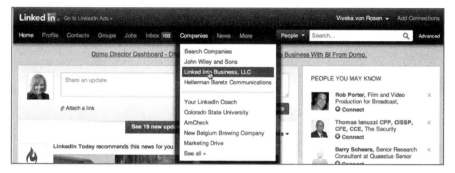

Figure 4.1 Admin Tools

If your meet all the qualifications, you should be able to edit your company profile.

Note: To help prevent spam, LinkedIn won't allow you to use common email domain names like Yahoo!, Gmail, and Hotmail. You cannot use these when you're creating a company page because they are not unique to an individual company.

You can always consider creating a group if your company profile does not have a unique email domain.

If you have done a search on LinkedIn and your company does not yet have a profile, select the Companies tab and click the Create A Company button on the right side of the page, as shown in Figure 4.2.

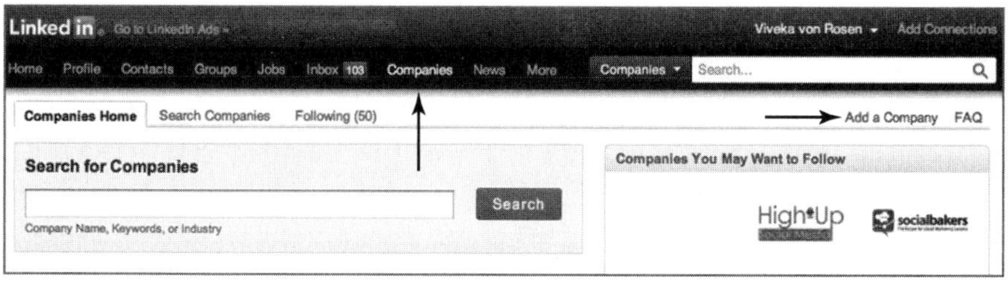

Figure 4.2 Creating a company

Tuesday: Name Your Company

The first thing you need to do is name your company (see Figure 4.3). I do not recommend including Inc., LLC, or Corp. in your company name. With most companies I recommend adding the entire name of the company, although IBM uses its acronym. Be careful with the name you choose, because it is not easy to change.

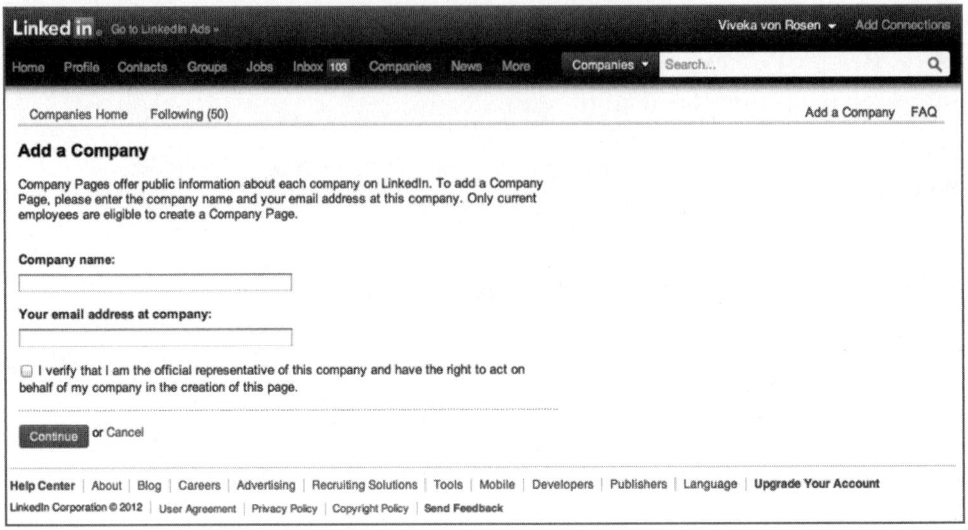

Figure 4.3 Naming your company

As you can see in Figure 4.3, LinkedIn will ask you for your email address. Make sure that the email address is the domain name associated with the company profile you are creating. Also make sure you have added it to your Settings section (Account tab › Add & Change Email Addresses). If your email address is not in this section, you will not be able to create a company profile. If you haven't yet done so, go there right now and add your email address to the Settings section.

You will also want to add your company logo. (Make sure you have permission to use that company logo.) You can add a standard logo and/or a square logo. We'll cover writing the company description tomorrow. Click Publish to save your company page.

Note: Unlike your personal profile—where just about every field is easily editable—your Company Name field is pretty much set in stone. If you do need to change your company name, you will have to write to CS@LinkedIn.com. Provide both the exact spelling of how the name currently appears on LinkedIn and how the name should actually appear.

Wednesday: Add a Company Description

Now you get to write your company description. Remember all those keywords we used earlier? Which ones apply to your company? Go through your list of keywords and put a check mark next to every keyword that is appropriate for your company.

To edit information on your company page:

1. Click Companies near the top of your home page and search for your company.

2. On the Search Results page, click your company name.

3. Click Admin Tools in the upper right and select Edit.

4. Make your changes and click Publish to save.

You get up to 2,000 characters to describe your company. As you did in the Summary section, be sure to use whitespace, special characters, bullets, and capitalization, as shown in Figure 4.4.

Welcome to our LinkedIn Company Page! I'm glad you found us! At Linked Into Business (LIB) we are here to "MAKE SOCIAL MEDIA WORK FOR YOU".

If you check our PRODUCTS AND SERVICES page you'll see we have all kinds of FREE resources, like eBooks and Tweetchats to help you succeed in your social media efforts.

As LinkedIn, Twitter and Social Media Training Consultants, we also specialize in training and consulting with companies and individuals in the utilization of social media for inbound marketing. It is our desire to make sure that everyone with an appropriate company culture has the ability to utilize social media to its fullest – creating a wider contact base, greater name recognition, increased conversion and better Google indexing and ranking.

We can work with you three ways:
• We can teach you to do it
• We can do it with you
• We can do it for you

We can help you create your social media presence on LinkedIn, Twitter, Facebook, YouTube and the Blogsite of your choice, and then show you how to optimize, manage and maintain your presence by yourself. We can create your social media presence for you, and teach you to manage it effectively, or we can manage it for you. It is our job to be invisible and let your authentic voice shine through.

If you have been thinking about becoming involved in social media marketing, contact our consultants at viveka@linkedintobusiness.com
(970) 212-4711

Specialties
LinkedIn Company Profile Optimization, Social Media Marketing, LinkedIn Marketing and Consulting, LinkedIn Professional Profile Optimization, New Media Marketing, LinkedIn Association Training, LinkedIn Corporate Training, LinkedIn Group Creation and Strategy
less

Figure 4.4 Company description

You probably already have a company description on your website. So by all means copy and paste that text into the word processing document you use to create your new company profile description. And add those keywords!

> **Note:** Try customizing your description specifically for LinkedIn. Is your company profile description speaking to your LinkedIn audience? You might even address them directly saying something like: "We are glad you found our LinkedIn company profile. Check out our Services and Products page for special offers! As a special offer to our followers we will be sending company updates with promotions and discounts as well, so follow our company! We are here to…" (and then give them a list of benefits).

Right under the Description section, you'll notice that you have the opportunity to add specialties. You have 256 characters to add keywords specific to your company, service, or product.

If you are the administrator of an existing company page and want to add more information to your company description or company Specialties section, you'll need to click the Admin Tools button on the right side of your screen and then click Edit. The Admin Tools will change according to the page you are on, so if you don't see the Company Description, Company Specialties, and Standard Or Square Logo fields, then make sure you are on the Overview page, which is the default (Figure 4.5).

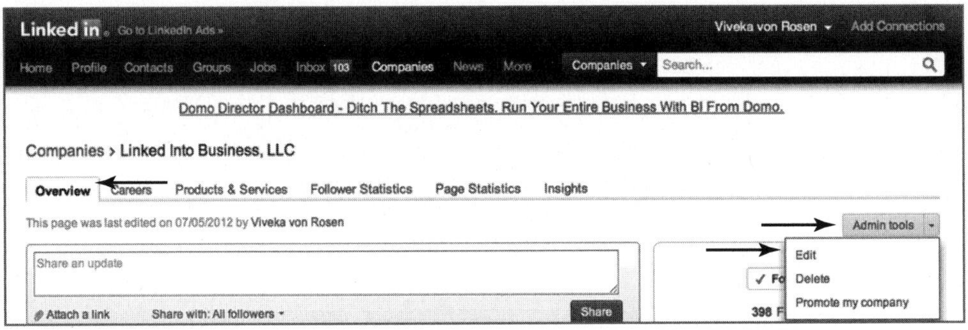

Figure 4.5 Editing an existing page

Other fields you'll want to fill in are:

- RSS Feed
- New Module (which pulls from the Internet and your company profile)
- Company Type (don't choose self-employed)
- Company Website URL
- Main Company Industry (choose the closest one)
- Company Operating Status
- Year Founded (optional)
- Company Locations (list up to five)

Note: If you are self-employed, I do not recommend using the self-employed option under Company Type because that will show up on your professional profile as well. You might want to choose either privately held or partnership.

Oracle and IBM both have very thorough traditional LinkedIn company page descriptions. I also admire the company profiles created by HubSpot and MLT Creative. In Figure 4.6, notice how HubSpot's company profile does the following:

- Speaks directly to its LinkedIn audience
- Calls your attention to its Products tab by capitalizing it
- Shares not only the features of its service, but who it has helped and how that has made HubSpot thought leaders

Welcome to HubSpot's home on LinkedIn! Follow us for regular updates about marketing tips, blog articles, free webinars and more. We pride ourselves for being friendly and helpful.

Also, check out our PRODUCTS TAB to see some of our most popular free webinars.

So ... What is HubSpot?

HubSpot is an inbound marketing software company that helps businesses transform their marketing from outbound (cold calls, email spam, trade shows, tv ads, etc) lead generation to inbound lead generation enabling them to "get found" by more potential customers in the natural course of the way they shop and learn.

Since founding in 2006 at MIT, HubSpot has raised four rounds of venture capital from Tier A investors, Matrix, General Catalyst, Scale Ventures, Sequoia Capital, Google Ventures, and Salesforce.com totaling $65 million. Despite being only 4 years old, the company already has over 4,000 paying customers. HubSpot has several free tools that you may already be familiar with including Website Grader and Twitter Grader.

HubSpot's blog (http://blog.hubspot.com) is one of the top 5 marketing blogs, the company has won over 50 marketing awards, and HubSpot has been featured in the Wall Street Journal, the New York Times, TechCrunch, ReadWriteWeb, Mashable, and a number of TV news programs.

Specialties
inbound marketing, marketing, internet marketing, online marketing, web marketing, software, blogging, SEO, marketing automation, social media, email marketing, analytics
less

Figure 4.6 HubSpot company profile

> **Note:** Pamela Vaughan wrote in a recent HubSpot blog post "13 Brands Using LinkedIn Company Page Features the Right Way" that the news module pulls in any news mentions of your company that LinkedIn finds on the Web and features them in the right-hand column of the Overview tab on your LinkedIn company page... Adding this module is a great way to highlight the media coverage your company has earned, adding third-party credibility and validation to your page." See more at:
>
> http://blog.hubspot.com/blog/tabid/6307/bid/31889/13-Brands-Using-LinkedIn-company-Page-Features-the-Right-Way.aspx#ixzz1r7fQ8iWX

As Figure 4.7 shows, you also have the opportunity to optimize your Overview page description for other languages. This tool enables companies to provide a more globally accessible page by including the company description in other languages, much as you choose to write your profile in alternate languages. This way, someone viewing the page from their default language will see the company description in their language.

Figure 4.7 Optimizing your page for other languages

That should give you a few ideas on how you can create a dynamic and engaging company profile description. Remember to create it in a word processing document so you can format it and catch any spelling or grammar errors.

Thursday: Designate Company Administrators

If you are the only administrator of your company page, you might want to consider allocating a few other individuals as administrators in case you ever leave the company or your profile gets suspended.

I *do not* recommend choosing the All Employees With A Valid Email Registered To The Company Domain option because that might land you in a world of hurt. You might have a helpful employee who altruistically tries to improve your branded message—or an angry employee who alters your company description to fit their opinion.

To designate administrators, click the Admin Tools link and then click Edit. In the Company Pages Admins section shown in Figure 4.8, under Manage Admins you type the names of other individuals on LinkedIn who you want to be administrators of your page.

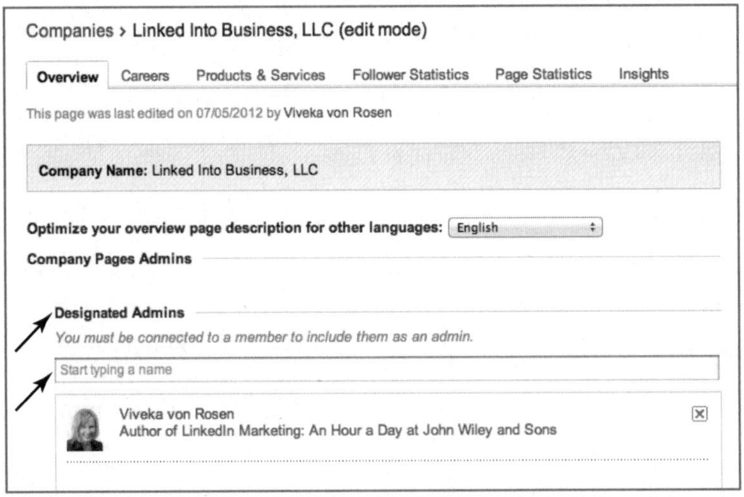

Figure 4.8 Assigning administrators

Note: Employees are linked to a company page when they add or edit a position on their profile and select a specific name from the Company drop-down list. If they fail to do this, they won't show up on the company page.

Here are the directions LinkedIn suggests sending to employees who don't show up as employees on your company page who you would like to make administrators:

1. Click Profile at the top of your home page.
2. Click Edit next to your current position.
3. Click Change Company and type the full company name.
4. This step is crucial: Click the correct company name in the drop-down list.
5. Click Update.

Friday: Edit and Revise

It's Friday, which means I'm giving you a break. If you've already created a company page, just take a moment to look through it. Select the Company tab and your company name should now show up in the drop-down box. Verify the following:

- Have you used all 2,000 characters in your description? Is it formatted?
- Have you added all the specialties relevant to your business?
- Are you showing up in the Company Search under your keywords?
- Is all the information accurate?

Don't skip these steps. Now that you've had a night to sleep on it, you might have come up with some new ideas or better phrasing.

The other thing I want you to do is take a quick look at your employees. Is there anyone listed as an employee of your company who is not? If the person is a previous employee, you can always just send them a message asking them to update their LinkedIn profile. If they don't do so in a reasonable amount of time or they have never been an employee, follow these steps:

1. Go to their profile by clicking on their name.
2. Copy their public profile URL and email customer service to let them know that the individual is not, or is no longer, an employee of your company.

Week 8: Adding Products and Services

I love this section of the LinkedIn company profile and a lot of people don't even realize it exists. You have the opportunity to add all of your products and services, as well as pictures or video of your products and services, special offers, and descriptions—you can even ask for recommendations for your products and services! So let's take a look at what you can do with this section of your LinkedIn company profile.

Monday: Add Photos, Descriptions, and Specialties

To get to Add Products and Services section, go to your company page and click the Products & Services tab; then click on the product or service you want to edit. You cannot edit your products and services from any other page. Once you click on the Products & Services tab, your Admin Tools change, and you can then click on the Edit link, as shown in Figure 4.9. If this option does not appear, make sure you are not still on the Overview page.

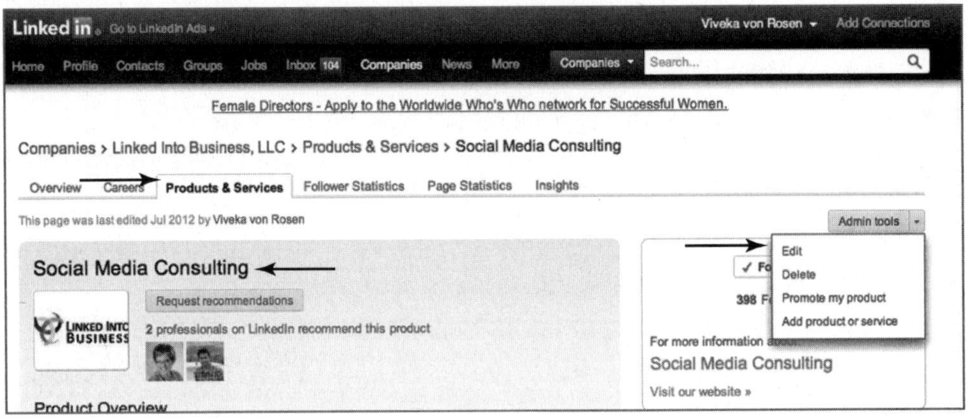

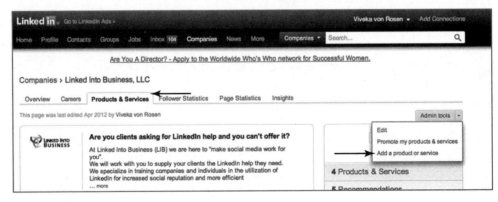

Figure 4.9 Editing existing products and services

If you are adding a product or service for the first time, make sure you are on the Products & Services page, click Admin Tools, and then click Add A Product Or Service. When you add a product or service for the first time, you need to specify whether it's a product or a service, as shown in Figure 4.10.

Figure 4.10 Adding a new product or service

Add your product or service's name. While you don't have to upload an image, I recommend that you do so. It's best if you have a vivid image that's 100 × 80 pixels. You can use a PNG, JPEG, or GIF file.

You now have 1,000 characters to describe your product or service. And you actually get to format this section! Your options are bold, italics, underline, numbered list, or bulleted list. (You are stuck with LinkedIn's font.) Make use of these tools so you can differentiate your Products & Services page and look much more professional than your competitors.

Even though you've already added specialties to your company description, you can add a list of product or service features. Use keywords in this section. They will show up as a bulleted list at the bottom of your page.

You can see in Figure 4.11 that MLT Creative does a great job of adding services to their company profile.

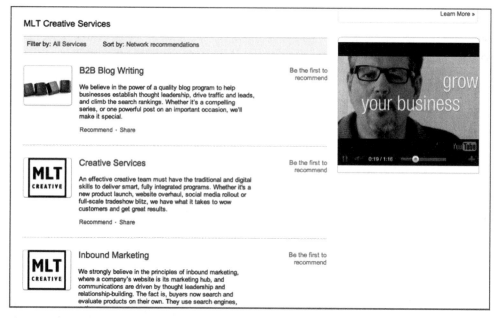

Figure 4.11 MLT Creative's company page

Tuesday: Create Offers

Did you know you can create special offers on LinkedIn? The Products & Services page has a special field just for that. As of yet I've not seen anybody use this feature. So why not you? See how in Figure 4.12.

Figure 4.12 Adding a special offer

On the right side of your LinkedIn company profile Products & Services page, you'll see the link Add A Promotion For This Product Or Service. You can give it a title, add a URL if you have a special landing page for this product or service on your website, and then write a brief description (500 characters) of the promotion.

As you add new products or promotions to your company, add them to your company page. I have seen very few companies making use of this section, but as LinkedIn ramps up its targeted follower updates, I think this section will get much more attention. A good example might be:

Free 15-Minute Consultation

Call us today for a free 15-minute consultation to uncover what you need to do to increase the ROI of your social media presence.

Miles Austin of www.fillthefunnel.com uses TimeDriver.com as a link to send people to in order to book a free 15-minute consultation with him. I think this is brilliant!

Wednesday: Add Disclaimers and Employee Promotion

Some companies have disclaimers on their websites. LinkedIn gives you the same opportunity to write a disclaimer right on your Products & Services page. This is not a bad idea at all! If you already have a disclaimer somewhere on your website, go ahead and add it to this section.

Industries that should definitely consider disclaimers include:

- Legal
- Medical

- Financial
- Marketing

Figure 4.13 shows a good example of a disclaimer.

Disclaimer

B *I* <u>U</u> | ☰ ☰

All quotes from LinkedIntoBusiness are valid for 30 days following the date of release. Our company accepts no liability for the content of LinkedIn page, or for the consequences of any actions taken on the basis of the information provided, unless that information is subsequently confirmed in writing. Any views or opinions presented in this email are solely those of the author and do not necessarily represent those of the company. Finally, the recipient should check any communications for the presence of viruses. The company accepts no liability for any damage caused by any virus transmitted by this email.

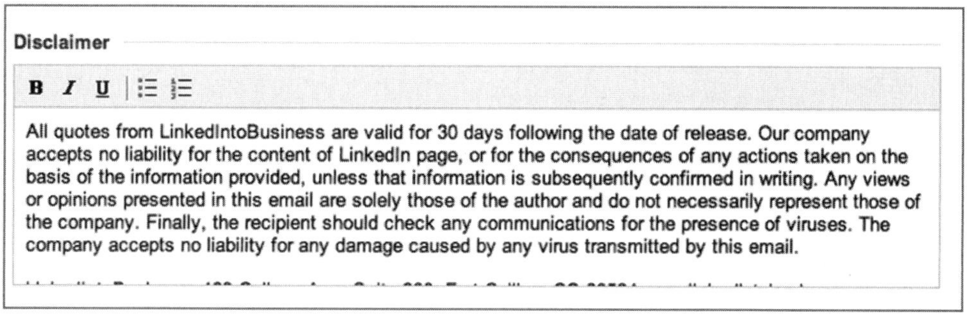

Figure 4.13 Example of a disclaimer

For a great list of disclaimers, check out `http://emaildisclaimers.com`.

You also have the opportunity to highlight or promote an employee in association with a particular product or service. Click on the product or service you wish to feature, and on the right-hand side about halfway down the page you'll see the Contact Us field. Start typing in the employee name that you wish to feature or promote. The only caveat here is that you must be connected to that individual on LinkedIn.

Thursday: Add Video and Recommendations

Did you know that you can add video to your LinkedIn company profile? What kinds of video might you add?

- Showcase your product or service
- Demonstrate it in use
- Share a video testimonial from a happy customer
- Show a funny viral video featuring your product or service

The only limitation is that the video has to be on YouTube.

In Figure 4.14 you can see how to add video. Here are the steps:

1. Click on the product or service where you want the video added.
2. Click Admin Tools › Edit.
3. Scroll down to (almost) the bottom of the right-hand side of your page.
4. Add a title for your video.
5. Add the YouTube video URL.

Figure 4.14 Adding video

You can also get recommendations from your fans and clients. According to a June 2010 CompUSA study, 63 percent of consumers indicate they are more likely to purchase from a site if it has product ratings and reviews.

If you click on the product or service you would like a recommendation from, you will have the option to request a recommendation. A message box will pop up (as shown in Figure 4.15) and you can request recommendations from anyone in your network. Don't be afraid to ask your existing customer base who is on LinkedIn to send you a recommendation.

Don't go with the default message shown in Figure 4.15. You have a great opportunity to individually connect with your customer and re-engage. It might be just the touch they need to call on you for more products or services.

When an interested party lands on your product page, they can also proactively write you a recommendation. Don't rely on this method to get recommendations. Unless your clients absolutely adore you, they might not be inspired to take time out of their day to write a recommendation.

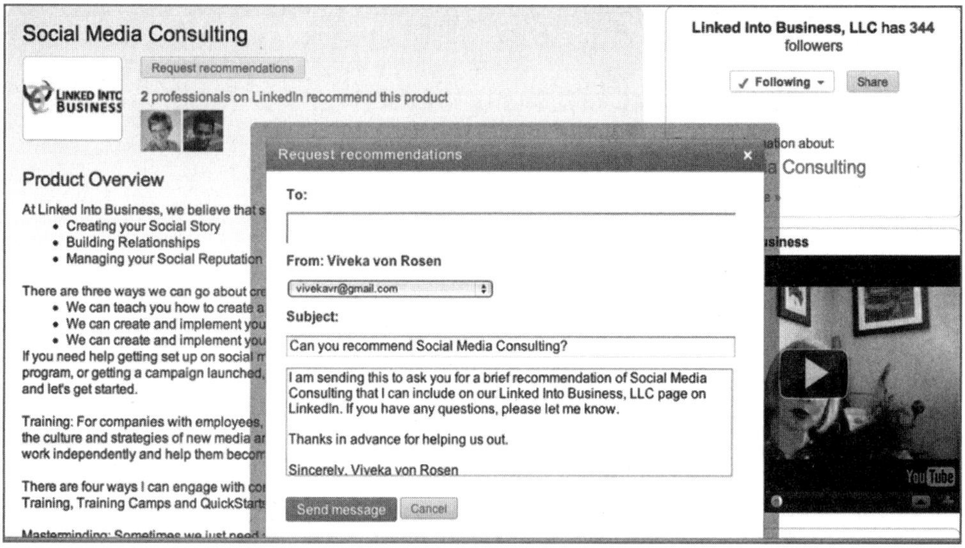

Figure 4.15 Product recommendations

Another way to ask clients and customers to recommend you is a Recommendations button for your product or service that you can put right on your website or in an email signature. You can get the code for such a button at `https://developer.linkedin.com/plugins/recommend-button` to proactively send your happy customers to your LinkedIn company profile.

When a LinkedIn user recommends one of your products or services, that message is displayed on that product or service page. The total number of recommendations from all your product and service pages are also displayed on the Products tab on your page as are the statistics impressions and engagement.

Friday: Use Targeted Product and Service Pages

Well, I have given you a few light Fridays, so this Friday I'm going to make you work! You can add for what all intents and purposes looks like a banner ad to your LinkedIn company profile. Most companies have not made use of this feature.

You can create up to 30 distinct landing pages for targeted audience segments based on a LinkedIn member's company size, job function, industry, seniority, and/or geography.

To add a targeted company page, select the Companies tab on your LinkedIn home page and click on your company. Then select the Products & Services tab and click Edit. Do not go to a specific product—just the general Products & Services page shown in Figure 4.16.

Figure 4.16 Creating a targeted company page

Note: You can create multiple variations of a particular page to focus on custom audiences based on their profile content. It's kind of like a targeted ad, except you don't have to pay for it. For example, you can create a version of your page targeted to legal professionals in the United States, a different version targeted to accountants in Canada, and another version targeted to doctors in Europe.

There are four steps to defining your products and services to a specific niche market using this tool:

1. The first step is creating your audience. Click the Create New Audience button. This will bring up a new screen that allows you to target your audience under categories like Company Size, Job Function, Industry, Seniority, and Geography. Many of these categories allow you to further refine your audience, so don't be afraid to target. See Figure 4.17.

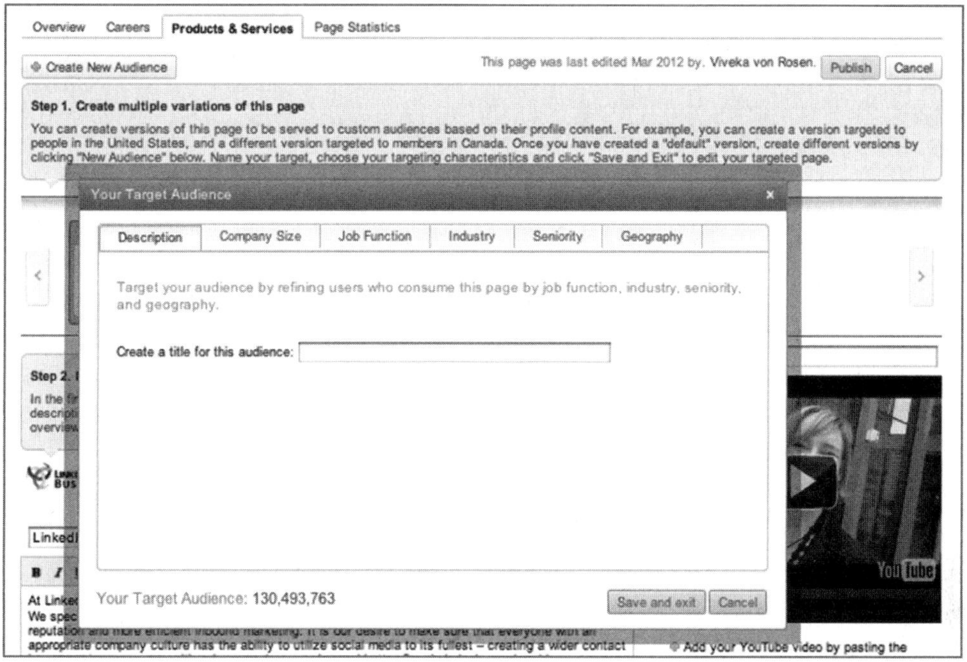

Figure 4.17 Targeting your audience

2. The next step is creating a title (using keywords) that will grab the attention of your audience. Then create a message that speaks specifically to your target audience. You would likely use different wording with your American attorneys than with your Canadian accountants. Now you have the opportunity to speak to your specific targeted audience. Remember your calls to action.

3. Choose up to three banner images (640 × 220 pixels) and add a URL that you want people to land on when they click on the banner. Use a call to action in your banner so people know they can click on them.

4. Remember, you can make up to 30 targeted pages, so why not get creative? You can quickly duplicate and easily edit and finesse a page by clicking on the duplicate link in the tab (as shown in Figure 4.18). Narrow down your focus. Play with it. Have some fun. Narrow focus means you are talking specifically to an audience that is more likely to listen to you because you are speaking to them!

To see a great example of the targeted company services page, check out MLT Creative's company profile. You can find it at www.linkedin.com/company/mlt-creative/products?trk=tabs_biz_product, or see Figure 4.18. Notice the call to action to Visit Now.

Figure 4.18 MLT Creative's banner

Week 9: Company Updates, Analytics, and Job Postings—Yours and Others

There are a few more things you can do with your company profile that we will cover in this section, including company status updates, analytics, and job postings. We will also look at how you can follow other companies.

Monday: Create Your Own (Targeted) Updates

You can now create your own updates within your company profile. It's similar to creating a status update on your home page, or on Twitter or Facebook. Open your company profile and make sure that you're on the Overview page. On the Overview tab you will see a field that allows you to share an update, as shown in Figure 4.19.

LinkedIn says this about company status updates:

You can post and share items like company news, promotions, relevant industry articles, and YouTube videos. Company status updates can have text in a link to a website, image or YouTube video. URLs will be automatically shortened by LinkedIn's URL shortener. Any LinkedIn member can comment on, like, or share a company status update. Once a member takes action on update, their network will also see the posting.

Figure 4.19 You can share an update.

LinkedIn members will be able to see your company status updates both on your company's Overview page as well as on their own home pages, as long as they are following your company.

LinkedIn recently released targeted status updates. These allow you to target and focus on the customers (followers) you want to talk to with information that is relevant to them. It's a great way to engage with customers who are telling you they are already interested in you because they are following you! And now you will be able to create specific and targeted follower lists based on several new criteria: Industry, Seniority, Job Function, Company Size, Non-company Employees, and Geography. With targeted company status updates, you can deliver highly relevant content and increase engagement. You must have at least 100 followers in your target audience in order to send a targeted Company status update, so start attracting those followers right now!

In addition to target status updates, you can use the new statistics to refine and improve your communications. Companies will be able to not only view follower count, but also track engagement metrics that include likes, shares, comments, percentage engagement, as well as follower demographic information. To see previous company status updates, scroll down below the Description and Network fields to see your recent company status.

You can also click on the Follower Statistics tab to see more detailed statistics of your followers such as:

- How many total followers you have
- How many new followers you have

- Impressions and updates on your status updates for the past 7 days
- Update engagement for the past 7 days
- Graphs of company update engagement
- Graphs of follower demographics by Seniority, Function, Region, Company size and Employee status

You can see what the Follower Statistics look like in Figure 4.20 below:

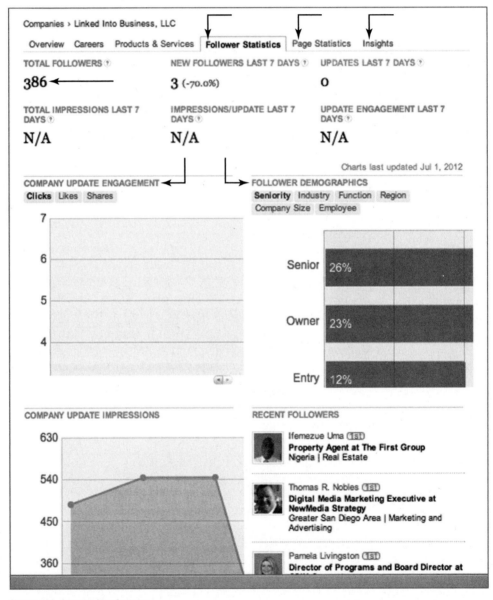

Figure 4.20 Company Page Statistics

It's a good idea to keep an eye on these posts, to see which kind of post best engages your audience. You will want to do more of that.

Note: Nathan Latka of Lujure.com wrote a great post on fan engagement. I will share some of his ideas with you here:

Try asking: Yes or No: Do you engage your online community? Sometimes getting a yes or no response is just as good as getting a seven-paragraph response. They are both opportunities for you to engage with your community and get feedback.

Fill-in-the-blank updates always increase responses. Try something like:

I enjoy [company name] because _____

Our company has _____ employees.

Links are shared much more often than unlinked posts. Cater to your audience's wants and needs by pulling in blog posts and articles that provide great value to those loyal folks.

The underlying theme is to just get people talking and facilitate conversation via your open-ended responses. Respond to every comment and ask questions to find out more about your audience. The most important element of engagement is the human factor. Don't be afraid to add your own flavor to spice up your content a little more!

Stay positive, be honest, and the rest will come naturally.

Tuesday: View Your Company Analytics

LinkedIn company profiles have their own set of analytics. I just mentioned the status update analytics, but your page has its own analytics as well.

To check these analytics you can click on the Page Statistics and Insights tab in the Company menu. Once you click on page statistics, you will see:

- Page views (All, Overview, Careers, Products & Services)
- Page visitor demographics (Seniority, Industry, Function, Region, Company Size, and Employee)
- Unique visitors (All, Overview, Careers, Products & Services)
- Products and Services Page (Clicks)
- Career page (Clicks)

You can see what the Page Statistics look like in Figure 4.21 below:

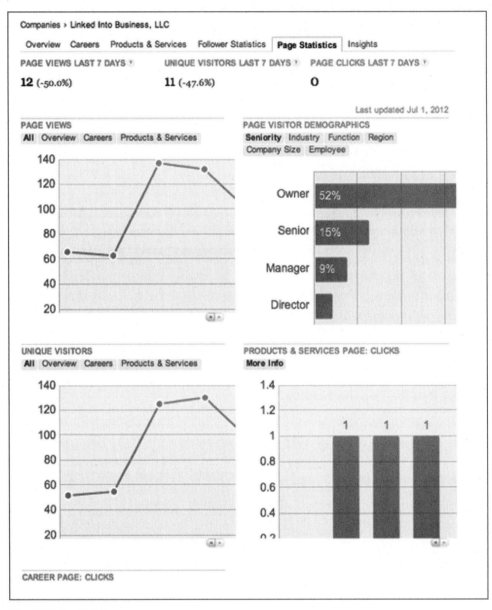

Figure 4.21 Page Statistics

Insights will show you:

- Other companies the people viewed who viewed your Company page
- Departures from your company
- Your connection graph to your employees

- Location that employees call home
- Most recommended employees in your company

It's a good idea to make sure that when someone leaves your company that they show up in the section. (If not, send them a gentle reminder to change their LinkedIn experience status.)

You can also see how you are connected to the members in your own company. It might be a good idea to have all your employees as first-level connections. If you work for a larger company, then make sure you are directly connected to key Influencers such as the executive team and HR.

Most people don't even know this page exists, much less use it to monitor and improve their LinkedIn company profile interaction with followers.

For those of you actively marketing your company on Facebook, consider using some of the same tactics on your company page to drive customers and business. (For a great book on Facebook marketing, check out *Facebook Marketing All-in-One for Dummies* by Amy Porterfield, Phyllis Khare and Andrea Vahl (Wiley, 2011).)

Wednesday: Create Job Postings

If you are looking to hire new employees, the Careers tab on your company page can be a great tool. One of the ways to post a job on LinkedIn is to go to your company page, select the Careers tab (if you have one), and click the yellow Post A Job button.

If you don't have a Career tab, select the Jobs tab at the top of your profile and click Post A Job. Any job you create on LinkedIn will automatically create a Careers tab and post to your company profile if you have one. See Figure 4.22.

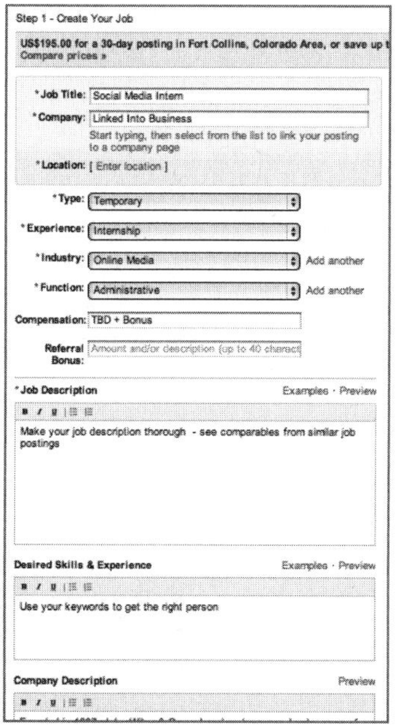

Figure 4.22 Posting a job on your company page

To post a job, you will need a job title. Remember that people are looking for jobs by job title, so make sure that you have all necessary keywords in your job title. Are you looking for an intern or a volunteer? A contract person or a consultant? A nurse or a caregiver? An accountant or a CPA or a bookkeeper? A social media manager or an inbound marketing strategist?

The required fields are as follows:

- The job title
- The company you are posting the job for (if you have more than one company profile or work for more than one company currently)
- The location of the job
- The type of job (full-time, part-time, contract, temporary, or other)
- The experience level of the employee you are looking for
- The industry
- The function
- The job description (if you are not clear about this, see what other companies are posting for similar positions)
- Applicant routing (who the applicant will contact)

In addition, you can add compensation and referral bonuses, desired skills and experience, company description, and job poster information. LinkedIn has partnered with NRD.gov to help veterans find jobs, so if you are committed to helping veterans, click the Veteran Commitment button.

 Note: You will definitely want to write a job description adding as many details and keywords as possible. LinkedIn's search algorithm will search through LinkedIn for possible candidates for you, but it can only do so if you take the time to fully fill out these sections.

According to LinkedIn, the average job posting is forwarded 11 times and gets an average of 30 applications. Because your LinkedIn job is searchable by Google, you also have a very good chance of finding people outside of LinkedIn. LinkedIn will also post your job on Twitter for you!

Thursday: Follow a Company

To follow a company, simply put the company name or company keywords into the company search field. Once you find the company you are looking for, all you have to do is click Follow Company. You will receive both updates from the company, as well as any information about jobs that might be posted.

As you can imagine, the Follow Company tool is an extremely useful tool for the job seeker as well as the entrepreneur, small business owner, or anyone who wants to keep an eye on a company (either your competitor's or a potential partner's). LinkedIn will send you not only an update, but also an email about the company's activity. Just think of it as insider information you won't get arrested for accessing!

> **Note:** By the way, if you ever want to "unfollow" a company, you just click the Following tab and it will give you the option to stop following the company.

As you can see in Figure 4.23, LinkedIn will notify you about several different activities within a company.

Here are some of the things LinkedIn will notify you about:

Staff Changes It's not a bad idea to keep an eye on the employees joining, leaving, or being promoted within the company. And following a company will allow you to do that. Why? Well, if you're looking for a job, and you see a job opening because an employee just left, there might be a void you can fill with your talents and skills.

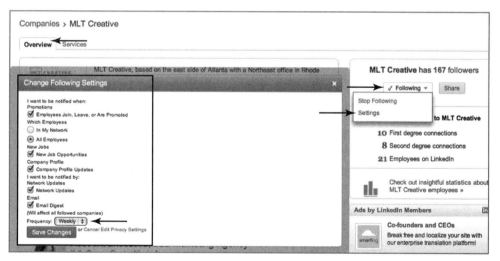

Figure 4.23 Follow Company Settings

If you are looking to build a partnership with a company, and you notice that someone you know has just joined that company, you now have an inside connection.

It's always nice to congratulate employees who were promoted within the company. It might come as a surprise to them (especially when their own family hasn't congratulated them yet), and it's a great way to start a conversation.

To see the employees of the company you're following, you can choose the In My Network option; then you can quickly and easily see who you are connected to, how you are connected, and who is influential in the company you might want to directly connect with. Alternatively, choose the All Employees option, which will give you a better view of all the employees who are in that company and also on LinkedIn.

Job Postings As I mentioned earlier, one of the things that you can be notified about is any new jobs that are posted.

Status Updates You can also be notified on company status updates. What I like about this is that you can see those updates both on your LinkedIn home page and through an email digest. If you choose an email digest, just know that you will get a daily or weekly email from *all* the companies you follow on LinkedIn.

> **Note:** To keep an eye on all the companies you're following, simply select the Companies tab and you will have the option to see those that you are following. You can also use the options on this page to stop following companies and change your notification settings.
>
> Because LinkedIn usually gives you two ways to achieve the same result, you can also see which companies you're following under Settings, and Groups, Companies, and Applications.

One of the things I really like about LinkedIn is the ability to see who works at a company and how you're related to them. It doesn't matter if you're looking at a company with 10,000 employees or two, you get access through LinkedIn to the very people you need to connect with to grow your business.

Although you can't follow employees on the company profile as you can within groups, you can certainly click on their name, which will take you to their profile. From their profile, you can connect with them, send them an InMail, or get introduced to them through a connection. You can also save their profile as a PDF or print or share it from this section. If you have a paid account, save their profile in the Profile Organizer.

Friday: Explore Other Company Analytics

As Figure 4.24 shows, LinkedIn also offers you insightful statistics about the employees of other companies. Just click on the company you are interested in, and then click on the Insights tab

Figure 4.24 Company Insights

You'll be able to look at statistics for an overview of the company employees as well as see all jobs posted for that company.

Unfortunately, LinkedIn recently reduced the statistics it was sharing with company followers, but you can still see:

- Who in the company is in your network (Who can you easily connect with by First-Degree, Second-Degree and Employees on LinkedIn?)

- Similar companies viewed by LinkedIn members (Similar companies might spark some ideas for clients, employers, or competitors to keep your eye on)

- Who has left the company (And are their positions now available?)

- A graph of your first- and second-level connections according to who still works at the company and who is new to the company

- Where the employees live (Is it time to move?)
- Most common skills of the employees (This is a wealth of information. As a job seeker, do you have the skills listed in your profile to match a company you are interested in working with? As a consultant, what skills is the company missing that you can offer?)
- Most recommended employees at the company (in case you are looking to poach an employee for your company)

This is a treasure trove of information for recruiters, job seekers, and people looking to make strategic relationships within the company.

So that is the company profile on LinkedIn. While you probably won't pay quite as much attention to your company profile as your professional profile, I recommend dropping in on it at least once a week to:

- Keep an eye on any changes that need to be made
- Find missing employees who need to be reminded to add the company to their profiles
- Remind employees who no longer work for you to move their position with you to their past position
- Alert LinkedIn to take nonemployees off your company profile
- Post your updates to targeted followers
- Monitor the growth and statistics of your followers
- Keep an eye on your competition
- Update any company or product and service descriptions
- Monitor recommendations

Your time investment in your company profile once it has been created does not have to be extensive—probably no more than 5 minutes a day for a quick review and follow-up. Even that little bit of attention could pay off big in the long run, so it's worth scheduling into your own calendar.

Next up: creating and managing a network that works!

Weeks 10–15: Creating and Managing a Network That Works

As I mentioned in Chapter 1, "Get LinkedIn," LinkedIn is only as usable as the size of your network (unless you have the $10,000-a-month membership and then you have access to pretty much everyone). This chapter will guide you through finding the people you need to connect to, what to do once you find them, when you should connect and when you shouldn't, and what to say when you do reach out.

Chapter Contents

Week 10: Using LinkedIn's Add Connections Tool
Week 11: Connecting to Strategic Contacts
Week 12: Using LinkedIn's People You May Know Feature
Week 13: Managing Your Network
Week 14: Monitoring Your Network
Week 15: Giving and Getting Recommendations from Your Network

Week 10: Using LinkedIn's Add Connections Tool

If you are following LinkedIn's suggestion to connect only to people you know, you might be missing out on some major opportunities. Let's look at how you can grow your network to a size that maximizes your professional opportunities.

Fortunately, LinkedIn gives you many tools to connect to folks you might know. But before we get started on adding people to your network, you need to know what *kind* of network you want.

Monday: Decide on a LION or LamB Network

You might have heard the terms *open* and *strategic networker* used when people refer to your network on LinkedIn. Let's clarify this terminology before moving on.

A LinkedIn open networker, also known as a LION (a term coined by Christian Mayaud, an early adopter of LinkedIn), encourages connections from other LinkedIn members whether or not they have had a previous business relationship. According to Wikipedia, LIONs are basically open to networking with people they have never met before, and they are important in the fact that they bridge networks of closed people.

I like what my friend (and LinkedIn aficionado) Neal Schaffer has to say about the role of LIONs: "If we all follow the standard rule of LinkedIn and say I Don't Know for every invite that we receive from someone who we have never personally met, it would be hard for closed networks to grow into each other and evolve into the great networking community that LinkedIn is today" (`http://windmillnetworking.com/2008/07/11/what-is-a-linkedin-lion/`).

So LIONs, in general, accept invitations from anyone, or at least won't give you the dreaded I Don't Know (IDK) as a response to your invitation.

> **Note:** When people say that they don't know you, or that your invitation is spam, LinkedIn penalizes you. Enough IDKs and you have to know the member's email address if you want them to connect.

With this in mind, it is *relatively* risk-free to invite a LION that you found in an Advanced Search into your network. I believe that most businesspeople fall somewhere between a LamB (defined in a moment) and a LION network.

The benefits to being an open networker are:

- Your network grows exponentially so you're more visible on LinkedIn.
- It's easier to contact the people you want to connect with on LinkedIn.
- You are likely to have more people reaching out to you because you have a big network.

The negatives are:

- Some people consider open networkers to be spammers and won't connect to you.
- Your network might become so big that you can't access your connections through LinkedIn.
- Your network might become so big that a lot of features and secondary applications won't work.

Laurie Macomber of Blue Skies Marketing coined the term LamB ("Look at my buds") to define strategic networkers. With some exceptions, a strategic networker is someone who connects only to people they know or can be introduced to. I like having some LamBs in the belly of my LION network because I know that these folks know almost all of their connections, and as long as I know and am on good terms with them, they will probably be willing to introduce me to folks I need to know.

The benefits to being a strategic networker are:

- Your network remains small enough to be manageable.
- You are able to connect either directly or through an introduction to the people that you need to.
- You're not disqualified as being a legitimate businessperson because your network is too big.

The negatives are:

- You might not be visible to the person you wish could see your profile.
- You might not be able to find the person you were looking for.

Not everyone should be an open networker. Open networking is great for recruiters, job seekers, people in sales and marketing, entrepreneurs, startups, and sometimes people in the nonprofit arena (because oftentimes if you run or work for a nonprofit or startup you end up doing the marketing, sales, and recruiting for your organization).

Strategic networks are best for executives, professionals who are not in sales and marketing, and people who simply don't want to be bugged with introductions on LinkedIn.

I usually recommend that strategic networkers reach out slightly beyond the people they know to those folks who can help them in their business ventures: existing and potential vendors, partners, Influencers, and mentors, as well as existing and potential clients, customers, employees, or employers. I think everyone should connect with a few LIONs or superconnectors so that you can bridge the gap, as Neal mentioned earlier, and grow your network to a visible size.

I'm going to give you tips on how to grow both types of networks. Choose a network size you are comfortable with.

Tuesday: Clean Up Your Email List

One of the easiest ways to grow your network is to invite the people on your existing email list to connect with you on LinkedIn. That might be a list of 20 or 20,000. In either case, you are going to want to spend a bit of time cleaning up your list.

First, LinkedIn allows you to send only 3,000 invitations. This is true if you send an invitation one at a time or are uploading your entire mailing list.

The second reason is that there are probably one or two people on your email list who really shouldn't be there—either an ex-spouse or customer service at Comcast. None of these folks needs (or wants) to get an invitation from you.

Note: Download and save your mailing list under another name (like LinkedIn Invites). I'm going to ask you to delete some names for the purpose of strategic connecting on LinkedIn, and you might not want them to be deleted from your original email file.

If you have to export your email to an Excel spreadsheet (as a CSV file), keep only three fields: first name field, last name field, and email address field. Make sure you delete every other column. If you don't, your import into LinkedIn is likely to be corrupted. Once you have created an Excel spreadsheet with just a first name column, last name column, and email column, save it as a CSV file. (This means that the fields of values of the Excel sheet are separated by commas.)

Note: If you're having difficulty creating and uploading a CSV file, LinkedIn gives directions on how to export from:

- A CSV file from Outlook
- A CSV or tab-separated file from Palm Desktop
- A CSV file from ACT!
- A vCard file from Palm Desktop
- A vCard file from Mac OS X Address Book

Click Add Connections in the top-right corner of any LinkedIn page, import your desktop email contacts, and then upload a contacts file from an email application like Outlook or Apple Mail. File formats must be CSV, TXT, or VCF.

Look carefully through the list and delete any names that shouldn't be there. If you don't think your mother-in-law or plumber will accept a LinkedIn invitation, go ahead and delete them from your list. Not feeling the love for an old neighbor? They can go too. You get the picture.

Once you feel that your email list for LinkedIn is clear of people you just don't want to connect with, you are ready to import it into LinkedIn.

If you are the executive of a large company, and/or you have a mailing list that's 20,000, 30,000 or 100,000 people long, consider divvying up that list among your employees, probably focusing on your sales and marketing team. As the CEO, you might want to remove your strategic connections, but your sales list should be shared with your team.

Wednesday: Import Your Outlook, iContacts, or CSV Email List

To import your email list into LinkedIn, go to the home page, and on the top right-hand side you'll see a green link that says Add Connections. Go ahead and click that. Ignore the screens you see, and look down at the bottom left of your profile where it says, "Do you use Outlook Apple Mail or another application?" Click the Import Your Desktop Email Contacts link.

> **Note:** The reason I want you to import your contacts rather than just upload them from your email list is because this way, you can be absolutely certain that you're inviting only people you really want to be connected with.

Once you click Import Your Desktop Email Contacts, a new page will open (see Figure 5.1) that allows you to choose the file. Choose the file from your file folder. (I usually keep my file on my desktop so I can find it easily.) Then click Upload File.

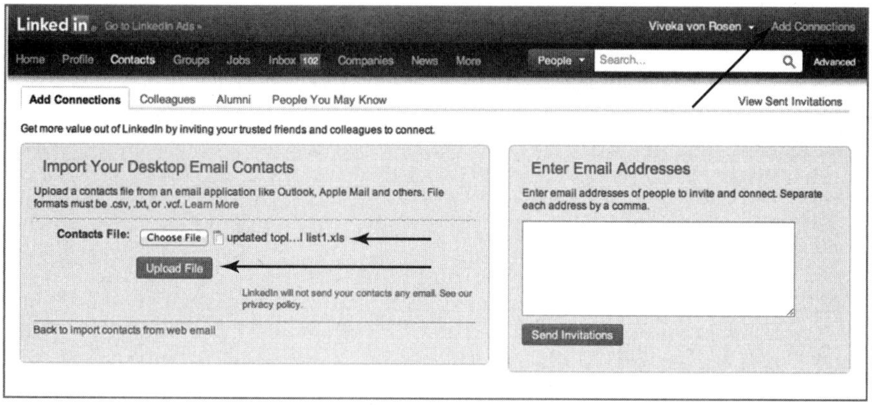

Figure 5.1 Import Your Desktop Email Contacts options

Even though you've already gone through this file and removed the people you don't want to be connected with, don't just hit Select All and Add Connections. The first screen that comes up will list people who are already on LinkedIn. Quickly go through the list and uncheck the folks you don't want to waste an invitation on. Remember you only have 3,000 invitations that you can send in a lifetime! You can't beg, borrow, or steal more invitations. (Well, you can actually beg for more from customer service, but you get my point.)

The second screen that appears lists people you're connected to but who are not on LinkedIn. This is where you want to be more discerning. Uncheck Select All. If you see someone in that list who you really want to connect to on LinkedIn, or who you want to get a recommendation from, then feel free to invite them to connect by checking the box next to their name. You should be inviting only a fraction of this list. Remember with just 3,000 invitations you probably don't want to waste an invitation on someone not likely to join LinkedIn anyway. If there is no one you want to connect to, click Skip This Step at the bottom of the page.

Over the next few days, depending on the size of your mailing list, you may find a lot of mail in your LinkedIn inbox and a lot of email sent to you through LinkedIn. Just be aware that this is relatively unusual activity and will end soon.

Remember you can always set the frequency of your emails in your Settings section. Click Settings › Email Preferences, and then choose either No Email or Weekly Digest Email for your invitations and messages from connections.

Thursday: Connecting with Email

If the whole CSV thing seemed too confusing, and you have a Gmail, Hotmail, AOL, or EarthLink account, you can always use the Add Connections link to see who you already know on LinkedIn (not to be mistaken with the People You May Know tab), as shown in Figure 5.2.

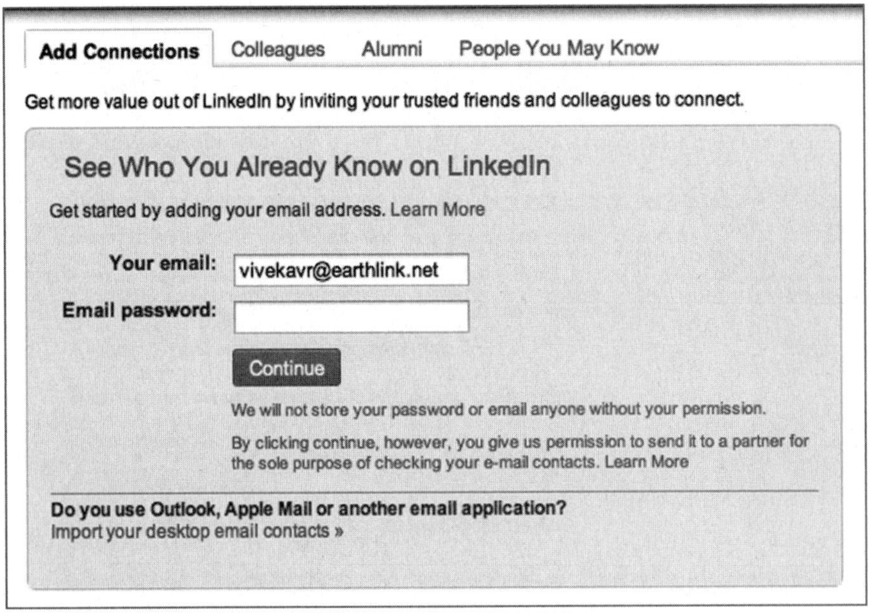

Figure 5.2 Seeing who you know

As you add your email address, LinkedIn will automatically upload your contacts from 39 email services, including Gmail, EarthLink, AOL, ATT.net, Mac.com, MSN.com, Hotmail.com, sbcglobal.net, Verizon.net, among others. Give it a try with your email service. If LinkedIn gives you an error message, you can always upload your CSV (more on that later).

As with the CSV upload, the first screen that shows up lists people in your email contacts list who are already on LinkedIn. If you didn't go through your list and remove everybody you didn't want to be connected to, take some extra time to review this list and make sure you connect only to the people you want to add to your LinkedIn network.

As you can see in Figure 5.3, the first thing you should do is uncheck Select All. This looks kind of confusing because immediately LinkedIn grays out all your connections. But have no fear—you can still go through that list and recheck the individuals you want to add to your LinkedIn profile. When you're ready, click Add Connections.

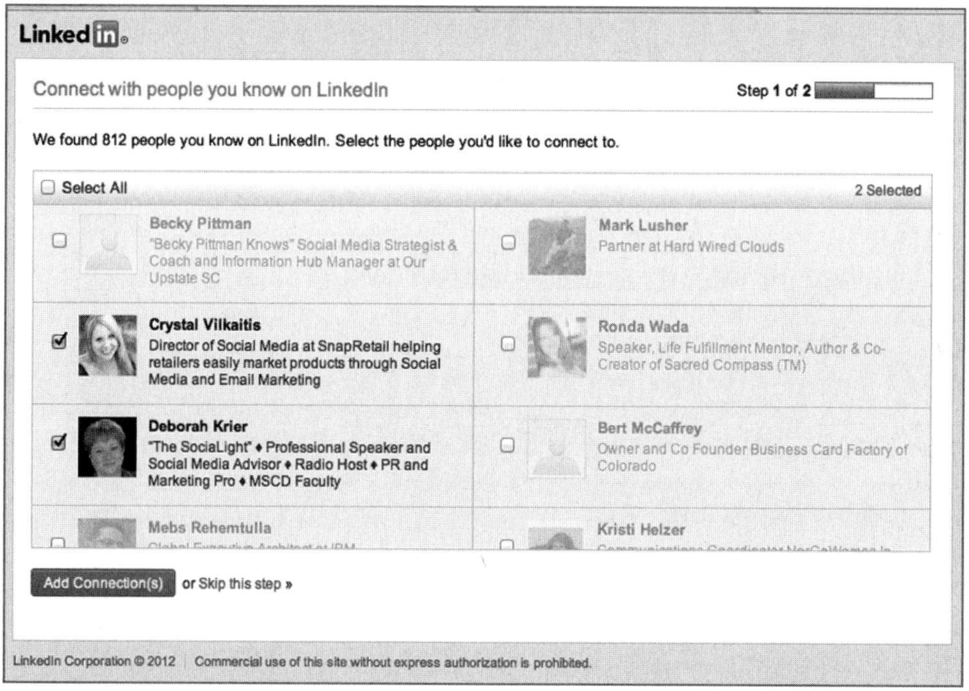

Figure 5.3 People you know already on LinkedIn

The next screen says "Why not invite some people?' These are your contacts who aren't yet on LinkedIn. I do not recommend hitting Select All and Invite To Connect. In my case, I have over 1,800 people on this list. That would've been two thirds of the entire invitation limit. Uncheck Select All and then go through the list and invite only those individuals who you really want to be connected with on LinkedIn or who you'd like to get a recommendation from. If there's no one in this list you want to be connected to on LinkedIn, click the Skip This Step link at the bottom of the page. If you find a few people to connect to, click on their name and then click Invite To Connect.

Unfortunately, neither of these options allows you to send a personalized invitation. I recommend using a personalized invitation, one where you get to create your invitation content, whenever possible. You have a better chance of someone actually accepting your invitation, and it's your first opportunity to build a relationship with that person.

Friday: Send Individual Email Invitations

The other option with Add Connections is Enter Email Addresses. This option allows you to enter the individual addresses of people who you want to invite and connect to. You can enter several email addresses at a time by simply separating each address with a comma, as shown in Figure 5.4.

Figure 5.4 Email invitations

 Note: If you had a problem uploading your CSV file, go to the column with the email addresses, and simply copy and paste them into this field.

When would this be useful? How about when you go to a networking event and gather all those business cards? A practice I recommend is asking the people who give you their business card if they are on LinkedIn. If they are, write LI on their card (if their LinkedIn URL is not already printed on it), and then invite them to connect when you get home. It's a great way to follow up with individuals you meet or reconnect with at networking events.

Maybe you just attended a huge trade show and you collected hundreds of business cards. Add their names to this field and invite away. Remember, you can't customize your invitation, so if it's a very important contact, look them up in a People search and invite them from their profile, which will allow you to send them a customized note.

If you have an iPhone, download the CardMunch app (`www.cardmunch.com`) and use this tool rather than entering email addresses. It will save you a great deal of time, allow you to send a personalized message, and even organize your new contacts, as shown in Figure 5.5.

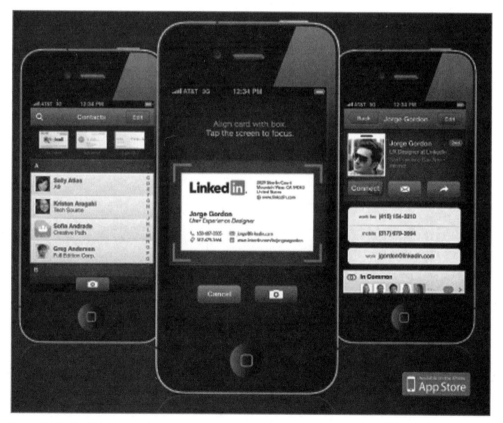

Figure 5.5 The CardMunch app

So now you have started building your network with people you already know! Some of my clients voice concerns that they're inviting people more than once and wasting invitations. Once you've sent an invitation, as long as the person you've sent it to has that email address in their profile, LinkedIn will not charge you for another invitation. (If they have not added all their email addresses in Settings as discussed in Chapter 2, "Weeks 1–2: Get Started on LinkedIn," then LinkedIn will invite them to create a new account and you will lose that one invitation.)

Note: LinkedIn will send three reminders to the individuals you sent an invitation to if they do not accept the invitation. After three reminders that person will no longer be contacted by LinkedIn saying that you want them to connect. Please note that withdrawing invitations doesn't return them to your available balance of invitations. Once you have sent an invitation, whether or not it is accepted, it is spent.

Week 11: Connecting to Strategic Contacts

Many people don't realize that LinkedIn has an Advanced Search feature for the free account. This is where I spend most of my time when I'm looking for new contacts.

Although I mentioned Advanced Search earlier, let's do a more detailed exploration of the page. First, in order to get to the Advanced People search, make sure the drop-down search box at the top-right of your page says People. Then click the Advanced link to the right of the search box, as shown in Figure 5.6.

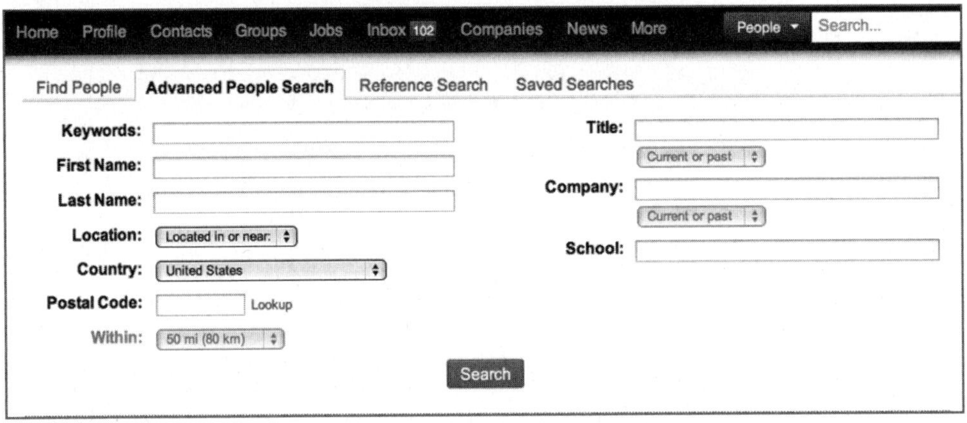

Figure 5.6 Advanced People search

This new search tool will allow you to search the entire LinkedIn network by:

- Keyword
- First Name
- Last Name
- Location (in, near, or anywhere)
- Postal Code (and there's a postal code lookup if you don't happen to know the postal code of the city you're looking for)

- Within (postal code) from a 10- to 100-mile radius
- Country
- Title (Current or Past)
- Company (Current or Past)
- School

As shown in Figure 5.7, you can also search by Industry, Relationship, and Language, and you can sort by Relevance, Relationship, Relationship and Recommendations, Connections, and Keywords. You can view either a basic search (which will show you their picture and, if available, their professional headline, city, and industry) or an expanded search (which shows you all of that as well as a snapshot of their connections, recommendations, current and past experience, and groups). I recommend the expanded search.

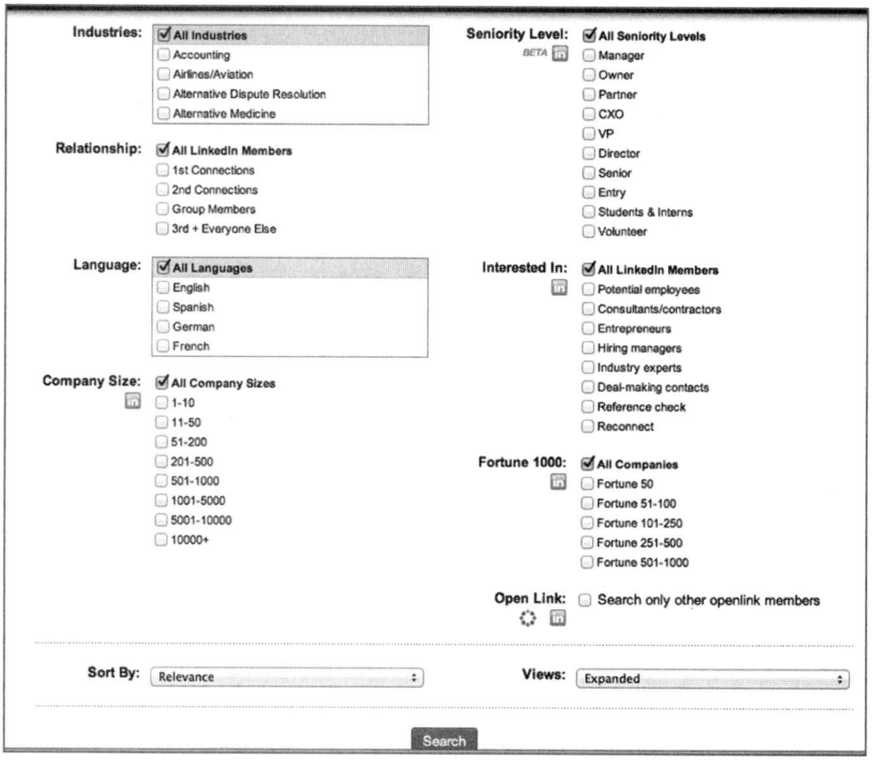

Figure 5.7 Additional Search options

If you have even the most basic paid business account, you can search by:

- Company Size (between one and 10,000+ people)
- Seniority Level (Manager, Owner, Partner, CXO, VP, Director, Senior, Entry, Students and Interns, Volunteer)

- Interested In (the types of people you might be interested in—All LinkedIn Members, Potential Employees, Consultants/Contractors, Entrepreneurs, Hiring Managers, Industry Experts, Deal-making Contacts, Reference Checks, or Reconnect)
- Fortune 1000 (All Companies, Fortune 50, Fortune 100, Fortune 250, Fortune 500, and Fortune 1000)
- OpenLink members

Boolean Logic and Keyword Strings

George Boole created Boolean algebra, which is the basis of all modern computer arithmetic. This logic is still used in searches today. (This works as well in Google as in LinkedIn.) You can use the terms OR, AND, and NOT as well parentheses and quotation marks to categorize a specific search for just the right person or website.

OR : People used different words to describe similar concepts on their profiles and you might not know which they chose: CPA OR Accountant.

AND: Use this when you want to find a person with both terms in their profile: CPA AND Accountant.

NOT: In conjunction with other terms, NOT will exclude people from your search who have that term in their profile: CPA AND Accountant NOT Bookkeeper.

Quotation marks: Keeps words together: CPA AND Accountant NOT "Bookkeeper."

Parentheses: Keeps phrases together: (CPA AND Accountant) NOT ("Bookkeeper" OR Secretary)

When doing a search, I start by filling in as many fields as I can to find the right people. If I get too few (or no) results, I start to open up my search by clearing some fields or opening the location.

For instance, I might look for the keywords "Graphic Artist AND Designer AND Photoshop AND WordPress" within 10 miles of an area code. If my search is too limited (or I get no results), I might expand my search to 50 miles, and/or take out the keyword "WordPress" and replace "Graphic Artist AND Designer" with "Graphic Artist OR Designer." That will give me a larger geographic area to search and is less restrictive as to whether the person has to be both an artist and a designer and know WordPress.

 Note: The first thing I do when I get no search results or extremely limited search results is make sure my spelling is correct. I always have to watch out for GIGO (garbage in, garbage out).

Take a few minutes to do a search for a strategic person who might make a great connection for you and get used to the Advanced People search. Don't invite them yet, though! There are still a few steps I'd like to walk you through to use LinkedIn most effectively and not waste your invitations or get the dreaded IDK!

Next, let's look at how to strategically use this search engine.

Monday: Create a List of Strategic Connections

The first thing I want you to do is create a list of strategic connections. You will make a list of people who you know, or know of, as well as types of people who might be influential in your business.

Of course, go through your contact list, but also go through your calendar. Have you been to an industry conference lately? Who were the keynote and breakout session speakers? Flip through trade magazines and journals. Has someone written an article that was important or influential to your business? If so, you might put their name down. Read any good books lately? Why not jot down the author's name?

Note: Some of my best connections are folks who I might have considered out of my league and yet I found them on LinkedIn and they accepted my invitations. Several have become my mentors and some are even now friends! (You'll hear more from a few of these folks in Chapter 11, "LinkedIn and You: Getting Specific.")

What types of people are useful for your business? What type of person makes a good contact? What type of person makes a good client? What type of person makes a good vendor? What type of person makes a good mentor? What type of person makes a good employee? What type of person makes a good employer? Write down the common characteristics of these people. This is an easy step to miss, but don't skip it. Taking the time to classify these folks will ensure you have a stronger and more usable network on LinkedIn.

If you've not done so yet, look at your existing top 20 clients. What characteristics do they have in common? What makes them different from everybody else? Make a list. Those are characteristics (keywords) you might want to search for on LinkedIn. You might find some new connections that way—and they might become your next clients.

Do your ideal clients:

- Live in a specific geographic location?
- Work in a specific field or industry?
- Work with customers or businesses?
- Make a certain income?

Take a look at your existing vendors. Why are you using them? What characteristics do they have in common? Use this list to look for new vendors on LinkedIn.

Look at referral and strategic partners in your business. What characteristics do they have in common? Add them to your list to search for on LinkedIn.

What are you looking for an employer or employee? What common characteristics? You're beginning to get the picture, right?

Use the Advanced People search to look for individuals by the characteristics you identified to do keyword searches. Of course if you know their name, search for them that way. When you find someone on LinkedIn who would make a good contact, download their profile as a PDF and save it in a folder named something like LinkedIn Strategic Contacts. Make a note if they are a first-, second-, or third-level connection or share a group with you. In case you don't yet know how to download a PDF on LinkedIn, I'll walk you through it step by step later in this chapter, during Week 13.

Tuesday: Identify Potential Connections

I apologize ahead of time, but I'm going to ask you to waste some paper. I'd like you to print out all the PDFs that you saved on your computer yesterday.

The next steps can either be done by you, or if you have an assistant, intern, or a volunteer, you can assign this task to them. You are going to go through all these PDFs and sort by hand all the profiles you downloaded.

Remember that on LinkedIn you can *easily* send a message only to a first-level connection. So the first thing you're going to want to do is go through the PDFs you downloaded and see which ones are first-level connections, and then sort them into a pile. If you forgot to mark down what level of connection they are to you, just do a quick search on their name and make notes on your printouts.

The second thing I want you to do is look through your remaining PDFs and see who you share a group with. These are also easy people to contact on LinkedIn (through the group).

The third thing I want you to do is go through the remaining PDFs and see who has a group that you might not (yet) share. Put these PDFs in a separate file. You might even consider sorting this pile into profiles that share membership in the same group.

The next group of PDFs I want you to sort are those profiles in which you share a common person. These are the people who you can get introduced to.

And the final pile of PDFs don't fall into any of these classifications. These are the folks who fall outside your network and who you will have to send an InMail to. Don't start reaching out to these folks quite yet—we have a few more things to go through.

> **Note:** If you have a paid account, you might consider using your Profile Organizer to divvy up your network into these categories. You'll learn more about the Profile Organizer later in this chapter, during Week 13.

Wednesday: Write Proper Messages and Invitations

I decided to start this section with messages rather than invitations since I find it easier to talk to someone rather than ask them for something the first time out (like asking them to connect with you). Also, there will be people you may want to have a conversation with who you don't necessary want to be connected to.

Sending a Message to Your First-Level Connections

When writing a message to your first-level connections, make them personal. If it's someone you don't really know, make them aware that you share a network on LinkedIn and that you're making an effort to reach out and get to know people.

Your message might read:

Dear Mark, I was going through my LinkedIn first-level connections and I found your profile. I see that you are an applications designer. Have you ever done any work in ABC industry? I'm pretty well connected there so if you ever need an introduction, please let me know. I'm very open to short conversations, so if you have time for a 10–15 minute phone call please feel free to reach out to me at (555) 555-5555.

Don't worry—very few people will take you up on the offer for a phone call, and the ones who do might make very good contacts for you. You might start with individuals who could clearly become clients or work in an industry or company that might provide a good client or employment base.

If it's someone you know who you haven't seen or talked to in a while, ask them how their family and business are doing. If it's a good friend of yours, just say you're dropping a line to say hi.

Don't use this first communication to ask them for anything. This is merely a way for you to get back in touch with the strategic businessperson you want to form a better relationship with.

Note: I'm a really big fan of Bob Burg's *Endless Referrals* (McGraw-Hill, 2005). He recommends that when you meet someone for the first time you ask them about themselves, about their business, and most importantly, about who makes a good referral for them. That way, the first thing you're doing, rather than asking for a favor, is provide them with value. It's much more likely that a LinkedIn member will respond to you if you ask the question, "Who makes a good referral for you?" You can even take it one step further and say something like "I noticed you are an accountant. I have several small business owners in my network. Would they make a good referral for you? If so, let me know and I'd be happy to facilitate an introduction."

Sending a Message to Other Group Members

For people you share a group with, reach out and send a message through the group. (Learn more about this in Week 17 in Chapter 6, "Weeks 16–18: Getting Strategic with Groups.") Remember, this is a message, not an invitation. You are making first contact with someone who you might want to later build a relationship with.

Ask them if they find the group useful, what other groups they like, and what discussions they have been involved with. Again, don't reach out to them this first time just to ask them for something.

Your message might look something like this:

Dear Mark, I noticed we are both in the Group LinkedStrategies. How do you like it? I've been impressed with the discussions lately. I saw that you commented on sharing Twitter names and I agree, it can be annoying. Are you aware of any Twitter groups that are good on LinkedIn?

Asking for an Introduction

According to LinkedIn, "Introductions let you contact members in your extended network through the people you know. If you want to contact someone who is two or three degrees away from you, you can request an introduction through one of your connections. Your connection will, in turn, decide whether to forward your message on to the desired recipient (if in your second-degree network) or on to a shared connection (if in your third-degree network)."

Here are a few things you might not have known about introductions:

- All LinkedIn members get introductions. Paid accounts have more.
- Introductions will expire after 6 months if there is no response.
- Once the member accepts your introduction, you can start communicating.
- An introduction is not an invitation. If you want to connect to (as opposed to contact) an individual, you must still send an invitation.
- You can use an introduction to ask if a member is open to an invitation.

Introductions are a great LinkedIn tool but must be used sparingly because you are given only five at a time with the free account. We'll talk more about introductions on Friday, but the same logic applies. When you reach out to someone through an introduction, let the introducer know what your interest is in the person you want to be introduced to. Reference their profile. Be clear.

InMail

When there is no other way to reach out to someone, you will have to invest in InMail. Even though you are paying for it, don't use your initial communication via InMail to pitch them. I don't know about you, but when someone I don't know sends me a sales letter on LinkedIn, I just delete it. Just like with those people you sent a direct message to, your first message to these folks should be a light touch.

Contact Template: Reaching Out for the First Time

Dear [Name],

I was doing a LinkedIn search on [Industry Type] experts and your profile showed up. I was very impressed with [something from their profile]. I know it's not easy in this business environment to [mention one of their achievements].

[Name], I am interested in both helping and learning more from you. How will I know if someone I am speaking with is a good prospect for you?

Please let me know if there is any way I can be of service to you.

[Signature]

[With credentials and contact information]

Once you reach out to someone through an introduction, a message through a group to a group member, or an InMail, and they respond, ask them if you can send them an invitation. (If you can send them a LinkedIn message, you are already first-level connections.) This might seem a little work intensive, but an assistant, intern, or volunteer can do much of it. Taking the time to make this first light touch might make the difference between a strategic connection accepting your invitation or sending you an IDK.

Thursday: Contact People You Don't Know

When reaching out to someone you don't know via an InMail, introduction, or a message in a shared group, it's a good practice to, at the very least, read their profile first. Depending on how important this connection is to you, you might want to do more research as well. Look at their website, look at their social profiles if they have them, do a Google search and read their articles and listen to their interviews. Become an expert on them. (This might sound like stalking, but on social media it's known as lurking and is perfectly okay!) We'll just call it research. If you have someone in common with the person you are wanting to contact, you might ask them if they have a minute for a phone call with you so that you can get some personal opinions about that individual. It's worth the time investment.

In your research you might discover they have a point of pain you can address, so try to provide the solution. Don't write something like "Your website is really badly keyworded and I know I can help you get better search rankings." It may be true, but it's offensive. Start with something like "I don't know if you are getting the traffic you need from your website, but I just found this article on SEO you might find useful." And it doesn't have to be your product or service. You are acknowledging their frustration and coincidentally (after lots of research) saw just the article, heard just the lecture, or talked to just the person who can solve their problem. And then give them the information for free. Of course if you're that person, offer your solution.

Naturally it's best to try to take the relationship to the phone, or even face to face if possible, as soon as possible. At the very least, see if you can wrangle an invitation out of them.

Friday: Get Introduced

I really like an introduction to someone I don't know, as long as I know the person who's introducing me. One of the downfalls of open networking is that I don't know most of the people I am connected to—meaning I don't know the person I want to introduce me to someone, and I usually don't know the person who other folks are asking me to introduce them to. However, in the lucky happenstance that I know the person who is going to introduce me to my strategic connection well, I use that option.

Remember, for the free account you get only five introductions at a time. That means if you ask five people to introduce you to John Doe, CEO, and none of them forwards the introduction, you're out five introductions until they are passed along or you withdraw them. Paid accounts get you more introductions (15 for the basic account and up from there). It is *not* five per month.

To ask for an introduction, go first to the profile of the person you want to get introduced to, and click Get Introduced Through A Connection, as shown in Figure 5.8. Do not just message your first-level connection and ask them for an introduction to someone in their network. Use the tool LinkedIn provides you.

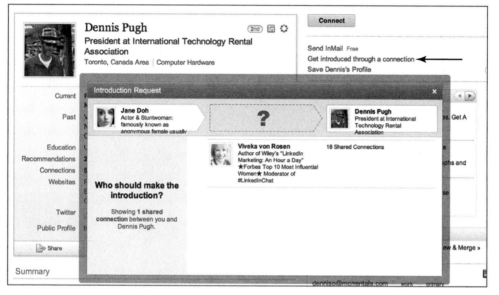

Figure 5.8 Asking for an introduction

Then choose the shared connection that you would like to ask to introduce you to the person. Make sure it is someone you know, who likes and respects you, and who uses LinkedIn regularly. If it's not someone you know, or they simply don't like you, they might not pass along your invitation. If they are not active on LinkedIn, they might not even see the invitation to pass it along. (Profiles that are less than 50 percent complete with only a handful of connections usually indicate someone who is not active on LinkedIn.)

LinkedIn recently changed the introduction process. You used to be able to write to both the person you wanted to get introduced to and the introducer. Now you can only write to the introducer and hope that they will pass along your message intact.

LinkedIn recommends (and I concur) that you state your intent and be clear about why you're asking for an introduction. Also give the introducer an out; be professional and give them a way to say no.

> ### Contact Template: Introduction
>
> Hi, [Name], I noticed you just got promoted. Congratulations! [Or make some personal comment to them]
>
> I see that you are connected to Jane Doh. I have need of an actress for a commercial I am shooting for a client. [Tell them why you are reaching out.] Do you know her well? Do you know if she's working right now? If you have a minute, I'd like to chat with you about Jane, but if you don't have the time, could you pass along this message? If you are uncomfortable forwarding this introduction, no worries. There are a few other people I could ask, but I thought of you first.
>
> Thanks in advance,
>
> [Your Name]
>
> [With credentials and contact information]

You will not have the option of asking for an introduction to someone you are already directly connected to. Just send them a message or email them since you will have their contact information via LinkedIn.

Week 12: Using LinkedIn's People You May Know Feature

Once you've added some connections, experience, and education fields to LinkedIn, it begins to come up with people you may know. I love this feature because it allows me to connect to people easily. Not only that, but LinkedIn is usually right! Often it will send me suggestions of people I actually know, who I might have forgotten about, who now work in a different position or company that I didn't know about, or who I never thought to connect with on LinkedIn in the first place.

Monday: Invite People Using Home Page Suggestions

At the top right-hand side of your home page you'll see a box that says People You May Know. What I like about this section is that LinkedIn usually does make some pretty logical suggestions.

In my network, I find the individuals are people I do know, probably stemming from mutual connections, or we share a company, a school, or an industry. Either way, these are some good folks for me to connect with. (If someone doesn't make sense, I hit the little X that gets rid of that person and LinkedIn pulls up some new people I might know.) If it's someone who makes sense for me to connect with, I'll click the Connect button, and then the usual LinkedIn Invitation screen (shown in Figure 5.9) appears.

You can connect to someone as a Colleague, Classmate, We've Done Business Together, Friend, Groups, Other, or I Don't Know. *Never, ever choose I Don't Know.* You might be penalized and at the very least LinkedIn won't forward the invitation. If you happen to have their email address, you can choose Other or Friend. If you don't have their email, you will have to choose Colleague, Classmate, We've Done Business Together, or Groups. Even though including a personal note is optional, write one specifically for that individual. You only have about 300 characters, so you can't get too in depth, but if it's someone you haven't talked to in a while then say hello and remind them how you know them.

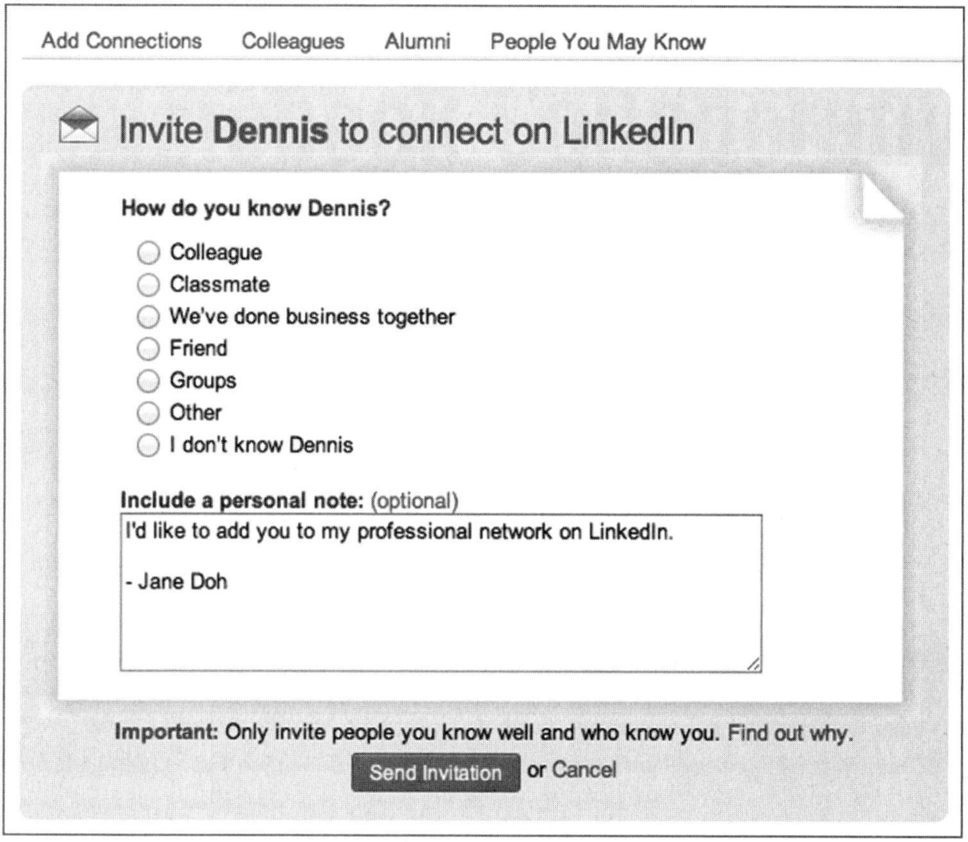

Figure 5.9 Invitation screen

If it's someone you don't know, you might say something like "LinkedIn suggested you as a person I might know. Even though we don't know each other I read your profile and LinkedIn is correct. You are someone I would like to know and invite to my network." And then just sign your name. You cannot add an email address or URL in an invitation.

Under People You May Know, you can also click the See More link and LinkedIn will take you to a brand-new page. The People You May Know page was recently updated and is currently in beta mode. See Figure 5.10 to see this new screen.

Figure 5.10 People You May Know

The first thing you'll see is a list of colleges and companies (and if you hit the + button LinkedIn will pull up an additional row of colleges and/or companies). These are people from different parts of your professional life. When you click one of those links, all the people associated with that college or business that LinkedIn thinks you might know will show up on the screen below. If you click Connect All, you'll be able to send an invitation to all the individuals at once.

Just be careful when using this function. Because you cannot send a personalized invitation when you choose Connect All, you might risk someone saying they don't know you, if in fact they don't know you. I know I've said it before, but *enough IDKs and LinkedIn will inhibit your ability to easily send invitations to other members.* I suggest taking the few extra minutes to invite those people individually by clicking the Connect button underneath their thumbnail. This will allow you to create a personalized invitation.

What I like about this new page is that you don't have to choose a path for connection (meaning you don't have to specify how you know them: Colleague, Classmate, Other, etc.). LinkedIn made the suggestion so it assumes you know the person. It makes connecting much easier. So rather than reaching out to the individuals on your home page's People You May Know section, just click See More and connect from that screen.

> **Contact Template: Sending a Personal Invitation through People You May Know**
>
> Hi, [Name],
>
> LinkedIn suggested I connect with you. I see you [work at, attend, teach at] [Company/College]. I've [gone there, spoken there, worked there] too. Would you like to connect on LinkedIn?
>
> [Signature]
>
> [With credentials and contact information]

This is a fantastic new tool with a great user interface, and I'm so glad that LinkedIn introduced it while I was writing this book.

Tuesday: Invite People Using Inbox Suggestions

If you click twice on the Inbox tab, and then click Invitations, you will notice a list at the bottom that also says People You May Know. What I've noticed is that this list is a little bit different than the list on your home page (and See More) that we just looked at. This section in your invitations inbox also lets you send an invitation without classifying how you know the person. In addition, it allows you to add a personal message.

At the very bottom of this page you'll notice the option See Who You Already Know On LinkedIn. This is the same option that appears in the Add Connections tool that we just looked at, and it will allow LinkedIn to search your email service (Hotmail.com, Gmail.com, Yahoo.com, and AOL.com, among others), as you saw in the previous section.

But you've probably already done this.

Wednesday: Invite Colleagues and Classmates

There are a few different places on LinkedIn that let you invite colleagues and classmates to connect to you.

If you scroll to the very bottom of your home page, you'll see a list of people who have just joined LinkedIn. The first list is colleagues at companies where you've worked. The second are classmates or alumni of places where you have received education. If *you* have not listed a company that you have worked at in the Experience section, or a school you have gone to in your LinkedIn profile, then it won't show up as a link here. Once you've added a company or a school, just click the link, as shown in Figure 5.11, and it will automatically upload up to 50 individuals who have recently joined LinkedIn.

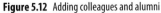

Just joined LinkedIn

Colleagues
Linked Into Business, LLC
Jane Doe: Girl with No Name
NBS Studios
Actor's Studio

Alumni
Julliard School of Acting
NYU Actor's Studio

Figure 5.11 Connecting to colleagues and classmates

Now you can go through the list and simply put a check mark next to every individual from that company or school who you want to invite to connect. Remember to add a personal note to this individual or group of individuals. It might be even something as simple as "I notice you work at my old company, [Name of Company], and that you've just joined LinkedIn. I'd like to welcome you to LinkedIn and to my network. Please accept my invitation and let me know if you would like me to make an introduction for you."

You can also find colleagues and alumni by clicking the Add Connections button, as shown in Figure 5.12.

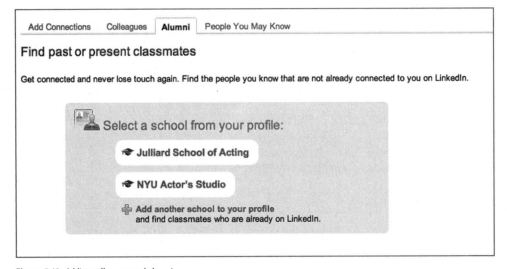

Add Connections   Colleagues   **Alumni**   People You May Know

Find past or present classmates

Get connected and never lose touch again. Find the people you know that are not already connected to you on LinkedIn.

Select a school from your profile:

☞ **Julliard School of Acting**

☞ **NYU Actor's Studio**

➕ Add another school to your profile
and find classmates who are already on LinkedIn.

Figure 5.12 Adding colleagues and alumni

If you select the Colleagues or Alumni tab, a list similar to what you just saw on your home page will appear, although these will be people who have been on LinkedIn for a while. Again, simply check off the people you want to be connected to and write a quick note saying that you both work at the same company and you're both on LinkedIn, and that you'd like to connect.

Go ahead and invite a few folks to connect right now.

Thursday: Understand InMail Etiquette

If you find a strategic connection that you would like to reach out to but you don't share a group or have any shared connections, are not a colleague a classmate, or have anything else in common, you can always send an InMail. (InMails cost money but might save you time.)

If you have a paid account, you can easily send an InMail by clicking the Send InMail link at the upper right of the member's profile page. If you have a free account, or if you've already used your InMails for the month, you can purchase up to 10 more InMails from LinkedIn. They do cost $10 each.

LinkedIn recommends using InMail, because it's fast and allows you to send messages to LinkedIn users you couldn't reach otherwise. LinkedIn claims that InMail is better than email or a cold call because it includes information about you and your professional background, giving the recipient the confidence to respond. And (this is probably the best part of an InMail) if you don't get a reply within seven days, you can send another InMail to the same or a new member on LinkedIn for no cost.

Personally, I consider InMail a last-ditch effort. But it's nice that you have the option.

> **Note:** Stacy Donovan Zapar, formerly of Intuit and now a private social recruiter, shared this tip in her blog on how to find the email addresses of your LinkedIn connections via Google. See www.stacyzapar.com/ 2010/11/how-to-contact-linkedin-users-without.html.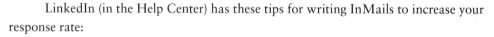

LinkedIn (in the Help Center) has these tips for writing InMails to increase your response rate:

- Design your InMail as a conversation starter. The goal is to discuss and explore an opportunity, not seal the deal immediately. Of course you want to mention the profile content that prompted you to write to them in the first place.

- Adopt a conversational and enthusiastic tone when you send InMail. Choose words that reflect your personal voice and express an interest in helping the individual reach their goals, rather than focusing on what you need from them.

- It's always good to be brief and to the point. Know that if you share too much, the person you've reached out to may not feel the need to reply to you.

- Focus on finding out their availability and interest in a job or networking opportunity. If you've read their profile you already know whether or not they're qualified, so it's a good idea to set up a meeting as soon as possible.

- Give them a reason to reply by asking them for advice, for their opinion, or even for referrals.

Friday: Get TopLinked—People You Don't Know but Should

Okay, granted this section is not people you know—just the opposite actually! But this is important information, especially for those of you who are open to having a larger or even an open network.

There is a website called Toplinked.com that features a list of Top Supporters on the left side of the page, as you can see in Figure 5.13. You do not have to pay TopLinked to contact and invite these people to connect with you on LinkedIn.

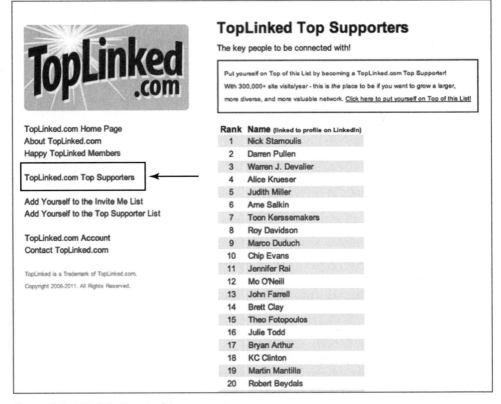

Figure 5.13 TopLinked's Top Supporters list

These are people who pay to be on this list. Why? So that you (and thousands of others) will invite them to connect. Why? So that their network will be bigger. Why? So that LinkedIn becomes a more usable tool for them—and for you.

What is nice about this list is that by clicking on a Top Supporter's name, you end up on their LinkedIn member profile, where you can easily check them out, and then if you want to, invite them to connect. Feel free to go through each profile and choose discerningly, or invite them all. By inviting even as few as 20 of these individuals your LinkedIn network size will likely grow 7–10 million members!

If you are interested in becoming an open networker, TopLinked also has a service where you can add yourself to the Invite Me lists of your choice (LinkedIn, Twitter, Facebook, etc.) and build your networks. You can choose just LinkedIn or any of the social networks in this list.

If you join TopLinked's $49.95-a-year service, you may receive several hundred invitations a week. I seem to average about 100. These people are inviting you, so you are not breaking the "Don't invite people you don't know" rule and you are not spending any of your invitations. To get an account go to `http://bit.ly/toplinkedviv`. (Just so you know, I am an affiliate member.)

When you sign up for this service, it is assumed that you will accept or ignore and *not* IDK or report as spam any member asking to connect. Of course you don't have to accept every invitation. I used to be completely open, but when I started getting spam messages on LinkedIn I became more discerning. But even though I only accept a fraction of the invitations I receive from TopLinked, I still add a few hundred people to my network every month—many of whom I do business with! *TopLinked is in no way affiliated with LinkedIn.*

Week 13: Managing Your Network

As you start to build your network, implementing these management tools might help you not only to organize but also communicate better with your connections.

Monday: Tag Your Connections

To those of you just getting started on LinkedIn, I am so jealous! One of the great tools that LinkedIn offers is the ability to tag your connections. Tagging is similar to lists on Facebook, and if you get into the habit of tagging your connections as you make them, you will be far ahead of folks like me who have too many connections to tag effectively, or those who just can't be bothered. Why? Well, not only does tagging allow you to group your connections into categories of your making, it also enables you to send targeted messages to each tagged grouping.

Where do you find tags? As you can see in Figure 5.14, under Contacts click My Connections, and you will see Tags to the left of your Connections list.

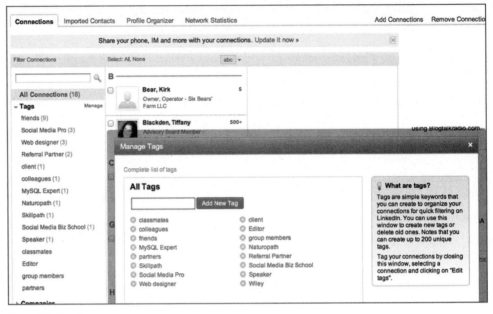

Figure 5.14 Tagging

LinkedIn will qualify and tag some of your connections for you depending on how you are connected: group members, friends, partners, colleagues, classmates, and untagged. But there is so much more you can do.

You can create up to 200 tags, and then classify your connections adding as many tags to an individual's profile as you want. Because most communications on LinkedIn are limited to only 50 recipients at a time, it's a good idea to add fewer than 50 people to each tag. That way, you can send a message to a group of people just by clicking on the tag.

Some tags you might consider creating are:

- Men
- Women
- Strangers
- Acquaintances
- Friends (real ones—not Facebook-like friends)
- Clients
- Prospective clients
- Competition
- Affinity partners
- Locals
- Association members (list different associations)
- Conference attendees (list different conferences)

- Network members (list different networking groups)
- Niche industry
- Former coworkers
- Fellow alum
- Potential candidates to hire
- Potential employers
- Twitter friends
- Meet-up friends
- Et Cetera

So I might have one person tagged as: Woman, WOI member, WLO member, Lawyer, Previous Client, and Prospect. And now I can use any of those defining tags when creating a list of people to send a message to.

Let's say I want to establish myself as a LinkedIn expert by sending out a new LinkedIn tip every week. I could export my contacts into my email program and send them all a tip at one time (this is somewhat frowned on by LinkedIn and I don't recommend it either), or I could take the time to customize the tip to the specific grouping of people tagged in my network, as shown in Figure 5.15.

Figure 5.15 Sending a message to tagged connections

So the same tip can be customized:

- As a legal professional on LinkedIn, did you know you can add your areas of practice to your professional headline? You have 120 characters to work with.

- As an accountant on LinkedIn, did you know you can add your special designations to your professional headline? You have 120 characters to work with.

- As a graphic artist on LinkedIn, did you know you can add your special skills to your professional headline? You have 120 characters to work with.

As you can imagine, tagging a big network can be quite a task, so don't wait until you have thousands of connections. If you start now and do a little each day, you can be done by the end of the month. (I know this is an hour-a-day book, but this task will definitely take you more than an hour depending on how many connections you have.) If you have an assistant or virtual assistant, you can even create some guidelines and have them do some of the work for you.

Note: You might notice that some of your connections are already tagged. LinkedIn automatically tags your contacts according to how you indicated you knew each other when you originally connected: Colleagues, Classmates, Friends, and Group Members.

Once your connections are tagged, start creating a communications strategy. Each week reach out to different groupings of people to keep them in the loop. You don't want these messages to always to be sales messages (at best you'll be ignored, at worst reported as a spammer). But if you have written a relevant blog post, have discovered a new strategy they might find interesting, or have valuable information to share, then this becomes a great way to reach out and touch someone and stay top of mind. And never forget WIIFM; when you are creating your communication strategy, remember that in order for them to open your note, they are going to want to know what's in it for them.

To help you with your communications strategy I have created spreadsheets you can download at www.sybex.com/go/linkedinhour. You'll learn more information about these spreadsheets and how to use them in Chapter 9, "Optimizing Your Time Using LinkedIn."

Tuesday: Use the Profile Organizer

The Profile Organizer on LinkedIn comes only with the paid premium accounts. It allows you to save and organize member profiles, add notes, and track your messages to clients, experts, job seekers, employees, candidates—just about any person of interest.

You'll find the Profile Organizer under the Profile menu bar at the top of your home page. If you have a free account and click Profile Organizer, LinkedIn will give the option of upgrading. If you have a paid account, LinkedIn will take you to the Profile Organizer page.

One of the reasons I started paying for LinkedIn was to get access to the Profile Organizer. Until tagging came out, it was the only way to organize your network.

The Profile Organizer allows you to bookmark a person's profile, either from the Save Profile link at the upper right of the member's profile, or from the Search Results page (just to the right of the person's information).

As shown in Figure 5.16, you can create a folder and put the profile in it right away, or you can just save the profile to the Profile Organizer and add that profile to a folder later. Kind of like in Google+ Circles, you can add individuals to many different folders.

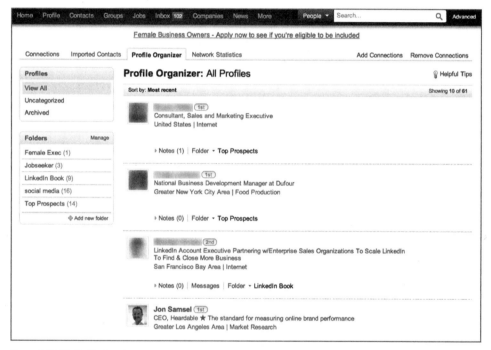

Figure 5.16 The Profile Organizer

As mentioned earlier, you can also add notes about where you met that individual or why they're important to you. No one will see the notes except for you.

If you have a premium account, you can save as many *profiles* as you like, but there are some limits to the *folders* you can add. With the basic Business account you get 5 folders, with the Business Plus account you get 25 folders, the Executive account has 50 folders, and with the Pro account you get 75 folders.

If you added a profile to a folder and you decide you don't want them in there anymore (maybe they went from being a top prospect to a client), then all you have to do is open your Profile Organizer from your home page, click on the folder with the link to the person's profile that you want to delete, and uncheck the box next to their name. You can also delete folders or rename them. Once you delete a folder, only the folder is gone—your profiles will be moved to an uncategorized folder that you can then rename.

The thing I like about the Profile Organizer is that you can place any profile in a folder, whether you are connected to that person or not. Until LinkedIn comes up with a real CRM system, this is at least one option of organizing and tracking your network and network communications on LinkedIn.

 Note: It might be worth noting that if you ever decide to downgrade your premium account to a free account, you will lose access to your Profile Organizer folders and notes. However, LinkedIn will save your notes for future reference if you should decide to upgrade your account again.

Wednesday: Manually Organize by PDF

As I mentioned earlier in this chapter, you can save a member's profile as a PDF. This can be any member on LinkedIn. They do not have to be in your network.

The nice thing about saving a profile as a PDF is that not only can you save it in your own folder, but also you can send that profile to anybody you want to. Consider saving your own profile as a PDF so that you can send it to people who are not on LinkedIn.

To save a member's profile as a PDF, click the PDF icon, as shown in Figure 5.17.

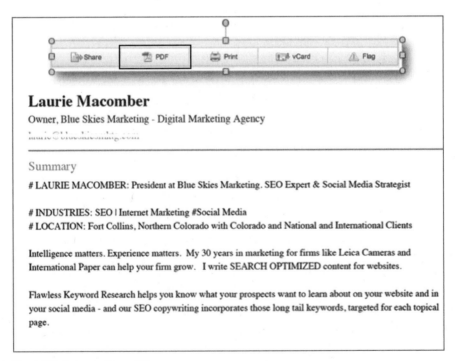

Figure 5.17 Saving a profile as a PDF

When you click the PDF icon, the LinkedIn member's profile will download into a nicely formatted PDF file. The header will include their name, professional headline, and if they are a first-level connection, their email address.

The document will also include the Summary and Specialties sections (if they are not a new member), Experience and Education, Skills & Expertise, Honors and Awards, Recommendations, and Areas of Expertise. To make life easy, LinkedIn has added a link that allows you to contact that person through LinkedIn. Why might you want to download someone's PDF?

- To organize your network when you don't have the Profile Organizer
- To keep a record of someone in case they leave LinkedIn (or your network)
- As research before an interview or meeting
- For some name/face recognition before a tradeshow or conference
- To keep a file for referral partners
- To keep a file for potential clients
- To keep a file for potential employees and candidates
- To keep a file on your competition
- To keep a file on potential vendors
- And as I mentioned earlier in this chapter, to help you organize and connect to a relevant and strategic network!

Thursday: Use the Outlook Social Connector Or Xobni

There are some pretty cool third-party applications that will help you organize your network. Let's look at a few of them now. (We'll explore more options in Chapter 11.)

Outlook Social Connector

The Outlook Social Connector allows you to manage your professional network on LinkedIn within Microsoft Outlook. Of course if you don't have Outlook, this isn't going to work.

To find the Outlook Social Connector, go down to the bottom of your screen and click Tools. Next to Overview is the tab for the Outlook Social Connector. Select that tab.

You can download LinkedIn for Outlook only in the 64-bit version on LinkedIn, but you can go to the Microsoft website to get the 32-bit version. In order for the LinkedIn Outlook Social Connector to work, you'll need to download Outlook Social Connector from Microsoft itself. To do that, go to http://g.msn.com/0Cr1033/80. (Just be aware that doing this will download the EXE to your desktop if you have a PC.)

The Outlook Social Connector allows you to keep track of what your LinkedIn connections are doing right at the bottom of an email you receive. You can see who they're connecting with, the articles they are reading and sharing, and the questions they're asking and answering. Another thing I like about the Outlook Social Connector is that it keeps you up-to-date on your connections' professional contact information. Profile details and photos from your connections will appear in your Outlook Contacts folder (which will be named LinkedIn), so you'll always have the latest contact information from LinkedIn.

Probably my favorite part of this tool is the green Add icon that will show up next to any email sender who you are not directly connected to on LinkedIn. What an easy way to grow your network!

Xobni

Xobni (*inbox* spelled backward) is a company that creates inbox and address book tools that make it easier for you to search for and discover all your contacts on various social networks—even those who might not be current members of your LinkedIn network. It shows you a connection's social media presence on Facebook, LinkedIn, Twitter, and Hoovers as well as when they communicate, what they communicate, and analytics as the best time to communicate with them.

At this time, Xobni will only work with Outlook (not Outlook Express), Gmail, and on your Android, iPhone, or BlackBerry. There is a free membership, but I recommend the paid account, which works out to less than $10 a month. You can find Xobni at www.xobni.com.

While similar to the Outlook Social Connector in function, one thing I loved about Xobni (which has nothing to do with LinkedIn) is its appointment scheduler. When someone asks you for an appointment in an email, Xobni will pull up your calendar for the day and the times you have available. When I bought my Mac I purchased Outlook for Mac just so I could keep using Xobni.

If you use Outlook, be sure to take a look at these two options.

Friday: Explore Paid Management Tools—JibberJobber and Salesforce

There are some awesome CRM tools if you are willing to invest some money in them. We'll take a look at JibberJobber and Salesforce here.

JibberJobber

I would be remiss not to mention JibberJobber, which is a job search organizer and personal relationship manager (PRM). I am not a job seeker but I find this system intuitive and easy to use. It has all the places to add notes and documents and reminders that I need to record and follow up with my contacts effectively. I might get a notice that a client is having an anniversary and I can send a note to them via LinkedIn right from JibberJobber!

You don't have to be a job seeker to use it, but if you are, you will be amazed at all the other tools this site offers (such as webinars, help with your 30-second introduction, insider information on companies you might want to work with). JibberJobber was designed by Jason Alba, who also happened to write one of the first books on LinkedIn, *I'm on LinkedIn, Now What???* (Happy About, 2008).

Because JibberJobber is a third-party application, if someone leaves LinkedIn (or you do) you will still have access to the community you built and the conversations you had. Get JibberJobber at `www.JibberJobber.com`.

JibberJobber is an excellent complement to LinkedIn. LinkedIn is about finding the right people to network and communicate with and develop these relationships. JibberJobber is a great tool to track who you are communicating with and what you are saying. It's a tracking system that lets you keep up with all the conversation.

Salesforce

As a business professional, you have probably almost certainly heard of Salesforce even if you are not using it. I mentioned the Salesforce LinkedIn app in the first chapter, and I highly recommend it for anyone using LinkedIn and Salesforce.

Let's get this out of the way: Salesforce is not cheap! I'm not telling you to go out and get a Salesforce account. But if you are already using it in your company, have your Salesforce administrator install the application into Salesforce and provide you with access.

The LinkedIn Salesforce application lets you view LinkedIn information about your network: leads, contacts, accounts, prospects, and business opportunities right in Salesforce itself. It also keeps all the information in one place so you don't have to move between multiple browser tabs to gather information. Not only will this save you time, but it will also keep you from losing crucial information when you click off a page.

According to LinkedIn, LinkedIn for Salesforce can help turn cold prospect information into closed deals by allowing you to:

- Quickly get accurate, up-to-date information on your leads and accounts
- Get real-time updates on your accounts and contacts so you know when to reach out and contact them (or not!)
- Gather information on LinkedIn without leaving Salesforce which, as I mentioned earlier, will save you time

This is not an inexpensive app. You need both a premium LinkedIn account and a Salesforce account. But if you already have them, definitely look into utilizing this application.

Week 14: Monitoring Your Network

Is your network growth in alignment with your goals? As we discussed in Chapter 1, it's important to monitor your network. Measuring your network growth allows you to see if you are in alignment with your goals. This week we're going to take a look at ways you can monitor your network on LinkedIn.

Monday: Use Network Statistics

Under Connections in the home page menu bar, you'll see the Network Statistics link. When you click that link, you'll see all the levels of your network.

Network Statistics show you the number of people who are first-, second-, and third-level connections. As you know, your first-level connections are the people who invited you or who you have invited to connect. These are the people you can easily contact and communicate with. Your second-level connections are friends of friends, as they're called on Facebook. Each one of these individuals is connected to you through one of your connections. To reach your third-level connections, you have to go through a friend and then one of their friends. Finally, you have the total number of users you can contact through an introduction, including people you share a group with.

You will also see the regional access of your network, as shown in Figure 5.18.

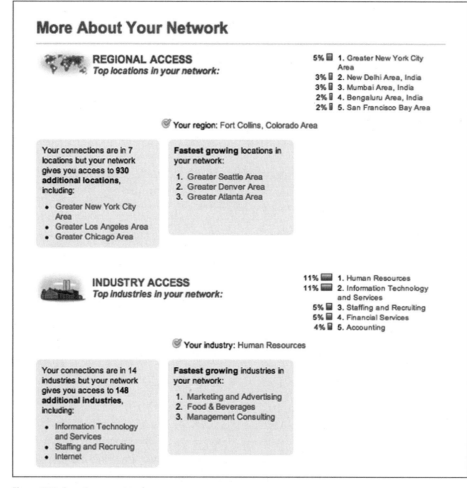

Figure 5.18 Accessing your network

LinkedIn will show you, by percentage, where your network resides. Taking a quick glance at this will tell you if you're focusing your efforts on connecting in the right place. Obviously if you are a location-based business and the greatest part of your network is outside of your particular area or state, you might want to take some time to find and connect with some locals. To do that, use the Advanced People search.

Searching for Members in a Geographic Region

In the Advanced People search, without filling in any other fields, go to the Postal Code field and type in your postal code (make sure you are in the right country). Choose the distance from your postal code (10-, 25-, 35-, 50-, 75-, or 100-mile radius) that you want to search. Click Search and LinkedIn will pull up all the individual members within that distance of your postal code. Use the methods described in the previous section to reach out to strategic connections in your local area.

If you're not a geographically based business, make sure that you're growing your network in the regions that you do work. Similarly, LinkedIn will show you your fastest-growing areas. Are they the areas you want to be growing?

LinkedIn also gives you industry access. Those are the top industries in your network by percentage. Are they the ones you work within and want to be growing? If your network is not weighted toward the industries with which you work, you may want to do an Advanced People search using industry keywords in the keyword field.

Tuesday: Use Your Home Page

There are also a lot of very useful LinkedIn statistics on your home page. On the right side of your profile you'll see the link Who's Viewed Your Profile. This will show you who has viewed your profile this month and how many times you've shown up in search results.

The first thing you're going to want to do is click Who's Viewed Your Profile, which will take you to a new page, as shown in Figure 5.19.

On the left you can see who those individuals are. People will often look at your profile in an anonymous mode so you can't see who they are. Sometimes, though, you will get an individual's name. All you have to do is click on their name and it will take you to their profile. If they are a first-level connection or they have a paid account, it's easy to reach out to them and thank them for viewing your profile.

You might say something like "I noticed that you were viewing my profile and I just wanted to say hi. Please let me know if I can answer any questions for you or be of service in any way." Of course if it's someone you know, pick up the phone or send them an email. You don't even have to tell them that you know they were looking at your profile—let them think its synchronicity at work!

Figure 5.19 Who's Viewed Your Profile

If you have a paid account, you can see the full list of who's viewed your profile. If you don't have a paid account, you can see the last five people who viewed your profile. So it's not a bad idea to keep an eye on this page every day.

The other thing I like about having the paid account is that you can see the top search by keyword. Make sure you have the keywords that are searched most often several places in your profile.

And while you can see the percentage of individuals by industry or by geography with the free account, with the paid account you can see how many views you have from those particular industries and geographies.

With both accounts you can also see, by the day, how many times your profile has been viewed. If you see a distinct increase in numbers on a particular day, consider what you did that day to get people to look at your profile. See if you can focus on the actions you took and replicate them if you can.

You can also see how many times you appeared in a LinkedIn search (but no one clicked on your profile). Is there a huge discrepancy? If you showed up in 100 searches and only five people clicked on your profile, what is it about your headline and photo (or lack thereof) that is failing to grab people's attention?

Wednesday: Monitor Your Connections

Let's take a closer look at your connections under Contacts in your menu. To the left of the screen you'll see the tags, which we just covered. Below Tags you can also see how your network is sorted by Company, Location, Industry, and Recent Activity, as shown in Figure 5.20.

Figure 5.20 Connections page

I recommend keeping an eye on the companies of individuals that you're connected to. You might have been trying in vain for weeks to get in touch with someone at a company that you want to be doing business with, not even realizing you already know someone who works there. So make it a weekly practice to glance at the Companies link in Connections. Just click the link and LinkedIn will pull up your first-level connections with an affiliation at that company. And because these are all your first-level connections (as opposed to the folks in your network who show up on the Company page), they will be easy to send a message to.

We've already looked at locations and industries on your Network Statistics page, but this section goes a bit more in depth and shows you all the locations and industries that your first-level connections are associated with. And if you click the link LinkedIn will pull up your first-level connections in that location or industry.

Make sure your network is located where you want them to be located and working in the industry you want them to be working in. If any of these are a little light, get searching for strategic connections.

Finally, you can see the recent activity of your network—your new connections, as well as their connections. Why do you want to look at the connections of your new connections? Because they might be people to whom you want to be connected. And your new connections may be able to introduce you to them. To see the connections of your new connections, just click on the number next to your first connection's name. It will be anywhere from 1 to 500+.

When you click on that number, a snapshot of the member's profile will come up, including their new connections and the connections you share.

Note: If the number of connections is not blue, that means that person has turned off your ability to see their network, so you won't get access to them. If the link is blue, just click it and it will take you to their new connections. You'll notice from this page you can just click the Connect button and add the shared person to your network without having to tell LinkedIn how you know them. What's cool about this feature is that you can send an invitation and add a personal message without having to ask for an introduction and without having to classify how you know that individual.

Why is it important to keep an eye on your connections? It's because you want to see the growth of your network and perhaps send them a quick message. Is your target geographic location stale? Invite more people in the cities you are targeting. No new growth at a company you want to target? Do a company search and invite a few folks. (This is a good task for an assistant.) LinkedIn doesn't have to be time-consuming, but your communications should be consistent.

Thursday: Getting Reports on LinkedIn

LinkedIn will email you certain reports about your network, as shown in Figure 5.21.

To set up these reports, you will need to head back into your Settings. Under Email Preferences, choose the frequency of emails you want to receive from LinkedIn with regard to:

- InMails, introductions, and OpenLink
- Invitations
- Profile forwards
- Job notifications
- Questions from your connections
- Replies or messages from your connections
- Invitations to join groups
- Network updates
- Activity notifications
- Referral suggestions
- Actionable emails
- Connection suggestions
- LinkedIn Today

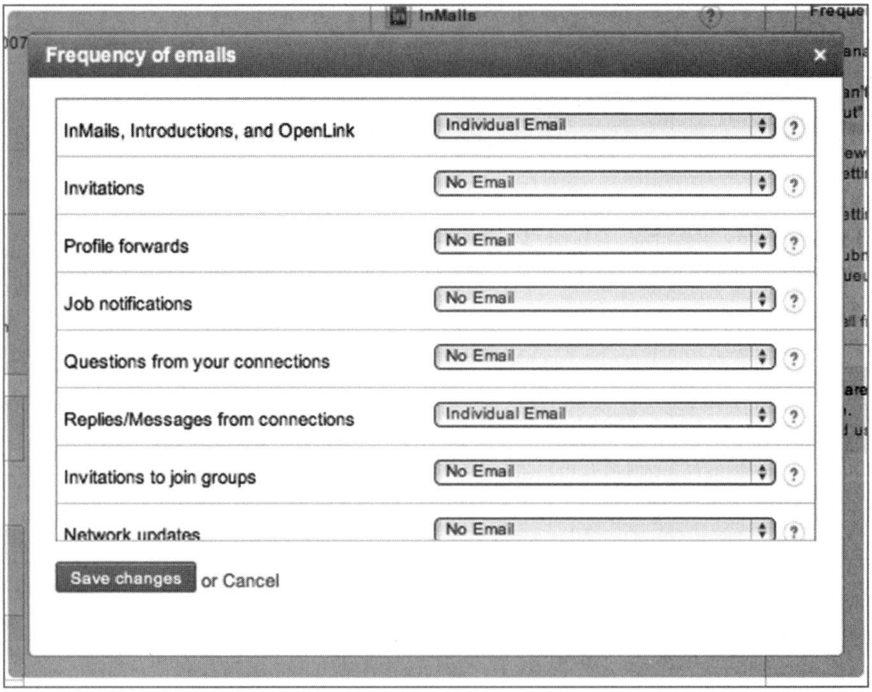

Figure 5.21 Email notifications

I choose to get emails from LinkedIn for InMails, introductions, and OpenLink because these messages *usually* come from users outside my network. Since these communications usually result in connections—if not business—these messages usually result in network growth. That means growing my network. Are some of these communications spammy in nature? Sometimes. But I'll put up with a few sales-y letters for the consultation and connection requests I receive.

Personally I don't choose to receive invitations in my email because being a TopLinked open networker I simply receive too many. So I know I have to go into LinkedIn and accept them every few days or so. If you are new to LinkedIn, or a strategic networker, I recommend getting the daily email. And don't just accept the invitation—send them a thank-you letter!

I also let LinkedIn send me emails regarding questions from my connections, replies/messages from my connections, connection suggestions, referral suggestions, activity notifications, and LinkedIn Today. This lets me keep in better touch with my existing connections and allows me to receive the information that I need in order to build relationships.

I no longer choose to receive email regarding invitations to join groups or network updates because it makes my email inbox too noisy. I can (and do) still receive these messages in my LinkedIn inbox. If you are starting with LinkedIn, you may choose to receive individual emails. When it gets too noisy, revert to weekly or no emails.

> ## Contact Template: Thank-You Letter
>
> Dear [Name]:
>
> Great to be connected and thank you for trusting me with your network.
>
> What do you use LinkedIn for? With so many valuable people on here, I'm always open to exploring new synergies to help one another out.
>
> In that vein, I recently completed [this free offer] which I would like you to have as a connection on LinkedIn. I hope you find it helpful, and of course feel free to share it with anyone who might find value from it.
>
> My specialties are: [describe your USP here]
>
> If you know anyone who I could be of service to, please don't hesitate to refer me.
>
> Thank you again for your connection.
>
> [With credentials and contact information]

Another individual email notification I choose to receive is not in this list but is very important, and that is the searches I save as shown in Figure 5.22.

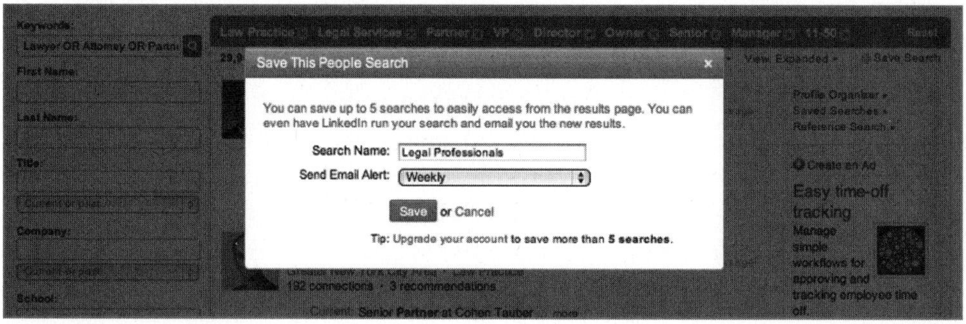

Figure 5.22 Saved Searches

Every time you save a search on LinkedIn (three for the free accounts, five for a basic paid account), LinkedIn will send you an email with new members who fall into that search category. Your first step should always be to look through these new search results and reach out to those individuals who will make strategic connections for you.

What I love about this function is that there are rarely more than 5–10 names in the email LinkedIn sends me, which means a small time commitment with huge results. Some of my best connections have come from reaching out to these folks.

Friday: Monitor Your Competition

Some of this information might get a little repetitive, but it is so important that I thought keeping an eye on your competition should have its own section!

Here are a few ways to keep an eye on your competition on LinkedIn (and a few more that I would be remiss in not mentioning):

- Company Searches
- Saved Searches
- Signal Searches
- Google Alerts

I mentioned in the previous chapter that you can follow a company and LinkedIn will send you a report on any new updates, promotions, and career opportunities posted by that company profile. It goes without saying that a job seeker needs to follow companies they are interested in working for, but how about keeping an eye on your competition? Your name *will* show up as a follower, so if you are Indra Krishnamurthy Nooyi (PepsiCo) you might choose not to follow The Coca Cola Company (although you might have one of your employees do so!).

LinkedIn recently released targeted company updates, which means you are getting more specific statistics about your company followers. Nonetheless, I think you are probably safe in following your competition. You can't follow anonymously, but the company you follow can't block you either. It's a personal choice, but I recommend following your competition (and clients, partners, vendors, and employers) on company profiles.

I just mentioned Saved Searches in the previous section. You are fairly limited in the searches you can save, so rather than saving a search on only one company (say, everyone who is currently or has worked at PepsiCo), you can create a keyword list in the Keyword search field of the Advanced search that would cover not only PepsiCo but Coca-Cola and any other soda company. Your Boolean search string (mentioned earlier in this chapter) might look like this:

```
Soda OR coke OR pop AND manufacturing (NOT Hansen's) Coca Cola OR PepsiCo
```

As you receive your search results you can refine this keyword string even more by adding more ANDs, ORs, and NOTs. I have a whole section on LinkedIn Signal in Chapter 8, "Week 23: Putting It All Together," but just know that by going to LinkedIn Signal at www.LinkedIn.com/Signal you can search on any keyword, including the company names, individual names, products, or services of your competitors. Not only that, but you can save the searches. As of this writing, LinkedIn was not sending you an email of your saved Signal search results, but we can always hope, right? So you have to go into Signal to see your saved searches, and I recommend doing this a few times a week. (This is also something an assistant could do for you.)

I would be remiss in not mentioning Google Alerts. Google Alerts, found at www.google.com/alerts, will send you an email alert of the latest relevant Google search results based on keywords you give it. You simply enter a keyword (Google calls it a query) that you wish to monitor. Google Alerts is free and you can create as many keyword or keyword search phrases as you like.

Week 15: Giving and Getting Recommendations from Your Network

A recommendation is a testimonial, referral, or comment written by someone on LinkedIn to endorse another LinkedIn member. Obviously, recommendations are good to have—and in the Advanced People search you can even search for someone based on their recommendations.

Monday: Find Recommendations

When you receive a recommendation from one of your connections (alas, LinkedIn has now made it so that you can get and give recommendations only from first-level connections), LinkedIn will send a message to your inbox and Manage Recommendations page (found under the Profile tab of the main menu bar).

Recommendations that *you* write for *other* people appear both on the right side of your profile in the box [Your Name] Recommends. It will appear on the recipient's profile in both their Experience section (as a number) and then in full in their Recommendations section.

Tuesday: Ask for Recommendations

The easiest way to ask for a recommendation is from the Request Recommendations tab that you get to from clicking Recommendations under Profile tab. The third tab on the page is Request Recommendations. This will bring you to a new page, as shown in Figure 5.23.

The first thing you will want to do is choose what you want to be recommended for from the drop-down menu. This list will only include experience and schools you have added to your profile. You can click the link that allows you to add a job or school, which will pull up either the Add Position or Add Education page that we covered in Chapter 3, "Weeks 3–6: Ready, Set, Profile."

The second field is Decide Who You'll Ask. These need to be first-level connections. You can either add their name into the text field or click the address book icon to search through your connections. You will check off the names of the people you want to get a recommendation from (and be sure to check on Finished). While you can choose up to 200 people, don't! One of my biggest pet peeves is someone asking me for a recommendation who I don't even know (one of the downsides of having an open network). To get better recommendations, ask for them one at a time. This is not a place to skimp on your hour!

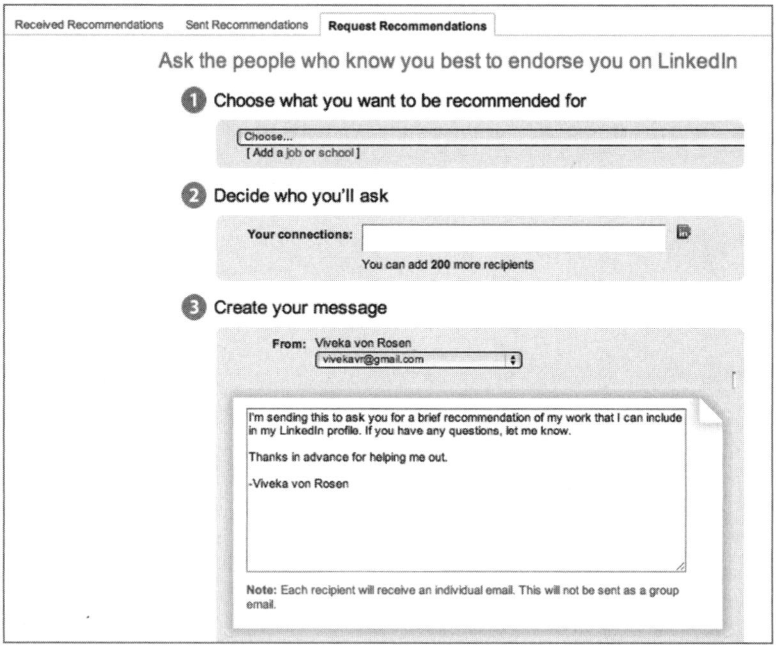

Received Recommendations   Sent Recommendations   **Request Recommendations**

Ask the people who know you best to endorse you on LinkedIn

1 Choose what you want to be recommended for

Choose...
[Add a job or school]

2 Decide who you'll ask

Your connections:

You can add **200** more recipients

3 Create your message

From: Viveka von Rosen
vivekavr@gmail.com

I'm sending this to ask you for a brief recommendation of my work that I can include in my LinkedIn profile. If you have any questions, let me know.

Thanks in advance for helping me out.

-Viveka von Rosen

Note: Each recipient will receive an individual email. This will not be sent as a group email.

Figure 5.23 Asking for recommendations

Contact Template: Requesting a Recommendation

Subject: Can you endorse me for the training I did at Company B?

Hi, [Name],

I hope things are going well at your company. Did your employees implement the suggestions I made? Please let me know if I can be of any more service.

I was hoping you would take a few minutes to write me a recommendation for LinkedIn. Please feel free to write whatever you like. If it helps, I've added a few talking points below:

- Knowledge of your industry
- Experience in my industry
- Ability to listen
- Timelessness
- Ease of use
- Effectiveness

If you have any questions, please don't hesitate to call. Thanks so much for your time. I really enjoyed working with you.

[Signature]

[With credentials and contact information]

LinkedIn will give you a default subject line, but I suggest writing something like this: "Can you recommend me for the work I did for you at [company name]?"

You then can go with the default message to your connection, but again, I suggest going with a personalized note. In fact, you might give them a few talking points to write about.

If you know the person well enough, you might call them first and ask them if they would write a recommendation for you on LinkedIn. If they say yes, go through the previous process.

Though it's a bit tricky, you might even offer to write the recommendation for them if you know they are busy and would not be adverse to the idea. Offer them the opportunity to customize it as they see fit.

The best recommendations are from industry leaders, executive-level employees, and then co-workers. Yes, you can get recommendations from friends or your employees, but it is likely to have less impact. A good number of recommendations is probably between 10 and 15. You no longer need three recommendations to have a 100 percent complete profile according to LinkedIn.

Wednesday: Give Recommendations

You can also give to get! It's nice to give recommendations—especially to the service providers or employees who deserve it.

Note: Be aware there might be compliance issues depending on what industry you are in. If you work within the legal, medical, or financial industries, there might be some restrictions in giving and asking for testimonials.

Click the Sent Recommendations tab and scroll down to the very bottom of your page, where you will see a blue box that says Make A Recommendation. To recommend one of your connections, click Select From Your Connections List and choose the person from your list. If you have their name and email address, you can choose them that way as well.

Click the button next to Colleague, Service Provider, Business Partner, or Student and click Continue. Then complete the recommendation form, as shown in Figure 5.24.

You will choose the basis for your recommendation (how you were connected to them at the time), their title, and your title.

When you write the recommendation:

- Take some time with it.
- Be thoughtful.
- Be thorough.
- Make it more than one line!
- Do it in a word processing document first to catch spelling or grammar errors.

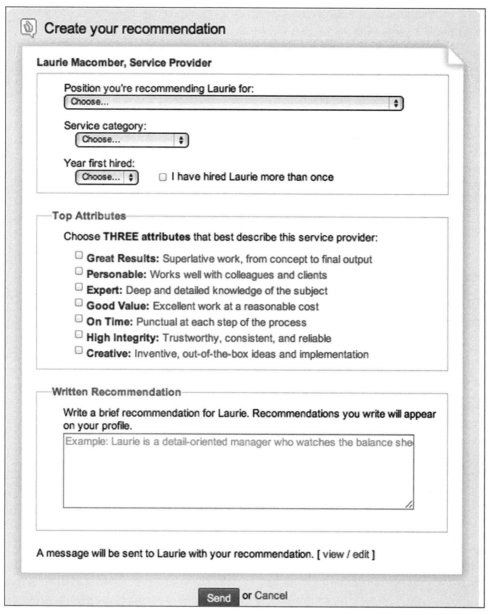

Create your recommendation

Laurie Macomber, Service Provider

Position you're recommending Laurie for:
Choose...

Service category:
Choose...

Year first hired:
Choose... ☐ I have hired Laurie more than once

Top Attributes

Choose **THREE attributes** that best describe this service provider:

☐ **Great Results:** Superlative work, from concept to final output
☐ **Personable:** Works well with colleagues and clients
☐ **Expert:** Deep and detailed knowledge of the subject
☐ **Good Value:** Excellent work at a reasonable cost
☐ **On Time:** Punctual at each step of the process
☐ **High Integrity:** Trustworthy, consistent, and reliable
☐ **Creative:** Inventive, out-of-the-box ideas and implementation

Written Recommendation

Write a brief recommendation for Laurie. Recommendations you write will appear on your profile.

Example: Laurie is a detail-oriented manager who watches the balance she

A message will be sent to Laurie with your recommendation. [view / edit]

Send or Cancel

Figure 5.24 Giving recommendations

Note: To recommend someone who is not on LinkedIn or who is not a first-level connection, enter their first name, last name, and email address in the fields provided. If you recommend someone who's not a first-level connection, the member will also be invited to join your network. The recommendation will appear on their profile if they accept the invitation.

Not only is this an opportunity to write a recommendation for someone who (hopefully) deserves it, but it is also a way to get back in touch. It's a win-win if done correctly. Also, LinkedIn will then prompt them to recommend you back! (And the Skip This Step link is pretty hard to see.) If you write them a thoughtful and glowing recommendation, they will want to write you one back!

The recipient can choose to hide a recommendation so it won't show on their profile. You can also edit or withdraw a recommendation you've sent at any time. Did you write a recommendation for someone who just made national news as a big scam artist? You might want to go remove that recommendation right now!

Note: The recipient will not be notified if you withdraw your recommendation. It is simply removed from their profile.

Thursday: Manage LinkedIn Recommendations

When one of your connections recommends you, LinkedIn sends a notification to your inbox and your Manage Recommendations page. From the notification message sent to your LinkedIn inbox, you can choose the following options:

Accept Recommendation This will allow you to either show or hide the recommendation on your profile. This is a good option if you don't want to hurt someone's feelings.

Request A Replacement I have certainly received excellent recommendations with spelling errors or incorrect information. This option will allow the person writing the request to correct the recommendation.

Archive If for any reason you do not want to accept the recommendation right away, you can archive it.

In Edit Profile, to view and manage your recommendations click the Edit link next to # Visible Recommendations For This Position.

As shown in Figure 5.25, with the recommendation visible you can accept a recommendation (if you haven't accepted it yet from your inbox). You can also show or hide the recommendation by clicking the Show option. If you need to, you can also request a new or revised recommendation from the individual and customize your message to explain why or what you'd like revised.

As I mentioned before, recommendations you've written for others can be withdrawn or revised using the Sent Recommendations page.

You can now also move individual recommendations around within the separate Experience sections. Let's say you received a recommendation from a co-worker and then later received a recommendation from your employer. You probably want the employer's recommendation first. In Edit Profile, drag your cursor over the recommendation you want to move, and then just drag it up or down. Unfortunately, you cannot move the whole Recommendations section this way. Recommendations will reflect the order of your Experience sections.

LinkedIn Expert (although I DO NOT work for LinkedIn) for the Social Media Business School
Social Media Biz School

1 visible recommendation for this position: Edit

"Viveka teaches a one-day seminar on social media that is interesting, thorough and fun. A comprehensive look at LinkedIn, FaceBook, YouTube, WordPress and other very helpful training is packed into about 7 hours. She keeps it interesting and it was a very productive investment of the time. Did I mention it was fun?" *April 6, 2012*

Top qualities: Great Results, Personable, Expert

(1st) Jeff Turner
hired Viveka as a Personal Trainer in 2012

Figure 5.25 Managing recommendations

Friday: Leverage Non-LinkedIn Testimonials

Have you received recommendations, testimonials, or referrals from someone not on LinkedIn? Your first action should be to ask them to join LinkedIn, but if you know they are not likely to do so, here are a few more things you can do.

Add their testimonial to Box.net (more on that during Week 20, in Chapter 7, "Weeks 19–22: Get Strategic with LinkedIn's 'Other' Options"). Briefly, save the testimonial as a PDF and upload it using the Box.net app (found under the More tab). Box.net is a free third-party application that plays well with LinkedIn. Make sure you name or rename your file something like *John Smith, CEO Recommendation* so it's clear what the file is.

Another option is to put your testimonials in either the Contact [Name] section or the Summary section. I recommend putting it in the Contact [Name] section and then just moving that section up in your profile by dragging and dropping in Edit Profile (unless the testimonial is short, very powerful, and from a very powerful Influencer—in which case you might want to put it in your Summary section!). Remember, you are limited to 200 characters in each of these sections.

So there you go! You now know how to find, contact, organize, and get recommendations from your network! Not bad for a few weeks' work.

Are you still having troubles connecting and engaging to the kind of network you want? Have no fear! I have more strategies for you next week in Chapter 6.

Weeks 16–18: Getting Strategic with Groups

In this chapter, we will take a look at best practices for interacting in groups. I'll also show you the step-by-step process for creating and setting up a viable, interesting, and engaging group.

Chapter Contents

Week 16: Building Your Network with Strategic Groups
Week 17: Creating Relationships with Groups
Week 18: Creating Your Own Group

Week 16: Building Your Network with Strategic Groups

Participating in groups is one of the best ways I know to start building strategic relationships. The nice thing about a group is that even if you are not connected with another member, you can still send messages without paying for an InMail. Beyond that is the fact that since you share a group, you already share an interest. This is why it is important to join not only industry- and company-based groups but a few skiing or golfing groups as well. We all know you can make as many deals (or more) on a golf course as you can in the boardroom. LinkedIn groups can work for you in the same way.

Monday: Learn Why Groups Are Important to You

LinkedIn defines groups as a "place for professionals in the same industry or with similar interests to share content, find answers, post or view jobs, make business contacts, and establish themselves as industry experts." I think this is a good definition, and it explains exactly why you want to join and be active in some LinkedIn groups.

Before joining a group on LinkedIn, take a look at some of the groups that LinkedIn recommends for you on your home page (see Figure 6.1).

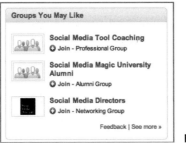

Figure 6.1 Groups You May Like

If you are new to LinkedIn, you won't have this option—yet! But once you make connections and join even a few groups, these suggestions will pop up. If you click See More, LinkedIn will direct you to the Groups You May Like page on the Groups tab; this page will have a long list of applicable groups for you to consider.

Another way to check out viable groups is to take a quick look at your existing connection's profiles. Is there anyone in your contacts list who you might want to get to know better? By clicking on their name and scrolling to the bottom of their profile, you can see what groups they are a member of. This option is not restricted to your first-level connections. Do a quick Advanced People search for an Influencer in your industry and you can see what groups he or she is a member of. Grab your notebook or iPad and jot a few of these groups down. Get a feel for the different types of groups available to you on LinkedIn.

Before you start joining groups willy-nilly, make a list of these things:

- Your industry and common keywords
- Your company and common keywords

- Associations you belong to
- Schools or educational forums
- Your ideal client and industries and subjects that they're interested in
- A person who would hire you, and their industries and interests
- Your own interests or hobbies
- Locations you or your business serves

This list will give you the fodder you need to start finding the groups that are right for you.

Open and Members-Only Groups

There are two types of groups on LinkedIn: open groups and members-only groups. The biggest difference between these two types of groups is who can see the discussions and interactions happening within the group. Open group discussions can be seen by anyone on the Web and shared with other social networking platforms. Members-only group discussions can only be seen by other group members. You will probably want to join both types of groups.

Open groups don't have the padlock icon next to their name, and although you can see the discussions, you still have to be a member of the group (and LinkedIn) to join in, comment, or post a new discussion. Discussions created in an open group are searchable and visible to anyone on the Web. Discussions can also be shared on other social networking sites like Twitter and Facebook.

Members-only groups are more private and are usually more focused. You will often find that college alumni and companies, people who want to manage their membership more closely, and folks who share sensitive or private information, will create members-only groups. When you join a members-only group, you'll notice that there's a padlock icon next to the group name that will indicate the general public is locked out. Or course, you can't join a LinkedIn members-only or open group unless you are a LinkedIn member.

Members-only group discussions don't show up in search engine results and are only visible to group members. This allows for more privacy when discussing situations that are sensitive or secret and where discretion is in order. So if you are thinking of creating or joining a LinkedIn group to mastermind new business ideas, you would probably want to keep it a closed group. If you are thinking of joining a group where you can brag about your extreme sports adventures with other hang-gliding enthusiasts, an open group might be the place for you.

At any time, the group manager has the option to switch a members-only group to an open group. Just be aware of that. Your previous conversations will be archived and unavailable to the general public, but any conversation from that point on will be open to the Web. So don't share the secret recipe for your Aunt Jane's cookies! You *will* be notified if your group is switched to an open group.

There are also subgroups of groups. At this time they are all members-only groups, although LinkedIn is thinking about allowing for open groups in subgroups at some time in the future. An example of a subgroup might be a mastermind group in a topic covered by the parent group but that the group manager creates for private and more focused conversation. For example, HubSpot's Inbound Marketing University Alumni Group on LinkedIn has a subgroup called Inbound Marketing Certified Professionals for those who have been certified in their Inbound Marketing University program. While it goes against the end-user agreement to have to pay to join a group on LinkedIn, you can certainly create a group just for the paid members of a service or product you already offer.

Tuesday: Find Groups

To find groups, select the Groups tab in your main menu bar. Here LinkedIn will give you suggestions for groups you might like, display your groups directory, and let you create a group.

You already have a list of groups you might want to join, so take a few minutes to look them up right now in the groups directory on the Groups tab. You can always do a groups search on the right side of your profile, in the People drop-down box. Either option will take you to the same search screen.

When you start to type your keywords into the group search box on the top-right side of the page, LinkedIn will come up with groups associated with those keywords in a drop-down box. You might want to check some of them out. (If you don't like these suggestions, you can click Turn Off Suggestions in your search drop-down box.)

If you have a specific group in mind, just ignore LinkedIn's suggestions, and once you have finished typing in the name of the group, hit Enter or click on the little magnifying box, as shown in Figure 6.2.

If you do your search from the Groups directory, you can also define your search by:

- All LinkedIn Members (1st Connections, 2nd Connections, 3rd + Everyone Else)
- All Categories (Your Groups, Groups You May Like, Open Groups, Members Only)
- All Languages (English, Portuguese, Polish, or type your preference in the Enter Language box)

Figure 6.2 Group search

Your group search results (in most cases) will be listed according to size. You will see the group name, a logo for the group, a brief description of the group, how active the group is, and how many members there are, as well as how many of those members are already in your network.

To the right of the list of groups you will see the options to view, join, or post to the group, as shown in Figure 6.3.

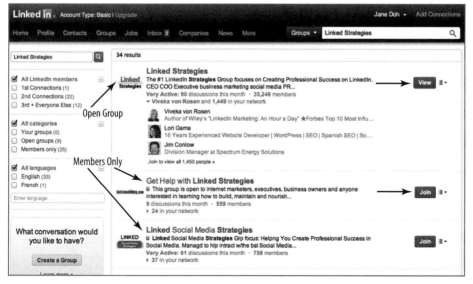

Figure 6.3 Groups You Can Join list

If the group is a members-only group, you will have the option of joining the group on this page. When you click Join, LinkedIn will take you to the Groups page, where you will see a brief group description and list of members. Sometimes groups are set up for Auto-Join. In that case, you will be taken right into the active Groups page and be able to see and immediately join in the conversation. If this is the case, you will probably want to change your settings. If the Members Only page requires membership approval, you will not be able to interact in that group until your membership is approved.

When you are first accepted into a group, you will see a green bar that says "You can adjust your settings here." You will want to click that link and change your settings. If you are already a member of the group and want to adjust your settings, select the More tab within the group (not to be confused with the More tab on the main menu bar) and click on your settings, as shown in Figure 6.4.

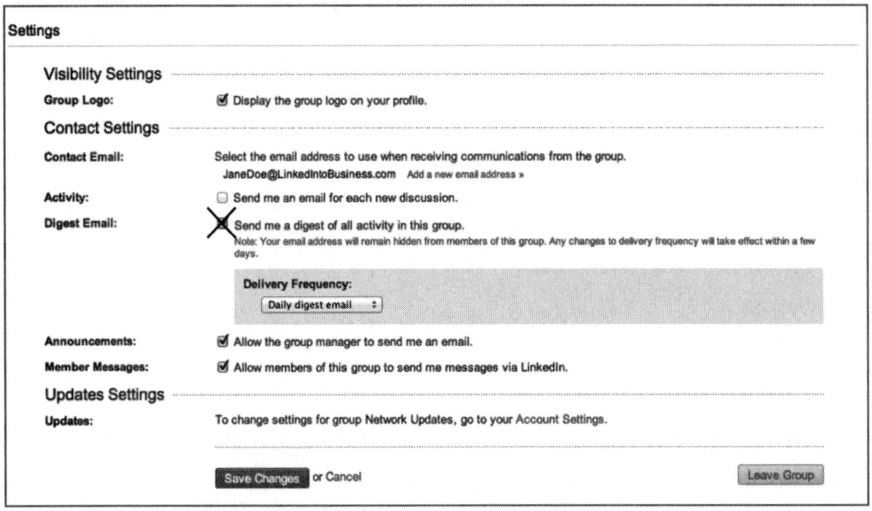

Figure 6.4 Adjusting group settings

You can decide whether or not you want to display your group logo in your profile. You can choose the email address that you want group members to use to communicate with you. (You can add new email addresses here too. It will just take you back into your LinkedIn Settings section on the top-right side of your screen, under your name.)

You can check the option "Send me an email for each new discussion," although I definitely do not recommend doing so if it's a noisy group. However, if it's a group that you want to be very active in, then you'll want to click this option to stay abreast of all that is going on. Just be aware that if the group is extremely active, you could be getting 10, 20, or even 100 emails a day! By default, this option is turned off.

You can also have LinkedIn send you a digest of all the activity in the group. The default is set to a Daily Digest email. Even this is too noisy for me, and unless it's a group I own or moderate or I'm very interested in, I choose the Weekly Digest option. You can uncheck this box and not get any email digests at all if you so desire.

You will have the option of allowing the group manager to send you an email announcement. I leave this option on because you can only receive an announcement once a week at the most from a group manager or owner and they sometimes share exclusive information or offers. If it becomes too spammy, you can always uncheck this option.

You also have the option "Allow members of this group to send me messages." I absolutely, definitely, without a doubt recommend you leave this checked. You *want* other members to be able to send you messages. This is one of the few ways that you can open up your network and receive communications from people who are not first-level connections. This page is also where you can leave the group if you find it is not useful for you. Be sure to save your changes.

If you are already a member of a group (as shown in Figure 6.4 earlier), then you will have the option of clicking Post. That will take you right to the group's discussion section, where you can post a discussion, reply, like a discussion, post a link, or post a poll.

Group Limits

Your ability to join groups is not limitless. While I tend to say "you can only join 50 groups," there are some exceptions:

Group Limits for LinkedIn Members (According to LinkedIn)

- Groups you can own and/or manage at one time: 10
- Subgroups you can own at one time: 20
- Groups you can join and be a member of at one time: 50
- Subgroups you can join and be a member of at one time: 50
- Groups you can moderate: 50
- People you can follow in your groups: 5,000

Group Limits per Main (Parent) Group

- Owners a group can have: 1
- Managers a group can have: 10
- Moderators a group can have: 50
- Members in a given group: 20,000 (maximum default, but there are exceptions)

Group Limits per Subgroup

- Subgroups created under a given parent group: 20
- Owners a subgroup can have: 1
- Managers a given subgroup can have: 10
- Moderators a given subgroup can have: 50

Wednesday: Decide Which Groups to Join

Let's take a look at some of the types of groups you might consider joining.

Industry Groups The first type of group I recommend joining is an industry group. Take a look at that list you created on Monday. What industry are your clients, customers, congregants, or constituents in? What industry groups are your potential employers in? What industry are you in? Use those keywords to start finding and joining groups. Remember you can leave any group that you don't find useful at any time.

Some groups you will join just to get access to the members, and some groups you will join so that you can start interacting and building relationships, as well as positioning yourself as a thought leader.

Company Groups Does your company have a group, or better yet, subgroups? It might be worth looking into. This will allow you to create stronger relationships with other employees within your own company. Are you looking for a job at another company? Do they have a group? If the moderator has set up an Auto-Join group, you might get access to it and create relationships with company insiders or mentors who can help you make the connections and find the information you need to find your next job. Many companies have career groups specifically designed to attract job seekers and potential employees. For example, Oracle has a group called Oracle Jobs.

Association Groups Are you a member of any associations in the real world? Do they have groups on LinkedIn? I love association groups on LinkedIn because they allow you to form and deepen relationships with other association members you would normally only see once a month or once a year—or not at all. Before or after an association event, use the group to research and reconnect with other members.

Alumni Groups Where did you go to school and work in the past? Are there university or company alumni groups that you might join? There's nothing better than an old school buddy to refer you or your business. Definitely join alumni groups to find and stay in touch with your old school or work associates. You never know where they might be working now, or who they might know who can help you in your career (or career search).

Local Groups Have you ever gone to a local meet-up group and found someone really cool about whom you thought, "Now this is someone I want to keep in touch with?" But then you lost their card, or you didn't put them into your calendar? Local groups are a great way to find and keep in touch with Influential locals.

Just type in your city's name, and a list of LinkedIn groups that are geographically located will come up. Not only might you find some groups you didn't know about, but also once you join the group, you will be connecting with other professionals in your own city. So it's easier to take a relationship to the next level by inviting them for coffee. (But don't invite them for coffee to pick their brain.)

> **Note:** Adrienne Zoble of A. Zoble and Associates has a great "Schmoozing Calendar" you can purchase online that is set up to help facilitate coffees and lunches with local businesspeople already in your "real life" (and I would add local LinkedIn network). This calendar helps you deepen your relationships and encourages better referral marketing. You can find out more about the Schmoozing Calendar here: www.azobleassoc.com/schmooze.htm.

If you are new to LinkedIn, you may find that you are not automatically accepted into some groups. Don't worry about it. Some group owners set up limitations on who can join their groups according to network size and date joined. If you've been rushing through this book, just give it a day or two and you will probably find that you have been accepted into many of the groups you had previously tried to join. You probably don't want to join more than a few groups a day (remember, you can join up to 70 groups, including the 20 subgroups).

> **Note:** You can see the group statistics of any group, whether or not you are a member. It's a good idea to check out the group's statistics to see if the group has the membership, interaction, and activity you are seeking. More on group statistics at the end of this chapter.

Take a little time in each group to see whether the discussions and interaction are of benefit to you. Some groups will be amazing places to build relationships. Some groups will be excellent places to position yourself as an expert in your industry, and some groups you will join merely to connect to its members.

Thursday: Explore Discussions, Polls, Promotions, Jobs, and More

So what do you do once you join a group? Well, groups are great because they allow you to start and contribute to discussions, promote your business, and even post jobs for free.

Discussions

Discussions are the best way to start building relationships with other group members. In fact, when you go to your group page, the first tab is Discussion, as you can see in Figure 6.5.

You can start a discussion in the first field, or you can see discussions that are ongoing and contribute to them there. You will also see the most popular discussions and can contribute to those as well.

Another option is the Choose Your View section, which will allow you to see What's Happening or the Latest Discussions. What's Happening gives you the true picture of what the group is talking about through a "carousel" of new topics and a ranked list of popular conversations. This will include previews of the most recent activity according to LinkedIn. Latest Discussions allows you to discover new topics that you might want to participate in or follow. LinkedIn will put these in a simple comprehensive list. You can change the views as often as you like. (The default is What's Happening.)

Figure 6.5 Group communications

You also have the option Show All RSS Discussions. RSS discussions are news-feeds (usually blog feeds) that the group owner or manager has chosen to automatically feed into the group discussion area. You'll be able to see pretty quickly if the RSS feeds are relevant or not. If they aren't, just click Hide RSS With No Activity and they will magically disappear.

If you're uncomfortable participating right away, then do a little lurking. Take a look at what people are writing about. Take a look at who's doing the writing. You can even follow group members and keep up with them. What a great way to keep an eye on a strategic connection or a competitor!

Group discussions are incredibly powerful for building relationships. As I mentioned earlier, you do not have to be directly connected to someone to have a conversation with him or her in a group. And while you can send a message to someone in your group (which we will talk about more in the next section), I recommend finding a discussion that the person you are interested in has participated in and responding to them there. Then take it to the next level. Yes, this approach is more time-consuming, but it's also more effective.

Polls

LinkedIn has also added its polling app to the Discussion section, as you can see in Figure 6.6.

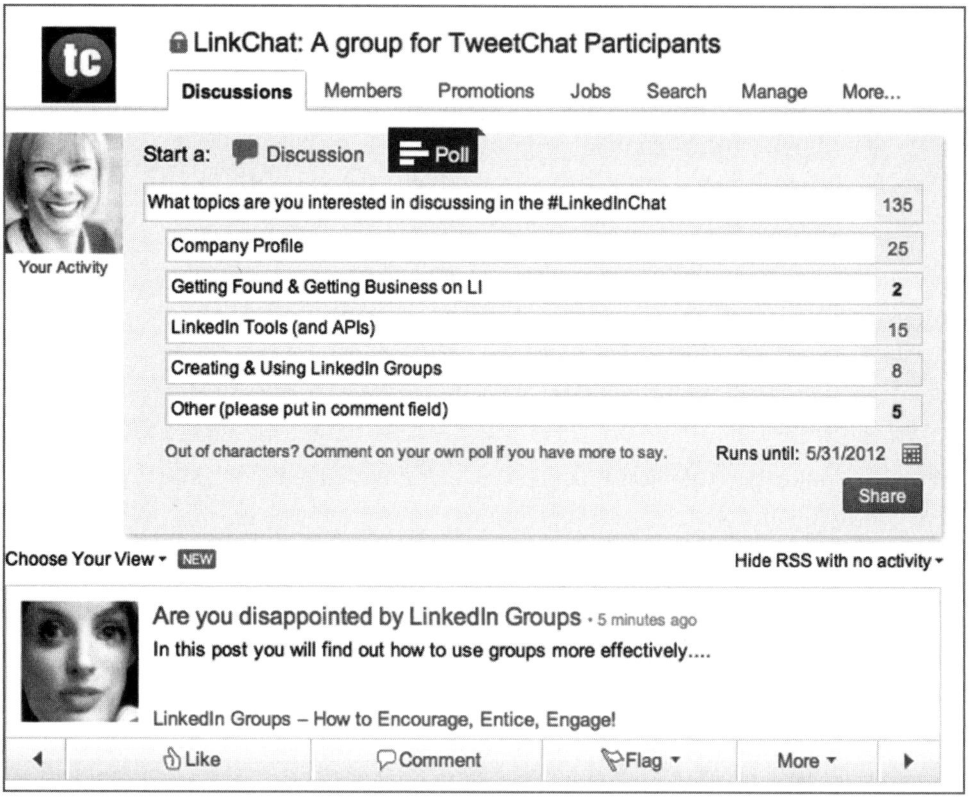

Figure 6.6 LinkedIn group polls

This is another fun and quick way to engage with your group members. You simply ask a question, and specify up to five answers or choices. Choose how long you want the poll to run. Keep it simple! The LinkedStrategies group often has people posting polls, and they seem to get more responses than a simple link or question. You will also see ongoing results as you post your answers. And you might even get some good (if slightly skewed) market research!

Promotions

If you have a promotion you want to post, simply select the Promotions tab, and on the right-hand side you'll see a little green cross with a Post A Promotion link. This is where you can enter your promotional title and additional details. By default, you will follow the promotion, and this isn't a bad idea, because you want to know what new comments are being made, especially if they're positive or even potential clients. If a group manager or owner hasn't enabled this feature, you won't see a Promotions tab.

Note: Just so you know, anything posted under Promotions will *not* be emailed out to anyone who has signed up for individual emails.

Jobs

You can also post a job in a group you are a member of (if this setting is enabled). It is called a Job Discussion (because LinkedIn wants you to pay for posting a new job), but go ahead and post your job in this section anyway. It will allow people to like your job, comment on your job, and even share your job with other members in their network. This is not to be mistaken with the Jobs tab that allows you to post a job on LinkedIn, which you will pay for.

The Job Discussion is another reason why it's an excellent idea to join an industry group that you want to be working in, because you will see jobs posted here that you won't see anywhere else on LinkedIn.

Members and Search

You will also notice a Members link and a Search link. I'll be talking about the Members link in the next section, but let's take a look at this new Search tab within groups. The first thing you can do is a member search, and this takes you right back to the Members page. But you can also search for polls, discussions, manager's choice, discussions you've started, discussions you've joined, and discussions you're following. You can also see if you have any submissions that are still pending and waiting for approval. So this is a great way to manage your interaction on your LinkedIn group.

I often find great information by using the search box (usually about my competitors so I can see what they are doing). Comparables are a powerful tool on LinkedIn.

More

Next, let's take a peek at the More tab. Here you can check on the following:

Updates A list of recent discussions including the person who posted the discussion, the title of the discussion, and the ability to like or add a comment to the discussion. If you don't have a lot of time, to enhance the impression of being active on LinkedIn take just a minute or two to quickly run through this list and like or comment on a few discussions.

Your Activity This will give you a list of your Recent Updates (Discussions You've Started, Discussions You've Joined, Discussions You're Following, Pending Submissions) so you can keep track of your communications. You can also keep an eye on the people following *you* in this group as well as the people you are following.

Your Settings This is the section we discussed in the previous chapter where you can choose logo visibility, frequency of digest email, and the ability to leave the group, among other things.

Subgroups If a group has any subgroups, they will be listed (and you can join them) using the options in this section. I like subgroups because they are both granular and usually private, which can mean deeper communications if you "work" the group by creating and responding to discussion and engaging the membership.

(Un)Following People in a Group

I recommend taking a few minutes to "unfollow" people who are no longer of interest to you. You probably aren't interested in following the activity of all your first-level connections or those you share a group with. Unfortunately at this time you can't Select All, Unfollow All, so this might be a good thing to do while watching TV (or have an assistant do it for you).

You can follow a group to get their activity updates for all the groups you have in common. LinkedIn automatically adds your connections to your follower list if you belong to the same groups.

To review and manage your follower list:

1. Click Groups at the top of your home page.

2. Click the group's name.

3. Click More in the row under your group's name and then select Your Activity.

4. On the left, look for your followers and people you're following.

5. Click the Unfollow link.

Group Profile This is the page you landed on when you first found the group. You can also see the group members here, the group statistics, and other groups LinkedIn suggests for you as well as similar groups other LinkedIn members have joined.

Group Statistics Are you wondering if a group is right for you? The Group Statistics section gives you a summary of the group as well as demographics, growth, and activity. This is a good link to share when you are trying to convince someone else to join a group. You can share the group statistics on LinkedIn, Twitter, and Facebook, or even add a URL.

Friday: Consider "Big" Groups

Finally, let's take a look at some big groups. Why do you want to join big groups? Because they're big. Big groups grow your network quickly and effectively. Big groups also work best when you are looking for a specific type of person in a search. You'll learn more about that in the next section.

In the previous chapter, I talked about TopLinked. So you want to join the TopLinked group on LinkedIn too (it's the first TopLinked group that shows up in the search: Toplinked.com – Open Networkers) in order to more easily connect with TopLinked's Top Supporters. Once you're a member of the TopLinked group and you go to the TopLinked Top Supporters' LinkedIn profile, you can simply connect to them as a shared group member.

To find the biggest groups on LinkedIn (that you might want to join just because they're big), go to the drop-down search box and click Groups. Don't type anything in the field—just click your cursor so that it's flashing in the search bar and then press Enter.

This will pull up the biggest groups on LinkedIn. The first group to show up is likely Jobs. This group has over 800,000 members. Join this group, and suddenly you have 800,000+ more people in your extended network. Surely one of those individuals can become a client, vendor, partner, or employer. *Remember to adjust your settings when you join this group.* Especially if you're not a job seeker, you probably want to turn off the group icon visibility in your profile. You also will not want to get a daily digest from big groups, or an email every time someone starts a new discussion.

Linked HR is also a great group to join. It also has close to 800,000 members. According to their group profile, Linked HR is the "largest professional HR group on LinkedIn" and a place where you can find "active HR Discussions that encompass the entire HR field and industry." All well and good if you are an HR professional or a job seeker, but why should a business consultant join the group? Because it's big. Because it expands your network out 800,000+ people. Because you never know which one of those folks will be your next client.

LinkedIn itself recently got into the groups game. While LinkedIn has had the groups feature for years, it is only recently that LinkedIn started creating their own groups that you can join. Not only are they big, but they tend to be well moderated and very informational. The groups that LinkedIn has created itself have been growing leaps and bounds. They seem to have a LinkedIn group for every industry (LinkedIn Accounting, LinkedIn for Android, LinkedIn Company Group, LinkedIn for Journalists, LinkedIn Mobile, etc.). You will want to join the LinkedIn group for your industry, mostly because it's really big—but also because you will have a shared industry interest with other members of that group.

Remember, you're going to want to join your own industry groups and the industry groups of those people you want to be working with—sometimes these are not the same people.

Now that you've joined a group, or 50 groups, let's look at best practices for creating relationships within these groups.

Week 17: Creating Relationships with Groups

It's a shame that people are mostly using groups to hawk their wares. This is making LinkedIn groups less relevant and less utilized by serious networkers. And yet I think groups are still one of the best places to have a conversation with serious business-minded networkers. Here are some best practices when engaging in groups. Let's see if we can't bring groups back to their glory days!

Monday: Understand Group Rules

Did you know your group had rules? Well, many don't! How can a group owner or manager expect you to play by the rules if you don't even know what they are? Group rules are simply guidelines for conduct within a given group. So it's important to learn the rules for the groups you join (if they have any).

Once you open a group (one you own or are a member of), take a look at the top-right side of the Group page. If the group has rules, you will see a Share Group link and then a Group Rules link just to the right of it. If you see these links, go ahead and click them. The group rules will show in a pop-up. If there are no group rules, consider sending a message to one of the group owner or managers.

Connecting to a Group Owner or Manager

To see who the group owner or manager is, simply click More and then click Group Profile. On the right-hand side you'll see About This Group and underneath that you'll see who the owner, manager, and moderators of the group are. To send a message to the group owner, select the Members tab, and in the Search Members box on the left-hand side of the screen, enter the name of the group owner or manager. Once they come up in the search, to the right of their name and professional headline, click Send Message.

If the Send message link does not show up, you will have to go into their profile and send them a message through an introduction or an InMail. It's always a good idea to be a first-level connection with a group manager or owner, so you can send them an invitation as well.

A good example of group rules appears in the Inbound Marketers for Marketing Professionals group, as shown in Figure 6.7.

I think this is as close to an ideal "group rules" posting as you can get. The tone of the group rules is conversational. Rebecca Corliss lets people know the purpose for the group: "A place to share ideas and ask questions about social media, SEO, blogging, email marketing, lead generation, marketing automation and content strategy." She lets you know that the group is closely monitored and that the conversation should be helpful and friendly. She also lets you know that "Any submissions containing spam including product offers, irrelevant links, false business offers, and inappropriate content will not be tolerated and that such content will be deleted and the member may even be blocked from the group."

I really like that members should make the assumption that people are posting with best intentions and respond accordingly. I also like that Rebecca encourages people to post jobs related to inbound marketing strategy in the Jobs section.

Keep this example in mind in the next section as we discuss creating your own group.

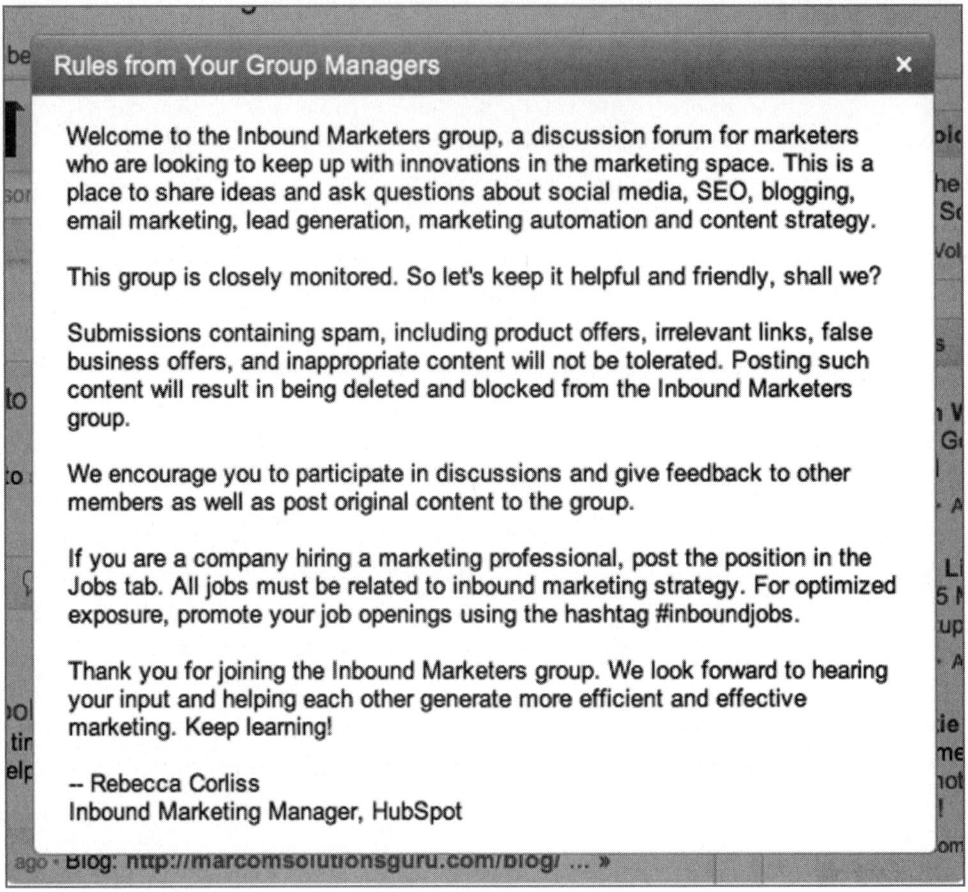

Rules from Your Group Managers

Welcome to the Inbound Marketers group, a discussion forum for marketers who are looking to keep up with innovations in the marketing space. This is a place to share ideas and ask questions about social media, SEO, blogging, email marketing, lead generation, marketing automation and content strategy.

This group is closely monitored. So let's keep it helpful and friendly, shall we?

Submissions containing spam, including product offers, irrelevant links, false business offers, and inappropriate content will not be tolerated. Posting such content will result in being deleted and blocked from the Inbound Marketers group.

We encourage you to participate in discussions and give feedback to other members as well as post original content to the group.

If you are a company hiring a marketing professional, post the position in the Jobs tab. All jobs must be related to inbound marketing strategy. For optimized exposure, promote your job openings using the hashtag #inboundjobs.

Thank you for joining the Inbound Marketers group. We look forward to hearing your input and helping each other generate more efficient and effective marketing. Keep learning!

-- Rebecca Corliss
Inbound Marketing Manager, HubSpot

Figure 6.7 Group rules

Group Owners, Managers, and Moderators: What's the Difference?

It's pretty simple. If you create a group, then you are the group owner. There can only be one group owner. As the owner of the group, you have the opportunity to promote your members to managers or moderators. As a group owner, you have full control over the membership, discussions, settings, subgroups, and rules. You can transfer ownership of the group to another group manager. Once you transfer ownership, obviously you are no longer the group owner.

A group manager has almost the same access to the group as the owner except they cannot close or transfer ownership of the group. But they can still have control over the membership, discussions, settings, group subgroups, and rules.

Group moderators are like discussion assistants, and they are limited to moderating discussions and comments and managing submission and moderation queues. They can also feature a discussion, but they have no control over the membership, the settings, the rules, or the subgroups.

Tuesday: Learn What to Do (and Not Do) in Your Group

If your group *does* have group rules, then obviously don't do anything in the group that the rules discourage. Since you'll probably discover that many groups don't have the group rules completed yet, you are going to have to moderate yourself.

As I mentioned earlier, one of the reasons groups are less effective than they used to be is all the spam and product offers out there. I'm not saying that you will never use a group to offer your product, but I don't recommend using the Discussion section to send a sales message.

Mostly you should be using groups to connect and build relationships with other members. If you have a question for the group, read an interesting blog that you think the group might be interested in, have a practice you strongly believe in, or have heard of an event you want to share, you can use the Discussion section.

Sometimes the event or the blog will be your own; sometimes it will be somebody else's. If you are going to post your own blog or article, let your readership know why it's important for them. Give them WIIFM. The same thing goes for posting an event. (If you are just promoting your event, consider placing it in Promotions.)

One cool thing about group discussions is that the manager can choose to highlight your discussion under Manager's Choice. LinkedIn will also list the discussions that have the most interactivity. Be interesting (or controversial) and get more visibility!

You can choose how often LinkedIn informs you about group discussions: daily, weekly, or not at all. From some groups you will want to receive a daily digest. These are the groups that you find stimulating and that seem to be a good source for relationships. These are the groups you will participate in daily—even if it's just minutes a day—so you can become an Influencer. That will get you some recognition, authority, and visibility.

Here are some things you should do:

- Do share your knowledge.
- Do help people out.
- Do express your true opinions.
- Do take time to answer and respond in a considerate manner.
- Do repurpose content you might already have that answers and adds to a group discussion.
- Do start your own discussions.

And some things not to do:

- Don't use groups as a place to place your sales letters.
- Don't use groups to share a "business opportunity."
- Don't use groups to solicit multilevel marketing or direct sales down-line. No one will participate in your discussion, you are likely to get flagged, and you'll just irritate people.

The only time it's okay to share your products or services with the group is when a member asks a specific question and your product or service might be the solution. But even then don't just say, "Buy my product or service at buymywidget.com." Give them some background, give them some valuable and useful information, and then add the link. You have to be very careful with this, or a group moderator, manager, or owner might put your discussion into the Promotions section, or another member might flag your discussion as inappropriate.

The Promotions section is the perfect place to list any product or service you think might be of use to the group. Just be aware that people don't visit the Promotions section that often, because promotions are often considered spam.

> **Note:** According to Wikipedia, spam is the use of electronic messaging systems to send unsolicited bulk messages indiscriminately. While the most widely recognized form of spam is email spam, the term is applied to similar abuses in other media, including social networking spam.
>
> A person who creates electronic spam is called a spammer.

Wednesday: Manage Your Groups

Too many people own groups where the spam spreads like wildfire because they are not paying attention to it. This makes your group irrelevant as a group owner, and chances are, if it's a group you've joined, it won't take you long to turn off your digest emails.

Help Manage Spam

Not only do I recommend *not* using groups as a forum to blast your sales message, I recommend that you become a social media NARC! Take free license to report any posts on a group you are a member of that are obvious spam. (UrbanDictionary.com defines a narc as "A person that turns you in for something you did wrong; specifically to any type of authority figure like parents, cops, teachers, boss.")

You can flag spammers or inappropriate content by clicking the Flag button beneath the discussion post. On the main page of the group, you will see the "carousel" and the Flag button is right beneath it. To flag an older post, click on the post name and LinkedIn will take you to a page just on that discussion. You will see the Flag button there as shown in Figure 6.8. This is also where you can Like, Comment, Follow, Share, Delete (if you are a manager), or Privately Reply to a post.

If it's a group you like, and you see the content going downhill, take it upon yourself to clean it up. One thing you can do if you're invested in the group is reach out to the manager or owner, and offer to become a moderator.

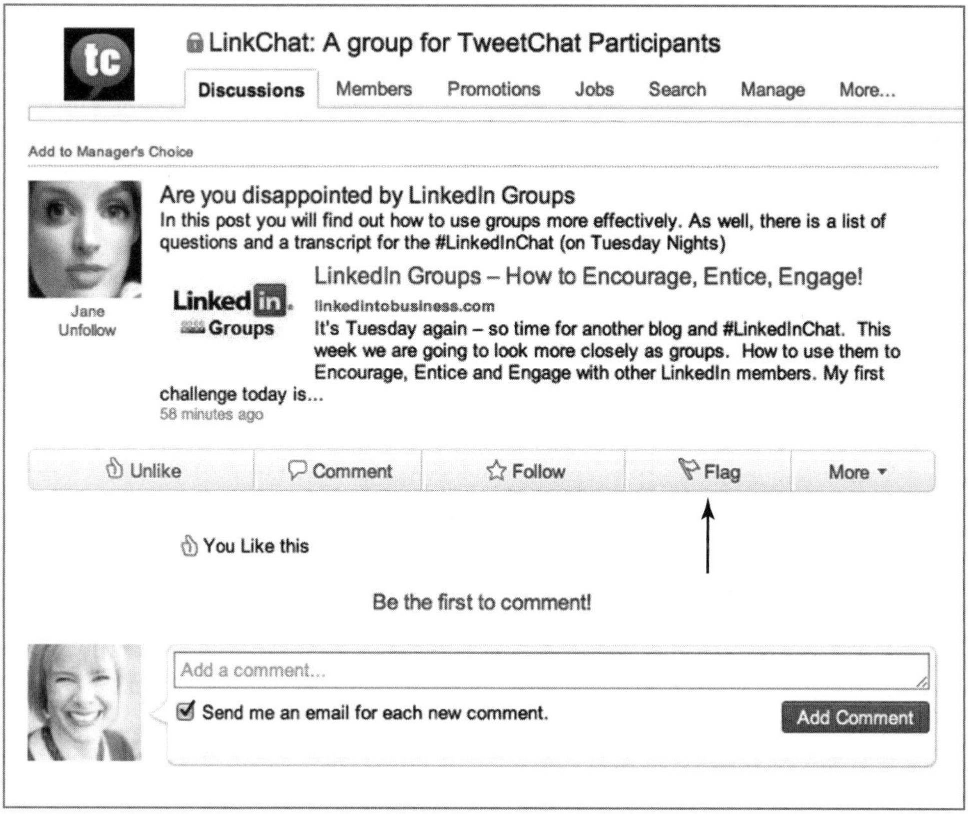

Figure 6.8 Flag those spammers!

> **Note:** A group owner or manager can choose how many flags a post must get before it is automatically removed from the group (I recommend three). They also may choose to allow all posts and only delete a post themselves. These can be very spammy groups if the management is not diligent.

Keeping a group clean of spam by refraining to use it as a sales pitch form—and keeping others from doing the same—will go a long way to making your group more useful for you and for everybody else.

Manage Group Order

Take a few minutes right now to go through your groups. Which ones have potential? Which ones are just one sales blast after another? Which ones represent the type of content and communications you want more of? Until you are using groups regularly, it might be worth it to organize your groups in such a way that the really useful ones show up first.

As shown in Figure 6.9, on the Groups tab, when you click Your Groups you will see a page with all your groups (and pending groups) listed. On the left you will see a Reorder link.

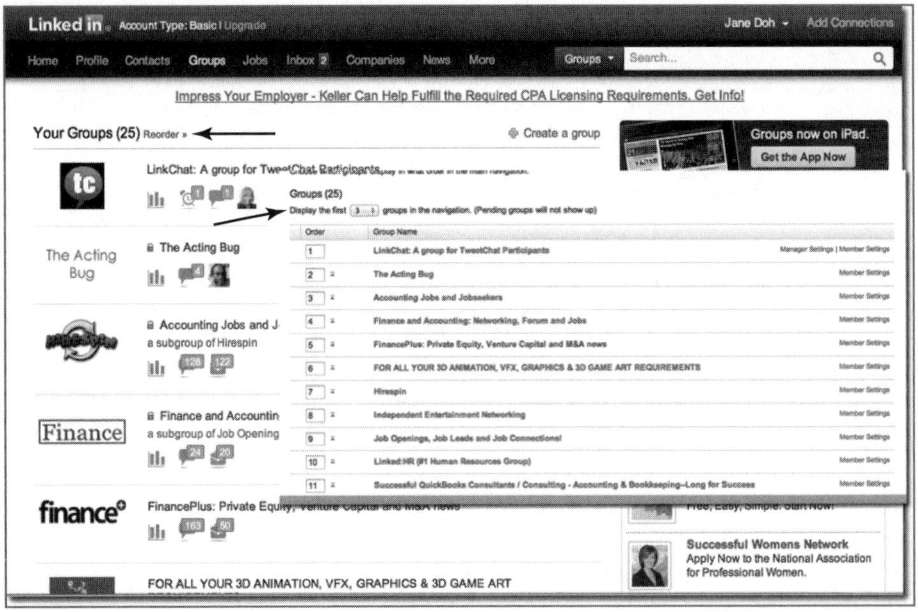

Figure 6.9 Reordering your groups

Click Reorder and you can go through and rearrange your groups in any order you prefer. By default, the groups you own or manage will show up first. But you don't have to leave them there. Order your groups from the most useful to the least useful and click Save Changes. You can also choose how many groups you want to display in the Groups drop-down field (up to 10). Now make it a daily practice to go into your top three or four groups and participate in the discussions.

Every once in a while, you want to take a look at all your groups, decide which ones are most relevant to you at this time, and reorder them accordingly.

Thursday: Search for Strategic Contacts

You can find a group member and send them a message or invite them to connect with you through groups. You can also follow a member. Following basically allows you to keep an eye on their activity but not communicate with them directly. It will give you some great information for when you are ready to send them a message or invite them to connect.

Searching, Messaging, and Inviting Strategic Members

I know I keep repeating myself, but groups are a great way to get in touch and build relationships with people who are outside of your first-, second-, or third-level connections.

What I like about groups is that you can search the membership by name or by keyword. To do this, go into a group that you think might have members who would make good contacts for you. Then click the Members link, shown in Figure 6.10.

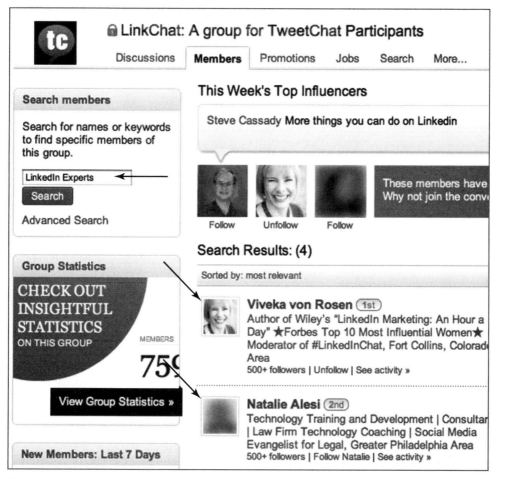

Figure 6.10 Searching for members

On the left-hand side you'll see the Search Members box. This is where you just looked for the group manager/owner by name to send them a message, but you can also use this box to search for individuals by keyword.

You can do a simple search in the search box by adding a string of keywords. For instance, if you work with a lot of medical professionals, you might search on **"medical professional" OR doctor OR "medical practice" OR Physician.**

LinkedIn will show you the results for any group member who falls into your search criteria. If they are first-level connections, you can just send them a message, and take this time to tag their profile as well. If the search result gives you second- and third-level connections, then simply hover your cursor to the right of their name to see the links Invite and Message. Some people have disabled this ability in their Settings section, but I estimate that well over half of the time, you can reach out to an individual who is not a first-level connection and send them a message from this search results section in your group.

The Advanced Search link right underneath the simple search will take you to a new Advanced Search page. This is exactly the same as an Advanced People search, except you will be defining the criteria to include the group you are searching in.

Try the simple search first because it is from the simple search results that you can easily invite or send a message to a member.

Following Members

LinkedIn recently improved its follow feature. Following a group member is similar to following someone on Twitter. You get access to their activity, although you won't necessarily get direct access to them.

If you find a discussion posted by someone you are following, you can comment on their discussion. That is a great way to initiate conversation with them.

To follow someone, simply click on their photo and it will take you to the follow screen shown in Figure 6.11.

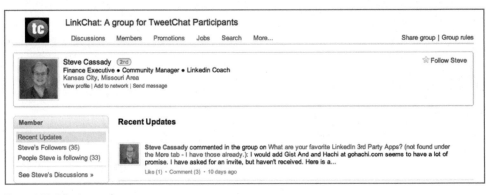

Figure 6.11 Following members

This will allow you to read and respond to their recent group activity, see who they are following (who might be influencing them), and who is following their group activity. You can get an email about the member's activity by clicking Your Activity on the group's More tab and then clicking the People You're Following link. Scroll through the members and click Email Alerts Are to turn on email alerts. You can also unfollow people on this screen.

While LinkedIn has had the follow feature for a while, this ability has never been particularly useful. But with the new activity page, you have an opportunity to easily comment on and like discussions, and that can certainly increase engagement and connection.

Friday: Employ Reverse Engineering

I mentioned in the previous chapter that I would give you a strategy for sending messages to people who are not first-level connections without paying for an InMail. The way to do this is what I call reverse engineering. It is just another way to communicate with individuals with whom you share a group. To do this, do a simple People or an Advanced People search. Or pull out the profiles that I had you sort in Chapter 5, "Weeks 10–15: Creating and Managing a Network That Works," of people who are group members. This is where reverse engineering comes in handy.

Click on the profile of the person that you want to connect with or send a message to. If they are a second- or third-level connection, or do not share a network with you, scroll down to the bottom of their profile and see if they're a member of the group. LinkedIn will tell you if you share a group with someone, because instead of the blue Join link, you'll see a green Already A Member message.

If you are already a member of a shared group, then all you have to do is click on the group name (which will take you to the group) and in the Member search box, type in the member's name as you did earlier. (Do not use the Advanced search.) Scroll to the right side, and click Send Message, as shown in Figure 6.12.

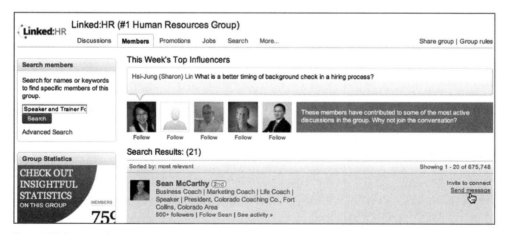

Figure 6.12 Reverse engineering

The ability to send a message is not available all of the time due to user preference (as a group member you can choose whether you want another group member to be able to send you a message or not). But it's a cheaper option than sending an InMail.

If you don't share a group with that member, just be aware you will have to join a group in order to send them a message. You can always leave the group by selecting More › Your Settings, and on the bottom right of your Settings page, clicking Leave Group.

I usually join about 45 groups so that I can add the occasional group to reach out to a member. As soon as I'm done communicating with that member, I'll leave the group.

Week 18: Creating Your Own Group

One of the best things you can do on LinkedIn to position yourself as a thought leader and attract new customers or clients is to create a group. (It also helps to get you found on Google!) Here are some ideas on how you can get started.

Monday: Name and Set Up Your Group

There are a lot of groups out there on LinkedIn—over 2 million of them. If you want your group to get any traction at all, people need to be able to find it! Here are a few tips to make sure you create a group that can get found and get members.

Create Your Group and Add a Logo

To create a group, select the Groups tab and move down to the Create A Group link. As shown in Figure 6.13, the first thing you have an option of uploading is the logo. If you have a company logo, and it's going to be a company group, then by all means use your company logo (as long as you have permission to use it).

If your group is not necessarily associated with your company (for instance, HubSpot's inbound marketing groups is not necessarily associated with their company, so while they use the same font and coloring as the HubSpot logo, they do not use the HubSpot logo) and you have the skills or the resources to create a new logo just for your group, you might want to do that as well.

By default, your logo (whichever way you go, company logo or unique group logo) is going to show up by default on the profiles of all your members (unless they turn off that option), so it might be worth the effort to make it look branded and make it look good.

Group Name

After you upload the logo, you'll have the opportunity to create a group name. (You cannot use the word *LinkedIn* in your group name.) The Group Name field is very important for the group search algorithm, so make sure that you have your company name or your group cause in this title section. After your name, you might tell them what you do. Use your keywords. You might name your group something like Marketing for Accountants: Best Practices to Get Your Accounting Business Found. You can change your group name up to five times. But try to go for the right name the first time.

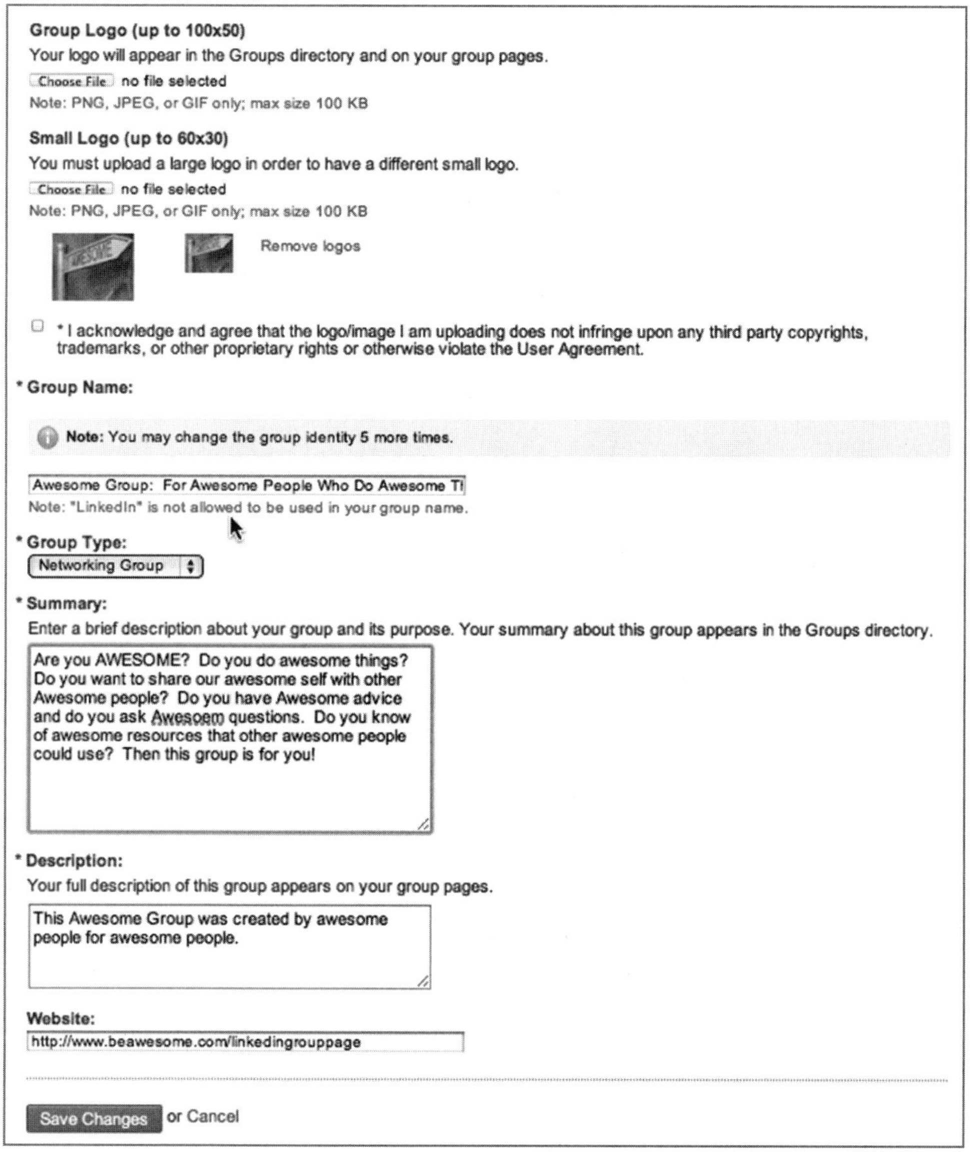

Group Logo (up to 100x50)
Your logo will appear in the Groups directory and on your group pages.
Choose File no file selected
Note: PNG, JPEG, or GIF only; max size 100 KB

Small Logo (up to 60x30)
You must upload a large logo in order to have a different small logo.
Choose File no file selected
Note: PNG, JPEG, or GIF only; max size 100 KB

Remove logos

☐ * I acknowledge and agree that the logo/image I am uploading does not infringe upon any third party copyrights, trademarks, or other proprietary rights or otherwise violate the User Agreement.

* **Group Name:**

ⓘ **Note:** You may change the group identity 5 more times.

Awesome Group: For Awesome People Who Do Awesome Tl
Note: "LinkedIn" is not allowed to be used in your group name.

* **Group Type:**
Networking Group ⬍

* **Summary:**
Enter a brief description about your group and its purpose. Your summary about this group appears in the Groups directory.

Are you AWESOME? Do you do awesome things?
Do you want to share our awesome self with other
Awesome people? Do you have Awesome advice
and do you ask Awesoem questions. Do you know
of awesome resources that other awesome people
could use? Then this group is for you!

* **Description:**
Your full description of this group appears on your group pages.

This Awesome Group was created by awesome
people for awesome people.

Website:
http://www.beawesome.com/linkedingrouppage

Save Changes or Cancel

Figure 6.13 Creating a group

Group Type

Once you create your group, you have to choose what type of group it is:

- Alumni group
- Corporate group
- Conference group
- Networking group
- Nonprofit group
- Professional group

Some groups are created for the long haul, like alumni, corporate, professional, and networking groups. Some groups, like a conference group or an event group, might have a shorter lifespan and are created for a specific time frame and purpose. I'm mainly talking about the more permanent groups in this section.

Summary

As shown in Figure 6.13 earlier, the Summary section comes next.

Your Group Summary is 300 characters and shares the purpose of your group. This is the section that shows up in a group search, so make sure that the first sentence is your most impactful. Let them know right away what's in it for them if they join this group. Make sure you get your keywords in this section and perhaps even capitalize any text you would normally put in bold print.

Group Description

Your Group Description section can be up to 2,000 characters. Make sure that you format this section with bullet points and capitalization. This is where you engage and entice your prospective members. Go more in depth about the benefit of joining your group. Let them know what they can expect from your group. Even though you'll be sharing similar information in your group rules and Welcome template (more on the Welcome template in the next section), people will receive that information at different times and in different ways. In this case, a little replication is not a bad thing.

Spend some time focusing on the type of group member you want. Who are they? What do they do for a living? What are they interested in? Put in your description who you think would make a good group member. Why? What types of discussions will you be encouraging? What topics? What kind of bonuses or offers might they expect from for joining the group? (LinkedInStrategies often offers eBooks and free LinkedIn webinars to its membership.)

I also recommend putting your contact information as well as your LinkedIn URL in the Group Description so that potential members or existing members can more easily connect and contact you with questions they might have. Don't think of this as a disturbance or annoying—think of it as a potential client or referral partner reaching out to you!

Website

Do you have a website associated with this group? Do you have a special offer for your group? If you have a specific landing page for the group, you can also put it in the Website field. If you don't have a website, consider putting your LinkedIn custom URL in this field…or your Facebook page…or your Twitter profile.

Email

You will also want to put a group owner email address in the next field. It does not have to be an email address that you have on LinkedIn. If you've created an email address just for this group, you can add it to this section. You might use something like LinkedInGroup@DomainName.com.

Access

Now you have to choose how people can access your group. Will it be an Auto-Join group, meaning any LinkedIn member may join the group without requiring approval from you first? Or are you going to demand a Request To Join, as shown in Figure 6.14?

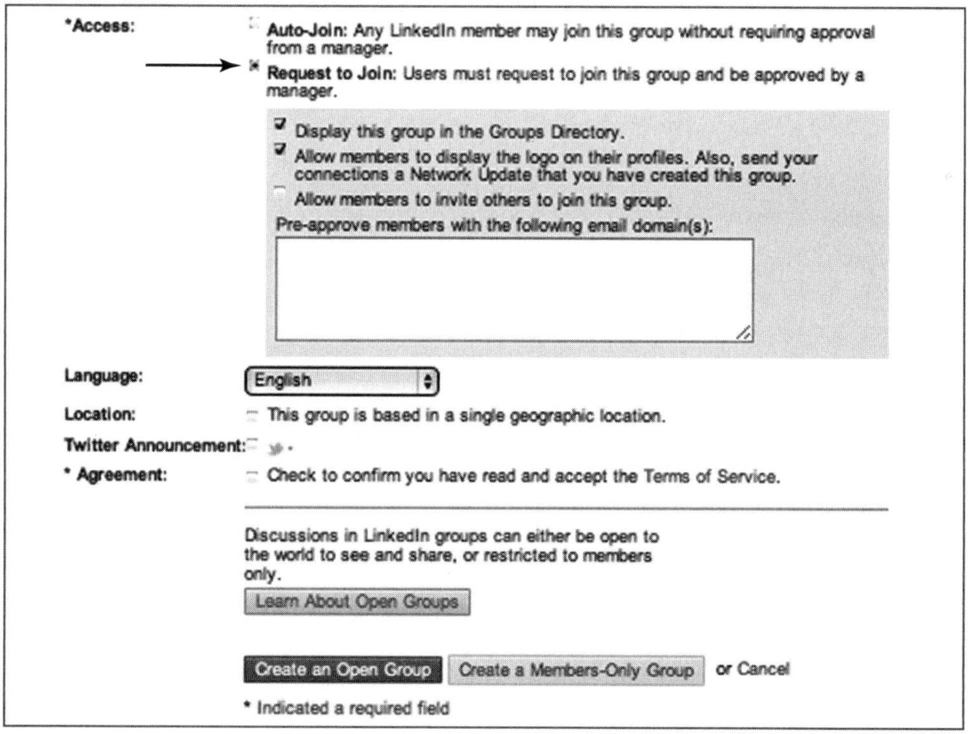

Figure 6.14 Group Settings

You can also choose whether your group members can display your group in their Groups directory listing, whether they can display the logo in your profile, and whether you can allow members to invite other members to this group. I recommend you choose all of these options unless you want a very private group for a specific number of people on LinkedIn and you do *not* want word of the group getting out.

You can also preapprove members at specific email domains (like yourcompany .com). So if you want to preapprove anyone who works for your company, put that email domain in this section.

Language

Choose your language, and whether this is a location-based group or not. You can even tweet an announcement of the creation of this group. And then check the box that allows you to agree to the terms of service.

This is also where you will specify whether your group is an open group or a members-only group. I recommend creating a members-only group first, and opening it up later when you feel comfortable with the whole LinkedIn group process. *You cannot change an open group back into a members-only group*, although you can change a members-only group into an open group at any time. Be very sure you want an open group if you choose this option. There is no going back.

If you ever want to change your group information (name, description, summary, etc.), click the Manage link within your group and then click Group Information.

In the next section, we'll take a deeper look at your group management options.

Tuesday: Select a Management Team and Create Group Rules

As you can imagine, it is much easier to manage and build your group if you have people helping you. These people are known as managers and moderators. To have a manager or moderator help you with your group, you need to have them join as a member (of LinkedIn and your group) first. Once they are a member, you will promote them to manager or moderator.

On the top right where it says Share Group | Group Rules, click Share Group and then choose Share On LinkedIn. Choose the Send To Individuals option, which will allow you to write a customized letter to the folks you not only want to join the group but you want to promote to manager or moderator.

Note: While you can make a person a manager or moderator without their permission, why would you? Build it up to be an honor and a privilege, and a wonderful way to position themselves as thought leaders and build meaningful relationships on LinkedIn. You may also send them an email or call them on the phone and ask them if they are willing to participate.

Promoting Managers

Once your future moderator or manager has accepted your invitation, you click on the participant's link to change their role from member to manager or moderator. Remember, a manager can do everything you can do as the group owner except delete the group or change ownership in the group. A moderator can just moderate the discussions, links, posts, and promotions in a group. It is from the Participants section that you can also block participants from the group.

Now that you have moderators and managers, you can have some help in managing your group. Let's take a look at the group settings you might consider for your group, and then we'll take a look at the Moderation Queue and Request To Join options.

When you click Group Settings, the first option is to make your group an open group if you have a members-only group (wait a bit on this). What you want to look at is the second option, the ability to enable discussions and news features, as shown in Figure 6.15. You will definitely want to do this.

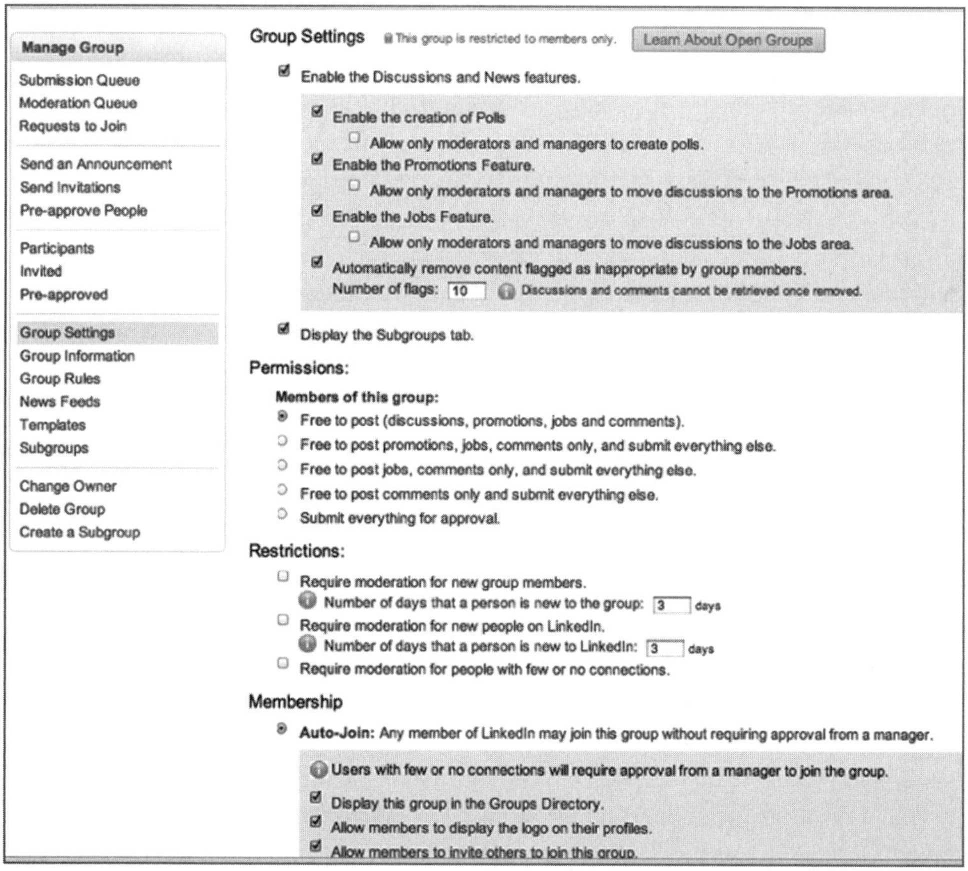

Figure 6.15 Enabling group features

I've already mentioned the polls option in the previous section. I'm a big fan. You can allow your entire membership to create polls (my recommendation) or only the moderator and manager to create polls.

You can also activate the Promotions feature here, allowing any member to promote a product or service. By turning this option on, you might reduce the spam in the Discussion section, so I recommend checking this box. You can allow moderators and managers to move discussions to the Promotions area or set a Flag meter.

You can do the same thing with jobs. Creating a Jobs feature allows members to post jobs. Make allowing members to post jobs a bonus of joining the group. I don't recommend limiting it so that only moderators and managers can move discussions into the Jobs area.

I mentioned that you have the option of automatically removing content that's flagged as inappropriate. The next area is where are you change the number of flags you need to remove the post. I think three flags is plenty. Let your group take some ownership in deciding what they think is spam. Just know that discussions and comments cannot be viewed once removed.

If you have a subgroup, this is where you can also display the Subgroups tab. If you notice your group is naturally dividing itself into factions due to interests, you might consider creating a subgroup. For instance, LinkedStrategies has three subgroups—LinkedStrategies: Career Development; Selling Is Social: Leveraging Social Media To Make Sales; and LinkedStrategies: Private Members Forum. These are targeted to three distinct markets within the LinkedStrategies membership.

You will also decide the permissions granted to your group members. Are members free to post discussions, promotions, jobs, and comments? Free to post promotions, jobs, comments, and submit everything else for approval by the group management team? Are they free to post jobs, comments, and submit everything else? Are they free to post comments only and get everything else approved? If you have no help in moderation, choose the first option. If you have a few managers or moderators to help you, choose the second and third option. This will help you limit spammy posts, but you *must* stay on top of it or your group will stagnate (and group members will possibly be offended if their discussions are not posted in a timely manner).

Some group owners and managers are uncomfortable with brand-new members joining their group. You have the option of requiring moderation for members who are new to the group or LinkedIn. You can also require moderation for people if they have no connections. I don't want to inhibit people from my group. In my mind you are innocent until proven guilty. But if you abuse my group you are out!

Once you have your settings in place, create your group rules using the Group Rules link. I recommend creating your group rules first in a word processing document and then cutting and pasting the group rules over. You can do a "conversational" group rules message as you saw earlier in this chapter, or you can create a simple list of group rules like the one in Figure 6.16.

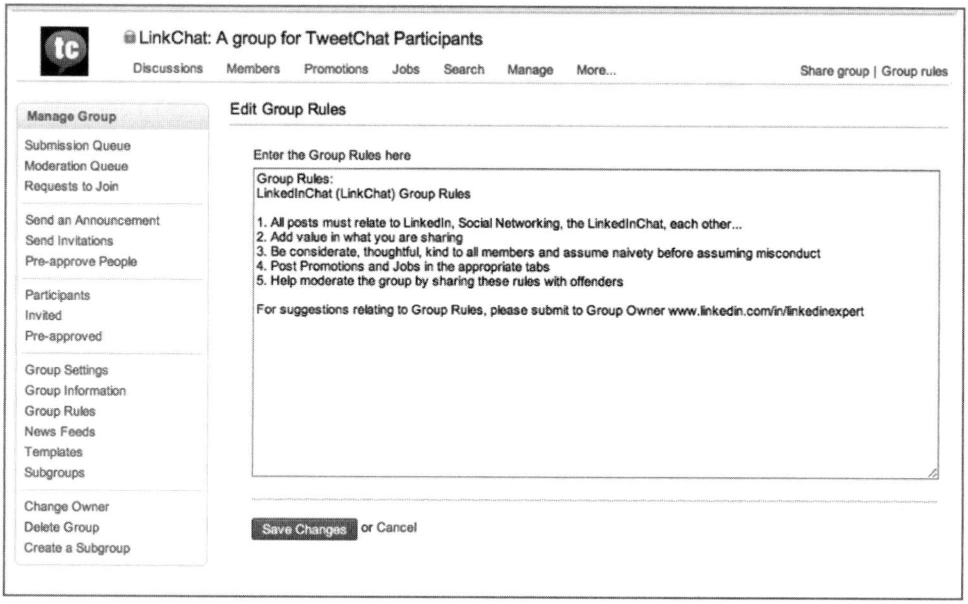

Figure 6.16 Creating your own group rules

Moderating Submissions

If you choose to require that people submit their discussions and so forth, you will need to moderate them in the Submission Queue, as shown in Figure 6.17.

Figure 6.17 Moderating your queue

Click the Submission Queue link and go through the Discussions, Promotions, and Jobs tabs by approving, moving, or deleting the submission.

The Moderation Queue contains submissions that have been flagged by other members. Again, you can either clear the flag or delete the post.

To have a healthy group, you need to regularly moderate the submissions on your queue. Groups with too many promotions in the Discussion section will lose the engagement of their membership. The more moderators or managers you have to keep up with submissions, the more likely you are to have a group that's very engaged.

Wednesday: Learn Best Practices for Inviting Members

As you saw earlier, you can invite members to your group by clicking Share Group at the top-right side of your Group page or on the left-hand side of your page in the Manage column.

The top-right side of your page allows you to share the group on LinkedIn in a status update, through a tweet, to other groups, or to individuals. I recommend inviting people to your group this way, because you can still customize your message.

You can also use the Send Invitations link on the left-hand side of your Group Management page. This tool allows you to invite potential members by email address or by choosing them from your first-level contacts. Unfortunately, LinkedIn is going to send a default message that says, "[Name] invites you to join [Group Name] on LinkedIn." And the invitation message simply says, "I would like to invite you to join my group on LinkedIn." Not very enticing, if you ask me!

If you are uploading a list, this is your only option *unless* you want to use your email service and send a real email to your contacts with a link to the group. You can find the Group Join Link on your Manage page. Click Send Invitations and on the bottom-left side you will see the link. You might want to make a customized Bitly.com link so you can more easily remember your group and share it more prolifically. Mine is http://linkd.in/linkedinchat. What I like about Bitly.com is that it will take your customized URL and add the LinkedIn linkd.in URL shortener automatically, so it looks more professional. I share my link in my email signature, on my Twitter posts, in the #LinkedInChat, on my Facebook page, and so forth. This feature is only available to group owners and managers.

 Note: I asked LinkedIn if there was a limit to the number of group invitations you could send out. Their reply: "If you are not the owner or manager of the group you do have a limit to how many invitations you can send from the group. If you are a manager or owner and are new you will have a limited number of invitations you can send for a little while…they change with each person and their history of sending invitations." So—really no answer at all. I guess a best practice is to invite with caution.

As with everything else on LinkedIn, when you invite someone to your group, let them know what's in it for them. They will see a similar message when they look at your group in the Description section, but that's okay. You need to entice them over there in the first place.

I already mentioned preapproving people who share a domain name, but you can also preapprove individuals. I don't use this option often, but for a very private group, if you don't want to risk someone getting in your group who shouldn't be, you will want to add a list of only those individuals who you want to be members of your group.

Getting your membership settings in place is probably the least exciting part of creating a group, but it's crucial to its success. Take the time to make sure your settings work for you. If you find you are getting too much spam or too few members, make a few adjustments. When you make an adjustment, let your members know. It might be just what you need to encourage more engagement.

> **Note:** Take a look at some of the groups that you are a member of for inspiration. What attracted you to them? What wording did they use in their description? Do you like their group rules? How are they set up? How do they encourage communication? Do the managers engage with the members?

Thursday: Use Templates, RSS Feeds, and Announcements

LinkedIn allows you to create some communications templates that automatically get sent to LinkedIn members who want to join your group, as well as weekly announcements you can send to your membership. You can also add some RSS feeds to your group. (Use this feature with caution.)

Templates

LinkedIn allows you to create templates for group communications. On the Manage tab, on the left side of the page, click Templates. The templates that you can create are:

- Request To Join
- Welcome Message
- Decline
- Decline And Block

The Request To Join template creates and automatically sends a custom message to people who request to join your group. If you have an Auto-Join group, this is not applicable. But for those of you who require that people request to join your group first, this is a great way to let them know both your group's expectations and when they can expect to hear from you.

In the subject line, you might say something like "Thanks for your interest in [group name]." In the message section, you might customize the message to say, "Thank you so much for your interest in the [group name] group. We are a group created specifically for [put who you created the group for here]. For more information on [subject matter or topic of interest] click on [put a URL here]. We moderate this group twice a week, so you should hear back from us within a few days. Please feel free to email me with any questions you have about the group."

Once you have customized your message, click Enable Auto Send. Be sure that you send yourself a test message first to verify that the formatting is correct.

As you can see in Figure 6.18, the second type of template you can send is the Welcome Message template. Far too few group managers and owners make use of this tool, but it's your first touch and a chance to engage with your new group member.

Figure 6.18 Welcome Message template

In the subject line, you might write something like "We are happy to accept you into [group name]." The Message section is where you're going to make an effort to connect with your new member:

- Ask them questions.
- Let them know that you are happy to refer them.
- Ask them who would make a good client for them.
- Ask them what they want to get out of this group.
- Ask them what they want to achieve in their business.
- Tell them your expectations for the group.
- Tell them what is allowed and not allowed in the group.
- Encourage them to post jobs on the Jobs tab (if you have one).
- Encourage them to put their promotion on the Promotions tab.

- Give them your contact information.

- Encourage them to connect with you on LinkedIn.

- You might share a product or service with them, but make sure it's just at the bottom of your message. You don't want to turn people off by appearing spammy.

If you add a URL to this message, it becomes a link that the person can click on in their email. Take some time formatting this welcome message. It might make all the difference in the world on the interactivity of the group.

The third template is the Decline template. Usually this is used when someone wants to join your private alumni or company group without being an alumni or current or former employee. It's usually a gentle refusal, and you might even give them some other options, such as following your company page.

The Decline And Block template creates and automatically sends a custom message to people when you decline their request to join the group. It will also block any further future requests. I don't recommend this template, although I am sure there will be times when it comes in handy (like when you have a very private, almost a secret group on LinkedIn).

RSS Feeds

Another thing that you can do on LinkedIn is add RSS feeds or newsfeeds to your group. Don't go crazy here! Even though you can add up to 25 RSS feeds, you shouldn't. Just choose two or three blogs that you think will serve your group membership. This, of course, can be your own blog, as well as other informational blogs that you find particularly useful.

> **Note:** In my LinkChat group, I added my own blog, the blog of my manager Austin Miles (who is a complete genius when it comes to social media), as well as the RSS feed to the SocialMediaExaminer, which I contribute to on occasion. I find that we are constantly referencing these blogs in the chat anyway, so I figure I might as well feed them here.

I don't recommend feeding too many blogs to your group. The blogs will show up in your Discussion section and have the RSS feed icon instead of your profile picture. I feed blogs because I am a bit lazy (busy). If you have the time, it's better to manually add these links yourself by clicking Start A Discussion and adding the link. It looks better, and it will probably get more interaction.

You can also feed jobs onto the Jobs tab (based on whatever criteria or keywords you set up). Stacy Donovan Zapar suggests this strategy and finds her group is more interactive and valuable because of it.

To add a job feed to a group you manage or own:

1. Go to your group and click the Jobs tab under the group name.

2. In the left pane, click Jobs.

3. In the Create A Feed box in the upper-right corner, click Get Started to create a jobs feed, or click Edit to make changes to an existing feed.

It's a little difficult to find, so see Figure 6.19.

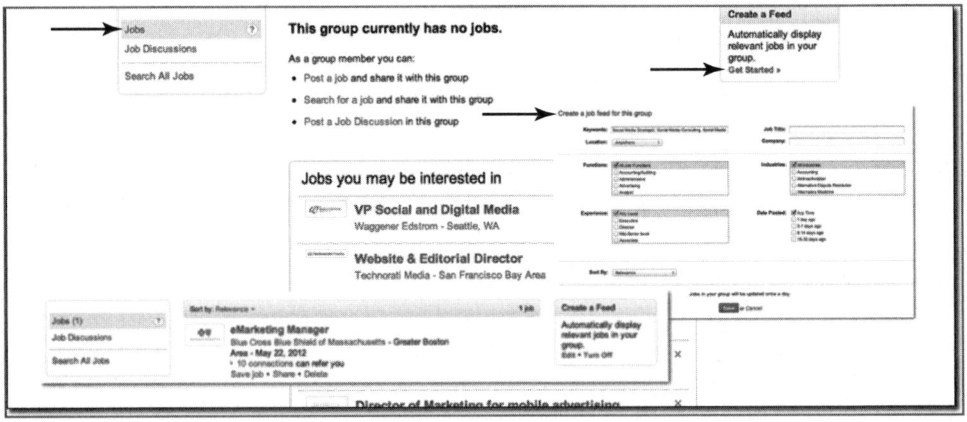

Figure 6.19 Adding a job feed

Once you have created a job feed, LinkedIn will have you do a job search. The saved search will feed results onto the Jobs tab automatically. You can turn the feed on and off at will.

Announcements

Another tool under the Manage section of your group is Send An Announcement. Unfortunately many group owners and managers either don't know this exists or don't make the most use out of it. What an unfortunate waste of a very powerful resource.

A group announcement allows you to send your membership a message once a week, as shown in Figure 6.20. It's yet another way to stay top of mind with your group members and position yourself as a resource and expert.

A good use of the group announcement is to recap the most popular discussions of the week, reminding people why they might want to interact in your group. You might let your group members know that you have a special offer just for them, and add a promo code or a link to that free video, webinar, or product. (Just don't send a sales pitch or promotion every week!) If your group is associated with a company or alumni, let people know the latest news, including job posts and events.

You can share a simple tip or trick and ask for feedback. For that matter, you should probably always be asking for feedback from your group members, in discussions as well as in your announcement. What did they like about your group? What did they not like about your group? What do they want to hear more of? Who do they want to hear more from?

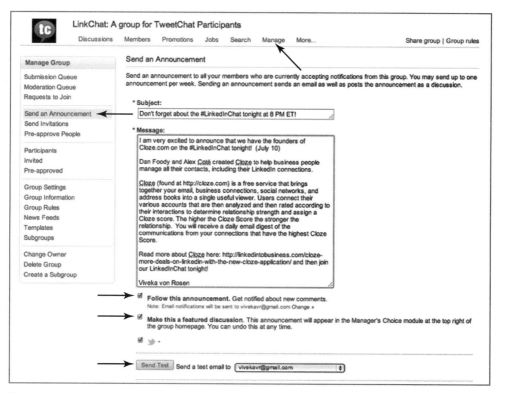

Figure 6.20 Weekly group announcement

If your group is associated with an event (like my #LinkedInChat), use the announcement to let people know about what's coming up. The more people who know about it, or are reminded of it, the more likely you are to get a higher attendance!

Are you getting some ideas?

Simply click Send An Announcement, change the subject line to read whatever you want it to, and write your message. You have 4,000 characters that you can add, though you probably don't want to use all 4,000 characters—at least not every week.

That covers groups: how to interact within them, how to use them to grow your business, and how to create your own group. Remember in the end it's all about being a source of valuable information. How can you help out other group members? How can you be of service to them? What can you do for them to help them grow their businesses? Keep asking and answering these questions and your group activity will surely help you grow and strengthen your network.

Friday: Group Statistics

LinkedIn now offers group statistics to both group members and management. To find the statistics for your group, click the group's More tab and then click Group Statistics, as shown in Figure 6.21.

Figure 6.21 Group Statistics

The Summary tab in Group Statistics will show you things like:

- When the group was started
- How many members you have
- The seniority level of your members
- How many comments were made
- Where the highest percentage of your membership resides
- What the highest percentage is for job function of your membership

This is invaluable information for a group manager. Is your group growing? Are your group members participating? Do you need to spark some discussion? If you are a location-based group, is that your largest concentration? If you created your group to attract certain industries, are those industries being represented? If not, you have some work to do in both engaging your membership and inviting new strategic members to your group.

The Demographics tab goes more in depth into the demographics of you membership according to the following:

- Seniority
- Function

- Location
- Industry

If you click the links on the right side of the page, you can dive even deeper and see the exact percentages of your membership through categories such as:

- Senior
- Owner
- Manager
- Director
- CXO
- Partner
- Entry

If this is your group, does it represent the membership you want? If it's a group you are a member of, are these the people you want to be connecting with?

Note: It's useful to note that you can check out a group's statistics before you even join the group. Just click View Group and under More check out the statistics. You might not want to waste your time with a group that doesn't have a membership focused (at least in part) on the seniority level, location, or job function that you are interested in communicating with.

If you click the Function tab, LinkedIn will show you the percentage of all your membership in the top six job functions within your group. (These will change according to the most popular functions.) Some popular functions in my groups are:

- Marketing
- Consulting
- Entrepreneurs
- Media and Communications
- Education
- Design

Again, it's a good idea to keep an eye on these functions or industries and make sure you are attracting the crowd you want to.

You can dive down into location and industry as well. Industry and function are similar, so it's a good idea to keep an eye on both. It might help to think of functions as the job functions within an industry.

The Growth tab shows you a graph of your group's growth. If you scroll over the graphs, they will display the membership number by date.

This tab will also give you the total number of members, how many members joined last week, and your week-over-week growth rate.

Finally, the Activity tab will show you activity according to weekly:

- Comments
- Discussions
- Jobs
- Promotion

There is also a handy graph that will show you the rate of discussions and comments over a 16-month period.

You can then share any tab on LinkedIn, Twitter, or Facebook, or through a link by clicking their icons on the top-right side of the page.

The Statistics page can be an invaluable tool in the growth and promotion of your group. Be sure to add a review of your group statistics into your weekly practices.

Next up: What "More" can you do on LinkedIn!

Weeks 19–22: Get Strategic with LinkedIn's "Other" Options

7

LinkedIn has several tools and applications you'll find on the More tab. I always tell people that if they're looking for something and they can't find it, check the More tab. Several of my favorite features (such as Skills and Events) are found here, so if you haven't explored these "other" options, let's take a look now.

Chapter Contents

Week 19: Using LinkedIn Answers
Week 20: Using LinkedIn Events
Week 21: Sharing with Applications
Week 22: Exploring Industry-Based and LinkedIn Apps

Week 19: Using LinkedIn Answers

I don't think people use LinkedIn's Answers as much as they should be when marketing their business. Answers can serve two roles:

- A great way to position yourself as an expert by answering questions in your area of expertise

- An excellent channel for creating relationships with people who are invested enough in your questions to answer them

I have found excellent resources and even clients through LinkedIn Answers, many of whom I had not previously known. Here's what I found out: There are a lot of really smart people on LinkedIn.

Where can you find Answers? It's your first option under the More tab on the main menu bar. When you click Answers, you will land on the Answers home page, as shown in Figure 7.1.

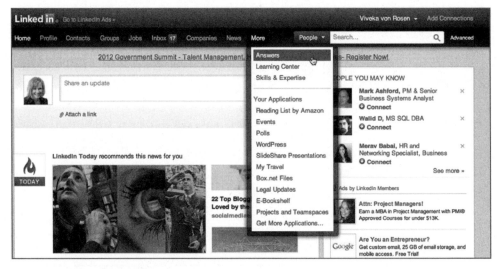

Figure 7.1 LinkedIn Answers home page

This page lets you ask a simple question or answer questions in categories recommended to you by LinkedIn, see new questions posted by your network, and view the This Week's Top Experts feature on LinkedIn.

Although you can ask a question from this page, I recommend selecting the Ask A Question tab to the right of the Answers Home tab. When you ask a question, LinkedIn will display the Ask A Question page anyway. This page allows you to add more detail and categorize your questions. Asking questions of the people who know the answers will get a better response. General questions tend *not* to result in deeply detailed and interesting answers.

LinkedIn offers general categories for you to answer questions under Browse on the right side of the page. Go ahead and click one of the links relevant to your business, as shown in Figure 7.2.

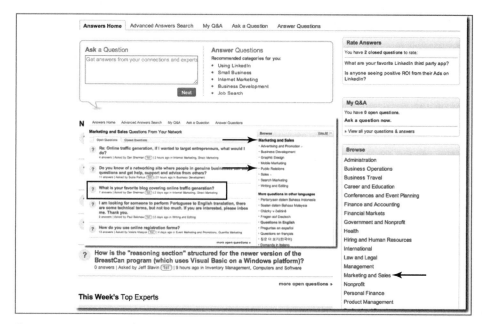

Figure 7.2 Answer categories

Are there any questions here you can answer? We'll take a look at how to answer questions in the next section, but are you seeing the possibilities?

Monday: Understand Answers

Next we'll focus on how you can use Answers for thought leadership positioning and leads.

Why would you care about questions from your network? Being able to answer a question will go a long way in forging a relationship with the person asking the question. One thing Jason Alba (author of *I'm On LinkedIn, Now What???* [Happy About Publishing, 2012]) taught me was that you can get to know a lot more about a person's interests by looking at the questions they post. Just because you're a project manager doesn't mean that you might not have a deep interest in financial forensics. When you look at the home page of your network, or this page on LinkedIn, take note of all the different categories of answers. People are more complex than we give them credit for.

I think some people use LinkedIn Answers as their primary marketing campaign. There are some LinkedIn members who answer up to 500–600 questions (I even saw 700 answered questions from a member) in a single week! With those numbers, it's no wonder many of these folks get Best Answer and are categorized as experts by

LinkedIn. What a great way to position yourself as a thought leader. (We'll talk more about that on Friday.)

The next tab is called Advanced Answers Search. This is where you'll go to find specific topics or questions that you can respond to. You can choose to search for a keyword match in questions and answers, or questions only. I'll talk about both choices in the next section.

The third tab is called My Q&A. This page displays the history and statistics of your questions and answers. Sometimes I'll post a question months in advance of the time I actually need the answer. This allows me to go back into that question and see people's responses. I can then follow up with whoever I need to when the time is right.

Next to the Ask A Question tab is Answer Questions. You can sort open and closed questions by level of connection—how many degrees away from you the person who asked the question is. Or you can sort them by date.

So now that you know where everything is, how do you take best advantage of Answers?

Tuesday: Use Answers to Build Relationships

What is the best way to build relationships using Answers? Ask questions. You can ask up to 10 questions a month and answer up to 50 questions a day. You can ask both public and private questions. Public questions will be visible to everyone on LinkedIn, or you can select the option Only Share This Question With Connections I Select to ask questions privately of your first-level connections.

Generally I recommend posting your questions to the public, but there will be times when you'll have a more focused or directed question for a thought leader or subject matter expert in your network. Do you have a public question and want to make sure it also gets posted to a first-level connection? You can do that as well, as you can see in Figure 7.3.

Let's say you are a professional development manager, and you want to build a relationship with other professional development authorities, as well as the people who might be able to use your services. You post a general question asking something like, "What is the best method that you have found to meet people face-to-face in a specific geographic location?" You post this question to the general public, and perhaps to a few folks in your network who would make good clients. The fact that you're asking for advice, rather than overtly telling people that you can help them in their practice with your professional development skills, means they are much more likely to respond to you—especially if they have the answer. And now you have established a first touch. When someone answers your question, you also have the opportunity to send them a private reply message. You should certainly thank them, and also take this relationship forward to the next level. Rather than a cold call, you now have a warm connection.

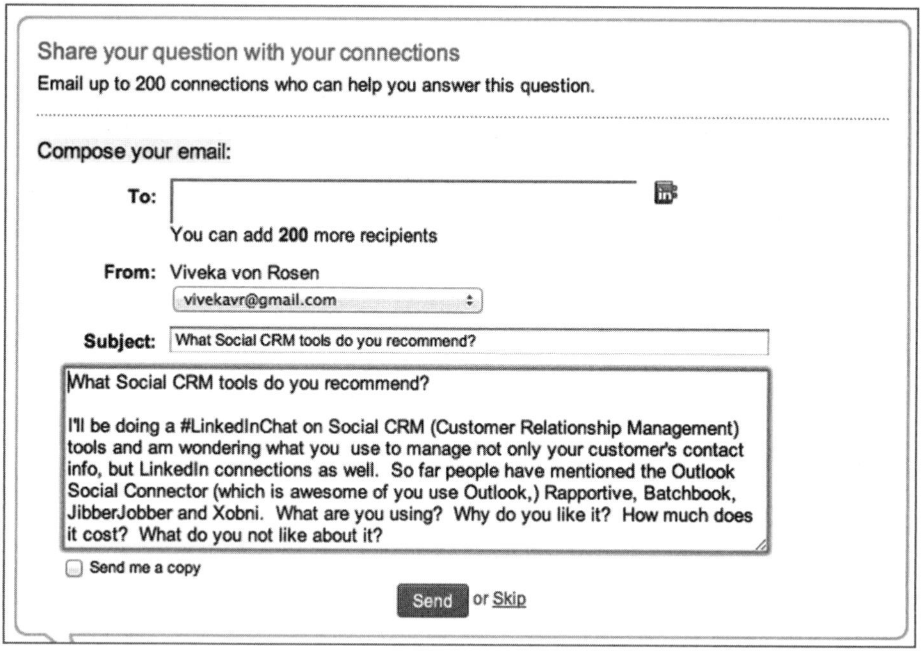

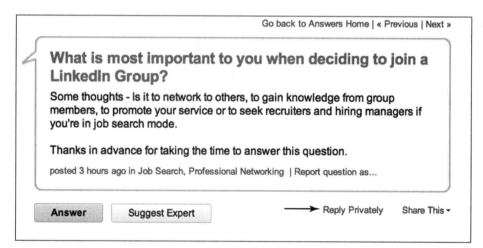

Figure 7.3 Asking a question of your network

Another way to build relationships using Answers is by doing someone a favor. You can of course answer their questions. You can answer the question publicly, which is a great idea if you want to get your name out there, but you can also reply privately, if it's someone you really want to build a relationship with, as shown in Figure 7.4.

Go back to Answers Home | « Previous | Next »

What is most important to you when deciding to join a LinkedIn Group?

Some thoughts - Is it to network to others, to gain knowledge from group members, to promote your service or to seek recruiters and hiring managers if you're in job search mode.

Thanks in advance for taking the time to answer this question.

posted 3 hours ago in Job Search, Professional Networking | Report question as...

Answer   **Suggest Expert**   ⟶ Reply Privately   Share This ▾

Figure 7.4 Answering questions privately

Replying privately takes the conversation offline, and it allows you to communicate with someone who may not be a first-level connection. As with a public response, you can also list web resources and recommend experts. Perhaps some of the web resources might be your own. (You used to be able to recommend anyone on LinkedIn as an expert, but now they have to be a first-level connection. Darn.)

Another way to help someone is to share their question. Suppose you see someone you want to grow a relationship with and you find they have asked an interesting question. At the bottom right of the page you'll see a Share This link. It allows you to email the question to somebody else, even if they're not on LinkedIn. You can share the question on del.icio.us, or you can paste the link right into Twitter or Facebook, or to your blog.

Why would you want to do this? Well, if you can help the person by facilitating a connection with someone in your network, either on LinkedIn or in their life, and something comes of that relationship, such as business for both of them, then you become more valuable in both their eyes. And with whom do people do business? People do business with people they know, like, trust, and value.

Wednesday: Use Answers to Repurpose SME Materials

Many of you write blogs, have newsletters, or post to professional journals. So you already have an enormous amount of subject matter expertise content on hand. Why not reuse or repurpose that content on LinkedIn? You can help out a lot of people. You can build relationships. And you can position yourself as a subject matter expert or a thought leader. It doesn't take a whole lot of work, because you already have the material.

Your first step is to go to the Answer page's Questions tab and look for open questions in your area of expertise. You can do so by browsing the right-hand side of the page and looking at the various topics. If you don't see a category related to your business, knowledge, or existing materials, then click the Advanced Answer search. This will allow you to search answers by specific keyword. (Choose Questions Only.)

You can search by a general topic, or you can define categories up to three levels deep. You can also choose to show only unanswered questions and be the first to the party (although in my experience these questions aren't usually very good). Once you find a question you know something about, take a quick look at your blog posts, newsletters, and articles to see which one would best answer the question.

Once you find a question you can answer, don't just share the link to your content. I recommend copying and pasting your post or article right into the response field (remembering you only have 4,000 characters). Make sure you customize your answer to fit the question being asked, or it might be considered spam. (Of course, your answer has to be relevant to the question being asked.) Once you have copied and pasted your customized response, go ahead and share the link to the article or the blog. If it's a physical journal, newspaper, or book, let people know where they can buy it.

Thursday: Use Answers for Blog Fodder

Is it only me, or have you ever been stuck staring at that white screen with nothing to say? One of my favorite tools for sparking the creative writing genius within is taking a look at LinkedIn Answers and seeing what questions are being posted. We already talked about this yesterday for repurposing content, but this is also a good strategy for *creating* blog content.

Why? Because the questions that people are asking might be something you want to write about, and they are *asking.* You already have an invested audience. Once you've written the article, you can respond to the answer with your content and a link to your article. So it's a win-win.

For example, I was recently asked to write an article on LinkedIn Ads. Quite frankly, at the time, my experience with LinkedIn's Marketing Solutions was pretty slim. I did a quick search on LinkedIn Ads in the Answers section and found an old question with some pretty good answers. I reached out to some of the folks who answered the questions and interviewed them for my article. In fact, one of the "answerers" is featured later Chapter 10, "LinkedIn Ads, Labs, Apps, and Tools."

Note: You might want to just search for open questions (because otherwise you won't be able to use the content you create as an answer). But if you're not getting any results, use the All Questions option, which includes both open and closed options. You won't be able to share your content in a question that has been closed, but you might still get some good ideas.

When I search for categories of questions to answer, I search for both questions and answers, as shown in Figure 7.5.

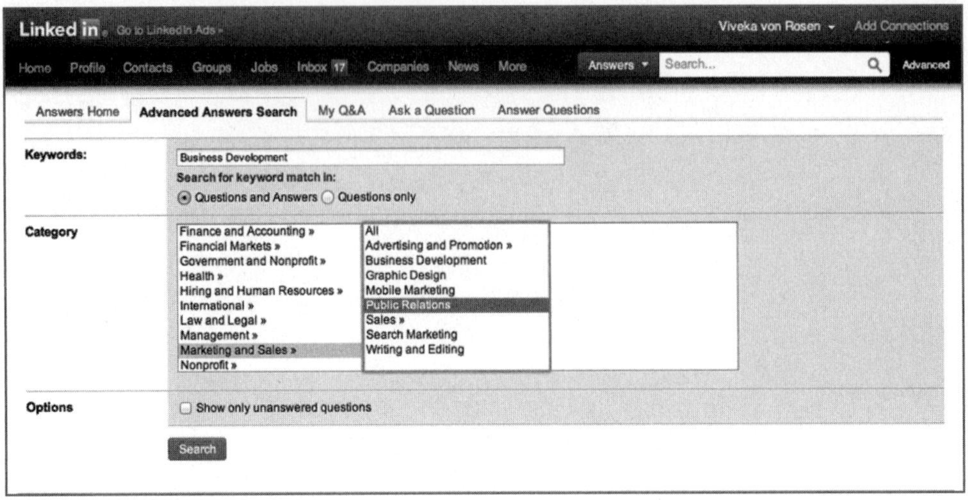

Figure 7.5 Finding questions to answer

The reason for this is that not only will I get a question that I can answer with my blog, but I might even use some of the answers that other people have posted in my blog post—with their permission of course. And why? Because it will help me build relationships with them too!

Your first step after finding a question of interest is to click on the question. (You might even use the question or part of the title of your post.) Look at the answers. If you really like one of the answers, then click on the individual who posted the question and send them a message in the usual way; if they are a first-level connection, send them a message, or maybe send them a message through an introduction, an InMail if you have one, or through the groups route that we talked about earlier. (You used to be able to comment or respond to someone's answer right in the Answer section, but you can't do that anymore.)

Friday: Identify Experts on LinkedIn

Do you want to create referral marketing relationships? Are you looking for employees? Are you looking for people to write guest posts on your blog? Well, Answers might be where you can find them.

If you are looking for an expert in a particular industry, you can go to the Answers home page and look for the category that your expert might be writing in. (Alas, this doesn't work in the Advanced Answer search.)

To look for answered questions, browse on the right-hand side of the page. Let's say I was looking for someone who could help me with my chapter on LinkedIn for lawyers. I would click on Law And Legal, and at the bottom of the page I would see who on LinkedIn ranks as an expert. Then I would click the link See All My Answers next to the person's name, as shown in Figure 7.6.

Figure 7.6 Expert answers on LinkedIn

This will take you to their home page. On the right side you'll see that person's activity, including their public answers. To see if they have written an update lately, you can also click the See All Activity link. This will show you not only the questions they've answered, but also who they're connected to, what groups they've joined, updates, and so forth.

If you click on questions they've answered, it will take you to a page that shows you the person's questions and answers. Take a look at their answers and see if this is a person with whom you want to be doing business. If it is, use the tools you've learned about in this book to reach out to them.

Week 20: Using LinkedIn Events

The LinkedIn Events feature has been around for a long time (since 2008), but it recently got an overhaul from LinkedIn and is now, I think, easier to use. If nothing else, LinkedIn Events gets great Google juice.

Monday: Learn Best Practices for Event Setup

To find the Events application, select the More tab and click Events. To the right of your page, you will see a yellow Create An Event button. (We'll check out other people's events at the end of this chapter.)

As with many applications on LinkedIn, take some time with the title of your event. Not only does a well-keyworded event title have a better chance of showing up in Google, but it is more likely to be found in an event search and clicked on by someone in the LinkedIn network. I find many people use the event title without describing the event: Mastering LinkedIn vs. Mastering Your Professional Network on LinkedIn for More and Better Business.

You need to let your audience know when and where your event will be held. LinkedIn supports both physical events (like trade shows or seminars) as well as virtual events (like webinars and virtual meetings). To choose a virtual event, simply click the This Is A Virtual Event check box, as shown in Figure 7.7.

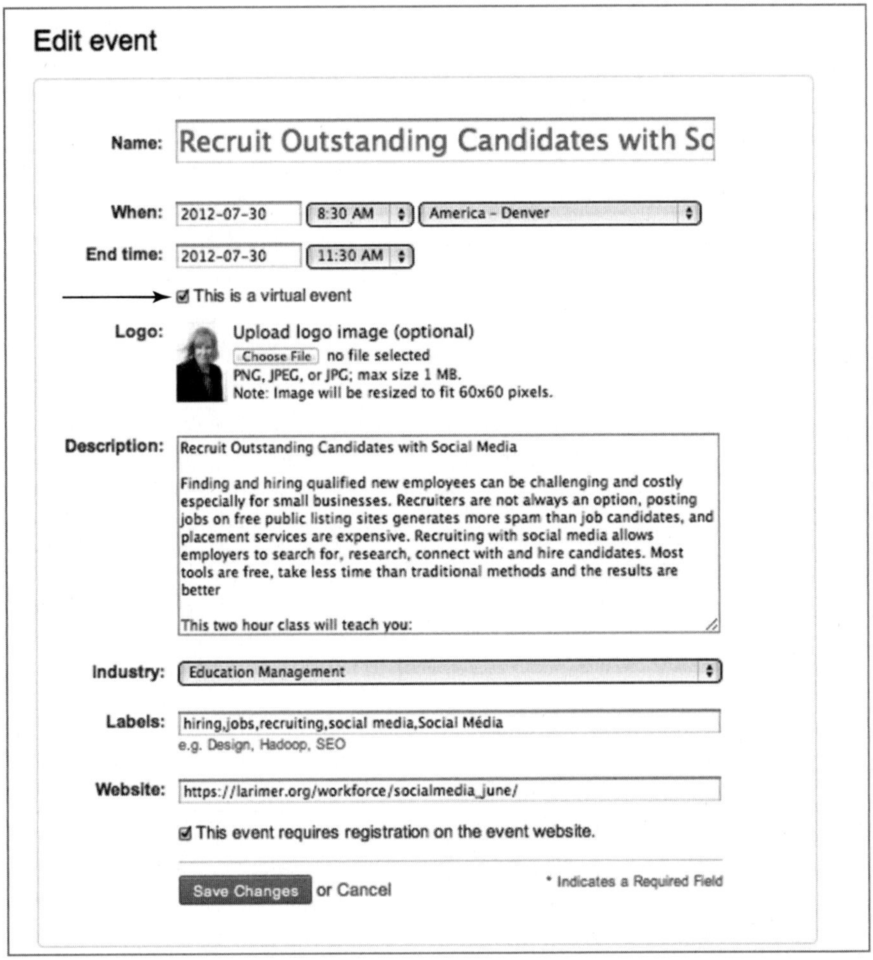

Figure 7.7 Creating an event

If it is not a virtual event, you can always share the physical address of the event in the Venue field. Upload a logo if you have one and you are ready for step 2.

Your next step is to add a description of your event. Make the first few lines captivating. What is the WIIFM for your audience if they attend your event? What will make your network participants want to share your event with their network? What's the value proposition?

I was testing the description fields and there seems to be a limitless number of characters you can use (I stopped at 6,000). A good rule of thumb when describing an event is to keep it to 500 words or fewer. Only the first few lines of the description will show up when you post the event, so make sure you are able to engage your audience immediately. The rest is details.

You can then choose your industry. I know this isn't a comprehensive list but you have to choose something, so specify the industry that most closely relates to your event. This is one of the ways that LinkedIn will categorize your event for the search algorithm.

Since the industry category is somewhat limited, you have an opportunity to better define your event under Labels. Think *keyword*. What are people going to type into the event search if they don't know about your event but are looking for an event just like yours?

If you have a website associated with the event, direct people there, especially if they have to register for the event. It's always better to put the exact landing page in this section. Some people might send you to a general website, but that is frustrating. Make it easy on them and send them to the right page the first time, as shown in Figure 7.8.

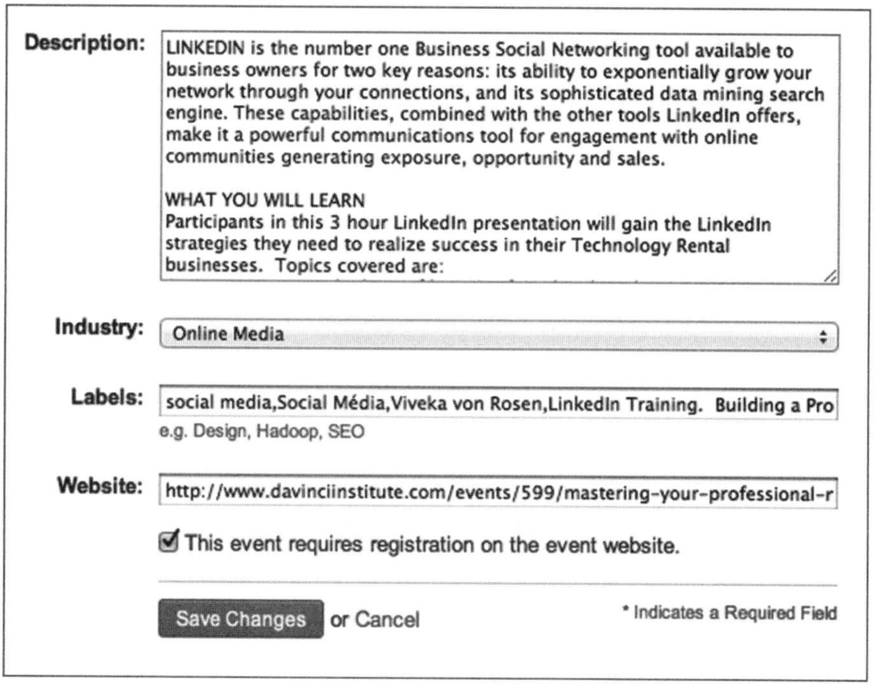

Description:	LINKEDIN is the number one Business Social Networking tool available to business owners for two key reasons: its ability to exponentially grow your network through your connections, and its sophisticated data mining search engine. These capabilities, combined with the other tools LinkedIn offers, make it a powerful communications tool for engagement with online communities generating exposure, opportunity and sales. WHAT YOU WILL LEARN Participants in this 3 hour LinkedIn presentation will gain the LinkedIn strategies they need to realize success in their Technology Rental businesses. Topics covered are:
Industry:	Online Media
Labels:	social media,Social Média,Viveka von Rosen,LinkedIn Training. Building a Pro e.g. Design, Hadoop, SEO
Website:	http://www.davinciinstitute.com/events/599/mastering-your-professional-r

☑ This event requires registration on the event website.

[Save Changes] or Cancel   * Indicates a Required Field

Figure 7.8 More event details

Once you have completed the general information for the event, you can easily share it on both Facebook and Twitter. Remember to save the event URL where you can find it for later sharing. LinkedIn will automatically post the event to your network, but don't rest on those laurels. Check out the next section, which shows you how to be proactive in sharing your event.

If you decide to edit an existing event, simply click the Events link and you will see all the events you have created on the right side of the page. Click on the event name and then click Edit, as shown in Figure 7.9.

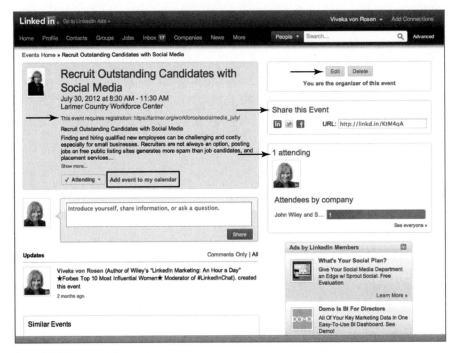

Figure 7.9 Editing an existing event

You will also see who has signed up for your event, by name and company and industry. In fact, if you click the See Everyone link, you can view a full listing of attendees. It might be a good idea to follow up with them if you can. Thank them for coming and encourage them to share the link to your event.

Other useful items on this page are

- Listings of similar events hosted on LinkedIn
- Sharing tools
- Calendaring link
- A map to the event (if it is a physical location)

As with Facebook events, you can easily share LinkedIn events with your network, and they are searchable on LinkedIn. A word of caution here: If it is a paid event, a LinkedIn member might feel that they have registered by clicking Attending. If it is a paid event, make sure the link you share in your LinkedIn event is to the actual registration page.

You cannot collect money on LinkedIn itself, but you can guide people to the page or application that will do that for you (like Eventbrite, www.eventbrite.com).

Tuesday: Share Events Through Events App and Updates

If you share your event using Twitter or Facebook, copy and paste the event URL somewhere that you can easily retrieve and share it. (You might even create a bitly link so you always have access to it and can track how often it is being shared.) But don't worry if you forgot to do that—you can find the link under My Events on the right side of the page, as shown in Figure 7.8 earlier.

Now that you have the event URL, you can continue to share it on Twitter and Facebook. And you will want to share it using LinkedIn's status updates as well.

Since you are limited to 600 characters in an update, (generous compared to Twitter's 140), make sure you make your update a call to action:

Come to our event if you are a_____ who needs _____. Join us for this awesome event at: [URL].

Another good tactic is:

Do you know someone who is a _____ who needs more_____?

Then let them know about this awesome event: [URL].
Or use something like this:

World-renowned specialist in _____ is offering a rare webinar on _____. Limited to the first 100 people who click Attend on LinkedIn. Get your place today at: [event URL].

In fact, why not try all three (or your own) updates? You should probably be sharing your event via status update a few times a week at least. Why not? It's free!

Don't forget to share your event with your groups. But don't just post a "Come to my event" discussion. Make it a discussion! Are you sharing an event for IT professionals? Then ask a pertinent question that your event will answer or offer a solution to and encourage a discussion. Add the link to your event in the link section. That way, it's not so much a hard sell as an intriguing proposition and a potential answer to their dilemma. (Plus you might actually get some information you can use in your event.)

Save some time by using the Sharing bookmarklet from the landing page of your event. Share it in one effort as a status update, on Twitter (with the 140-character limit), with your groups, and with your connections.

Wednesday: Use Messages to Share Your Event with Key People

Why stop at status updates and groups to share your event? Use your very powerful LinkedIn message tool. Remember that you can send messages to your network by tags, industries, companies, and location, as shown in Figure 7.10.

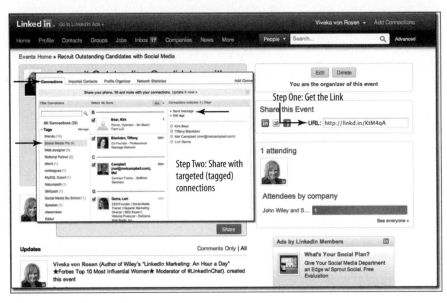

Figure 7.10 Event sharing with messages

Let's say you have created a live event on graphic design for Internet marketing professionals: Creating Infographics for Your Clients. Record the URL and then click Your Connections on the Contacts tab in the main menu. Now click Locations and choose the city where you are holding the event. If you have fewer than 50 people in that location, you can click Select All and then Send Message. (Remember that LinkedIn's Bulk Messaging will let you send up to 50 messages at a time.) Make sure your message title is engaging and then describe the event. You might say something like this:

> Did you know that infographics have a 67% better chance of grabbing your customer's attention than an ordinary graphic? I am hosting a live event for graphic artists in Richmond, VA to teach you how you can better engage your audience (and get more business and money!). If you know a graphic artist in the Richmond area, or you are intrigued by the art of the infographic, please consider attending this event. [provide event URL]

And then add more details and sign with all your contact information.

Although it might take more time, you could even search in this list for connections who are graphic artists (it will say so in their profile). You can always prepare your list ahead of time by tagging the graphic artists in your network who live in Richmond and send that specific tagged group a message (especially if that is a niche market of yours that you plan on creating other events for).

Your limits are that you can:

- Only send messages to first-level connections
- Only send messages to 50 people at a time

The more specific you can be when sending a message, the more likely people are to open it.

If you *really* want to target an audience for your event, do an Advanced People search by keyword and location (or whatever specifics are relevant).

Thursday: Use Share Profile to Highlight Your Speaker and Sharing with LinkedIn Ads

If you have a speaker at your event who is influential in your subject, industry, or location, then use that to influence others to join your event.

Go to the Influencer's profile on LinkedIn, and then click the Share link on their profile, as shown in Figure 7.11.

Now you can follow the steps from Wednesday and send the Influencer's profile, with a link to your event, to the connections you want to inform about the event. You can also attach the Influencer's LinkedIn Public Profile URL and the event URL via a status update, Twitter, or Facebook, and in an email as well.

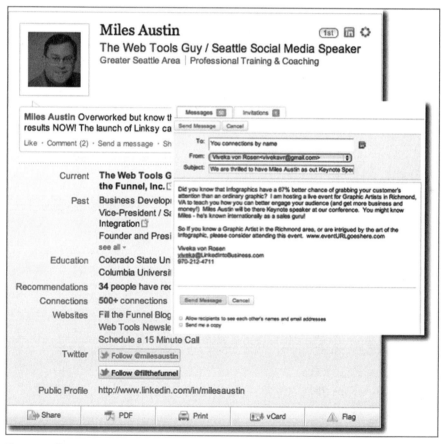

Figure 7.11 Sharing a speaker's profile

Friday: Connect Through Other's Events

So now you know how to create your own event, but what about others' events? Do you need to know how to use Excel more effectively, create an infographic, learn how to use Facebook's Timeline to market your business, find the right bookkeeper for your business, start an LLC, use your iPad more efficiently? These were all free events I found with a short two-minute search in LinkedIn's events!

To find an event, click Events, and in Search Events type a search term for an event you would be interested in joining, as shown in Figure 7.12.

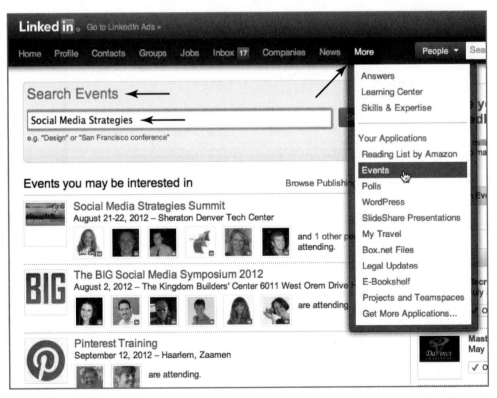

Figure 7.12 Searching for events

LinkedIn will also make event suggestions for you according to your profile and previous events attended or created. Click the link and it will take you to the event's page. If it's a free webinar, then sign up!

You will also see who else is attending the event by clicking Attendees you might want to meet. If it's a physical event, then why not reach out to some of the attendees and plan for a coffee or dinner meeting? Get more bang for your buck. You will also be able to see and sort attendees by company and industry. (You may want to connect with folks in a certain industry or company only.)

If you think the event might be useful to your tribe on social media or your network on LinkedIn, then by all means share the event using the tools provided: Twitter, Facebook, and event URL, as shown in Figure 7.12. LinkedIn will also make suggestions for similar events and throw a few ads your way as well.

> **Note:** Don't take tax advice from me, but how about using LinkedIn events to find an event somewhere that you want to go on vacation? Maybe you can attend the event and write off the entire trip! Or if you are a recruiter, you might find an event in an industry you are searching in. If you are a job seeker, you might find an industry- or location-based event that will help you network with folks face to face.

Week 21: Sharing with Applications

I love LinkedIn's applications. To find applications on LinkedIn, go to the More tab and click Get More Applications. You can view all of LinkedIn's applications, those that they've created or own (such as Skills, Polls, Events, GitHub, SlideShare) as well as third-party applications (such as Box.net, My Travel, Legal Updates and Lawyer Ratings, Amazon Reading List, WordPress and BlogLink, Projects and Team Spaces, E-Bookshelf, Creative Portfolio, Real Estate Pro).

Monday: Learn More about Applications

LinkedIn says you can have a total of 15 modules or applications on your profile, and six will show up on your home page, although many people have commented that they are unable to add more than six or seven apps. Personally I've never been able to add more than eight applications. Look through the apps offered and choose the best ones for you.

From Get More Applications, LinkedIn will open a page where most of their commonly used applications are listed. You can then choose the application icon you are interested in, which will also give you more information on the application itself, as shown in Figure 7.13.

Figure 7.13 Get More Applications

Choose whether you want to display the application on your profile and/or on your home page. What's the difference between adding an application on your home page and adding an application to your profile? When an application displays on your profile, anyone with access to your profile URL can see it. These are the people in your network. If you are using an application and are not interested in anyone else knowing about it (maybe you are using Projects and Team Sharing to develop a project with other LinkedIn members), choose to display the app only on your home page so you can easily access it.

Now click Add Application. To remove an application, just go back to the application in Get More Applications, click its icon, and click Remove. Or you can go into Settings and in Groups, Companies, And Applications, remove the app.

Let's look at the various applications next.

> **Note:** When you to add an application to LinkedIn, be aware that you are allowing that application to access your profile information and information about your connections. Mostly the applications use this information in order to tell you about the service they offer. Just be aware that this and other information the application accesses may be displayed publicly. If it makes you feel any better, applications are contractually obligated to respect your privacy settings. LinkedIn's APIs terms of use do restrict some of the information that applications can use. If you want to read more about terms of use, go to `https://developer.linkedin.com/documents/linkedin-apis-terms-use`.
>
> If you want to create applications for LinkedIn, go to `http://developer.LinkedIn.com`.

Tuesday: Use Box.net

LinkedIn has a few applications you can use to share and repurpose your existing content. One of my favorite applications is Box.net.

Box.net allows you to upload any type of office-type document (Word and text files, Excel and spreadsheets, PDFs, MP3s, etc.), and then manage and share your files on LinkedIn. Remember all those marketing assets I had you gather in Chapter 1 (and share in Answers)?

What existing marketing documents have already rendered you excellent results?

- Are you known for a specific white paper or article?
- Do you have an audio interview that can give you credibility and position you as an expert?
- Do you have a useful checklist that you would want people to share, thereby promoting you and your business?
- Do you have a portfolio?
- Do you have a résumé?
- Do you have testimonials from people who aren't on LinkedIn?
- Do you have an intake form?
- Do you have an e-book?
- Do you have a calendar you'd like to share?
- Do you have a brochure?
- Do you have JPEGs of certifications, awards, or degrees?
- Do you have job descriptions of current openings?

If you answered yes to any of these questions, then Box.net is for you.

Box.net is a third-party application, so you will have to create an account at www.Box.net to use it in your LinkedIn profile. It's free. I suggest opening up Box.net in a new browser window and creating your account there, but you can create it from within LinkedIn as well.

Once you create an account with Box.net, you'll be able to upload files, create new folders for them, rename your files, and arrange them in any order that makes sense to you. LinkedIn will tell you which folders are visible on your LinkedIn profile, so make sure that any file or folder you want seen by your network is in this LinkedIn profile folder. I choose to display my Box.net contents on my profile and on my home page. At the very least make sure you display the contents on your profile—otherwise what's the point?

To upload a file, click the Upload link to open the dialog shown in Figure 7.14.

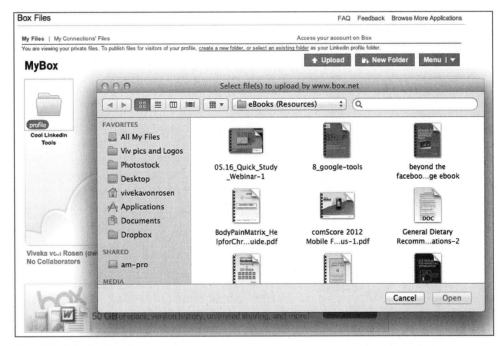

Figure 7.14 Uploading files to Box.net

Choose a file from your computer and click Open. Make sure you have permission to share that file.

Note: When I first started with Box.net, I was so excited about the program that I uploaded all my presentations—including the ones I usually charge for. Oops! Remember, these documents are visible to anyone in your network.

If you upload a lot of different documents, you'll probably want to divvy up those files into different folders. When you create a new folder, name it in such a way that people will want to click on it. You could name it Awesome Accounting Resources or Everything You Need to Know Before Hiring a Lawyer. And then make sure that folder holds relevant information.

Some of the ways to manage your Box.net account within LinkedIn are to create a List view as opposed to an Icon view, as shown in Figure 7.15. You can sort by type of file, you can click Subscribe (which will send you an email whenever content is added to your Box.net account), and you can go to Settings (which will allow you to edit the settings as seen by your network). You can edit the profile folder name, the default order, the default view, and if you have MP3s listed here, whether you'll allow visitors to download them.

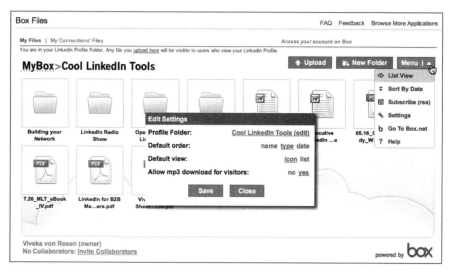

Figure 7.15 Box.net settings on LinkedIn

Unfortunately at this time Box.net does not let you know who has viewed or downloaded your materials. So make sure each piece has your contact information in case that person decides to contact you or share your information with others.

Besides uploading your own content, Box.net shows you your connections' files. This is another great source for finding experts to connect and partner with.

You can go to Box.net to do things like add more memory, manage your folders, invite collaborators to add content to your folders, leave comments on other people's folders, or even add applications. I won't go into detail here, but Box.net plays well with your iPhone, Salesforce, Zoho, and more. (If you use Dropbox, you will find Box.net to be similar—except that Box.net is a LinkedIn app and Dropbox is not.)

Take a look at how your Box.net files show up in your profile, as shown in Figure 7.16, and make any necessary changes.

Figure 7.16 Box.net in your profile

On my profile only 10 of my 15 files are showing. You may want to create folders if you have too many files. I have folders with documents on Building Your Network, LinkedIn Radio Shows, LinkedIn Tools, and Videos. I also have important files pulled out of folders (such as Testimonials, my LinkedIn Executive Profile Questionnaire, e-books, and my speakers one-sheet).

Go ahead and add some documents to Box.net right now.

Wednesday: Showcase Your Business with SlideShare

LinkedIn bought SlideShare in May 2012 and got rid of Google Presentations, so now there is only one app for uploading presentations and video: SlideShare. Even though LinkedIn bought SlideShare, it is still a standalone application and I recommend creating an account at www.slideshare.net if you do not already have one. According to their website, SlideShare is one of the world's largest presentation-sharing communities, and it allows you to share presentations and documents with your LinkedIn network. If it's in a presentation format, you can upload it: your résumé, testimonials, portfolio, conference presentation, marketing and sales presentations, and so forth. As long as it is in Microsoft PowerPoint, PDF, Word Document, Keynote, or iWork format, you shouldn't have a problem. One of the things that makes SlideShare exciting is that (at this time) it is the only way you can also upload video to play automatically on your profile (you can upload video into Box.net but people have to find the video and then click on it to play). SlideShare is much more effective.

To upload a presentation from within LinkedIn, find SlideShare under Get More Applications, click the SlideShare app icon, and click Add Application. As soon as you add SlideShare, you can choose the presentation you want to upload.

Adding Video to SlideShare

To upload a video into a presentation, which you can then show on SlideShare, open your PowerPoint presentation (or your Keynote presentation or your Word document), click Insert, and add a video. Resize your presentation so that it fills most of your slide. Save your presentation somewhere that's easy to find. I save my presentations on my desktop.

Upload your presentation into SlideShare. You may want to rename it with a call to action before you upload it into LinkedIn. For instance, you might name it something like **Accounting Skills: Click Here to Learn More**.

To add a presentation at SlideShare.net, visit www.slideshare.net and upload the presentation. Once your presentation is uploaded into SlideShare, go into LinkedIn and open the SlideShare application. Since you now—or if you already have—a SlideShare account, click the Account link. Choose the presentation you want to upload. If you don't have a SlideShare account yet, you can also choose to upload your presentation that you've created from your desktop. Click Upload, and then select the file you want to upload, as shown in Figure 7.17.

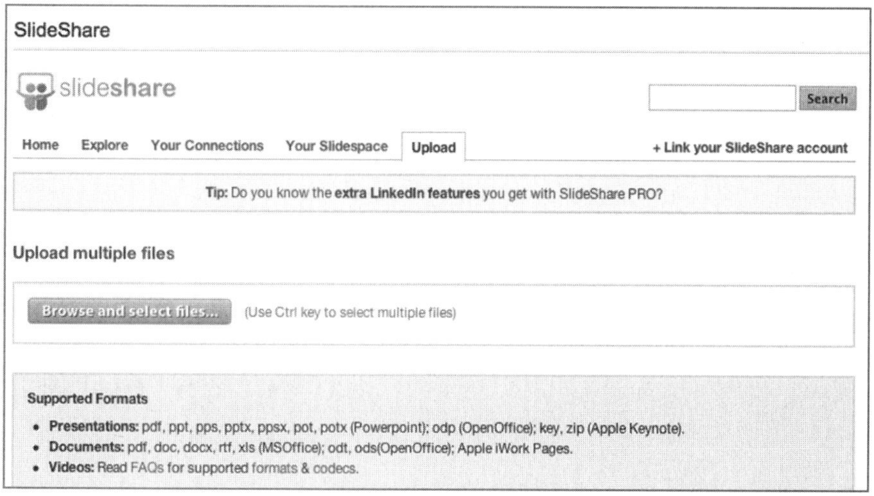

Figure 7.17 Uploading SlideShare

Finally, click View Profile to make sure that your presentation uploaded correctly. Sometimes it takes a few minutes for your presentation to upload, so if it's not there right away check again in 10 minutes or so.

Note: With LinkedIn's purchase of SlideShare, SlideShare has added a few more options for its Pro users. If you pay for your SlideShare account (even if you have a free LinkedIn account), you will receive a complete dashboard with SildeShare's Pro analytics, showing the number of uploads, views, favorites, and comments you are receiving on LinkedIn, and you will get a customizable and interactive widget called Portfolio Widget for displaying your portfolios on their LinkedIn public profile. Pro accounts start at $19 a month.

Thursday: Share with Projects and Teamspaces

A company named Manymoon (recently purchased by Do.com) has created an application called Projects and Teamspaces that works well on LinkedIn, allowing you to create projects, assign tasks, and share documents with people in your professional LinkedIn network. On their original home page, Manymoon said that the Projects and Teamspaces app can be used by professionals for any purpose in any industry: sales for lead management, recruiters for applicant tracking, consultants to manage client projects, and nonprofit to coordinate volunteer initiatives. You can use the Projects and Teamspaces app solely within LinkedIn, or you can track it from your Manymoon.com or Do.com account.

If you already have a Manymoon account, click the "Already have a Manymoon account?" link. If you don't have an account, click Create Project. Name your project and then you will get the opportunity to register to get more features.

Once you have set up your account, you can start assigning tasks to somebody in your network. You can give them a due date and under Additional Options choose the priority level of their assigned task. You can even add the project to your personal calendar. In addition, you can add comments, files, or Google Docs, as shown in Figure 7.18.

If you want to skip the endless email train back and forth between project participants, and you all are on LinkedIn (or have this application), you might consider Projects and Teamspaces. I like it because it adds the element of tracking and accountability to a project. Since I use Google Docs anyway, this is a natural fit.

Let's say you are doing a website redesign for a client. You have a web designer, a social media strategist, a coder, an email marketing specialist, yourself as project manager, and of course your client. You all use LinkedIn. You can use Google Docs to share information, and then assign tasks through Projects and Teamspaces to all your contractors and consultants. You give them By When dates and then add those dates to your calendar (and tell them to do so as well). When a date comes up and their contribution has not been added, you have proof of the conversation and of their duties. And leverage.

Figure 7.18 Projects and Teamspaces app

If you use have a virtual assistant (VA), you are going to *love* this tool! If you're collaborating on a project, you can track who is doing what and their progress. And because there's so many due dates and calendaring tools, it adds another level of accountability.

Friday: Get WordPress or Blog Link

If you write a blog, you will definitely want to consider adding either the WordPress or the Blog Link app to your profile. Both can be found under Get More Applications.

If you have a WordPress blog, use the WordPress app on LinkedIn. Click the WordPress link and then click Add Application. LinkedIn will ask you for your WordPress URL. You can use this tool with a myname.wordpress.com account as well as with a vanity URL like www.linkedintobusiness.com. Once WordPress is linked to your LinkedIn account, it will automatically populate on your profile and LinkedIn home page if you choose to view it there.

If you don't have a WordPress account but you do have a blog, use the Blog Link app. As with the WordPress app, all you have to do is click the Blog Link app icon and then choose to display it on your profile or LinkedIn home page. Unlike with

WordPress, you can add your blog to at least one of your websites (in Edit Profile). Blog Link will pull content from that link.

Given the two choices, I prefer WordPress. I think the layout looks better. However, Blog Link will import pictures as well as text, so it is a personal choice as to which blog application you use and the layout you prefer.

If you are a content creator, you might choose to pull your blogging application up higher in your profile so that people see it sooner.

Note: If you don't have your own blog, you can import someone else's blog into your profile. For instance, you as an individual might not have a blog but maybe your company has a blog. Import it. Or maybe you don't have your own blog, but you often write guest posts for another blog. Import it.

Coders: Read This!

Here's a brief overview of GitHub, a LinkedIn app.

If you are a coder, you might want to check out GitHub, because it allows you to show off your programming projects with other coders and, on LinkedIn, with your network.

To get started, add the GitHub application on LinkedIn. Then choose the Link option so that your GitHub account will post your projects on LinkedIn. If this sounds like Greek to you, don't worry. GitHub probably doesn't apply to you. However, if you do coding, you may very well want to create a GitHub account if you haven't done so yet.

The GitHub open source tool is free. For similar tools you'd pay anywhere from $7 to $200 a month. Not only can you list your own projects with GitHub, but you can see other projects you are following and send updates on projects you're working on. When you link your account to GitHub, just make sure that you uncheck any project you don't want to be seen on LinkedIn! It takes about 24 hours before updates can be reflected on your LinkedIn profile.

Coders may also want to check out `http://developer.linkedin.com` to view LinkedIn's APIs and Developer programs. While LinkedIn is fairly conservative with its APIs, it is also open to working with coders and even offers a Certified Developers Program.

Week 22: Exploring Industry-Based and LinkedIn Apps

Let's take a look at some more industry-based third-party apps.

Note: More beta applications (which we'll be talking about in Chapter 11) can be found at http://www .linkedinlabs.com. In addition, you can see other third-party applications that are using LinkedIn's APIs to develop apps you can use with LinkedIn at `https://developer.linkedin.com/` `certified-developer-program`.

Monday: Explore Apps for Legal, Business, and Creative Professionals

Take a quick look at all the other third-party apps that LinkedIn has to offer.

JD Supra Legal Updates

I'll spend a lot more time on JD Supra's Legal Updates later in Chapter 11, but for now, those of you who are attorneys or work in the legal field, know that Legal Updates will likely be an incredibly important application for you.

The Legal Updates feature allows you to post and read legal updates relevant to your area of legal expertise:

- Legal documents
- Court filings
- Legal articles
- Newsletters
- Client alerts
- Repurposed blog posts
- Legal forms
- Checklists
- Templates
- Fillable forms
- Contracts (for public record)
- Other transactional docs

These can be read and uploaded directly on your LinkedIn Legal Updates page, as shown in Figure 7.19.

What I like about Legal Updates is that you can customize your legal updates with the subjects and the specialties that are relevant to you. You don't have to read about banking and finance law if your focus is real estate law.

Another excellent thing about JD Supra is that when you upload an article, your name and profile is attached to that article. This increases top-of-mind awareness, and also makes it easier for the people reading the article to get in contact with you (or for you to get in contact with the writer of an article that interests you). This is obviously much easier than trying to track down the contact information for the author of an article you might have read in a journal. If you have any questions about the article, or would like to make a connection, all you have to do is click on the author's name and LinkedIn will take you to their LinkedIn profile, where you can send them a message, an InMail, get introduced to them, and so forth.

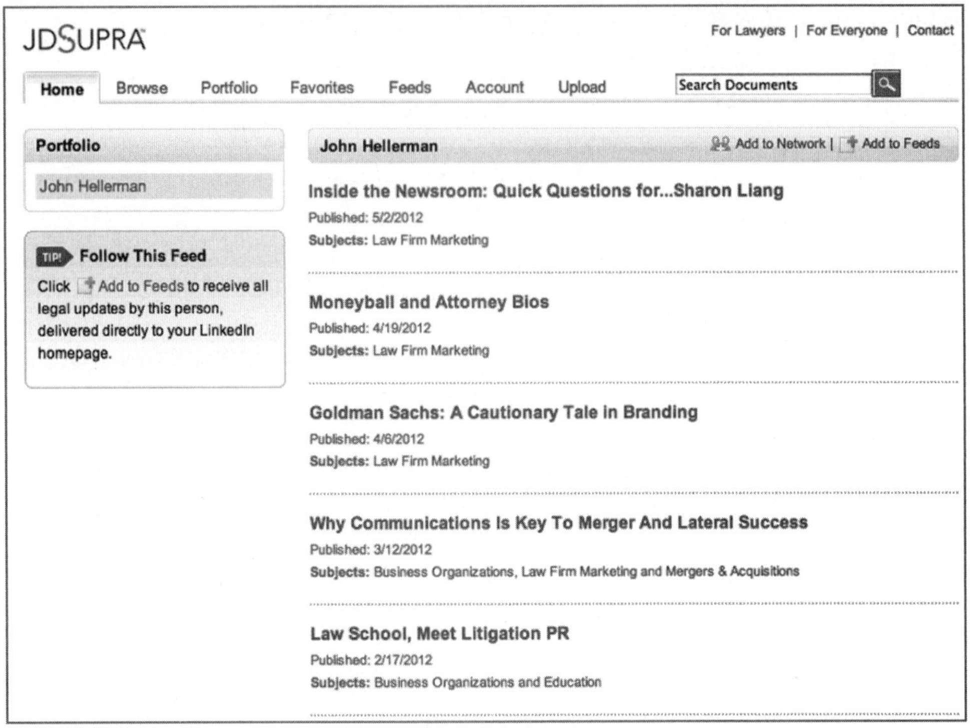

Figure 7.19 Legal Updates

To find Legal Updates by JD Supra, just go to the application on your LinkedIn profile, where you will be able to, according to JD Supra, upload documents, search documents, browse articles by subject or popularity, create a portfolio of your own documents, access legal eagle feeds, and even create favorite documents so that they're easy to come back to.

Martindale-Hubbell Lawyer Ratings

Another legal application that LinkedIn offers is Lawyer Ratings by Martindale-Hubbell. If you have already received client review and peer review ratings, why wouldn't you link those to your LinkedIn profile? This will help to substantiate any stated credentials on your LinkedIn profile. You can also provide a link so that your clients can create a client review just by clicking a button right within your own profile.

The Martindale-Hubbell ratings review is a free service, so if you are a legal professional, especially if you're starting out, consider this service and application.

FT Press E-Bookshelf

FT Press created an application for LinkedIn called E-Bookshelf. This application allows you to find quick and concise business and career lessons from top experts, as shown in Figure 7.20. Although you have to buy credits to purchase these articles, FT Press gives you three free credits to get started on LinkedIn.

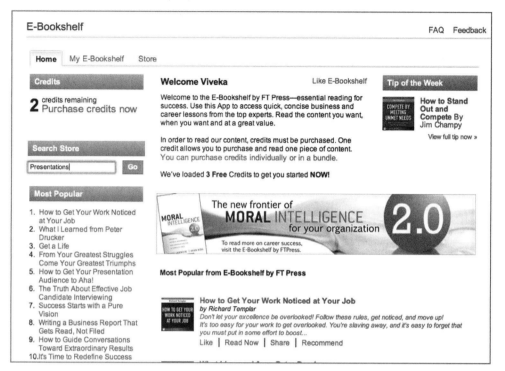

Figure 7.20 E-Bookshelf app

I've only played around a little with this application, mostly using the free credits, and it does look like there are some decent articles by top experts. E-Bookshelf can tell you how to do everything from buying a car to creating a really awesome Microsoft PowerPoint presentation. You might as well upload the application, try it out, and remove it if you don't find it useful.

To see the articles you have purchased, click My E-Bookshelf. If you want to find an article, use the search field on the Home or Store tab.

Credits start at $1.99 each (and go down in price when you buy in bulk).

Rofo's Real Estate Pro

Real estate professionals can use Rofo's Real Estate Pro to list and promote client real estate transactions on their LinkedIn profile. According to LinkedIn, Real Estate Pro allows you to share the completed deals with your business connections as well as check your market, create a following, and promote your expertise while developing new business. Just be careful not to share any private information.

If you are looking for real estate or office space in the local marketplace, you might consider downloading Rofo for finding office space listings and property for sale. Sometimes you'll find listings that you won't find anywhere else. At the very least, it will give you some comparables.

Behance Creative Portfolio Display

According to LinkedIn, Creative Portfolio Display is a professional way to showcase your creative work in your LinkedIn Profile. Many of the cultural creatives are already using Behance as a social portfolio display of their work, so why not link it to your LinkedIn profile so that your LinkedIn network can see examples of your portfolio? Because it is a free and easy way to display your visual work and allows you to present creative projects done for past clients (or for your personal portfolio), it's a great application to consider.

While it is a little work intensive to create, once you have Behance Creative Portfolio Display up and running, it won't take much effort to update. If you have a great portfolio, you have a great opportunity to be hired through LinkedIn!

After installing the application, upload your portfolio in the Behance Network. Behance says on their website: "You can create an unlimited number of multimedia projects that include still images, video reels, text, and/or audio samples. You can select which projects are displayed on your LinkedIn profile."

Tuesday: Create an Amazon Reading List

As an author, I'm a big fan of Reading List by Amazon. It's surprising to me that many authors don't even have their own books listed here. So if you are an author and your book is listed on Amazon, then by all means make sure you upload your book, as shown in Figure 7.21.

The Amazon Reading List can be found on the More tab. To link the Reading List to your LinkedIn profile, select the Your Reading List tab and where it says "What Are You Reading?" start typing the name of your book. If you're not an author, you can type the name of any book you're reading right now.

Once you type your book name (or your name to find what books you have listed on Amazon), select the book that you found. Then click one of these:

- Read It
- I'm Reading It Now
- I've Read It

If you've read it, you'll also want to click I Recommend This Book, especially if it's your book. You now have 5,000 characters to tell people why they should read your book.

The other cool thing about Reading List is you can also see what your network is reading. How do you use this? If you know what books people are reading, you know their interests and it gives you some good talking points when you reach out to someone for the first time or when you reconnect with someone.

You can check for updates by industry or by connection. You can also go right into your connection's profile and check for books they've been reading recently.

Figure 7.21 Reading List by Amazon

Note: If you're a job seeker, and you've managed to find the profile of the person who will be interviewing you, check their LinkedIn profile to see what they've been reading. And then read it yourself. When they interview you, you might quote the book, or mention the author's name (which is why you should read it first). They might be amazed at the synchronicity of you knowing the book they just read, or just how intelligent you are because you read the same types of books they do!

Wednesday: Engage Your Audience with Polls

LinkedIn polls can be an excellent tool to collect feedback and engage with your audience. I think polls have become more popular for two reasons: First, they don't take much time; you can read and answer a poll in less than 10 seconds. Second, LinkedIn polls provide immediate the demographic feedback of who answered the question (and what they answered).

As LinkedIn says, "Add the Polls application and leverage the wisdom of millions of business professionals on LinkedIn." LinkedIn polls allow you to easily find answers to your business and market research questions. How do CEOs respond to your question? Do 25-year-olds answer differently than 45-year-olds? Do men and women answer differently? Once you ask your question, LinkedIn will distribute your poll to your connections, and even make it viewable to your entire LinkedIn network. You can share your poll through Facebook or Twitter, and embed the voting module on your own website or blog.

Consider your goals when creating your poll:

- To engage with your tribe in general.
- For market research. (Be aware this is not going to be statistically accurate.)
- To engage with an existing client or customer (for top-of-mind awareness).
- To engage with a potential client or customer (by asking leading questions).

LinkedIn polls can:

- Help you get more information about your market
- Clarify your message to be more impactful
- Test receptivity to new products or services
- Find new clients
- Keep you top of mind with your connections

Like with all social media and indeed marketing in general, you will want to measure the results of your poll very carefully. Apart from the results of the poll, you can see a few demographics as well such as age, seniority within a company (based on job title), and gender. Polls are a great source of general information, but not all polls are statistically valid. If you're simply posting a poll on your website or letting it run viral, that sample is not truly random. It's generally self-selected and that means that you have to read that data with care.

To create a poll, click the Polls link on the More tab. This allows you to see your existing polls as well as polls you've created, answered, or added to your profile.

Ask a question and give up to five responses. (I recommend using Other › Please Comment as your fifth option.) Use a conversational tone when creating your question and answers.

Here are the limitations, according to LinkedIn:

- Questions can be no more than125 characters.
- Up to five responses are allowed at 40 characters each.
- Responders can choose only one answer.

Once you've created your poll, you can share it on LinkedIn, Twitter, or Facebook. You can also create and share your polls in your Group Discussion field, as mentioned earlier in this book.

Once you have created a poll, you can keep an eye on it in the Polls section, as shown in Figure 7.22.

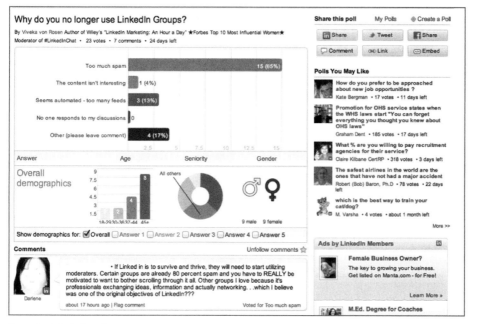

Figure 7.22 LinkedIn polls

You can see the answers and the demographics of the people who responded. You can continue to share your poll from this page. Note that the LinkedIn Share button on this page acts like the Sharing bookmarklet by allowing you to share in a status update, on Twitter, in groups, and with individuals. This feature is a lot more substantial than the LinkedIn Share when you first create the poll (which just goes out to the general LinkedIn membership).

You can share the link and even embed the poll in your blog. You can comment on the poll yourself and see the comments of those who took your poll. LinkedIn will email you any poll comments.

I just love the Polls feature and always have success connecting and re-engaging with my tribe when I use it. Go ahead and create a poll right now. Send it to me! I'll be happy to respond.

Thursday: Organize Your Travel with My Travel

TripIt.com has created the My Travel app that organizes travel plans into an itinerary that has all of your trip details in one place. According to TripIt, the free account allows you to automatically create itineraries by forwarding confirmation emails to plans@tripit.com; create custom itineraries; add maps, directions, travel notes, photos, recommendations, and more; and easily access your itinerary online, via mobile devices, calendar feeds, or social sites (like LinkedIn!). You can also share itineraries with family, friends, and co-workers to keep them in the know and connect with them on the road, as shown in Figure 7.23.

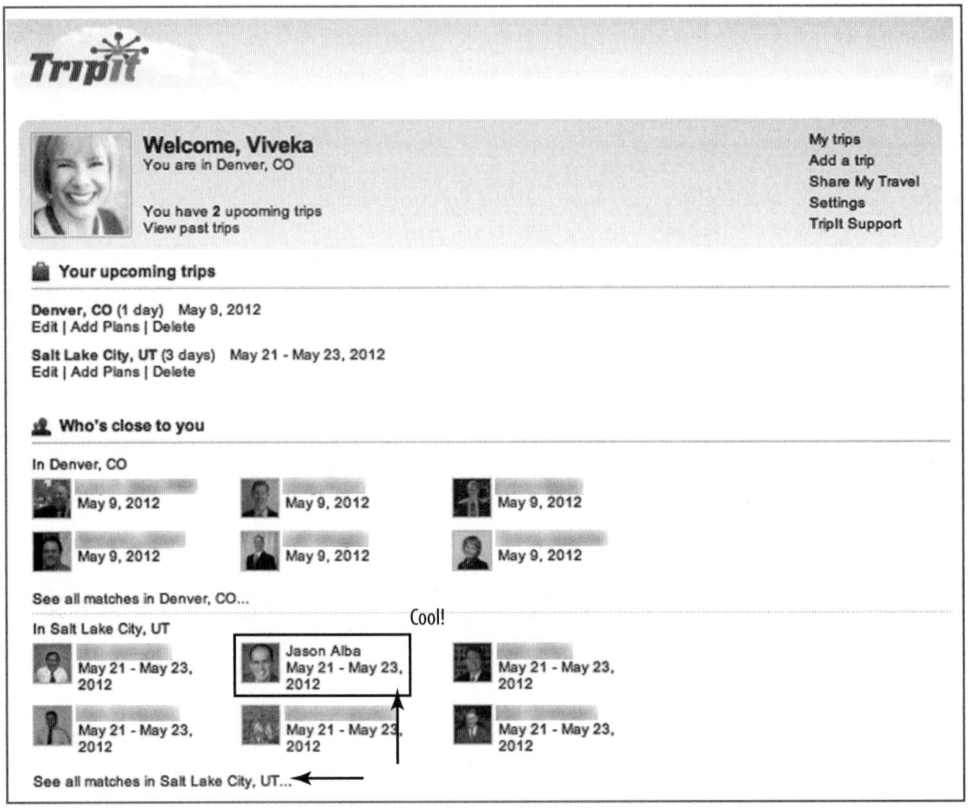

Figure 7.23 My Travel by TripIt

Use the My Travel app by TripIt. It lets people in your network know where you are going to be so they can contact *you* for a meeting. One of the best things to do with LinkedIn is find individuals to meet with face to face (F2F). However, even if you live in or near a big city, it's not always the local person who is the perfect person.

Fortunately my job allows for a lot of travel, and so I use My Travel to turn my URL LinkedIn experience into an IRL (in real life) F2F meeting. And you don't have to travel as much as I do to make it work. Any trip you take—even a family vacation—can result in a game-changing meeting.

My Travel not only tells you when your connections are traveling, but also lets them know when you are traveling. And what else are you going to do on the 6-hour layover in Phoenix? Might as well meet with a LinkedIn connection who also has a layover in Phoenix at the same time! Alan Martin, an Oracle professional, uses TripIt to plan and organize trips with colleagues in order to facilitate meetings and save on resources and expenses.

My Travel is on the More tab. Once you have created an account with TripIt, you can check out these features:

- My Trips
- Add A Trip
- Share My Travel
- Settings
- TripIt Support

My Trips are the trips you have booked (and previous trips). You can add a trip here (although if you set up an account with TripIt, it will automatically add any trip you send to plans@tripit.com and even that can be automated). I think the Share My Travel link is pretty nifty too. You can pick who in your network you want to share your travel with, and LinkedIn will allow you to send a link (to sign up for TripIt) in a message to up to 50 people at a time. You can customize the message to say whatever you want it to say. If you don't want LinkedIn to share your travel in an update, you can adjust those settings in Settings. And if you have any questions, TripIt Support is there for you.

The other really cool feature is your travel stats. When someone asks you if you travel much you'll have the number of trips you've made, cities and countries you have traveled to, miles you have traveled, and days you've been on the road all in one place (year-to-date [YTD] and Total).

Friday: Use Skills

The Skills feature allows you to add your own unique skills to your LinkedIn profile. We already looked at Skills (on the More tab) to find Related Skills you can use as keywords. But what else does this feature do?

First, LinkedIn pulls a description of the skill from Wikipedia. If you are having a hard time finding things to put into the Experience section of your profile, consider using information from this section to describe your skills in more depth.

LinkedIn also lets you know the relative growth (popularity) of your skill on LinkedIn. Don't let this keep you from adding a skill; it's some good information to tuck away.

LinkedIn shows you which of its members are most proficient in your skill. I find this section particularly useful. LinkedIn gives you members' first and last names—which you can't get in a search unless they are a first-level connection (with the free account). It's good to be connected to Influencers, and that's exactly who these people are!

To the right of the LinkedIn professionals, you will see companies to whom this skill is relevant. They might be good prospects for you to follow. You can follow a company right from Skills. Then LinkedIn informs you of both updates and job opportunities from these companies.

LinkedIn also suggests groups you might be interested in based on your skills. Sometimes these are more relevant than groups you find on your own in the Groups directory. You can join a group right on this page.

If you are a job seeker, Skills will suggest jobs that have been posted that need people with your skills. You can apply for the job (or at least check it out) right from this page.

Skills is pretty much one-stop shopping on LinkedIn! If I only have a short time to show people the power of LinkedIn, I'll give them a quick tour of Skills and that is usually all I need to do to convince people of LinkedIn's significance.

So there you have it! Who knew so much was hidden on the More tab on LinkedIn? Keep an eye on this section since this is often where LinkedIn will stick its newest services or applications—all of which can be extremely important in marketing your business!

Guess what? This concludes the architecture of LinkedIn. Now you know where everything is and how to use it. It's time to get into the really fun part of strategizing your marketing with your new LinkedIn knowledge.

Week 23: Putting It All Together

Even though you have spent the previous chapters learning all the tools and practices you can implement using LinkedIn in an hour a day, we haven't really gotten into specific, repeatable, daily practices.

One of my favorite parts of working with clients is helping them to create daily LinkedIn strategies to produce powerful connections and dramatic increases in business resulting from those relationships based on their goals and strategies.

How you communicate on LinkedIn will be a direct result of these goals and strategies, as well as your new daily, weekly, and monthly practices.

Chapter Contents

Monday: Use Updates for Inbound Marketing
Tuesday: Use LinkedIn Signal
Wednesday: Create a Powerful Inbound Marketing Connections Strategy
Thursday: Showcase Your Skills in Answers
Friday: Understand 3 and 3

Monday: Use Updates for Inbound Marketing

If the concept of inbound marketing is, as described by Wikipedia, "earning the attention of prospects… by producing content [that] customers value," then it becomes very important on LinkedIn to create and share content that your network finds valuable and might want to share with their network. Fortunately, the tools LinkedIn gives us—status updates, messages, group discussions, and Answers—make this simple (if not easy). The key is to set up a system helping you to create and share content in an organized, efficient, regular, and effective way. So here's what we'll be doing in this chapter:

- Pulling together your content
- Setting up a system
- Setting up your schedule
- Using both LinkedIn and third-party tools to share information

Planning Status Updates Related to Your LinkedIn Goals

In this section I will walk you step by step through the process I use to plan status updates that will specifically help you reach your LinkedIn-related goals. I like to use a table or spreadsheet to help me plan and keep track.

Open a new document. It can be a Word document or if you are comfortable working with spreadsheets, I recommend opening your spreadsheet application of choice. (I use Excel.)

At the top of your page enter **LinkedIn Goal**, and then in a second column enter your primary goal or goals for being on LinkedIn. It can be for any of the reasons that follow, or something we haven't stated. Remember, your goal goes beyond the promotion of a single product, service, or event company. Why are *you* on LinkedIn? How are you using LinkedIn to promote all that you are and all that you offer? How are you using LinkedIn to promote your personal brand? Perhaps you are using it to:

- Attract new clients and customers
- Create new referral partner relationships
- Attract affiliates/downlines
- Position yourself as a thought leader or subject matter expert
- Drive traffic to your website
- Share information about your company
- Attract donors and sponsors to your charity
- Position your Internet marketing business
- Find candidates
- Find a job
- Other

In a third column enter any URL you want to reference in your updates (your blogsite, website, About Us page, etc.). If your status update gets found in a Google search, you want there to be a link for folks to click on, right?

In a fourth column, include the keywords that are relevant to your LinkedIn goal(s). Why? As I just mentioned, search engines love social media, and if you have your keywords in a post you have a good chance of that post showing up on a web search. And of course LinkedIn Signal will definitely pick up on those keywords. Use a few of these keywords in each of your weekly status updates.

Open your calendar, or if you use one, a scheduling tool like BufferApp.com or Hootsuite.com. Some of my clients like to write their monthly updates ahead of time and post them in column 5. I usually just make a note of what I will reference or write about. If you use a scheduling tool like Hootsuite, you can also write all your updates ahead of time and upload them to be posted over time. (Be aware there are sometimes glitches and Hootsuite will release the posts all together.)

Now all you have to do is schedule and/or post your status updates for the week or month. Creating status updates to support your overreaching goal for being on LinkedIn is a continual process of sharing relevant information on a regular and steady diet to your network.

By scheduling them ahead of time, or at least by creating a road map of your status updates, you will be building a firm foundation for your inbound marketing strategy. Think of it as painting a picture one steady brushstroke at a time. You can always "impulsively" add a status update or use LinkedIn's sharing bookmarklet to post any article you find interesting. But using this simple planning method will ensure that you have no gaps in your update stream for potential clients to fall through.

You can see my workbook in Figure 8.1.

Status Update Worksheet				
Goal for LinkedIn		URL	Keywords	Updates
	Thought Leader Positioning		LinkedIn Expert, LinkedIn Author, LinkedIn Speaker, LinkedIn Trainer, LinkedIn Profile, LinkedIn Optimization, LinkedIn B2B	Tips
	Engage with Prospective Clients		B2B, Legal Professionals, Professionl Women, CEO, CMO, Entrepreneurs, SMB	Article for LIL and JD Supra
	PR		LinkedInChat, MediaChat, SMManners, MASHABLE, SME, LinkedNinja	Reference
Campaign Strategies				
May	Events	URL for event	Keywords	Updates
5/17/12	Social Media Buzz Club Webinar	www.socialbuzzclub.com	LinkedIn Tips	post event
5/23/12	Keynote for Phototronics - Utah		LinkedIn Sales Tips	
5/24/12	Social Media Lab	www.larimer.org/jobseeker	Social Media, Jobseekers, LinkedIn for Jobseekers, Facebook rules	post event
5/30/12	Webinar for Marketing Profs	www.marketingprofs.com	LinkedIn things you may not know	tips and event
5/31/12	WBOnline Bootcamp Webinar	www.wbonline.com/linkedin	LinkedIn for women, LinkedIn Strategies	event and tips
5/31/12	BeFoundJobs Webinar	www.befoundjobs.com	linkedin for jobseekers	tips and event
June				
6/2/12	HBC Seminar - New Jersey			

Figure 8.1 Status update calendar

Planning Campaign-Specific Status Updates

You can either create a new workbook or a new area in the workbook you created for goal-related status updates. The first column should be called **Campaign Strategies** (or whatever you want to name your time- or event-sensitive campaigns).

To refresh yourself, open your calendar to see what events, product launches, tradeshows, or projects you have coming up that will influence your status update campaign strategy:

- Share information about your products and services
- Sell your books
- Share information about an event
- Get speaking gigs
- Other

> **Note:** If you use an editorial calendar, it will give you a better overview of what is going on and what holes you might have in your schedule. An editorial calendar as social media content creators use it (that is, you) helps control your media, what you are saying, and where you are sharing by the different social media platforms over time. Some people like to attach or even merge this worksheet with their editorial calendar (Evernote is a good tool to use), although I prefer to keep my editorial calendar, status update worksheet, and Scheduler as separate documents.

You can create a monthly, bimonthly, quarterly, or even yearly spreadsheet. It just depends on how much you have going on that you want to promote. I try to do a few months at a time, listing both month and date in the first column. Needless to say, this is an ever-changing worksheet as I add last-minute events, PR opportunities, and webinars to it.

Add the event or campaign title in the second column. In a third column, list any URLs relevant to your campaign. In a fourth column list relevant resources and any keywords that are pertinent to your upcoming campaigns. You might want to create a fifth column to keep track of the status updates. Have you posted it yet?

You can get the spreadsheet I use with clients at www.sybex.com/go/linkedinhour.

When it comes to time-sensitive campaigns, you'll create more focused bursts of communication in the hopes of generating excitement and energy for your event, launch, tradeshow, job search, candidate recruitment, tax season, and so forth.

Some people will choose to schedule reminders for themselves right in their Microsoft Outlook or business calendars. This is useful if you are disciplined, or are concerned about the changing nature of your business and want to keep things a little more fluid.

Some people will utilize third-party applications to schedule and post their status updates. Tools like Bufferapp.com and Hootsuite.com will allow you to not only schedule your updates strategically, but also post them for you. The paid account on Hootsuite even allows you to upload a "bulk scheduler" so you can upload all your posts in one fell swoop! Here is an example of a Hootsuite posting in Figure 8.2.

The key is having a system and sticking to it!

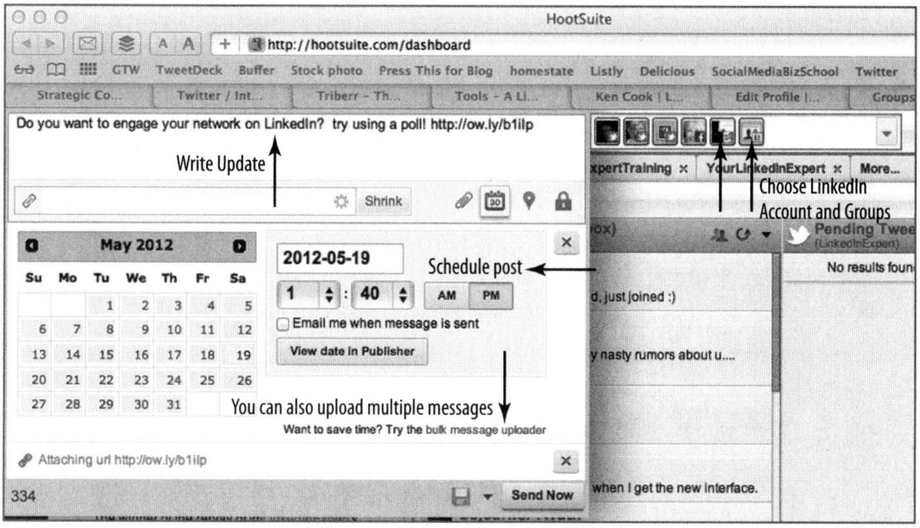

Figure 8.2 Schedule your updates with Hootsuite.

Tuesday: Use LinkedIn Signal

I briefly mentioned LinkedIn Signal in Chapter 2, but let's do a quick review here. To find Signal, you can either go to www.linkedin.com/signal or click Signal on the News tab. Now you have the ability to search any status update or tweet that you network has posted on LinkedIn. And respond to them!

LinkedIn Signal is one of my absolute favorite tools for monitoring my brand, as well as finding, connecting to, and building relationships with potential clients customers, vendors, employees or employers, or partners. According to LinkedIn, Signal casts a professional lens on LinkedIn and Twitter updates by:

- Letting you see what industries, companies, and geographic locations are saying about any topic

- Showing you a quick survey of links that are trending around any topic

- Narrowing down your search to see only links shared by your immediate connections

I like Signal because it allows you to communicate and build relationships with people who are not first-level connections.

To prepare for using LinkedIn Signal effectively, we need to first create, implement, monitor, and respond to our search lists. In this chapter, I will walk you step by step through:

- Creating search lists: Critical, Important, and Somewhat Relevant

- Monitoring your lists daily, weekly, monthly, and quarterly

- Responding to your search

Creating Your Lists

By now you probably realize that I'm a big fan of repurposing content. So let's take a look at some of the lists you pulled together in Chapter 5, "Weeks 10–15: Creating and Managing a Network That Works," Week 11 (when I had you create a strategic list of connections):

- Make or review your list of the Influencers in your industry you would like to create a relationship with
- Make or review a list of executives in your company
- Make or review your list of clients
- Make or review a list of potential clients
- Make or review a list of the products and services you offer right now
- Make or review a list of products or services you've offered in the past
- Make or review a list of products or services that you are considering offering
- Make or review a list of competitors
- Make or review a list of your competitors' products and services

Go through all of these lists and create a master list of those companies, people, products, or services that are most important for you or your company to keep a daily eye on at this time. Create another list of companies, people, products, or services that are not crucial to your business but that you still might want to keep an eye on. Create a third list of people, products, and services to keep handy just in case.

Monitoring Your List

Go to www.LinkedIn.com/signal and do a search for every company, person, product, or service in the first list, and then save those searches. You will probably want to click on these saved searches weekly, if not daily (Figure 8.3).

Save the second list to your desktop. Put a reminder in your calendar to do a monthly Signal search on these companies, people, products, or services. In some cases you might want to schedule a weekly search.

Finally, calendar a quarterly review of the third list. You can do a Signal search on these individuals, but you might also want to see if there are any people, products, services, or companies that need to be moved to list 1 or 2.

Responding to Your Searches

I know I've mentioned more than once that one of the issues people come up against when using LinkedIn is the inability to easily interact with people who are not first-level connections. We looked at using groups to do that, and here is another solution.

Figure 8.3 LinkedIn Signal searches

When you find an individual on Signal with whom you want to interact, all you have to do is comment on their status update or tweet. Now you have that "first touch" and can send them a request to connect, referencing how you "met" via Signal. You can just carry on a conversation on Signal. Let's look at some of the people you can interact with.

Influencer

When you get a search result on an *Influencer* you've been wanting to connect with, go ahead and comment on their update. If you are using a customer relationship management (CRM) tool, make a note that you responded to their comment. As soon as possible, ask if they would be open to connecting, and then send them an invitation. Because this is Signal, you can respond to a comment (or a tweet) even if the person is outside your network.

If you are not currently using a CRM, then consider ConnectedHQ or JibberJobber. More details on those tools appear in Chapter 10, "LinkedIn Ads, Labs, Apps, and Tools."

Note: Ninja Trick: If you are having a hard time connecting with someone on LinkedIn, see if they are on Twitter and connect with them there.

Client/Customer/Candidate/Constituent/Congregant

If you see a key *client* or *customer* has posted a status update (on anything), or has been mentioned *in* the status update, then comment or respond to that status update.

If it is an important client, make a note in your CRM. This lets them know that you are interested in them, keeping an eye on them, and are sharing their good news. It only takes a moment and it might go a very long way in enforcing Top of Mind Awareness (TOMA) and goodwill.

If you see that an *existing or prospective client* or *customer* has been mentioned in a status update in a *positive way*, perhaps send them an email, give them a phone call, or send them a message through LinkedIn congratulating them.

Mentions of Your Company, Product, or Service or a Competitor's

Just as you would use Google Alerts to monitor mentions of your competition or your company, products, and services on Google, you can use Signal to monitor those mentions on LinkedIn.

Make a list of the people, places, companies, products, and services you want to monitor. Monitor them weekly (or even daily). Use the opportunities provided to reach out to the person of interest. Use LinkedIn's communications tools to develop your relationship. As soon as possible, take the communication to email, a phone call, or a face-to-face meeting.

Compliments and Opportunities

If someone has complimented your company, product, or service in a status update, thank them by commenting on their status update, emailing them, phoning them, or sending them a message through LinkedIn. If you thank them by responding to their comments on Signal, it will be visible to the public and that is good publicity. But if you phone or email them, your communication will be more personal and will probably do more to build your relationship with the person. You know the best way to respond to your customers or clients. Maybe do both?

If someone has mentioned needing a product or service that you offer, by all means reach out to them through status updates, or if you can, through Twitter or a message via LinkedIn.

Complaints

If someone has complained about a competitor or a competitor's product or service, and you feel comfortable doing so, you might reach out to that individual and let them know about your product or service that will meet their needs. At the very least, you might want to keep a file of complaints.

If someone has complained about your product, service, or company, whether justified or unjustified, handle it. Immediately. Thank them for their response, apologize for the breakdown or misunderstanding (or clarify the misunderstanding if they are wrong), and then, if necessary, do what you need to in order to make it right. And do this publicly if possible. One of the best things you can do is turn someone unhappy about your product or service into an advocate by listening to them, acknowledging their complaint, and making it better!

Of course there will be some haters out there. Fortunately, they leave behind them a stinky trail of dissatisfaction and negativity that everyone can see. I rarely give haters the time of day. However, if a complaint is valid, address it.

Note: While I was teaching a class on how to use LinkedIn Signal, one of the participants did a keyword search on the words: "I need a (service)." This search resulted in a tweet that showed up in LinkedIn Signal that read: "I need a (service) for an event this weekend." He immediately commented on this person's update letting them know he was local (he looked at her profile) and could provide the service she needed. They connected on LinkedIn and he was able to create a relationship with her. They ended up doing business together, and she became one of his best clients. All through LinkedIn Signal. Not all LinkedIn Signal searches will result in communications that lead to great business relationships, but some might!

If you are diligent in searching and monitoring LinkedIn Signal, you have an amazing opportunity to find and connect with exactly the right people to build your business, and it only takes a little prep work. To get the Signal Lists worksheet, go to www.sybex.com/go/linkedinhour.

Wednesday: Create a Powerful Inbound Marketing Connections Strategy

If you've ever used Facebook lists to send messages to targeted "friends," then you will be familiar with LinkedIn's tags. Use them to group your network into categories of people (they won't see what you have tagged them as) and then prepare a messaging campaign to those targeted connections. Let's look at how to:

- Use tags
- Craft your messages
- Create a PR calendar
- Send your messages

In the beginning of this book we talked about inbound marketing as a strategy you could use to attract clients, customers, constituents, colleagues, classmates, and congregants to you. That's what this next section is all about: creating a powerful, personalized inbound marketing connection strategy.

The formula to a successful inbound marketing is:

- Consistency
- Interesting, intriguing, and valuable information, shared in palatable portions
- Invested connections who hold you top of mind

Fortunately, LinkedIn is set up so that you can do this easily.

That being said, this isn't going to work unless you've gone through your network and tagged your connections. So if you've not yet done so, go back to Week 14 in Chapter 5, where we talked about how to manage your network by using tagging, and get to it!

Create Your Message Worksheet

Once you have all your connections tagged, copy and paste those tags from your profile into another document. I recommend the worksheet I shared in the previous section.

To get the LinkedIn Daily Practices Master worksheet, go to www.sybex.com/go/ linkedinhour.

For each LinkedIn tag, write a brief description of the *content* that a tagged group of individuals would find interesting. Then create another column with links to resources you can share over a period of time.

I don't recommend sending a message to your tagged group of connections more than twice a month. For each tagged group, find 24 pieces of content that you're going to want to share with them over a period of a year. You can replicate content, use your own content, or use a tool such as Technorati to find blog posts that would be relevant to your tagged connections.

Once you have created this document, you have an excellent road map for engaging with your niche markets on a consistent basis with content they're going to find intriguing, relevant, interesting, and valuable. And once you have created this document, you can always hand it off to an assistant and make sure they schedule the messages.

Craft Your Message

So now you know who you're going to write to, what you're going to write about, and when you're going to write them. But what is your actual message?

Note: Although LinkedIn messages won't allow for images, you can add links.

You probably don't want your messages to be any longer than two or three short paragraphs. Keep it under 300 words if possible. And remember, this is not a sales pitch! You want to write your targeted group a message that speaks specifically to their specialty or industry, that speaks to their point of pain, that speaks to their business and even personal needs. (And they don't need a sales pitch from you.)

Take a look at your tagged group, address them directly, and share the valuable piece of information (that you have listed in your worksheet). Add your signature. Under your signature you can write something like, "For more information about this topic, please feel free to contact us. This is what we love to do, and we'd love to do it for you."

Sample Message

Your message might look something like this:

"As a medical professional, you're far too busy to deal with the daily marketing of your practice. But you have a front-line defense. And it's literally your front office! Marketing your medical practice might make the difference between success and failure. Here's an interesting article I found about 10 easy ways your office staff can communicate with your patients to increase visibility and promote your business. [URL here]

I've used these tools with my clients over the years to great success. Wishing success to you!

[Signature Line]

For more information on how you can market your medical practice, please don't hesitate to call us at: (555) 555-5555 or email us at name@businessname.com.

Do you want to know how I came up with this simple yet powerful strategy? Because of three people in my network. I had over 24,000 first-level connections as of this writing. Do you want to know how many of those folks spring to mind when you say the term "recruiter" or "social media strategist" or "business development special-ist"? Even though there are literally thousands of those individuals in my network, I can name three. Why? Because about every two weeks these connections send out a message with a valuable tip focused on my industry. I almost always open those mes-sages. And when I need to use a recruiter, refer a social media strategist, or contact someone about business development, who do you think is going to spring to the top of my mind? That's how this works.

Sending Your Message

I've already had you create a schedule for your updates, so it's time to add your mes-sages to your calendar and schedule them for posting. At this time there is no way that I know of to automatically schedule and post messages to your tagged groups of connections, so you have to do this the old-fashioned way. Manually. (Or give it to an assistant or VA to do it for you.)

You can either write your message in full or compose a brief note describing the message. (I'll typically write something like "Send Potential Client Group a LinkedIn Tip on Keywords.") Because I have a worksheet that has the tagged groups and recommended resources referenced, it's just a matter of quickly looking at my document, writing the message, and sending it out.

Just as a refresher, in order to send messages, go to your Contacts tab and click Connections. Find the tagged group of connections that you want to send a message to and click on it, as shown in Figure 8.4.

Figure 8.4 Sending messages to tagged connections

Remember, if your tagged group of connections is under 50 people, you can just click Select All and Send Message. If you have more than 50 individuals in a tagged grouping, you will have to manually click on the names of the individuals to whom you want to send a message. Once you've checked off 50, click Send Message.

Craft a subject line and your message. Make your subject line and message intriguing or interesting. Grab your audience's attention. (May I note here that using the word free is 1: overdone, and 2: cheesy?)

For an excellent book on email marketing, consider *Email Marketing: An Hour a Day* by Jeanniey Mullen and David Daniels (Sybex, 2008).

At the bottom of the message, by default, LinkedIn will allow recipients to see each other's names and email addresses. This is a very bad idea. It's like accidentally CCing instead of BCCing your email list. Uncheck this please. You might also want to send yourself a copy, both to see your formatting and to keep as a record.

Over the years you will probably duplicate some of these messages over and over. Don't worry—no one is going to remember that you sent that exact same message two and half years ago. That being said, make sure you customize your content to your designated tagged group of connections. While I might send the same LinkedIn tip to five different tagged groupings, I will make it relevant to their industry or specialty.

The key is consistency when targeting your tagged connections with information that is relevant to them. Once they know, like, and trust you, they are far more likely to open the (very occasional) message that has your product or service offer or business request.

Thursday: Showcase Your Skills in Answers

I hate to belabor the point, but consistency is key when it comes to communicating and marketing with LinkedIn. We spent an entire week talking about Answers in Chapter 7, "Weeks 19–22: Get Strategic with LinkedIn's 'Other' Options," Week 19, so I want to spend this section helping you to:

- Find and create a litmus test for answering questions
- Create an Answers/blog schedule

Marketing via Best Answers

The first thing I recommend is taking a look at some of the individuals who have been vetted as experts by LinkedIn and by the members asking the questions. Look at that what they're doing; look at how often they're doing it. For some of you this is going to be an excellent strategy. You are full of information, you are considered experts in your field already, and answering questions on LinkedIn might be a natural channel for you to express your expertise and attract new clients.

Just a reminder: Answers is found on the More tab. The Experts are found on the bottom of the home page. These are the Top Experts (those who answered the most "Best Answer" questions that week) on LinkedIn.

If you would like to see the Experts for specific topic on LinkedIn, browse the topics on the right-hand side of the page. Click on a topic that you are interested in, or knowledgeable about, and the Experts will appear at the bottom of the new topic-specific page, as shown in Figure 8.5.

Choose an Expert, and click See All My Answers. This will take you to their home page, and on the right side, about halfway down, you will see a box that has their Q&A listed. Click the See Q&A link. This will take you to yet another page that has all their questions and all their answers.

This will give you a litmus test of the type of answers you need to be providing in order to be considered an Expert by the people asking the questions, and consequently by LinkedIn.

This strategy is not for everyone. But it can still give you a good idea of what kinds of answers are getting the most attention on LinkedIn.

Figure 8.5 Experts in LinkedIn

Scheduling Your Blog Using Answers

We already mentioned using Answers as blog fodder in Chapter 7. For those of you who blog regularly and have an editorial calendar, you already know that you're going to be writing about a certain topic at a certain time. You can use Answers to find other individuals asking similar questions and answering similar questions, and use that content, (with their permission) to bulk up your blog post if needed. You might even get one of the "answerers" to write a guest blog post for you.

If you know you are going to be writing a blog post about a specific topic, ask a question about that topic at least a few weeks ahead of time. Often you will get responses you might not have thought of yourself, and use these responses in your blog post. This is a great way to create new relationships and to get information you might not have thought of previously, and you can then refer to your blog post in your answer.

> **Note:** Don't forget to use Answers if you are looking at hiring a contractor or an employee. If you're vetting a candidate for your HR department, Answers truly will show you people's knowledge in a specific area, so it's a great way to research these individuals.

Friday: Understand 3 and 3

I can't remember where I heard about this technique, but it's a useful one for staying top of mind with your existing connections. I call it the 3 and 3 technique. It involves going through your list of connections, reaching out to three people you don't know and three people you do know (who you haven't talked to in a while), and sending them a simple message.

I know some of you will only be connected to people you know, and so just get rid of that second three. (By this I mean, don't worry about reaching out to three people you don't know, since you won't have any first-level connections you don't know.) Schedule the time to regularly reach out to three people you know, who you haven't talked to in a while, and ask them how they're doing through LinkedIn's messages.

You have access to their profile, so you can look at their recent activity and comment on a post, comment on an answer or question, comment on a job change or promotion. That's the great thing about LinkedIn. It provides you with the information you need to start a conversation.

I cannot tell you how many times I've used this technique and immediately heard back from a person who said, "I was just thinking about you." That's what I love. The synchronicity of social media. Even if we have to force the fact.

If you are not first-level connections, consider using introduction requests to get back in touch (and invite) people you know but haven't talked to in a while, or people you know peripherally or casually. It's a great way to generate "random" interactions and makes it less awkward if you need to ask for help later. Fill the funnel and stay in touch with people who can help your business before you actually need them!

I think it's pretty obvious why you might want to reach out to someone you haven't contacted in a while on LinkedIn, but why in the world would you send a message to a stranger? So you can get to know them! We don't know who we don't know who might make our next great employee, an excellent client, or a valuable referral partner. By simply going through your connections list and sending a quick message to someone you don't know, you're opening the lines for communication.

I usually write something like this:

I was just looking through my connections list on LinkedIn for people I'm connected to who I don't really know. I'm making an effort to turn names into valuable connections. In this spirit, I was hoping you might tell me more about who you are, what you do and who makes a good referral to you.

I noticed in your profile that (you do this thing/you work for this company/ you are interested in/you are skillful in).

I often (work with this industry/blog on this topic/need people with these skills). Can I use you as a referral?

Please feel free to write me back at any time and let me know a little bit more about yourself and what you do. I'm always trying to make my existing connections on LinkedIn more valuable and relevant.

Thanks for accepting my invitation and being in my network. I appreciate you.

Note: If you use a social CRM system such as Rapportive, Outlook Social Connector, Salesforce, or ConnectedHQ, quickly make a note in the CRM you are using. If you don't use a CRM, make a note in that person's profile. It would look weird if you sent them the same message two or three times in a row. Then you wouldn't look like an interested contact—you would look like a stalker! If you don't use a CRM, consider upgrading to a paid account so you can make notes on anyone in your network, not just first-level connections.

None of these techniques is particularly sophisticated; it's simple commonsense communications set to a regular schedule. As I mentioned at the beginning of this chapter, consistency is key.

Yes, this can be time-consuming, especially when you're setting up your system. But once you have a system in place, your communications shouldn't take you more than a couple minutes a day. And as you can see, much of this can be relegated to an assistant, a VA, a volunteer, or an intern.

In fact, in the next chapter, I will be sharing the checklist I use with my clients to keep them on task and on schedule.

Optimizing Your Time Using LinkedIn

*This chapter provides you with the checklists
I use with my clients. You will want to customize them to reflect your goals and campaigns
on LinkedIn.*

Chapter Contents

Getting Started on Your Checklist

Monthly, Daily, and Weekly Checklists

Checklists for Each Day of the Week

Getting Started on Your Checklist

If you have not yet completed your worksheets from Chapter 8, "Week 23: Putting It All Together," do so now. You will need to reference them when you start creating your checklists. The more thoroughly you have filled out your worksheet from the previous chapter, the easier it will be to get LinkedIn done—potentially 15 minutes a day or less!

You will notice that I have made a column to delegate some of the tasks to an assistant or virtual assistant (VA), which will certainly save you time. If you do have an assistant or VA who is going to help you with your LinkedIn presence, then make sure they have read this book and will work with you setting up the checklist.

The following tables are collected into a single reusable checklist, available on the book's download page: www.sybex.com/go/linkedinhour. Each table should be envisioned with check-off columns out to the right such as "VA or Me," "To Do," and "Done."

Tables 9.1 through 9.8 show the following:

- Profile and Network
- Updates
- Groups
- LinkedIn Answers
- Events
- Polls
- Applications
- Company Profile

Tables 9.9 through 9.13 show the following:

- Daily Action: Monday
- Daily Action: Tuesday
- Daily Action: Wednesday
- Daily Action: Thursday
- Daily Action: Friday

Monthly, Daily, and Weekly Checklists

Even though you have probably created your profile and network by this point, you will want to keep an eye on both, as shown in Table 9.1. I often see profiles that are sorely out of date. As you add businesses, products, or services to your business, make sure they are reflected in your profile as well.

Also, continue to strategically build your network according to your industry and location, and see Who You Might Know, people new to LinkedIn who might be colleagues or classmates, and who in your network you should connect and build relationships with. Be proactive. As Stacy Donovan Zapar says, "Whether you are a job seeker or business person, it is much more effective to build your network before you need it."

▶ **Table 9.1** Profile and Network

Focus	Action	Frequency
Profile	Check headline for accuracy.	Quarterly
Photo	Update photo. No 1970s glam shots!	Quarterly or as needed
Add Sections	Update Add Sections (Publications, Patents, Languages, Organizations, etc.).	Quarterly
Summary	Update Summary.	Quarterly or as needed
Skills	Update skills as you learn or master new ones.	Quarterly or as needed
Contact Me	Update Contact Me.	As needed
Search	Check for "Findability"—keyword people search.	Biweekly
Viewed My Profile	Check and respond to "Viewed My Profile."	Daily
Network Location	Check location and industry of your network.	Weekly or as needed
Add People You May Know	Check People You May Know and add connections.	Weekly
Network Statistics	Check for growth.	Daily
Recommendations	Add recommendations.	As needed
LinkedIn Blog	Check LinkedIn's Blog.	Weekly

In Chapter 8 you created worksheets for your Goal and Campaign updates. Implement those worksheets (and schedulers) by posting or scheduling your updates daily.

LinkedIn doesn't offer much in the way of monitoring and statistics, but you do have Signal. Make sure you are keeping an eye on what people say about you, your competition, and your clients, as shown in Table 9.2. This information can change daily.

▶ **Table 9.2** Updates

Focus	Action	Frequency
Updates Topics	LinkedIn Goal Status Updates, daily or upload into Scheduler.	Daily or via Scheduler
	Campaign Status Update, daily or upload into Scheduler.	Daily or via Scheduler

Continues

Focus	Action	Frequency
Signal	Add to (Edit) and Save Critical List Worksheet.	Monthly or as needed
	Search LinkedIn Signal for "Critical List."	Daily or Weekly
	Respond to updates when necessary.	Daily or Weekly

Your groups (Table 9.3) can be one of the best ways to engage your target audience and build relationships with relevant LinkedIn members. But you must be proactive in moderating your own group and participating in groups of which you are a member.

▶ **Table 9.3** Groups

Focus	Action	Frequency
Create Group	Create group following guidelines in Chapter 6.	One time
RSS Feed	Search for up to 50 RSS feeds (Technorati).	Monthly
Rules	Create rules and templates.	One time or as needed
Invite	Invite members.	One time
URL	Create bitly URL for group.	One time
Share URL	Share your group in email signature, on LinkedIn, Facebook and Twitter updates.	Daily
Announcements	Create weekly announcements and calendar.	Weekly or biweekly
Monitor	Monitor your group's discussions; make sure you moderate as needed.	Daily or weekly depending on your group's activity
Spammers	Delete those spammers. Be proactive! Keep your group interesting, relevant, and free of spam.	Daily or weekly as needed
Create Website for Group	Some people create a website or blog page describing their group (LinkedMinnesota is a good example).	One time
Other Groups	Participate in groups you are a member of. Read discussions. Respond when applicable. Most people only keep up with 3–5 groups.	Daily

LinkedIn Answers (Table 9.4) are a great way to find "blog fodder" and position yourself as an expert in your area or interest or industry. You can be very active in Answers, answering several a day, or just use them selectively for certain projects. In either case, having a system and a schedule will make your time in Answers more effective.

▶ **Table 9.4** LinkedIn Answers

Focus	Action	Frequency
Repurpose Content	Search questions asked in Answers on your area of expertise.	Weekly
Create Editorial Calendar	Create a list of blog topics/ Editorial Calendar (see worksheet from Chapter 8 or use your own).	Weekly/monthly/quarterly
Answer Questions	Answer questions with blog article link.	Several times weekly
Create new content	Research "hot" questions in your area of expertise (those with a lot of answers).	Weekly—create list
	Use question as your new post (use the content of the answers—ask for permission if you do).	1–5 times weekly

While LinkedIn events (Table 9.5) should not be the only way you market your event, you should definitely create an event for any business occasion you are offering. Not only might you drive some traffic to the event, you might even get some "Google Juice" (visibility). Events can also help support your positioning as an authority in your industry.

▶ **Table 9.5** Events

Focus	Action	Frequency
Create Event	Make a list of upcoming events.	Monthly
	Event titles: compile keywords.	As needed
	Event dates: schedule.	As needed
	Create description of event.	As needed
	Landing page/registration page for event.	As needed
	Create summary with a call to action.	As needed

Continues

Focus	Action	Frequency
	Post event in updates. (Also consider putting into a status update scheduler.)	Every few days until event
	Invite your first-level connections.	Weekly until event
	Post event in relevant groups. (If you have your own group, make sure to put event URL in an announcement.)	Weekly until event
	Pay for an events ad (send to specific people: industries/search terms).	One time

Polls (Table 9.6) might not be statistically accurate and I would never use the results to substantiate my claim in a lawsuit, but they sure are great for garnering interest in your network and building relationships. Plus, the results are cool and people love the pie charts!

▶ **Table 9.6** Polls

Focus	Action	Frequency
Polls	Monitor existing polls.	As needed
	Respond to participants.	As needed
	Share in groups.	As needed
	Use in blog post.	As needed
Create New Polls	Look at editorial calendar. Do you have a blog, or a project that a blog could enhance?	As needed

Keep an eye on your applications (Table 9.7). Some are a one-time-only addition (like WordPress) and some might require daily or weekly interaction (like Projects and Teamspaces). Another reason to monitor your applications is that occasionally LinkedIn will have glitches and your apps might simply disappear and need to be replaced or re-added to your profile. In addition, LinkedIn will delete entire programs and add new ones. So keep an eye on Get More Applications as well as the existing apps on your profile.

▶ **Table 9.7** Applications

Focus	Action	Frequency
Video	Create a file of videos to feature on LinkedIn.	Monthly or as needed

Continues

Focus	Action	Frequency
Presentation	Create a presentation and insert video.	As needed
SlideShare	Upload using SlideShare.	Monthly or as needed
Blog	Add WordPress or blog link.	One time or as needed
Creative Portfolio Display	Compile portfolio and upload (link) with creative portfolio display.	Update weekly with new content
Box.net	Create a file with existing e-Docs you already have (testimonials, checklists, questionnaires, white papers, research, résumé, etc.). Upload relevant files. Create and organize into appropriate folders.	Upload new content when available
TripIt My Travel	Sync TripIt's My Travel with your travel booking site or add travel manually.	Schedule travel monthly
Amazon Reading List	Amazon: Update when you read (or write) a new book.	Monthly
FT Press eBookShelf	Search and download relevant articles.	According to subscription
JD Supra Legal Updates	JD Supra (if applicable).	Check daily
Rofo Real Estate Pro	Rofo (Real Estate) (if applicable).	Check daily
Manymoon Projects and Teamspaces	Manage projects with your team, follow up with team members, add new projects.	Daily or as needed

LinkedIn is very invested in making company profiles (Table 9.8) more interactive and more viable for its membership. Make sure you are using all company profiles have to offer (Targeted Status Updates, Statistics, Targeted Service pages). And don't forget to add any new products or services you have to your company profile.

▶ **Table 9.8** Company Profile

Focus	Action	Frequency
Company Profile	Create company profile. (Make sure the email address for your company is added to your settings; under Account, add email.)	One time
	Create description.	One time; review yearly

Continues

► **Table 9.8** Company Profile *(Continued)*

Focus	Action	Frequency
	Add administrators.	As needed
Products and Services	Add products and services, logo, and description.	As needed
	Add video and special offers to products and services.	As needed
	Create targeted audience and banners for products and services.	As needed
Status Updates	Create status updates for company.	Daily
Statistics	Check follower statistics.	Weekly
Other Companies	Follow other relevant companies (clients, prospects, competition).	Receive daily or weekly email

Checklists for Each Day of the Week

Tables 9.9 through 9.13 list daily tasks (including many from the previous tables). Customize them to reflect your own business, campaigns, and interests. They are a great place to get started and get organized!

You will notice there is some replication throughout the following tables. That is because you will want to repeat some tasks daily, some every other day or so. Remember to customize these tasks to a table that works for you and your business.

In addition, if you have a resource like a VA, secretary, volunteer, or intern, be sure you delegate some of these tasks to them. With the creation of your checklists from Chapter 8, they should be able to take a lot of these tasks off your shoulders.

The tasks for Monday, Wednesday, and Friday focus more on connections and group interaction, whereas Tuesday's and Thursday's tasks focus on research, monitoring, and blogging.

► **Table 9.9** Monday's Tasks

Inbox	Delete "spam."
	"Archive" interesting but not important.
	Respond to requests.
	Forward introductions.
	Accept "unknown" invitations.
	Accept "known" invitations.

Continues

Groups—Manager	Moderate queue.
	Post a discussion (blog).
	Respond to requests.
	"Like" or comment on discussions in group.
Groups—Member	"Check in" with top groups.
	"Like" or comment on discussions in group.
	Post appropriate blog.
3 and 3	Create list of "knowns" to respond to.
	Create list of "unknowns" to respond to.
	Send message to one known.
	Send message to one unknown.
	Note in profile or in CRM.
Communication	Letter to "Group A" (Define tagged groups—communication strategy).

Depending on the amount, or even if you blog, you may need to add more (or delete) the tasks found in Tuesday and Thursday to your weekly actions. I know some people blog every day (how do they do it?), in which case I would add the Answers tasks to Monday, Wednesday, and Friday as well. If you don't have a blog, then you probably won't need to do them at all.

▶ **Table 9.10** Tuesday's Tasks

Answers—Repurposing Content	Create list of available blogs.
	Create list of areas of expertise.
	Check Answers for questions on areas of expertise.
	Create a list of applicable Answers.
	Attach appropriate blog response to Answer.
	Research person asking question: possible client, joint venture (JV), or partnership?
Answers—Creating Content	Research Answers for good blog post options.
	Look at content; connect with people posting answers for content.
Advanced Search	List of "ideal" clients.
	Search and create list of people found.
	Create message to send to contacts.
	Send message to appropriate contacts.

Continues

Company Search	List of "ideal" companies.
	New hires and promotions.
	Message to new hires, etc.
Communication	Letter to "Group B" (define tagged groups—communication strategy).

If you don't have your own group, some of the following tasks won't apply. Just delete them form your checklist. But you will be a member of groups, so don't forgo those daily or weekly actions!

▶ **Table 9.11** Wednesday's Tasks

Inbox	Delete "spam."
	"Archive" interesting but not important.
	Respond to requests.
	Forward introductions.
	Accept "unknown" invitations.
	Accept "known" invitations.
Groups—Manager	Moderate queue.
	Post a discussion (blog).
	Respond to requests.
	Post an announcement.
	"Like" or comment on discussions in group.
Groups—Member	"Check in" with top groups.
	"Like" or comment on discussions in group.
	Post appropriate blog.
3 and 3	Create list of "knowns" to respond to.
	Create list of "unknowns" to respond to.
	Send message to one known.
	Send message to one unknown.
	Note in profile or CRM.
Communication	Letter to "Group C" (define tagged groups—communication strategy).

Answers—Repurposing Content	Create list of available blogs.
	Create list of areas of expertise.
	Check Answers for questions on areas of expertise.
	Create a list of applicable Answers.
	Attach appropriate blog response to answer.
	Research person asking question: possible client, JV, or partnership?
Answers—Creating Content	Research Answers for good blog post options.
	Look at content; connect with people posting answers for content.
Advanced Search	List of "ideal" clients.
	Search and create list of people found.
	Create message to send to contacts.
	Send message to appropriate contacts.
Company Search	List of "ideal" companies.
	New hires and promotions.
	Message to new hires, etc.
Communication	Letter to "Group D" (define tagged groups—communication strategy).

▶ **Table 9.13** Friday's Tasks

Inbox	Delete "spam."
	"Archive" interesting but not important.
	Respond to requests.
	Forward introductions.
	Accept "unknown" invitations.
	Accept "known" invitations.
Groups—Manager	Moderate queue.
	Post a discussion (blog).
	Respond to requests.
	"Like" or comment on discussions in group.
Groups—Member	"Check in" with top groups.
	"Like" or commented on discussions in group.
	Post appropriate blog.

Continues

3 and 3	Create list of "knowns" to respond to.
	Create list of "unknowns" to respond to.
	Send message to one known.
	Send message to one unknown.
Communication	Letter to "Group E" (define tagged groups—communication strategy).

LinkedIn Ads, Labs, Apps, and Tools

LinkedIn offers several features that users may not take full advantage of (like ads and tools). Some are not even a part of the user interface (such as LinkedIn Labs and other third-party applications).

If you have been waiting to hear more about LinkedIn ads and Labs or third-party apps (including Mobile), read on! I thought this might be a great place to write about them, although this section does not fall into the "Hour-a-Day" format. This book would not be complete without their mention.

10

Chapter Contents
LinkedIn Ads
LinkedIn Labs
LinkedIn Mobile
LinkedIn Tools
LinkedIn Third-Party Applications

LinkedIn Ads

After reading about Facebook ads and how effective they can be in *Facebook Marketing: All-in-One for Dummies* by Amy Porterfield, Phyllis Khare, and Andrea Vahl (John Wiley & Sons, 2011), I had renewed hope for the effectiveness of LinkedIn ads. I quickly posted a question in LinkedIn's Answers to find out how many people were experiencing great success with the ads feature.

Alas, the response was dismal. Most people saw no ROI and considered LinkedIn ads to be a waste of money and time. In fact, many of the responders indicated that Facebook ads were much more useful than LinkedIn ads—*including* B2B folks!

The responders did seem to like the Post A Job ads. Nearly everyone thought the job postings were well worth their investment and saved them a great amount of time in finding employees and candidates.

I will warn you right now that my own experience with ads hadn't left a great taste in my mouth. Even though I tried to keep an open mind and interview as many people as possible on the topic, I received only one positive response from the 100-plus people I queried.

I did try repeatedly, through every LinkedIn connection I had, to get a quote or input from LinkedIn Corporate, LinkedIn Marketing, and LinkedIn Sales on the effectiveness of buying ads on LinkedIn, but no one would respond for comment. So if there are stunning examples of how this works for the average businessperson with an average budget, you won't see them in this book.

LinkedIn has some "Success Stories" on their website: `http://marketing.linkedin.com/success-stories/case-study`. However, the companies that had success with using LinkedIn ads were all large companies with, one assumes, bigger budgets.

Apparently LinkedIn does fine with their marketing monetization, because according to their websites, Hiring Solutions revenue was $102.6 million this year, increasing 121 percent compared to the previous year. Marketing Solutions revenue was $48 million, increasing 73 percent compared to the prior year. I'm glad someone is making money with their LinkedIn ads!

Nonetheless, since ads are an important aspect of any marketing campaign, I want to cover them here. You'll have to decide whether you want to make the investment. I will also touch on LinkedIn's Marketing Solutions. However, in most cases, the $25,000-plus price tag will render this option irrelevant to many of the readers (myself included).

Here's what we'll cover:

- Where to find LinkedIn ads and how to get started
- What you can advertise on LinkedIn
- How much you will have to invest
- Case studies

Where Are LinkedIn Ads?

LinkedIn has two types of ads: self-service ads (those similar to the ones many of you are used to seeing on Facebook) and Marketing Solutions (the expensive ones).

To create a LinkedIn ad, first go to www.linkedin.com/ads. If you have a paid account, click Go To LinkedIn Ads at the top left of any LinkedIn page (just to the right of the logo).

If you have a LinkedIn account and a credit card, you can start or manage an ad campaign by clicking on the "Advertise on LinkedIn" link under you Home tab, and then click on the yellow "Start Now" button if this is your first ad, or the "Manage your ads" link on the top right side of the Ads page. Once you have started a new campaign, create your ad as shown in Figure 10.1.

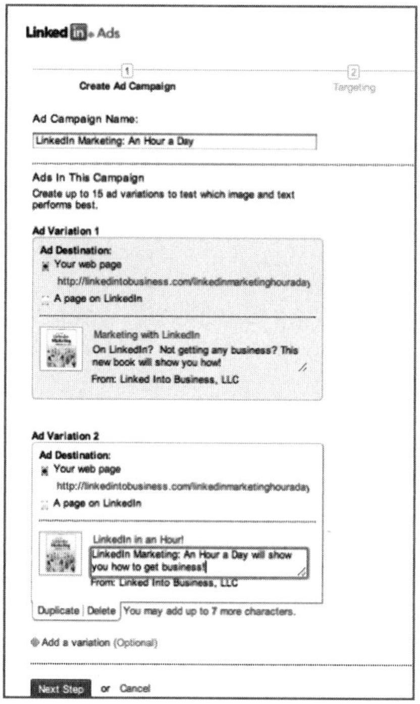

Figure 10.1 Creating an ad

These are the steps you must take to create a LinkedIn ad:

1. Name your ad campaign so that you and others can easily refer to it for editing and monitoring.

2. Give your ad a title (using up to 25 characters). This is the first line of text that will show up in an ad (for example, Confused About LinkedIn?).

3. Upload an image (no greater than 50×50 pixels).

4. Write a description of up to 75 characters (for example, "Would you like to learn how to monetize your time on LinkedIn? Click here.").

5. Add a URL link (if you have a landing page) of up to 500 characters specific to the product or service you're advertising. (The domain must match the display URL.)

6. Select a target audience for your ad.

7. Create and test up to 15 variations of the same ad.

8. Set a daily budget and bid on how much you're willing to pay for clicks or impressions.

9. Pay LinkedIn.

10. Wait for their approval.

 Note: Cost-per-click (CPC) and cost-per-thousand-impressions (CPM) are two different styles of billing you can choose for ads.

Your ad might appear on a variety of pages on LinkedIn. Unfortunately, I received no response from LinkedIn as to what their algorithm was or even what we could expect to see. Nonetheless, in the Help section LinkedIn assures that your ads may appear on any or all of these pages below:

• Profile page (when users view profiles of other LinkedIn members)

• Home page (the page users see when they log in to LinkedIn)

• Inbox (the page users use to see messages and invitations to connect)

• Search Results page (the page that you see when you search for a member by name)

• Groups (on pages in LinkedIn groups)

Once you have created an ad, you can edit and manage it from your settings page, as shown in Figure 10.2.

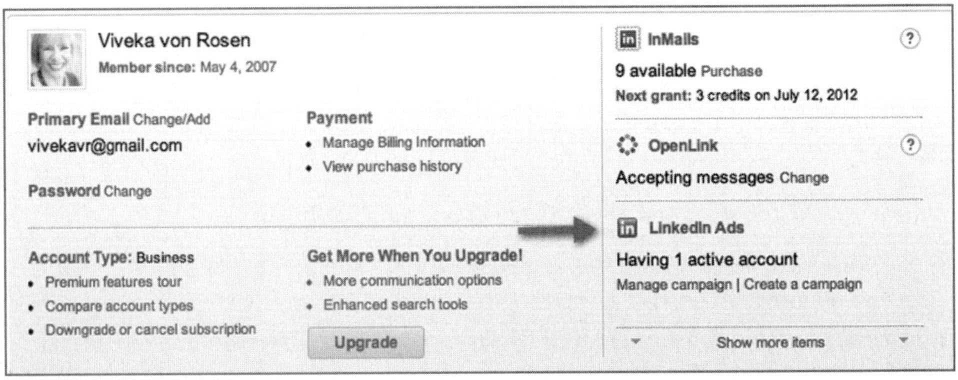

Figure 10.2 Managing your campaigns

> **Note:** If more than one person is going to need access to your LinkedIn Ad campaign, you will need to create a business account. That way, anyone in your company who is on LinkedIn will have the ability to create, edit, and manage your campaign.

What Can You Advertise on LinkedIn?

You can advertise pretty much any product, service, website, LinkedIn page, or job on LinkedIn. You just can't advertise anything that mentions LinkedIn. I received this note: "Please know that we do not allow members to mention LinkedIn, unless the landing page (URL) of the Ad is a page on LinkedIn."

You can find LinkedIn's ad guidelines here: `www.linkedin.com/static?key=pop%2Fpop_sas_guidelines`. You can find LinkedIn's ads agreement here: `www.linkedin.com/static?key=pop_sas_terms`.

Or you can check the Customer Service link at the bottom left of LinkedIn (which used to be the Help link). Type the search terms **Ad Guidelines** or **Ads Agreement**.

One technique that seems to work well is to advertise a whitepaper, a free item of perceived value, or a job. For instance, if you are a business coach you could provide a link to free business assessment. Anyone who downloads that assessment is a likely candidate for your services.

Share the link where the LinkedIn member can download the file to access your item of value. If you choose to share a valuable resource with them (in the form of a whitepaper, article, checklist, evaluation, etc.), then the only cost to them should be giving you their email address and contact information. Don't hit them with a price tag when they land on your page.

Once you have that information, you can enter it into your email marketing system (for email marketing tips, see *Email Marketing: An Hour a Day*, by Jeanniey Mullen and David Daniels, Sybex 2008).

It's difficult to get people to simply click on the product or service you wish to sell, but they may click on something that they perceive as having value. Get them into your sales system. LinkedIn ads work best for filling the funnel. See a sample "free stuff" ad in Figure 10.3.

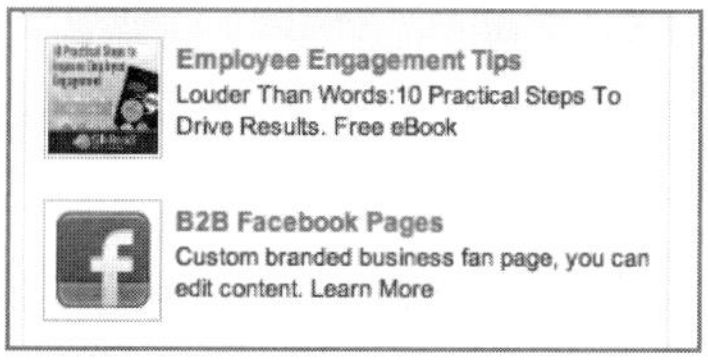

Employee Engagement Tips
Louder Than Words:10 Practical Steps To
Drive Results. Free eBook

B2B Facebook Pages
Custom branded business fan page, you can
edit content. Learn More

Figure 10.3 Sample LinkedIn ad

How Much Will You Need to Invest?

Here is LinkedIn's answer to how much you'll need to invest:

- For larger budgets ($25,000 plus), try LinkedIn display advertising.
- For smaller budgets (less than $25,000), try ads for targeted text advertising.

In my Ads (self-service) campaign, I can create and post an ad for as little as $2.00 per click or $2.00 per 1,000 impressions. The recommended amount for me is between $2.12 and 2.36 in both cases. Of course, the more you spend, the more visibility LinkedIn will give you.

Note: Another friend of mine invests over $20,000 a month in LinkedIn self-service ads. He does CPC rather than CPM ads with this strategy. He advertises his product at a higher cost on the ad than the price people receive when they click through and land on his landing page. Only people interested in his product click through, although he gets a lot of impressions. When people land on his sales page they get a nice surprise with a significant discount. He has a higher-than-average sales rate and great ROI. But again, he has spent up to $20,000 a month on ads.

In its Help section, LinkedIn shares this useful advice: "There are a number of factors that affect how many impressions and clicks your ad receives, including the competitiveness of advertisements in our system and the size of the audience you're targeting." Not terribly helpful if you ask me.

Note: Interestingly, even the companies I interviewed who were using LinkedIn's Marketing Solution display advertising ($25,000-plus ads) were not getting many metrics back from LinkedIn regarding visibility and click-through rates. One of the people I interviewed told me, "I don't even know what we are paying for. And no one at LinkedIn seems able to tell me." 'Nuff said.

Is It Worth It? (Case Studies)

Let's take a look at a few case studies from the Stevens Institute of Technology and Sitecore (`marketing.linkedin.com/success-stories`).

Note: While the term *self-service ads* implies they are cheap, this is not necessarily the case. Sitecore invested what many smaller businesses and entrepreneurs might consider a significant amount for an online ad.

The Stevens Institute of Technology display ads and self-service pay-per-click ads to increase brand awareness and encourage people to click through to their inquiry form. They target members without graduate degrees in the New York and New York area with group affiliations and job functions related to their degree program.

Since mid-2011 when they launched their ads, the Stevens Institute of Technology achieved open rates as high as 21 percent and click-through rates as high as 12 percent (http://marketing.linkedin.com/sites/default/files/pdfs/LinkedIn_StevensInstitute_CaseStudy2012_0.pdf.

I also interviewed Ted Prodromou, who manages Sitecore's marketing campaign on LinkedIn and saw good results with his company's self-service ad campaign. Ted is the Online Marketing/SEO Analyst. (Sitecore is a leader in web content management and online engagement, and it builds business application software that solves modern-day problems for a wide range of companies and organizations.)

I interviewed Ted about his experience with LinkedIn ads, since he was the only person to answer positively of all the people I questioned.

Sitecore started with the self-service ads because they wanted a lower monthly budget to start. Because an average Sitecore license is about $100,000 and it takes anywhere from 6 to 12 months to close a sale, Ted had the time to use LinkedIn ads to build a network of interested, or warm, leads.

Sitecore's strategy was to market a valuable whitepaper (for programmers), targeted at a specific audience. They were quite successful and gathered, on average, 60–70 leads a day. Ted says a high number of the people who came to their landing page through the LinkedIn ad ended up clicking through, providing their email address, and were then put into Sitecore's email marketing system. Once the leads warmed up, they were turned over to the sales department for a very high closing ratio. So in Sitecore's case, LinkedIn ads definitely provided an ROI.

Sitecore was excited by the results and decided to launch a similar campaign in Sweden. And even though Sweden is apparently notorious for not responding to CPC or CPM ads, Sitecore once again experienced substantial success with their campaign.

Ted figures Sitecore's success correlates with the fact that LinkedIn members are exactly their market. With the targeting feature, they were able to get in front of exactly who they needed to. They did try LinkedIn Marketing Solutions, but so far, Ted says, the results for the much higher-priced ads are inconclusive.

> **Note:** On the positive side, LinkedIn ads are so expensive you don't get the glut of "Change your life and make a million dollars and find your life mate by clicking on this ad" spammy ads that you see on Facebook.

LinkedIn Labs

LinkedInLabs (http://linkedinlabs.com) is a really cool resource that highlights some of LinkedIn's applications that they are not ready (or never will) launch in the LinkedIn platform itself. Often designed by LinkedIn employees and interns, these applications are worth noting.

What Is an API and Why Should You Care?

Even thought LinkedIn has a fraction of the third-party apps that Facebook and Twitter have, according to LinkedIn's website there are more than 60,000 developers using LinkedIn APIs.

 Note: According to Wikipedia, an API is "a specification intended to be used as an interface by software components to communicate with each other." In other words, if you want your application to "talk to" and "use" LinkedIn's data, you have to use their application programming interface. Think of is as a translator between programs that speak different languages and don't know the etiquette of each other's cultures!

If you want to find out more about LinkedIn's API, go to `https://developer.linkedin.com/apis`.

Labs

LinkedIn's employees, programmers, and partners are working on some new applications, many of which you can see and try out at `http://linkedinlabs.com`.

LinkedIn Labs posts a small set of projects and experimental features built by the employees of LinkedIn, as shown in Figure 10.4.

I have a list of their current offerings (straight from the website). Check the website often because LinkedIn will add and remove these apps over time based on popularity and support. In fact, I recommend visiting the website to see what LinkedIn Labs is offering now.

Also, check out `http://engineering.linkedin.com` to learn more about the engineering teams at LinkedIn.

- The Veterans feature allows people to reconnect with military veterans on LinkedIn. You can find out where they work, what types of jobs they have, and where they live. See `www.linkedinlabs.com/veterans`.

- MOCHA Veterans is an online tool that allows veterans to search for job postings on LinkedIn using their military credentials: `www.linkedinlabs.com/mocha`.

- Aid Patrol Veterans connects people with local organizations to bring care and hope to homeless veterans: `www.linkedinlabs.com/aid-patrol`.

- The Hero Connect Veterans features aims to connect veterans to other veterans in companies and locations they are interested in: `www.linkedinlabs.com/heroconnect`.

- SpeechIn helps you to get your personalized LinkedIn Today headlines read to you on your mobile phone. Requires Safari or Google Chrome: `www.linkedinlabs.com/speechin`.

- TextIn helps you access the power of LinkedIn through text messaging: `www.linkedinlabs.com/textin`.

Veterans

Veterans Hackday 1st place, November 2011

Reconnect with military veterans on LinkedIn. Find insights such as where they work, what types of jobs they have, and where they live.
http://www.linkedinlabs.com/veterans

in Share 22

MOCHA

Veterans Hackday 2nd place, November 2011

Online tool that allows veterans to search for job postings on LinkedIn using their military credentials.
http://www.linkedinlabs.com/mocha

in Share 12

Aid Patrol

Veterans Hackday 3rd place, November 2011

Aid patrol connects people with local organizations to bring care and hope to our homeless veterans.
http://www.linkedinlabs.com/aid-patrol

in Share 4

HeroConnect

Veterans Hackday finalist, November 2011

HeroConnect aims to connect Veterans to other Veterans in companies and locations they are interested in.
http://www.linkedinlabs.com/heroconnect

in Share 16

SpeechIn

Hackday Winner, May 2011

Get your personalized LinkedIn Today headlines read to you on your mobile phone. Requires Safari or Chrome.
http://www.linkedinlabs.com/speechin

in Share 45

TextIn

Hackday Winner, March 2011

Access the power of LinkedIn through text messaging! (US only)
http://www.linkedinlabs.com/textin

in Share 153

Swarm

Hackday Winner, November 2010

An eerily beautiful visualization of popular company search queries on LinkedIn.
http://www.linkedinlabs.com/swarm

in Share 564

Year in Review

November 2010 Hackday Winner

The most popular email in LinkedIn history. A visual representation of everyone in your network who changed jobs in a given year.
http://www.linkedinlabs.com/yearinreview

in Share 633

Figure 10.4 LinkedIn Labs

- Swarm is a graphic visualization of popular company search queries on LinkedIn. This one is pretty cool and worth playing with—if only for screen shots: www.linkedinlabs.com/swarm.

- Year in Review provides a visual representation of everyone in your network who changed jobs in a given year: www.linkedinlabs.com/yearinreview.

- The InMaps LinkedIn Analytics feature allows you to see your professional network, clustered in real time, based on their interrelationships. (Unfortunately, if your network is too big, this doesn't work. It's a very cool tool to see where your network is strong and where it might need some growth.) Go to www.linkedinlabs .com/inmaps.

- Connection Timeline allows you to view your connections across the timeline of your career. I loved going through this app and placing people and dates together. It sparked me to call a few folks: www.linkedinlabs.com/timeline.

- DropIn is a game similar to Tetris that allows you to learn about your professional connections. (Be careful—this one is addictive: www.linkedinlabs.com/dropin.)

- Resume Builder allows you to build, save, and share beautifully formatted résumés based on your LinkedIn profile. This one comes highly recommended for job seekers: www.linkedinlabs.com/resumebuilder.

- Infinity is another visualization of your professional network: www.linkedinlabs.com/infinity.

- NewIn Pure Energy is an application that shows new members joining LinkedIn from around the world and requires Google Earth. This is less effective with a super big network, but I love anything Google Earth-y: www.linkedinlabs.com/newin.

- ChromeIn integrates LinkedIn directly into Google Chrome: www.linkedinlabs.com/chromein. Just be aware that if you click on the Chrome app it will try to download the app onto your computer.

- Signal is aimed at making it easy for all professionals to glean the most relevant insights from the never-ending stream of status updates and news. By now you are well acquainted with Signal! It is also found under the News tab: www.linkedinlabs.com/signal.

LinkedIn Mobile

You can find a *Forbes* article about the massive shift to mobile technologies here: (www.forbes.com/sites/markfidelman/2012/05/02/the-latest-infographics-mobile-business-statistics-for-2012/). Right now mobile devices like tablets and smart phones are taking over.

Here are some interesting facts:

- This year, more than 50 percent of network devices will ship without a wired port (Morgan Stanley Market Trends: www.forbes.com/companies/morgan-stanley/).

- By 2015 there will be 7.4 billion mobile devices in the market (ABI Research).

- 1.2 billion smart phones will enter the market over the next five years, about 40 percent of all handset shipments (ABI Research).

So if you have a mobile device, it might make sense to get LinkedIn's mobile applications.

LinkedIn for Your iPad

Let's take a look at LinkedIn for your iPad. While I love the look and intuitiveness of this application, one thing I've noticed, as with many features of LinkedIn, is that it doesn't work so well for people who have a super large network.

That being said, it's definitely worth downloading onto your iPad. One of the features I really like is the new calendar feature. When you're in the iPad app, you can check your calendar easily without having to leave the app (if for no other reason than when I look at my calendar I know I have to stop spending so much time in LinkedIn Today).

Another thing I like about the iPad app is that when you're looking at someone else's profile, you can easily see their activity in a beautiful newspaper-style layout. It is much more visually appealing (and easier to find) than the browser version of Activity, as you can see in Figure 10.5.

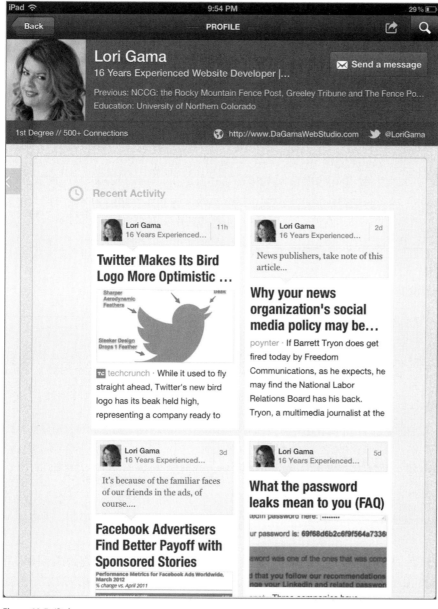

Figure 10.5 iPad app

Here's another bonus: The web addresses that they have in their Summary (and website and Twitter) sections are linked—even though web addresses that you put in the Summary section of your browser-based LinkedIn profile are not! That's an incentive to put web addresses in your summary.

You can easily see who's viewed your profile. Click their icon or thumbnail, and if they are a first-level connection, send them a message (or if they're not first-level you can invite them to connect with you). This saves you a few steps compared to connecting to folks in the LinkedIn website.

LinkedIn Today is set up beautifully on the LinkedIn iPad application, looking more like a magazine than ever. I have a feeling that the new LinkedIn website user interface (UI) is going to be based strongly on the iPad application interface. You heard it here first!

LinkedIn on Your Smart Phone: iPhone, Blackberry, Android, and Palm

While the iPhone application does not do everything that your LinkedIn website profile can do, it's a great tool to have "in between times." I'm a big fan of using 5 or 10 minutes here and there to accept invitations, respond to messages, do a little browsing, and read some news. My iPhone application lets me access LinkedIn practically anywhere and any time. You can also look at groups and even participate in groups on your iPhone.

The BlackBerry Android and Palm applications are very similar to the iPhone application, with the exception that they have not implemented the Groups features yet.

LinkedIn Tools

To find LinkedIn tools, just scroll to the very bottom of any page on LinkedIn. The middle link is Tools—click it.

The first page that comes up is the overview page. You'll find links to the Email Signature and will be able to download the Mac search widget.

Email Signature

If you use Outlook, Outlook Express, or Thunderbird, then you can use the Email Signature tool on LinkedIn. It will create a signature by pulling your information from your LinkedIn profile and plugging it into different templates. There are four templates:

- Executive
- Ingot
- Plastic curve
- Simple

Each of these has different color schemes to match your branding.

Besides adding information like your name, company website, address, tagline, and logo, you can add your professional profile link, a "See who we know in common" link, and for those of you who are hiring, "We're hiring" link, as seen in Figure 10.6.

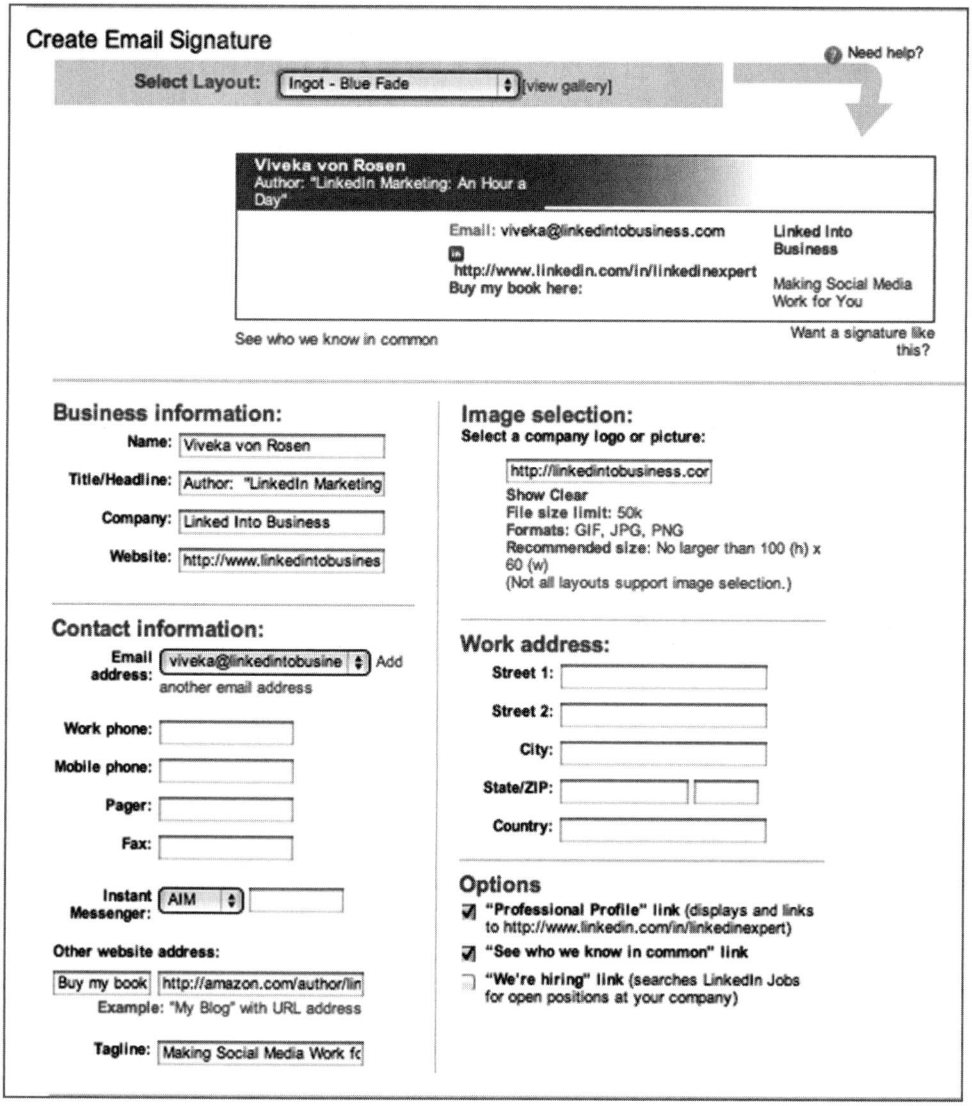

Figure 10.6 Email signature

Many of you reading this book already have a corporate signature or have designed a nicely branded signature for your email. But if you haven't, this tool is worth taking a look at.

Mac Search Widget

The Mac search widget is a quick download that allows you to search LinkedIn from anywhere on your Mac. Think of it like Spotlight for LinkedIn.

> ### Google Toolbar
>
> While LinkedIn offers the Google toolbar in the Tools section, it doesn't exist anymore. This is what they say on their website: "At LinkedIn we want to provide a simple and efficient experience for members like you. So from time to time we take a look at our set of features to evaluate how your members are using them. Part of this process sometimes means we decide to eliminate a feature so we can better invest in those resources in building more great LinkedIn products." Why they take away functional tools that work I don't know.

Outlook Social Connector

I love the Outlook Social Connector. It's the main reason I miss having Outlook. I've already mentioned the Outlook Social Connector, but it bears mentioning again. It allows you to:

- See the latest LinkedIn activity and profile photo from any connection that sends you an email
- Easily connect with those connections from within Outlook
- Use your Outlook CRM system to manage LinkedIn connections
- Email your LinkedIn connections directly

LinkedIn Widget for Lotus Notes

The LinkedIn widget for Lotus Notes lets you get your email and LinkedIn updates all in one place. Much like Outlook Connector, it allows you to learn more about the people who send you the email. You also get thumbnails of their LinkedIn profile. Unlike Outlook, Lotus Notes allows you to search for people you want to connect with on LinkedIn and work with as well as share your status and see what your connections are working on.

I don't use Lotus, but if I did, I would check this out. It looks like a really cool tool, as shown in Figure 10.7.

Sharing Bookmarklet

I've also already mentioned the Sharing bookmarklet. As you'll recall, the Sharing bookmarklet is the tool that allows you to share articles and links with your network via status update and group discussion. If you haven't done so yet, pull the Share On LinkedIn button onto your browser toolbar.

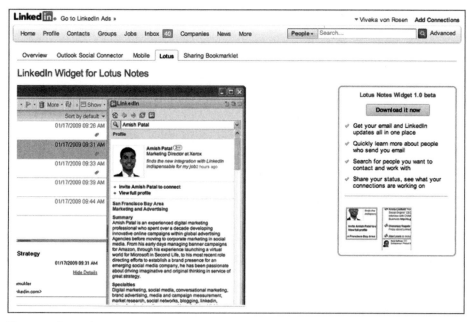

Figure 10.7 Lotus widget

LinkedIn Third-Party Applications

Obviously, if there are over 60,000 apps using LinkedIn's API, this is far from a conclusive list. However, these are apps I use regularly and highly recommend.

CardMunch

I've already mentioned CardMunch several times in this book, but since it's an application I use a lot, I thought I'd mention it one last time. To get CardMunch, you can go to www.cardmunch.com, or you can find it in the iTunes application library.

To use CardMunch, simply take a picture of a business card. The business card will be uploaded into a contact list. From there you can invite the individuals to connect with you on LinkedIn, or if you're already connected, send them a message or give them a phone call. It's a great way to follow up with people you've met face to face.

I don't know about you, but I have a shoebox (okay, I'll be honest, a boot box) full of business cards and good intentions... which gets me nowhere. CardMunch allows you to easily capture the contact information on a business card and then utilize it however you see fit.

Here on Biz

Here on Biz is another great iPhone application. (I promise that not all the applications I mention will be iPhone or iPad applications.) Here on Biz is still in beta mode, and I was lucky enough to be one of the few people who got to test it out. I love it!

Here's how it works: When you turn this application on, your iPhone picks up your location. Then it does a search for anyone else on LinkedIn using the app in your vicinity. From that screen you can click on their thumbnail and invite them to connect. Or if you're already connected, send them a message, as shown in Figure 10.8.

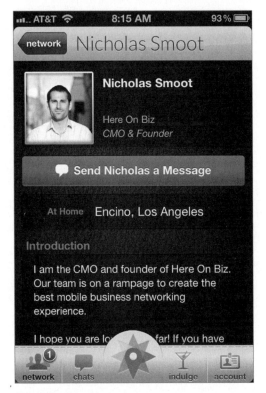

Figure 10.8 Here on Biz app

Think of it as Foursquare for business but much more effective. If you are traveling (say at a conference or at an event), the application will pick up the LinkedIn users in your vicinity. Then it is simply a matter of reaching out. What I like most about Here on Biz is that it facilitates face-to-face meetings.

Connected HQ

Connected HQ is a CRM system (also recently acquired by LinkedIn). What I find so amusing is that Connected HQ has some of the functionality of the CRM that I was wishing for in Chapter 1!

Connected HQ allows you to download all your LinkedIn contacts, as well as email contacts, and it will even link with Twitter and Facebook, as shown in Figure 10.9.

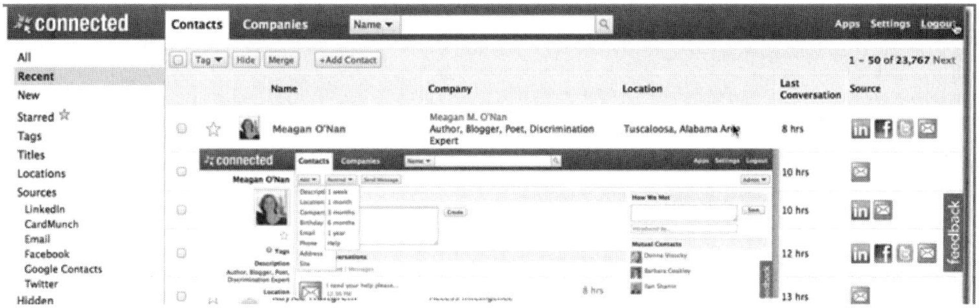

Figure 10.9 Connected HQ

From there you can see whom you've been interacting with and where those interactions occurred. As with a true CRM, you can tag your connections, you can make notes about them, and you can even schedule reminders for email or callbacks. It might not have the functionality of a full CRM (like Salesforce), but it has a lot going for it. And it's free!

Rapportive

Another free CRM you might consider if you use Gmail is Rapportive (recently purchased by LinkedIn). It pulls your social network into your Gmail account and lets you see social profile information about your connections. This gives you more intelligence on them when it's time to send an email. Not only that, but Rapportive keeps their contact information updated (even when the person doesn't).

JibberJobber

JibberJobber (more details on this tool in Chapter 11, "LinkedIn and You: Getting Specific") is a very functional CRM designed especially for job seekers. I highly recommend the $10-a-month investment in JibberJobber. To obtain it, just go to www.jibberjobber.com.

Hachi

One of the limitations of being an open networker on LinkedIn is that I often don't know the people from whom I want to get an introduction. Or I might know them, but I'm not as aware as I should be of their social media engagement. So if I ask for an introduction, I don't know if it's going to sit in their inbox for an hour, a day, a week, or a year!

Hachi solves all those problems for me by looking in all my networks and finding—through some magical algorithm—the best person to introduce me.

The other benefit in addition to LinkedIn introductions is the fact that Hachi goes four levels deep, not just three.

Hachi (pronounced "Ha-chee") can be found at www.gohachi.com and searches through all your professional and social networks to give you the smartest way to reach anyone you want. *Smartest* is the key word here, because not only does Hachi give you all the possible paths to reach your target, but it also recommends the smartest of those paths, based on intelligence about you and your networks. It goes further to get you communicating with your target.

- Connect your social and professional networks with Hachi.
- Start searching for the person you want to connect with. You can search by their name, title, company, education, industry, or location.
- Hachi will display people from your network who meet your search criteria.
- Click on the person's name to learn more about the searched person.
- Click the Find Path button to find out how you can reach that person.
- Hachi will display the various ways you can connect and will suggest the smartest way.

Cloze

Cloze (found at http://cloze.com) is a free service that brings together your email, business connections, social networks, and address books into a single useful viewer. Users connect their various accounts, which are then analyzed and rated according to their interactions to determine relationship strength and to assign a Cloze score. The higher the Cloze score, the stronger the relationship. You will receive a daily email digest of the communications from your connections that have the highest Cloze score.

You can also search to see who in your networks has the best relationship with someone you might want an introduction to (similar to Hachi). The score helps to separate proven relationships from passive, one-time connections.

Then it's simply a matter of using those relationships that mean the most to you to build new relationships that will help grow your business.

Hootsuite

Hootsuite is, in my opinion, the best tool for scheduling LinkedIn updates, as well as posts to your LinkedIn company profile and LinkedIn groups. I use Hootsuite with the checklists and the calendar I provided for you in Chapter 9, "Optimizing Your Time Using LinkedIn."

At this time Hootsuite Pro costs $9.95 a month, but you might be able to get away with the free Hootsuite offer.

BufferApp

If Hootsuite is out of your price range, consider BufferApp for scheduling posts to LinkedIn. Not only will BufferApp post updates to LinkedIn, but it'll also tell you the best times to do so. While BufferApp does not let you post updates to groups or your company at this time, it's still worth looking into since it's free.

Grading Tools: Klout, Kred, and PeerIndex

The social media grading tools like Klout, PeerIndex, and Kred should also be mentioned here. All three applications look at your social media interaction and give you a grade based on it. None of them give much weight to LinkedIn, so I don't like them that much.

I think it is definitely worth your time to look at some of these auxiliary apps and features for LinkedIn. Not all of them will be appropriate to you and what you do for a living, but some of these apps might increase your productivity and save you some time.

I continue to introduce new LinkedIn and social media applications I think my readers will find useful in my blog at http://LinkedIntoBusiness.com and on my LinkedInChat on Twitter on Tuesday nights (http://Tweetchat.com/room/linkedinchat) at 5 p.m. PST. I recommend checking both of these resources a few times a month to keep up with the latest offers.

So that is pretty much it with my contribution to the book! But there is one more chapter where I have "mined" some of the best minds out there when it comes to using LinkedIn for business, and asked them to contribute their favorite LinkedIn strategies for specific industries and businesses. Even though you might think an industry does not pertain to you (for example, you are a recruiter and not interested in real estate), I still recommend reading each section, since the strategies often cross practices.

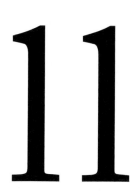

LinkedIn and You: Getting Specific

While I would love to write a book about LinkedIn for each and every industry, business type, and businessperson out there, I just don't have that much time. Nevertheless, there are some businesses and businesspeople that I feel need a little more focus in this book. Fortunately, I have been quite blessed in my relationships with other LinkedIn thought and industry leaders, and it occurred to me that I could tap into their extraordinary wealth of information for this last chapter of the book.

Chapter Contents

LinkedIn and Job Seekers
LinkedIn for Entrepreneurs
Recruiters, HR Personnel, and Hiring Managers
Legal Professionals
Women on LinkedIn
Real Estate Professionals
Not-for-Profits and LinkedIn
Some Final Tips on LinkedIn for Marketing

LinkedIn and Job Seekers

I really am passionate about job seekers using and getting employed through their use of LinkedIn. I teach a few classes on the topic in our local workforce center in Fort Collins, Colorado (please feel free to sign up; it's the bargain of the century), as well as traveling around the United States speaking on the topic. That being said, I am not the only expert when it comes to using LinkedIn for job seekers!

My friend and mentor, Jason Alba (www.linkedin.com/in/jasonalba), is the author of *I'm on LinkedIn, Now What???* (Happy About, 2008), the first non-workbook-style book written on LinkedIn. Jason offers wonderful resources for job seekers at www.JasonAlba.com. He was kind enough to share some of his ideas with me in an interview I did with him.

Brett Fairall (www.linkedin.com/in/bfairall) has designed several applications for job seekers (www.Mobbios.com, www.WOWsume.com) and has great tips for job seekers as well.

Jason Alba's Tips for Connecting and Engaging

Jason is just one of those people who is incredibly generous with his time and information. He is truly one of the first LinkedIn experts and the most knowledgeable person I know when it comes to LinkedIn for job seekers.

He created JibberJobber.com, a tool to organize and manage professional relationships and help job seekers organize their search. It was one of the earliest "personal relationship managers" available to professionals to use during their career and career search. Here are a few tips Jason had to share with us.

I interviewed Jason Alba for this section, and the content is taken almost verbatim from our interview. Enjoy!

Get Serious About Your Profile

Jason feels that the most important thing a job seeker needs to do is get serious about their profile on LinkedIn. Too many people do the bare minimum on their profile and that can hurt rather than help you on LinkedIn.

If a job seeker's profile gets found in a LinkedIn search (or someone happens upon their resume, or finds them on Google), they need to be impressed with the job seeker's profile. They need to be "sucked in" and engaged. A well-planned, complete, and optimized profile has a better chance of attracting a recruiter, employer, or hiring manager. (For a refresher course in how to optimize your profile, reread Chapter 3, "Weeks 3–6: Ready, Set, Profile.")

Proactively Search, Connect, and Engage

Jason mentioned that there is often a mentality with many job seekers that to find a job all they have to do is apply, apply, apply to job boards and then wait for the phone to ring. But Jason feels that doesn't work anymore. "Job seekers need to get out of their comfort zone and proactively look for the right connections. They need to figure how to move from reactive to proactive."

Job seekers need to be proactive about connecting and engaging on LinkedIn. Jason feels they are either searching or they are stagnant: "Too many job seekers create a profile and then sit there and do nothing. Every job seeker should be using LinkedIn's Advanced Search feature to find the hiring managers, business owners, or HR professionals they should be prospecting. They should be taking a few minutes every day to make a list of company executives, HR professionals, recruiters, potential mentors, and Influencers in their industry, potential mentors—and then reach out and contact them! Job seekers have to start developing relationships before they need the job." Or as I like to say, fill the well. (For more tips on how to grow and engage with your network, read Chapter 5, "Weeks 10–15: Creating and Managing a Network That Works.")

Don't Rely on LinkedIn's Job Board!

Jason feels that LinkedIn's job board (on the Jobs tab) puts job seekers back into comfort zone mentality. He warns us, "Don't just rely on LinkedIn's job board by finding a job, applying, and waiting for the phone to ring."

Instead, he feels that job seekers should use LinkedIn to find who works at a company they are interested in, or how they are connected to the person who posted the job. Then they should reach out to that person. What else do they have to lose? (For more on how to search company profiles, read Chapter 4, "Weeks 7–9: Use Your Company Profile for Branding and Positioning.")

Use LinkedIn Groups

Jason is a big fan of LinkedIn groups: "One way job seekers can reach a lot of people, without sending invitations to a lot of people, is through a LinkedIn group. Once a job seeker is a group member, they become 'one of them.' So they should join groups in their areas of interest."

He feels that there is something powerful about starting a relationship with someone who didn't know you previously, and "then they get to know you, as you want to be known, not as your experience has cubby-holed you previously."

Note: As I mentioned in Chapter 6, "Weeks 16–18: Getting Strategic with Groups," a job seeker can start a discussion and leave comments in up to 50 (although I recommend about 45) groups in industries that interest them. The reason I recommend joining a few less than 50 groups is because you want some "wiggle room" when it comes to joining and leaving groups. I have found when I keep my group level at 50, I spend too much time trying to figure out which groups to keep and which to leave—which inhibits the flow of my search and connecting.

Jason acknowledges that "it might seem work intensive, but compared to the time job seekers spend on job boards, the few minutes I spend every day building relationships in my group produces much greater results."

How powerful are the relationships job seekers are making in the industries that interest them compared to the time they take pouring their résumé into the black hole of the job board or company database? Jason believes that "groups are truly a way to tap into the hidden job market."

Find Out Where the Person Hiring You Is Comfortable

Jason firmly believes that to communicate with the person who can potentially hire them, a job seeker needs to find out where they are comfortable. Are they active on Twitter? Then maybe the job seeker should reach out to them on Twitter.

When reaching out, ask the new contact where they would like to have the conversation: via email or a phone call. If a job seeker can send their prospect a direct message on LinkedIn, that is the best bet.

Jason adds, "I also like Introductions a lot, getting your message and branding in front of multiple people. However, if it's a time-sensitive message, be aware Introductions can take a long time."

I agree with Jason that invitations will work, but a job seeker's first conversation shouldn't be an invitation. The relationship should come first whether or not the job seeker sends an invitation to the prospect.

Be Clear on Personal Branding

When I asked Jason how he defined branding, he said, "I define personal branding as how others perceive you. With LinkedIn, job seekers can develop their personal brand—how they want to be perceived. For instance, when I think of my brand, I want people to think of me as a Subject Matter Expert or Thought Leader (or both)."

Jason thinks that one of the biggest problems job seekers have with personal branding on LinkedIn is that they often misbrand themselves. "They pigeonhole themselves. When creating your brand on LinkedIn, make sure people perceive you correctly."

I liked the strategy that Jason suggested to position and brand yourself: "Ask a question every week that helps people understand what your interests are. Questions subtly assert your interests." (For more on how to use Answers, read Chapter 7, "Weeks 19–22: Get Strategic with LinkedIn's 'Other' Options.")

Jason continues: "For instance, the job seeker could write something like this in Answers: 'I'm preparing a presentation on_____ for_____. What are three things you think I should include?' That indicates an area of interest and also stimulates engagement. Then their network will begin to see the job seeker's interests and their perception might shift to include all the job seeker's interests (their branding), not just the fact that they are looking for a job in a particular field."

Get a Personal Relationship Manager (PRM)

Jason created JibberJobber.com to help job seekers manage their network. According to Jason, "JibberJobber is an excellent complement to LinkedIn. What job seekers are doing in their job search is finding people to network and communicate with and then developing these relationships."

According to Jason's website, JibberJobber allows them to track who they are communicating with and what those people (hiring managers, recruiters, principals, insiders, etc.) are saying. JibberJobber is a tracking system that lets them keep track of all conversations. It's a true personal relationship manager (PRM). I think it's an amazing tool and have been using it for years.

Last Words

To wrap up, Jason adds: "I already mentioned creating a barebones account and waiting for the phone to ring is a bad idea. Also, job seekers shouldn't spend too little time or too much time on LinkedIn. Don't forget real life. Go to networking events. Meet people in real life. Call them on the phone. Connect. Engage."

Brett Fairall's Tips for Getting Noticed

I was thrilled to interview (and be interviewed by) Brett Fairall of Mobios.com and WOWsume.com. It was a completely different type of interview; it went on for hours and was great fun. I pulled the nuggets of the interview out for you here.

Research Your Potential Employer

Brett says that the first and most important thing any job seeker should do is research. He suggests using LinkedIn to research your potential employer, what they are interested in, and what they want.

He emphasizes that "You need to make sure that the company and/or person you want to work for is, well, who you want to work for! Can you, and do you, want to speak in their language? For instance, if you have strong political beliefs and the company you work for swings the other direction, can you put your own opinions aside?"

You don't want to turn off the person interviewing you. Brett asks, "Is someone going to dislike who you are? Can you curtail your message around them instead of focusing on your own interests and beliefs? Can you mold your message around their mentality? If you can, and you are comfortable doing so, it will make the interview more comfortable and the interviewer will be more receptive to you."

He gives this example: "If you were interested in going into journalism, then you would want to be wordier in your interview. Drop the names of the books you've read, drop the names of the authors you've worked with. Build connection with the interviewer. What that does is naturally and inherently separate you from the pack. According to the U.S. Bureau of Labor Statistics, there are 3.4 job seekers per available job (www.bls.gov), so you *must* differentiate yourself from those other applicants.

Build Your Network

Brett agrees with Jason Alba that you need to build your network and build your connections. He says that it's about who you know. But more than that, on LinkedIn it's about who knows you (who can find you in a search). "And I mean actually 'knowing' them. Knowing what they like. Knowing what they want because you have done your research on them. If you have the same persona, same MO, same interests (or at least share similar interests), you then become known, liked, trusted, and remembered."

Tell Stories

People remember stories. Brett says to use your LinkedIn profile to tell stories. Use your interview to tell stories…relevant stories.

- Stories build relationships with people.
- Stories allow people to empathize.
- Stories build commonality.
- Stories build trust.

Use the LinkedIn Summary section or the Description section of your Experience page to tell the people looking at your profile the stories of your success, as we discussed in Chapter 3.

Remove the "Blind Date" Effect

I really liked what Brett had to say about the "Blind Date" effect: "LinkedIn is a safe social media community for business owners (especially those who shun Facebook). Think of it as the eHarmony to skankydate.com. Potential employers can look at your profile and see if you are the right fit for their business, their company community, and their company culture. You can show people that you are right for them by providing useful updates, answers, and discussions on LinkedIn. And make sure your photo is up-to-date so they recognize you!"

Get Recommendations

Brett agrees that you must use LinkedIn for thought leadership positioning and branding. However, he thinks you should go beyond just telling people you are: "Prove it. Self-proclaimed thought leadership is miserable. In my opinion it's great to position yourself as someone who is knowledgeable—but let other people call you an expert. Get recommendations, but make sure they are realistic."

Recommendations are a great place to let others talk about you and uplift you. Brett says, "While I prefer video or audio testimonials, written recommendations are better than nothing (as long as they are not from your mom, brother, or cousin). Make them good, relevant, professional—and no spelling errors!"

He also emphasized not to use your positioning or branding to elevate yourself above others. You are positioning yourself to help people, to provide valuable information, and support others so that people are drawn to you.

Some Do's and Don'ts

Don't paint a different picture of yourself online different from whom you are in person. That means no 1970s glam shots. Own your faults and your awesomeness. Hold yourself accountable for what you have done. Don't:

- Post anything that will turn off an employer
- Post anything completely irrelevant
- Distract them with irrelevant facts
- Be fake or vulgar online
- Over-post or overshare

  Do:
- Dedicate yourself to your passion
- Research your audience; know who can you help as a job seeker and who can help you find a job
- Position yourself as an expert
- Be focused
- Keep current with your industry and your profile
- Create content
- Share content
- Answer questions and post helpful status updates
- Help people
- Be a leader in helping people out
- Be humorous, playful, and lighthearted (for the right audience)

Tools to Use: Mobbios and WOWsume

Brett has created a few tools that might be useful for the job seeker. Mobbios (translation: mobile biographies) is a mobile and quick response (QR) code marketing tool that helps "increase audience engagement and ease of connectivity, and revolutionizes the way consumers interact with real-world brands and products." I just think it's a nifty video and QR tool that is becoming more and more relevant in this day and age.

Brett created the Mobbios WOWsume tool specifically for job seekers. He says that "WOWsume is one cool way that job seekers can 'one up' their competition by creating a nicely formatted and impressive video résumé."

I also recommend job seekers have a video resume, and this tool makes it more professional than some talking head captured on your computer's camera!

As Brett says, "Your paper résumé is not a reflection of your potential. WOWsume, on the other hand, gives hiring employers the ability to see who you are, how personable you can be, and engage with your potential all before meeting you in person."

I recommend you add the link to your WOWsume in the websites section.

- Get Mobbios at `www.mobbios.com`.
- Get WOWsume at `www.wowsume.com`.

Never Give Up!

To wrap things up, Brett advises, "Keep trying! Keep following up. Remember, on average, it takes seven 'touches' to make a sale (or sell yourself to an employer). People have to feel they know and trust you in order to hire you. LinkedIn is about building relationships."

He also recommends that you have your elevator pitch down. What are you doing? What are your skills? Don't undervalue your skill set. If you don't value your skills, no one else will. But also, never forget to focus on your potential employer. How you are going to help them achieve their goals?

Go forward boldly. You have to believe in yourself. Have passion and have fun!

LinkedIn for Entrepreneurs

I met Miles Austin (`www.linkedin.com/in/milesaustin`) when he came to Denver to run a business I had invested in and was blown away by his knowledge, generosity, and business acumen. He has been a mentor to me ever since, and I am thrilled to share some of his secrets for entrepreneurs using LinkedIn here.

As Miles says in his LinkedIn summary, he is "The Web Tools Guy" and a popular Seattle social media, social business, and social selling speaker. He takes his audience from the theory to the implementation of the tools and social platforms that are transforming society. Miles has extensive sales and leadership background (from the Fortune 500 market leaders to three of his own start-ups), so he is the perfect guy for this chapter. Read his "Fill the Funnel" blog at `www.fillthefunnel.com`.

We already talked about keywording your profile to get found earlier in the book, but Miles takes it one (very useful) step further.

Find High-Traffic, Low-Competition Keywords Using Google's Keyword Tool

One of the things I find people just don't do on LinkedIn is correctly keyword their profile. As I have mentioned throughout this book, one key to success on LinkedIn as an entrepreneur, especially if you are a new entrepreneur or are starting a new business, is to get found.

Miles adds a little more depth to the strategy I shared with you in Chapter 3. He says, "The first step is to go to the Google keyword tool (`https://adwords.google.com/o/Targeting/Explorer?`) and type in the keywords *your clients would be searching for.* Even though you might consider yourself a dental technician, I guarantee that at 3 a.m. when they wake up with tooth pain they are looking for a dentist, not a dental!"

Of course, use the keywords that get massive searches. In this case: dentist vs. dental. But here is the trick. Miles says you should "find the keywords that get high volume (lots of searches) but don't have a lot of competition (those words or phrases are not on as many websites)" as seen in Figure 11.1.

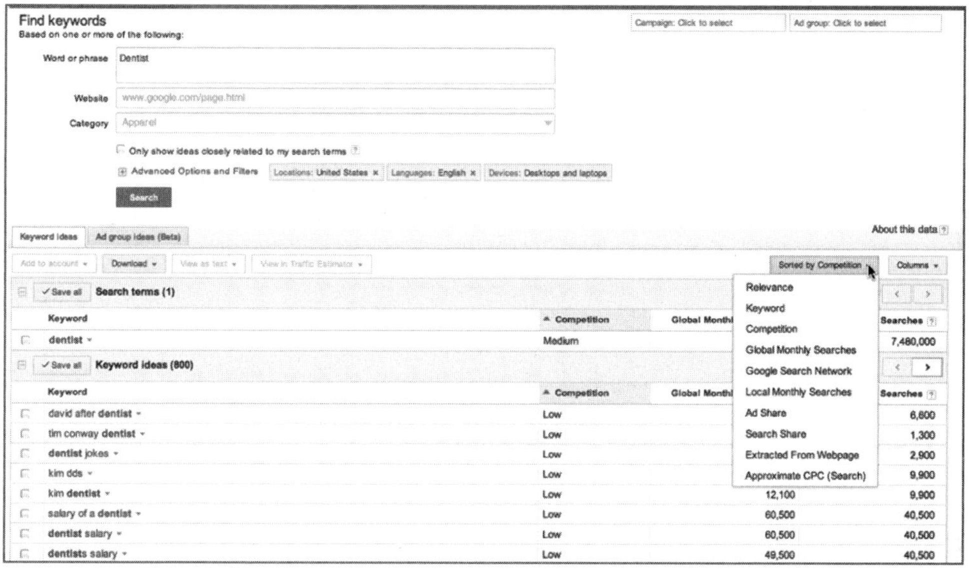

Figure 11.1 Find the keywords that get high volume but not much website competition.

In this case, "Dentist Salary" had a lot of hits but not much website competition. So you could use the phrase "Is your dentist worth her salary?" on LinkedIn and have a better chance of getting your profile seen. (Obviously this works for your website too!)

Miles also shares that you can sort the results by global or monthly searches to get the highest volume and sort the results by competition to get those well searched for but less used keywords. He says, "A commonsense businessperson will incorporate those words throughout their activity on LinkedIn—not only in their profile, but also in their status updates, group discussions, etc."

Create Subgroups

Most folks know that groups help brand you and position you as a thought leader in your community. They can also help you get found in searches. Miles says he often has entrepreneurs complain that all the good groups have been started or taken. So here is what he tells them to do:

1. Find a relevant geography-based group on LinkedIn.

2. Join and become an active participant.

3. Pay special attention to the activity of the owner or manager of the group. Read their posts; comment, like, and share them to increase top-of-mind awareness with them.

4. Establish a relationship with the individual to build trust.

5. When you feel you have established a relationship, ask them if you can create a subgroup to manage. Be clear you don't want to own it, but just manage it with the owner's support.

6. Create the subgroup.

7. Nurture and grow it.

Now you, for all intents and purposes, have your own group! What you do with it is up to you.

Miles recently did a search on some top industry groups and what he discovered was that very few of them had subgroups. A lot of group owners hadn't created subgroups because they didn't know how to or didn't have the time to manage them. Miles says, "You might find that the group owner is happy to let you create a subgroup because it will help to grow and substantiate their 'mother' group."

Once you manage your subgroup, you can bring additional value to it by bringing value to its members. Provide interesting content. Nurture relationships and conversation. Activate the Polls, Jobs, and Promotions tabs.

Note: Miles shares that one thing he has done to add value to his groups is to use his Promotions tab to encourage members to post promotions or special offers that are only available to other group members. It becomes a Groupon-type thing. Now instead of being a tab that people avoid like the plague, it becomes a reason to check into the group daily! As a group manager, you must be diligent in monitoring this tab and deleting spam.

Amazon Reading List

Miles has found that more and more people are utilizing the Amazon reading list, so this is how he uses it in his business strategy:

- Read the books that your prospects are reading.

- Read the books that your prospect's bosses are reading.

Here's an example of what Miles has done:

"Say I wanted to connect with Director of Global Development at Starbucks. I would go to the company page or do an advanced search to find her profile. If she were reading anything, I would buy it. But then I would go one step further. I would do a search on who her boss might be and see what he/she was reading. Then I would order and read the book. And then I would mail the same book to the Director of Global Development and say something like: 'I noticed that your CEO is reading [book name]. I also am reading it and found it very useful. Because you are the [title] of [company], I thought you might find it very interesting if you haven't read it yet. The book talks about [relevant content here], which is a practice I employ myself. I hope you enjoy it. Of course if you have any questions, please don't hesitate to contact me at [email address]."

If you can, you might try following up with them via LinkedIn through a message, introduction, or a group.

Why does this work? According to Miles, it gets their attention. It alludes to your interests and thought leadership. It separates you from the pack. It shows you are business and social media savvy. Plus, very few people will throw a book away. (Make sure your contact information is in it—not just a business card, but handwritten in the cover.)

Miles says, "You might invest $19, which is even cheaper than buying someone coffee these days. You might get their attention. You have a much better chance of them calling you back. It takes the barriers down. It builds relationships."

Subscribe to SlideShare

You'll recall from Chapter 7 that I am a big fan of SlideShare, but I never thought to use it the way Miles suggests! Since LinkedIn now owns SlideShare, I think this is a relevant strategy.

According to Miles, the first thing you should do is subscribe to SlideShare. Don't just use it to upload your own content, but subscribe to the SlideShare feed of your target audience. Miles adds that many companies have their own SlideShare page and will upload presentations about their product or service, how-to presentations, as well as shareholder presentations. You can gain a lot of good business intelligence through SlideShare:

- Search SlideShare for the profile of a company you are targeting.
- Skim through their presentations until you find one that is relevant to you.
- Find your target person on LinkedIn.
- Send them a message or InMail, or ask for an introduction and say something like "I really enjoyed flipping through the presentation you presented to your shareholders on SlideShare. I see that you are active in [industry, charity, etc.].

I participate in [something in common] and have found [add content of value here—a tip, statistic, etc.]."

- Hold off making a pitch right away, but do encourage engagement by asking questions.

SlideShare can be a huge source of information.

Consider a Paid Account

Both Miles and I have changed our minds about LinkedIn's paid accounts and now recommend that people enroll in at least the basic business account:

www.linkedin.com/mnyfe/subscriptionv2?displayProducts=&family=general&compare_acct=&trk=acct_set_compare

Here's why:

Who's Viewed My Profile With the free account, you only get to see the last five people who viewed your profile. With even the basic paid account, you get to see everyone who is checking up on you. These are people you need to follow up with. Reach out to them. Ask them how you can help them. And of course with the paid account you can use your InMails, as well as messages, introductions, or contacting through groups.

Top Searched Keywords With the paid account you get to see the keywords people used to search for you and the percentage of popularity. Miles says, "For instance, when I check these statistics (also found under Who's Viewed Your Profile), my name (Miles) comes up first with 20 percent of the searches, Twitter comes up second with 4 percent, and then the keyword phrase I want to be searched under, 'Professional Development,' is only 1 percent. That tells me that I need to start talking about and using the keyword phrase 'Professional Development' more in my profile LinkedIn Activity."

Better Searches With the paid account you get better access to people's information on LinkedIn. You can find people faster and you can save more searches. This saves you time and effort and makes you more effective.

Profile Organizer When you find a good prospect, you can organize them (first-, second-, and third-level and group connection), keep notes on them, and add contact information to the Profile Organizer. It almost becomes a customer relationship management (CRM) tool.

OpenLink The paid account allows you to use OpenLink so anyone can reach out to you for free. Open the floodgates. Will you get people who are not of value to you? Yes. Will you get people of value contacting you? Yes.

Other Tools Miles Recommends

Since Miles is known as "The Tool Guy," I asked him what additional tools entrepreneurs using LinkedIn might invest their time and/or money into.

IntroRocket

Introrocket.com integrates all of your LinkedIn connections; it builds a visual map of how you and they, and all of their connections, are connected together. It also gives you the "strength" of your connections and rates or ranks your connections according to relevance. It gives you a visual map of the best people in your network to use to introduce you to a prospect. According to their website, you are 12 times more likely to connect with a lead by using IntroRocket. As you read in Chapter 10, "LinkedIn Ads, Labs, Apps, and Tools," both GoHachi and Cloze have a similar offer, but I must say I really liked IntroRocket's interface. I think it's worth trying all three and seeing which one you prefer.

TimeTrade

Miles says you should use all three of your website links on LinkedIn to:

- Get found by your network
- Give your network information as fast and as easy and painless as possible (link to a download)
- Engage with your network

I think this is a brilliant deduction! I plan on stealing it and sharing it with my webinar guests and readers!

Miles says, "I use one of my website links to give LinkedIn members a way to easily set up an appointment with me using www.TimeTrade.com. A TimeTrade account lets you set up appointment times (it syncs with your calendar) so that all a person has to do is click on a link to see when you are available. Then they book their appointment. I have set my account up so that anyone who finds my LinkedIn profile can book a free 15-minute exploratory call with me. This tool has generated one meeting or more every single week. And that means more business and more income. Also, because I am on the West Coast, I set some early appointments in TimeTrade so that my East Coast prospects can easily schedule a time with me. Making it easy on them means more business for me."

Final Words of Advice

Miles' final words of advice are these: "As an entrepreneur, you ignore LinkedIn at your own peril. You will never know if you are losing business opportunities and/or connections if you do not have a strong LinkedIn profile and activity plan. If you are still on the fence, search for a few of your competitors. If you find them easily on LinkedIn, then your customers and prospects are too."

Recruiters, HR Personnel, and Hiring Managers

If you've been on LinkedIn for a while, then you know my friend and technical editor, Stacy Donovan Zapar, known as "The Most Connected Woman on LinkedIn" (www.linkedin.com/in/stacyzapar). She is a longtime corporate recruiter who is about to launch her own business as a social recruiter. And she is just a really, really cool woman!

Her statement in her Summary section tells it all: "I love to meet new people through LinkedIn and pay it forward by helping them to grow their businesses, reconnect with former coworkers, network with industry peers, share best practices, find their next position, etc."

Here are some really cool tips for recruiters and hiring managers from my interview with Stacy.

Share Your Contact Information Clearly on Your Profile

Stacy says that it is very important to make sure that your contact information can be easily found on your profile. "There is nothing more frustrating than finding the perfect candidate and not being able to contact them easily, and vice versa. As a hiring manager, recruiter, or HR professional, you want to make sure your contact information is clear on your profile."

She suggests you add your email to your Summary section or Contact [YourName] section, as we covered in Chapter 3. "You might say something like: 'I accept all invitations. Please feel free to send me an invitation or email me about a position at name@domainname.com. To see available jobs, click on the 'Available Jobs' folder in Box.net below."

LinkedIn Recruiter Alternatives

While it's fantastic to have access to the entire LinkedIn membership (currently over 180 million users), Stacy doesn't think you need a LinkedIn Recruiter account if money is an issue and your network is robust enough on its own. She suggests that you can get creative by leveraging traditional networking/sourcing techniques and using your LinkedIn account in conjunction with other tools at your disposal (Google, Twitter, Facebook, your applicant tracking system, and so forth).

As Stacy says, "Even though you don't have as wide of a net to cast as with LinkedIn Recruiter (where you have access to the entire LinkedIn network), you can still do a lot with a free or basic paid account."

The basic paid business account is only $19.95 a month (if you buy it for 12 months) and gives you access to the Profile Organizer, which gives you the opportunity to organize your network and write notes. Why is this important? Well, as Stacy says, "You don't want to keep sending the same message to the same candidates time and time again. And you want to keep track of any relevant information that candidate shares with you (i.e., open to relocation, only wants $150K+, wants to move into a different field, asked to not be contacted again, expects to get his XYZ certification by the end of the summer, needs visa transfer/sponsorship, former employee, fired from previous position, blocked my InMail, etc.)." The notes you make on your candidate profiles and in the Profile Organizer can work as a pseudo-applicant tracking system.

"Mine" the Knowledge from Your Own Company

Here's an effective strategy from Stacy that works well for corporate recruiters:

"When I am recruiting for a remote office location where I may not have a very robust network, I will build relationships and network with current employees in that department who work in the target office location. The handy thing is that you don't even have to use LinkedIn to contact these people (which can be slow and/or costly); you can simply contact them through your company email system, one by one if you prefer or send a bulk message to all relevant employees in that location.

"Ask them who they might know who's a fit for that opening. Ask if they have any contacts who might be a good resource for referrals. Reference the employee referral bonus, if your company has one. Ask if there are any relevant, reputable companies in the area that would be good targets to source from. Where did *they* used to work before joining your company? Are there any local professional organizations—online or in person—that might be strategic to join (JUGs—Java User Groups, Perl Programming Meetups, local marketing organizations, etc.).

> **Note:** Because you're not local to that location, have the hiring manager and/or some of the team members attend those meetings. I've found that hiring managers and peers in their field are often much more approachable and therefore better at attracting candidates at these meetings than a recruiter (who may be viewed as an outsider and/or "salesy").

"After emailing a group of employees, I'll follow up with a LinkedIn invite to connect to those who took time to respond with helpful advice. For every new connection I make in that location, I now have a multitude of second- and third-degree connections who have worked with this person in the past (hopefully in that same location and in that line of work)! Perfect, huh? I now have a more robust, very targeted network in that location, along with a built-in employee referral mechanism. Great news since a warm-lead/employee referral is statistically a higher-quality hire with a lower cost-to-fill."

Join Local and Big Groups

As do Jason, Brett, and Miles, Stacy loves groups. In her opinion, the biggest advantage to joining LinkedIn groups is the free messaging feature to fellow group members. This awesome feature can save you so much time and money (compared to Introductions and InMails). And think outside of the box when it comes to LinkedIn groups. Don't just source within the groups themselves, but also when doing candidate searches in LinkedIn. When you find a profile of interest and want to reach out, look in the right column of that profile for the Groups You Share With *Name* box. If you have any groups in common, then you can message that member for free. And if you notice one or two particular groups showing up time after time, then that's a great indicator that you should try to join that group. That's where your top candidates are hanging out! (For a refresher on the power of groups, read Chapter 6.)

Stacy continues: "The first thing I'll do when I hear that I'll be recruiting for a new geographic location or new skill set is to go on LinkedIn and join several relevant groups, local to that opening. It often takes group owners several days or even weeks to approve your membership, so do this first to get the clock running. Don't wait until you're desperate for candidates and feeling pressure from the hiring manager."

Don't forget that, as recruiters, it's also important to join a few of those really big megagroups (with several hundred thousand members) because it enables you to message so many more people for free. Stacy suggests that some of the best groups for recruiters are:

- Jobs (950,000-plus members)
- Linked:HR (715,000-plus)
- eMarketing (440,000-plus)
- Executive Suite (250,000-plus)
- Consultants Network (225,000-plus)

It seems like just about *everyone* is a member of at least one of these! Of course, find the ones that best suit your needs and your typical recruiting focus.

Stacy also suggests that you consider joining (or trying to join!) the company alumni and/or company careers groups of your competitors. These employees are often fantastic candidates for your openings, and they are probably familiar with your company, making them much more likely to respond.

Remember, you can only join 50 groups, so be strategic in your choices. You can always leave the group if it proves fruitless or once the position is filled and you're no longer recruiting for that discipline or location.

She recommends that you don't use up too many of your 50 spots joining recruiting or HR groups—fellow recruiters aren't the people you're trying to target!

Use Templates

Stacy is a big fan of templates. (So am I!) She says, "I have a Word doc on my desktop with message templates that I use in my communications on LinkedIn. There is no sense in re-creating the wheel so I create templates for the messages I send out over and over, often customized for the position at hand."

Once Stacy finds a candidate of interest, she will paste the template and then further customize it based on the candidate's profile. For instance, she might write something like, "Dear *John*, I had an opportunity to view your profile today and was very impressed with your background and experience, especially your time at *XYZ Competitor Company*." She has found that taking the few extra seconds to customize the message makes a big difference in the response rate from cold-call candidates.

Another tip Stacy gives when reaching out to cold candidates on LinkedIn is to use the Expertise Request option (if using InMail) rather than the Career Opportunity option. If using Introductions or messages, cater your subject line along those lines ("PR Networking" or "Finance Expertise" instead of "PR Opening" or "Looking for a Financial Analyst"). Instead of blasting your position at them (which comes across as spammy), appeal to them as a relevant, well-connected expert in their field. Let them know that you are impressed with their background and value their opinion as it relates to XYZ (Java, Marketing, PR, Accounting, etc.). Ask them if they can point you to any of their peers or other experts in their field who might be interested in your amazing opportunity. Many times, they will respond to learn more and oftentimes will throw their hat in the ring. And even if that person doesn't work out, you can still network with them, get additional leads/referrals from them, and link up with them, gaining access to their entire network of industry peers.

Stacy's Email "Hack"

You can burn through a lot of InMails on LinkedIn or waste time sending lengthy introductions that may or may not ever get passed along to your target contact. Or, once you get a candidate's name, you can use the following Google "hack" to get their email.

Most companies have a set email pattern (`jsmith@acme.com` vs. `john.smith@acme.com` vs. `john_smith@acme.com`, etc.) that is consistent for all of their employees. Once you figure out that company's pattern, you can then plug in your target's name and email that person directly.

The company's email address format usually matches up with the company's website address (i.e., `www.acme.com` matches `xxxxx@acme.com`), so do a quick Google search to find out the company's website address. To do this, search with `*.*@acme.com`.

Scan through the search results until you find two or three employee email addresses listed. You will usually be able to see a pattern within the first page or two of search results (i.e., `robert_brown@acme.com`, `michael_jones@acme.com`, `stephanie_black@acme.com`, etc.). Voilà! You now know that that company's email pattern is `firstname_lastname@acme.com`!

Simply plug your target contact's name into the email pattern and reach out to them directly. This trick has saved me lots of time, money, and InMails, especially since I've kept a running Excel file of all of the email patterns I've researched over the years. Very handy!

When you send them a message, make sure you still reference their LinkedIn profile and use your templates.

Do's and Don'ts for Recruiters

According to Stacy, here are some key things not to do:

- Don't just use your status updates to *only* post jobs. Don't be a one-trick pony.

- Don't be a spammer.

- Don't be a job blaster. Instead, post valuable, interesting, and engaging content. Then you can sprinkle in job posts every five or six status updates.

- Don't break the rules in groups. Don't hijack discussion threads (comments) to post your job.

- Don't post jobs on the main discussion board. Use the Jobs tab to post jobs (and don't overpost, keeping in mind that postings expire in two weeks).

- Don't post jobs in the regular Discussion section. Do use the Jobs Discussions tab in your groups to post jobs (they expire after about two weeks).

- Don't give recruiters a bad name. Lots of people will block recruiter requests because of all of the irrelevant spam that comes their way, and many groups no longer allow recruiters to join, all because of a few bad eggs.

- Don't forget about saved searches! Let LinkedIn email you when a new candidate joins LinkedIn.

- Don't just include a link to your LinkedIn profile in your email signature.

  Here are some important do's:

- Keep good notes. Use your notes.

- Reconnect—it's all about warm leads.

- Grow your network. Be strategic but remember that the larger your network, the wider your candidate pool.

- Use an email address when you can.

- Do your homework; make sure someone is a good fit before you reach out to them or ask for an introduction. Don't contact a Java Developer in the Bay Area about a QA Tester role in Minneapolis…. This is the number-one complaint I hear from LinkedIn users regarding recruiters! It makes us look lazy or incompetent.

- Start locally in your search and then expand it.

- Be targeted in your search. Use your keywords.

- Think about who your audience is. Your audience isn't just active job seekers. Cater your message to appeal to those passive job seekers who might not otherwise respond to you.

- Target those who are gainfully employed. Even better, identify those who are experts in their field and develop relationships with those people. Groups and Answers are both great tools for doing this.

- Add content that is relevant to your audience. (Looking for a candidate in a marketing position? Post articles about marketing in marketing groups.)

- Build your network before you need it!

- Join groups before you need them.

- Connect with LIONs in the area or industry you are moving in. Even if you're not an open networker, just adding a few superconnectors to your network can greatly increase your network size and overall reach.

- Use Hootsuite or similar tools to manage your LinkedIn presence.

- Post job descriptions in Box.net.

- Use SlideShare to post jobs or upload a video. Evangelize your company culture or share some of your company's amazing benefits/perks.

- Use all three of the website fields—one with your company career page with job postings, one with your personal blog/website (Don't have one? Change that!), and one to post your Twitter name or a particularly *hot* opening: "HOT: Java SWE - Bay Area." Don't waste any of your available options.

- Be proactive and diligent about inviting candidates to link up. And don't wait until the interview, offer, or on-boarding process! The sooner they join your network, the sooner their peers and colleagues become part of your candidate pool.

In conclusion, Stacy says to use LinkedIn like a Lego. "It's not the only tool in your arsenal but it's the most powerful one to build on, in my opinion. Use it as a building block, pairing it with other social networking platforms (Twitter, Facebook, Google+, Pinterest, Blogs, YouTube, Meetups), online resources (Google, Bing, etc.), and internal corporate tools (email, CRM, applicant tracking system, etc.).

"And when at all possible, pick up the phone! You don't have to use social media to be social!"

Legal Professionals

Legal professionals tend to be a conservative group. So when it comes to adopting social media into their practices, I have found that attorneys and other legal professionals gravitate more to LinkedIn than any other network. In fact, when I did a search on the keyword "attorney OR lawyer" back when I started using LinkedIn six years ago, there were barely over a hundred thousand members using the words attorney or lawyer in their profile. Now there are over a million.

In 2010, attorney Kendra Brodin and I wrote an ebook called *Linked into Law*. We recently refreshed some of the key content so that we could release the best parts in this section. (To order the new Linked Into Law ebook, you can email me at Viveka@LinkedIntoBusiness.com.)

Kendra (www.LinkedIn.com/in/KendraBrodin) is the Director of Career and Professional Development at the University of St. Thomas School of Law in

Minneapolis, Minnesota, where she helps students and alumni prepare for and build a meaningful career. She is also a law firm consultant and executive coach for lawyers on personal and professional development topics such as individual and organizational leadership, goal setting and achieving, and career and life success and satisfaction.

Here are the key benefits of being a lawyer on LinkedIn:

Ability to Be Known The ways you participate in the marketplace will help define your personal and law practice brand. If you contribute and share in a positive way, you can develop a heightened reputation and become a credentialed authority in these communities.

Ability to Find Others With a moderately sized network (which is easy to build), you can develop a sufficient reach when performing advanced searches. With functional search fields, your results are more targeted so you find the people you need. You can begin your research and evaluation immediately, saving time and money when looking for vendors, employees, partners, Venture Capitalists (VCs), joint venture partners, and so forth.

Opportunity to Learn and Share LinkedIn group discussions are an excellent place to showcase your knowledge and advice. With the introduction of JD Supra Legal Updates, attorneys and legal professionals are now able to share their articles and filings across the Web. This creates authority, referrals, and the ability to generate new clients.

Ability to Connect with Group Members There are many exclusive groups, both legal- and client-industry related, that give you access to other members and people who share commonalities.

Opportunity to Show You Are plugged Into Current Technology Active participation in LinkedIn tells others you are serious and competent about networking and new technology.

Mistakes to Avoid

Lawyers are conservative for a reason. They have ethical issues that many other professions just don't have to deal with. For that reason, we have added this section to make sure that legal professionals don't inadvertently land in hot water using LinkedIn. Here are some mistakes to avoid.

Be Careful when Specializing

In many states, attorneys may not "specialize" unless they are specifically licensed or registered to claim specialization in a certain area of the law. And yet many—hopefully most—attorneys have a specific area of focus. When you create your list of keywords for optimizing your profile, focus on the specific areas of law you practice.

Instead of a "specialty," try something like "My practice focuses exclusively on bankruptcy" rather than "I specialize in bankruptcy." If you don't have a specialty in patent law, don't say that you have one on your LinkedIn profile; you will always want to be mindful of your state's rules on this and abide by them.

Don't Break Client Confidentiality

Here are some tips on avoiding breaking client confidentiality:

- Don't post about clients. You may be tempted to post something like "Just off the phone with client who lied to me about all the facts." Remember that the time and date of your posting is preserved with the post, so it has the potential of revealing information to someone who might know that the client was meeting with the lawyer that day.

- Don't post what you are working on. Simply tweeting that you are working on a summary judgment motion (especially if you relate facts that might be unique to the case) could be a breach of confidentiality.

- Remember that words spread. On LinkedIn and other social media, you may think you have a limited, controlled audience, but you don't really know how many or which of your friends are connecting with and distributing your updates to people you don't know.

- If you wouldn't say it to your neighbor, don't post it!

Don't Create Attorney/Client Relationships

LinkedIn can be an absolutely amazing place to share your knowledge and experience. But as you begin to connect with potential clients online, that very thin line of perception may be crossed. What might have been an "off the cuff" answer for you becomes a client/attorney relationship to the person with whom you are communicating. Make very clear, with disclaimers if necessary, that the information you are sharing should not be taken as legal advice.

Don't Connect to Everyone

Normally, we recommend connecting with everyone on LinkedIn because the larger your network, the more visible you are. The more visible you are, the more likely you are to find the contacts you are looking for and be found by those looking for an attorney. In almost every case, this is a good thing. The exception is when a connection in your network disqualifies you from a case because of conflict of interest. Be selective when choosing to connect with someone.

Don't Forget "Legal Updates"

The Legal Updates InApp enables lawyers to gain visibility on LinkedIn outside of their own networks by distributing their written work (blog posts, articles, clients alerts, etc.) to people who have opted to receive legal updates on whatever interests them or matters to their professional lives. When someone in financial services installs the app, they start getting all manner of legal content from JD Supra on banking and finance issues. People in the insurance field receive legal updates on insurance matters.

Tech folks get IP, technology, and other such related updates. Anyone using the app can customize this feed with any other subjects that interest him or her. But more than that, the content always ties back to the person who wrote it, the lawyer. And if that lawyer has also installed the Legal Updates app, in a single click a reader outside of that lawyer's network can connect to the lawyer directly on LinkedIn.

Also, lawyers who use this app can include a portfolio of their JD Supra publications directly on their LinkedIn profile—and they can upload content on either JD Supra or LinkedIn. With each upload, the legal update is also announced to their network (with a LinkedIn status update). So, you're able to share content with your own network *and* grow your network by making sure your writing reaches targeted readers outside of your network.

One user of Legal Updates says, "This is networking at its best. LinkedIn users are eager to share articles of interest, recommend them to friends, and network with the authors. And Legal Updates is a nearly endless source of that sort of credentialing content."

Ethical Considerations for LinkedIn

There is a lot of information available on the Web about ethical considerations, and I will try to pin down the most salient and important ones. Then I will leave it to you to do your own research and investigation of your state rules and their implications for your LinkedIn usage. Social media is unchartered territory for most state bar organizations, so this is fair warning to be thoughtful and above-board in all of your social media interactions.

Just as with anything else you do as an attorney, you are subject to your state ethics regulations and rules. Being online and communicating virtually may feel different than face-to-face interactions or print communications, but your online actions are just as subject to ethics rules and regulations as in-person interactions.

While you might refute the fact that social media sites like LinkedIn are intended to attract clients and should thus be exempt from these ethical considerations, that argument won't get you too far. To try to simplify things a bit, let's consider the three main categories that are governed by state ethics regulations:

Communications Email and other web-based interactions (like social media) constitute communications. So, just as with all other communications, be honest. Make sure what you say on any profile or web page is true and accurate. The American Bar Association (ABA) Model Rule of Professional Conduct 7.1 instructs lawyers to avoid false or misleading communication about lawyers and their services. You must be hyper-vigilant that you don't mislead others about yourself or your services—when in doubt, downplay rather than exaggerate.

Solicitations The ABA's Model Rule 7.3 now states that "a lawyer shall not by in-person, live telephone or real-time electronic contact solicit professional employment from a prospective client when a significant motive for the lawyer's doing so is the lawyer's pecuniary gain." Although not all states have the "real-time" language, it is likely that many states will begin to follow suit on adding this kind of verbiage to their rules. The rule forbids using real-time electronic contact to solicit business directly from a potential client.

Advertisement If you are using LinkedIn for professional purposes, you should operate under the assumption that what you do will be governed by your state's advertising rules. Some experts assert that if you're going to put your firm's name on your LinkedIn page (which most of us would do), your profile has thus immediately become an extension of your firm's website and now requires a legal disclaimer akin to your website.

I suggest these strategies to help legal professionals avoid ethical snags on LinkedIn:

Use Disclaimers If you are concerned that others might perceive this as a specialization, you can always put a disclaimer in your Summary section, in the Description section of Experience, or even at the bottom of any communication you have within LinkedIn (messages, profile forwarding, introductions, InMails, group comments, etc.). You may want to create a few disclaimers and keep them handy on your desktop for quick cut-and-paste responses.

Testimonials On LinkedIn, you can post testimonials in the form of recommendations. This is great for most professionals, and it makes sense on a professional networking site like LinkedIn. But it's sticky for lawyers. Testimonials on LinkedIn can be a good thing, as long as you don't make (or permit others to make) false or misleading statements. Also, don't participate in an "I-recommend-you, you-recommend-me" game since that could violate Model Rule 7.2 by offering value in exchange for a recommendation. It is important to note that LinkedIn actually plays this game by recommending that you write a testimonial for the person who just wrote one for you. If you truly want to do so, play it safe and wait a few weeks.

Ghost Posting Think twice before someone else "ghost posts" on your behalf. If someone else posts for you, it is arguably misleading because clients might think that you have written the material and are therefore knowledgeable about a particular topic. This approach is tempting, but it could break ethical rules.

Your State's Ethics Rules If you haven't read your state's ethics rules in a while, it's time for a refresher course. Every state has specific rules about legal marketing and social media. You must take some time to read and become familiar with your specific state's rules, interpretations, and opinions. Period.

You must comply with the ethical marketing rules for the state in which you have your primary law practice and law office. Also, it is critical to know the rules of any other state that you may be actively soliciting clients or are licensed to practice law. With social media so pervasive and accessible, you must be familiar with the rules in other states, especially if you are intentionally marketing to clients in another state in which you are licensed to practice.

LinkedIn can be an absolutely amazing place to share your knowledge and experience. Not only can you attract clients and clients' referrals, but it's also an excellent credentialing tool. As Adrian Lurssen of JD Supra said in a 2011 interview with me: "Potential clients and referring attorneys are looking to Google. When JD Supra members continuously show up in searches because of the content they are sharing across many online mediums like LinkedIn, they become more authoritative."

For law firm administrators and managing partners reading this, don't ban LinkedIn for your employees. Social media sites can be great legal advertising tools. Some helpful social media policy and guideline links are available with a quick Internet search. Make sure you are in compliance, and then use this tool for business development and client retention. Final words:

- Know your state rules.
- Be honest.
- Think about the rules before you post anything.
- Use appropriate disclaimers.
- Limit "advertising" language.
- When in doubt, leave it out!

Women on LinkedIn

One of my passions, and a book I really do want to write, is on how women are using social media: what they should and should not being doing; how their innate skills make them amazing users, curators, and creators of social media content; and how some common traits of many women might be holding them back. Rather than interview someone for this section, I decided to share my thoughts and beliefs.

One thing I have found—and I am generalizing a great deal—is that many women tend more toward care-taking than self-promotion, both in life and in the world of social media. Yes, some of the smartest and most savvy marketing people I know are women. But when working one on one with some of the amazing female entrepreneurs I've had the privilege of knowing, I often come up against "I could never say that about myself—that's bragging!" You know what? Brag away!

Get Over the "Little Ol' Me" Syndrome

I have no doubt that if you Google something like "Find self-esteem in five easy steps," you'll find dozens of websites that can help you get to where you need to be in presenting yourself in life as well as online.

Do you want to feel more successful and create a more confident voice on LinkedIn? Then read Gail McMeekin's *The 12 Secrets of Highly Successful Women* (Red Wheel/Weiser, 2012).

Work with a personal coach if you have the resources. I have been working with Susan Somerset Webb (www.linkedin.com/in/susansomersetwebb) and she has helped me move into an exciting and powerful time in my life. Even as an international speaker and author working with Fortune 500 clients, I still woke up some mornings thinking, "But what if they knew who I really was?" Many women, like me, feel like frauds no matter how successful we are. So we need to do whatever it takes to get over that feeling.

I read a lot, take workshops, and work with a coach. There are many free resources you can find if money is an issue to get over whatever is keeping you from fully acknowledging the awesomeness that you are. If you have low self-esteem and low confidence, or you're stuck in caretaking mode, you need to shake it off and find your stride in order to be more successful on LinkedIn. And in life.

"Who Does She Think She Is?"

Ava Diamond (www.bigimpactspeaking.com) is a speaking mentor and messaging strategist. She is also a popular speaker and addresses what I call the "Little Ol' Me" syndrome in many of her writings.

She has this to say about "bragging": "Many of us heard this refrain as young girls when one of our friends would brag or even say something good about themselves. We were taught not to talk about ourselves because people wouldn't like us.

"Today, we see 'obnoxious braggers,' and tell ourselves, 'I never want to come across that way.' So we don't self-promote. We fly under the radar. We get no visibility. And that's a big mistake.

"As women, learning to authentically self-promote is an art and a skill we must master to be successful in today's world. When you do it right, the rewards are tremendous."

LinkedIn is a tool that allows you to promote yourself, your business, and your products and services. Don't be shy. Tell your audience why they should work for, buy from, or hire you. Tell them what you bring to the table that no one else does.

Get a Good Photo

Invest in yourself when it comes to your profile photo. That glamour shot from your high school graduation is not going to cut it on LinkedIn. If you can, spend some money and get a professional photographer to take you profile shots. By professional photo I don't mean a hokey background and paste-it-on smile. I mean investing in a professional photographer who's got the right lighting, the right angles, and the knowledge to make you look your best.

Note: My photographer, Christina Gressianu, is one of those natural talents whom I wish everybody had access to. The things that she can do with lighting and angles is amazing. She makes me look like myself, but better. Why do I mention this? Because having your photograph taken by a professional might be the boost you need to see yourself the way others see you. It might just give you the confidence you need to shine in your work life.

If you don't have a lot of money to spend on a professional photographer, then keep an eye out for Groupon, Living Social, or Daily Deals specials. I often see offers for photo sessions at a fraction of the cost.

If you don't have any money to invest in yourself for a professional photo session, then at the very least find a friend with a digital camera, spend some time on your hair and makeup, find a place you love, and have your friend take dozens of photos of you. Choose the best one.

If you're not a fan of your body, don't worry about it. The best LinkedIn photograph is a close-up on your face. Be smiling from the inside. As hokey as it sounds, it really comes across.

Get Video

Get used to yourself on video. I know this is hard for many of us...myself included. But this is a world of video: videos on YouTube, videoconference calls, video chats, Skype, Google+ hangouts, WOWsume, and so on. We have got to get used to what we look like on film. What can you video?

- If you are a speaker or trainer, get some video of yourself doing your thing.
- If you are a consultant, shoot some video of your work with a client (make sure no proprietary information gets shared without consent).
- If you are a job seeker, put together a video résumé.
- If you are an executive, speak to your clients and customers about the benefit of hiring your company.
- If you have a product, let your customers know why they should buy it.

Many laptops have video cameras built in, and many even come with software. When no one is looking, start making videos of yourself. Test out lighting, test out angles, test out clothing choices, test out makeup and hair choices. And when you're ready, shoot a short video that you can use on your LinkedIn profile.

I got one of my biggest speaking gigs to date because of the video on my LinkedIn profile.

If you can afford a professional videographer, that's a great route to go. If you've had professional video taken of you, by all means post that video on your LinkedIn profile.

Shooting a Flattering Video of Yourself

Victoria Fricke has a very helpful article in her blog post, The Crimson Crow, on how to shoot flattering video of yourself. Although I have summarized some of the key points below, I recommend you read the whole article here:

> www.thecrimsoncrow.com/2012/05/how-to-shoot-a-flattering-webcam-video-of-yourself/

Lighting

- Move the video screen as close to the camera as possible.
- Make sure the room is well lit and that you are not casting shadows.
- Play with the lights until the desired effect is achieved.

Adjust Computer Light

Adjust your computer's brightness setting to eliminate glare and keep it from interfering with the video.

Start Recording

- Sit directly in front of the lens.
- When recording, be sure to look directly at the camera lens or eye—it is important to give the appearance of direct eye contact.
- Be sure to sit up straight and maintain good posture.
- Speak clearly without being too loud or too fast.
- Leave your hair alone!

Until my PR firm Hellerman Baretz shot an amazing professional video of me, I used the video I shot and edited on my Mac, sitting in my living room.

By the way, that was the video that got me the gig. You don't necessarily need a crew of eight, a make-up person, and a green screen. You need just a willingness to invest some time and shoot, reshoot, and reshoot until you are happy with the results.

I know, as a woman, that video can be downright scary. It doesn't add 10 pounds—I'm pretty sure it adds 30. But we just have to get over it. And get that video up there!

Give Yourself Credit

Don't be afraid to give yourself credit for your accomplishments. Don't be shy of posting awards, honors, or any kind of mention of your magnificence! Too many women have the "little ol' me" syndrome, and you know what? It just doesn't fly on LinkedIn. You need to be confident in who you are, the business you work in, and the products and services you sell. If you're a job seeker, trust me, this confidence comes across—even in a text-based site like LinkedIn.

Don't be afraid to position yourself as an expert or thought leader. That's not to say you need to put expert or guru next to your name like I did (although there's no better way of getting over "little ol' me" syndrome than publicly acknowledging your expertise in a public area like social media!). But don't be shy about posting articles or sharing flattering articles about yourself, pictures of the awards you've won, or examples of your work in Box.net.

Get Recommendations

Share the successes you've had and the honors you've won in LinkedIn's honors and awards sections. Don't be shy. You've earned them!

Final Words

If you are having a hard time representing yourself in your best light, ask you friends and clients what they like best about you. Use their words to create the Professional headline, Summary and Experience sections that represent you in the best light.

My friend Dennis Moss (who is obviously not a woman, but I like this anyway) wrote in his Summary section, "Why you should hire me—(Things I Can't Say About Myself:)" and then listed several short testimonials. How brilliant. Let other people brag on you!

Final thoughts:

- Make sure you have a flattering picture (and don't overexpose your assets!).
- Make sure your profile is complete.
- Make sure your profile represents you in the best light.
- Make sure your profile represents all your honors and awards.
- Use your website to post flattering articles written by or for you.
- Mention social media mentions of you.
- Showcase your work using Box.net.
- Showcase yourself in a video using SlideShare.
- Don't be afraid to speak your mind in status updates, group discussions, and Answers.
- Stick to your guns! Not everyone is going to agree with everything you say all they time. In fact, Gail McMeekin suggests that the more successful you become, the more people are likely to attack. So stay strong!
- Don't be a victim to "Little Ol' Me" syndrome.

- Get help if you need it (there are lots of women and mentors on LinkedIn who can help you).
- Join the group "Connect: Professional Women's Network." I just discovered it and I love it!

  www.linkedin.com/groups/Connect-Professional-Womens-Network-4409416?gid=4409416&trk=hb_side_g

Real Estate Professionals

Brad Hanks (www.linkedin.com/in/bradhanks) was one of the first folks I met through LinkedIn back in 2006. He speaks nationally on social media and LinkedIn for Realtors and kindly agreed to let me interview him for this section.

Here are a few tips he shared with me for Realtors and real estate professionals.

Participate

This seems to be a common war cry, but it bears repeating. Like every other section in this chapter, Brad encourages you to participate! "Being successful on LinkedIn is much more than just putting your profile out there. Don't just create your profile and expect the offers to come rolling in. You must participate by sharing status updates, by commenting in groups, by interacting with your network."

Participate in Groups

When you are actively participating and communicating what you are doing in your groups, that's when the activity starts. Brad says that participating in groups is not just finding a group and lurking. You must engage. He says this about himself: "I instruct and do short sales, so I joined the CDPE group (Certified Distressed Property Experts). When someone asks a question or needs help, I try to respond. And when I have questions I will post them. Groups are a great way to stay up-to-date on what's happening in your industry. I was doing short sales back in the 90s, and now that I'm getting back into it, I realize it's a new critter. So I needed to 'get in' with people who were actually doing short sales—source them for research and information."

Brad recommends these groups:

- To Our Short Sales Success!
- General Certified Residential Specialist (CRS)
- Accredited Buyer Representative (ABR)
- Certified Distressed Property Expert (CDPE)

Remember, you will get more value if you participate!

Brand Yourself

Everyone wants more exposure for their listings, but social media is not the place to be blasting them. Social media is an exercise in branding.

Like Jason and Brett, Brad defines branding as "getting your name out there, being the 'go to' person in your marketplace." And once you've done that, you have to let people know what markets you are in.

Brad adds, "I leverage my social networks from my live presentations. I've already made the connection with my audience through the event, so now they feel like they know me. And the more they feel like they know and trust me, the more likely they are to listen to and engage me."

Make Use of LinkedIn's Features

Take advantage of some of LinkedIn's applications:

- Use SlideShare for additional exposure.
- Make your profile more engaging and interactive with:
  - Video
  - Testimonials
  - A presentation of "How-Tos" (like "How to do a short sale")

Brad emphasizes that "you want to make sure your content is consumer facing. Of course other Realtors will see your content and realize you are an expert in a particular area. This will help build trust with other professionals. And that could lead to referrals."

Share Valuable Content

Brad says he never posts his listings. I did not expect to hear that from a Realtor! But here's why: "I don't see the value in it. Right now there is no targeting with status updates (from your professional profile) except to 'Anyone' or 'Connections Only,' and that means if I were to post a listing I'd be spamming 20,000+ of my connections who have no interest in buying a house. Why would I do that?"

What does he post instead? "I consider myself a curator as well as a content generator. I am happy to share valuable information that other people write. For example, I might share a link to an article from Realtor Magazine. It's not my content. But I find it useful and so do others. I often get comments like 'Thanks for sharing' even though they have the same access to the content. But in their minds, I am the source of that content even though I am not the creator of it."

Limit Your Time

Don't spend hours a day on your social networking. Your focus should be to get in, communicate and interact, and get out. Do bits and bites throughout the day; do a few minutes here and there. Brad spends less than an hour a day on his social networking.

Brad reminds us: "Remember, social networks are there to facilitate real face-to-face meetings with people. Spend your time being social! You use social media to open the door, but the focus should always be on getting to face-to-face interaction."

Nonprofits and LinkedIn

LinkedIn recently wrote a blog post, 5 Tips for Nonprofit Professionals (`http://learn.linkedin.com/nonprofits/`), highlighting several things we've covered in this book. It's worth reading the article in full, but in short, LinkedIn suggests using its platform to:

- Establish your professional brand by creating a complete profile and using it to convey passion for your cause and showcase your unique expertise.
- Drive support to your organization by adding the Volunteer and Causes section to your profile.
- Expand your network and influence by connecting with colleagues and partners.
- Share updates regularly with your network so they know what your organization is doing and what it needs.
- Create a company page for your nonprofit organization and encourage people to follow it. Be sure to fill out the Products and Services page.
- Collaborate with peers, volunteers, and potential donors by joining groups.

Groups to Join

One group they recommend is LinkedIn Nonprofit Solutions (`www.linkedin.com/groups/LinkedIn-Nonprofit-Solutions-4181975`), which enables nonprofit professionals and organizations to tell their story, recruit relationships, and engage key audiences like supporters, partners, or future staff and board members.

The other group they mentioned is The Chronicle of Philanthropy (`www.linkedin.com/groups?home=&gid=1188667`) with amazing members like Libby Gill (`www.linkedin.com/in/libbygillcompany`) who you can learn a lot from. Libby is an internationally known executive coach, brand strategist, and bestselling author. Her latest book is *You Unstuck: Mastering the New Rules of Risk-taking in Work and Life* (Travelers' Tales/Solas House, 2009).

I also recommend the group LinkedIn Nonprofit Solutions (`www.linkedin.com/groups/LinkedIn-Nonprofit-Solutions-4181975?`) with members like Beth Kanter, a well-known expert on how nonprofits should use social media.

Join these groups. Engage with these people!

LinkedIn and Nonprofit Tools

LinkedIn has two offers for nonprofits. One is called LinkedIn Nonprofit Solutions, headed by Bryan Breckenridge, and the other (which was disabled but LinkedIn says they are going to reintroduce it) is called LinkedIn for Good. Stay tuned to the LinkedIn blog for news on both programs.

Beth Kanter had a great guest post about nonprofits using LinkedIn on her blog (www.bethkanter.org) written by Geri Stengel (www.linkedin.com/in/geristengel). You can read the full article at http://www.bethkanter.org/linked-in/. I decided to interview Geri for this book, and she shared some very valuable insights I hope your nonprofit can make use of!

Geri Stengel is the founder of Ventureneer and Stengel Solutions. Ventureneer (http://ventureneer.com) is an excellent resource for nonprofits, and if you work with or for a nonprofit, I definitely recommend you take a peek at her site, free webinars, articles and studies.

LinkedIn is an On-ramp

Geri says that nonprofits should consider LinkedIn to be an "on-ramp for building long-term relationships." Nonprofits can use LinkedIn to find and establish connections with major donors and volunteer including board members.

IRS 990 Form and LinkedIn

The government necessitates that nonprofits fill out a 990, which is a tax form that discloses their major donors. These forms are public, and you can use them to see who is donating to nonprofits with a similar mission to yours. Geri recommends using www.GuideStar.org as a one-stop resource for 990s.

Once you identify prospects using the 990 form, you can research which social medium those donors use. Geri says that, "if your donors are Millennials, they are more likely to use Facebook, but Baby Boomers tend to use LinkedIn." On LinkedIn you can find out "what they care about" and are interested in by reading their profiles. If your donor, volunteer or prospective board member is active on LinkedIn, there are many ways to engage them. You can engage with them in LinkedIn groups. Or, ask to connect because you share a common interest or group. Once connected you can respond to their updates.

Reaching Out

Geri is adamant (and I certainly agree) that while LinkedIn is a great place to find and engage a prospect, to take that relationship to the next level you need to go old school by talking on the phone or better yet meeting in person. She says to, "Use LinkedIn to find out where a prospect lives, and if they are in a city that you live in or are going to you can reach out to them using LinkedIn and let them know you would love to grab coffee with them!"

Geri makes it very clear that you shouldn't use LinkedIn to ask for money. "It's not about asking for donations! It's about building the relationship and starting the conversation. When the time is right, ask for the donation on the phone or face-to-face."

To help nurture relationships, Geri likes to send relevant articles to her connections. "To stay top of mind, I recommend sending articles on topics of relevance to potential donors and board members. LinkedIn Today is a great source of those articles. It automatically sends me relevant articles from publications and industries I've preselected, which I then forward to appropriate people."

That's how you start to build long-term relationships!

Advanced Search

Geri is currently searching for board members an organization she services on the board of. Using Advanced Search, first Geri will search within a geographic radius. Then she will search via business category or industry. "For example my nonprofit needs an attorney and real estate professional." Finally, Geri will search for specific keywords relevant to her nonprofit. In the interview she said, "you know, it was interesting I didn't get good results when searching for keywords such as 'homeless' and 'supportive housing.' But when I broadened the search to the keyword 'volunteer' my results improved dramatically."

Geri also cites her friend Marc W. Halpert, a LinkedIn Trainer and Evangelist at www.connect2collaborate.com, who used the keyword "birding," among other SEO keywords, when helping the Connecticut Audubon Society (www.ctaudubon.org). Marc helped them research potential new board members, one of which took the position, using LinkedIn. You can contact Marc at www.linkedin.com/in/marchalpert.

Connecting

How does Geri connect on LinkedIn? "I also tell folks that LinkedIn a no-cost or low-cost day-to-day tool for finding people you want to know." She uses it to get that "all important introduction" to looking to source a gift for an auction. However, because the world of nonprofits can be competitive—there are only so many people and so much money to go around, Geri will use InMails to bypass the middleman. She says, "We have this mutual interest, and I am going to be in town—would love to grab coffee with you."

When I asked Geri if they had the free or paid account, she said that both she and Marc have the free LinkedIn account. However, to save time for the board recruitment project, Geri will upgrade to the paid account to send InMails.

Groups

Geri also thinks groups are important. "They are a great way to build your network. Also, if I have a question I might post it in a group to get answers. Groups are a great way to source expertise."

We mentioned a few groups earlier in this section, but here are three more groups Geri recommends:

- Board Source (`http://www.linkedin.com/groups?home=&gid=131626&trk=anet_ug_hm`) is a good group for governance issues.
- Bridgestar (`http://www.linkedin.com/groups?home=&gid=126919&trk=anet_ug_hm`) is a good general group for nonprofits.
- Social Media for Nonprofit Organizations (`http://www.linkedin.com/groups?home=&gid=1172477&trk=anet_ug_hm`) is a great group if you want to explore using social media to market your nonprofit.

Final words

If you are doing a "big ask" for a big donation, or for someone to be on the board, take your communication offline! Try and meet on the phone, or face to face if possible. Remember that LinkedIn is a useful on-ramp, but it is only a tool. *You* have to nurture and build the relationships with the people you find online.

You Might Want to Pay for LinkedIn

The benefits of paying for a LinkedIn membership include:

- Access to more people (not just those who are within a few degrees of separation)
- Additional search filters
- The ability to view the full profile of everyone
- The ability to connect with people directly through InMail

Wrapping Up

Don't think of LinkedIn as a technology, even though it is. Think of LinkedIn as an on-ramp to building relationships with people who can become funders, board members, employees, or strategic allies.

Some Final Tips on LinkedIn for Marketing

LinkedIn was created "to help you make better use of your professional network and help the people you trust in return." So why isn't every businessperson using LinkedIn, and why is it not topping the headlines as the best business tool ever created for the practice of marketing? The reason is that, despite its enormous potential, few people know how to use LinkedIn effectively, which is why I wrote this book.

As I wrap this book up, remember these things:

- Give yourself the credit you deserve for investing in yourself! You've done it!
- Always be of value to your tribe—and be clear on the value. No playing small. You rock!

- Remember it's about relationships. Keep generating those relationships.
- Fill the well! Do the work before it's needed. Build your network and establish relationships now that you can utilize in the future.
- Be yourself. Though the word gets overused in the world of social media, being authentic—regardless of your industry—shows through.

Index

Note to the Reader: Throughout this index **boldfaced** page numbers indicate primary discussions of a topic. *Italicized* page numbers indicate illustrations.

A

ABA (American Bar Association) Model Rule of Professional Conduct, 324
About Us section, 80
Accept Recommendation option, 176
access to groups, **205**, *205*
Account tab, 52
accounts
  Box.net, 237–239
  creating, **29–33**, *29, 31–32*
  home page, 33
  managing, **52–54**, *53*
  paid, 314, 316–317
  types, 9
activities
  Group Statistics, 218
  in profiles, 88
activity feeds, 46
Activity tab, 218
Add A Product Or Service option, 110
Add A Promotion For This Product Or Service link, 112
Add A School link, 85–87
Add & Change Email Addresses option, 104
Add And Change Email Addresses option, 54
Add Application option, 237, 243
Add Connections link, 33, 37, 39, 133–135, *133–134*
Add Education page, 173
Add Position page, 76, *76*, 173
Add Sections option, 90
Additional Notes section, **88**
administrators in company profiles, **108–109**, *109*
ads, **284**
  case studies, **288–289**
  creating, **285–286**, *285–286*
  ethical considerations, **325**
  guidelines, **287**, *287*
  investment in, **288**
Ads by LinkedIn Members section, 36
Advanced Answers Search tab, 222
Advanced People Search feature, **138–141**, *138–139*, 165
advanced search
  fields, **10**
  home page, 35
  and network size, **11**
  nonprofits, **335**
  strategic members, 200
Advertise on LinkedIn link, 38, 285
Aid Patrol Veterans feature, 290
Alba, Jason
  answering questions, 221
  experience descriptions, 80
  JibberJobber, 163
  job seeker advice, **304–307**
All Employees With A Valid Email Registered To The Company Domain option, 108
All Questions option, 225
Allow members of this group to send me messages option, 185
alumni groups, **186**
Alumni tab, 152, *152*
Amazon Reading List app, **248–249**, *249*, 312–313
American Bar Association (ABA) Model Rule of Professional Conduct, 324
analytics, **22–23**
  company, **121–123**, *122*
  other companies, **126–128**, *127*
AND operator
  Advanced People Search, **140**
  competition searches, 171
Android apps, 294
announcements for groups, **214–215**, *215*

Answer Questions tab, 222
Answers
    for blogs, **225–226**, *226*
    checklists, **275**
    designating experts, **64**
    identifying experts, **226–227**, *227*
    overview, **220–221**, *220–221*
    for relationships, **222–224**, *223*
    repurposing SME materials, **224**
    working with, **221–222**
Answers option, 44
Anyone On LinkedIn option, 51
APIs, **290**
applications
    Box.net, **237–240**, *238–240*
    checklists, **276–277**
    home page, 37, *37*
    industry-based. *See* industry-based apps
    learning about, **235–237**, *236*
    profiles, 92
    Projects and Teamspaces, **242–243**, *243*
    SlideShare, **240–242**, *241*
    third-party. *See* third-party applications
    viewing, 52
    WordPress and Blog Link, **243–244**
Archive option, 176
article shares on LinkedIn Today, **62**
Ask A Question page, 220
associations
    customizing, **88–89**, *89*
    groups, **186**
attainability of goals, **57**
attendees of events, 235
attorney/client relationships, **323**
Austin, Miles, 112, 213, **310–315**
Auto-Join groups, 205
autonomous business pages, 22
awards
    customizing, **89–90**
    profiles, **91**

B

B2B (business-to-business), 17–18
B2C (business-to-company), 17–18
backing up profiles, **98**, *99*

Behance Creative Portfolio Display
    app, **248**
BeKnown app, 8
Best Answer
    experts, 222
    marketing by, **267–268**, *268*
    ranking, 64
big groups
    joining, **191–192**
    recruiters, **317–318**
biographies, mobile, **309–310**
Bitly.com link, 210
Blackberry apps, 294
blacklists, 63
Blind Date effect, **308**
Blog Link app, **243–244**
blogs
    Answers for, **225–226**, *226*
    scheduling, **268**
Blue, Allen, 5
Board Source group, 336
Boole, George, 140
Boolean logic
    Advanced People Search, **140**
    competition searches, 171
Box.net application, **237–240**, *238–240*
bragging, 326–327
BranchOut app, 8
branding
    companies. *See* company profiles
    personal, **306**
    real estate professionals, **332**
Breckenridge, Bryan, 333
brick-and-mortar businesses, **19**
BridgeStar group, 336
Brodin, Kendra, 321–322
browser edit function, 98
BufferApp app
    post scheduling, **300–301**
    update scheduling, 257–258
Burg, Bob, 144
Business Account, 9
business focus, 8
business-to-business (B2B), 17–18
business-to-company (B2C), 17–18
businesses. *See* companies

C

calendars
: campaign-specific status updates, 258, *259*
: goal-related status updates, 257, *257*
: Schmoozing Calendar, 187

calls to action for events, 231

campaigns
: goals, 55
: status updates, **257–258**, *259*

candidates in Signal, 262

capitalization, 82

CardMunch app, 20, 137, *137*, **297**

Careers tab, 123

CDPE (Certified Distressed Property Experts) group, 331

certifications in profiles, **90**

Certified Developer's Program, 21

Certified Distressed Property Experts (CDPE) group, 331

Change Your Profile Photo And Visibility option, 52

checklists, **272**
: every day actions, **278–282**
: monthly, daily, and weekly actions, **272–278**

ChromeIn tool, 292

Chronicle of Philanthropy group, 333

Cinco de LinkedIn, *5*

classmates for invitations, 151–152, *152*

click-throughs, **62**

clients
: confidentiality, **323**
: Signal, **262**

Close Your Account link, 54

Cloze service, **300**

coaches, searching for, **142**

colleagues for invitations, 151–152, *152*

Colleagues tab, 152

comments on updates, **64**

communications, ethical considerations for, **324**

companies, **17–19**
: document gathering, **26–27**
: following, **125–126**, *125*

groups, **186**
: new accounts, **30–31**, *31*
: page follows, 62
: recruiter information, **317**
: Signal mentions, **262–263**
: in Title fields, 77

Companies link, 52

Companies tab, **43**, 115

Companies You May Want To Follow section, 37

Company Pages Admins section, 108

company profiles, **16–17**
: administrators, **108–109**, *109*
: analytics
:: other companies, **126–128**, *127*
:: your company, **121–123**, *122*
: checklists, **277–278**
: descriptions, **104–108**, *105–108*, **110–111**, *110–111*
: disclaimers and employee promotion, **112–113**, *113*
: editing and revising, **109**
: following companies, **125–126**, *125*
: job postings, **123–124**, *123*, 126
: names, **103–104**, *104*
: offers, **111–112**, *112*
: photos and specialties, **110–111**, *110–111*
: starting, **102–103**, *103*
: targeted product and service pages, **115–117**, *116–118*
: targeted updates, **118–121**, *119–120*
: videos and recommendations, **113–115**, *114–115*

comparables, 190

competition
: monitoring, **170–171**
: Signal mentions, 262

complaints, 263

compliments, 262

CompUSA study, 114

confidentiality, **323**

congregants with Signal, 262

Connect: Professional Women's Network, 331

Connected HQ app, 20, **298–299**, *299*

Connecticut Audubon Society, 335

Connection Timeline, 291
connections
    email, **134–136**, *134–135*
    inbound marketing strategies, **263–267**, *266*
    introductions, 147
    monitoring, **167–168**, *167*
    setup, **31–32**, *32*
    statistics, **59–61**, *59–60*
    tagging, **155–158**, *156–157*
Connections option, 39
constituents with Signal, 262
Consultants Network group, 318
contact information
    profiles, 97
    sharing, 316
Contact Me section, **92–94**, *93*
contacts
    imported, **39**, *40*
    strategic. *See* strategic contacts
    templates, **145**
Contacts tab, **39**, *40*, 66
contractors, 268
Corliss, Rebecca, 193, *194*
cost-per-click (CPC) billing, 286
cost-per-thousand-impressions (CPM) billing, 286
costs
    ads, **288**
    job postings, 124
courses in profiles, **91**
CPC (cost-per-click) billing, 286
CPM (cost-per-thousand-impressions) billing, 286
Create A Company button, 103
Create A Feed box, 214
Create A Group link, 202, *203*
Create A Profile Badge option, 49
Create An Event button, 227
Create New Audience button, 116
Creative Portfolio Display app, **248**
credit for women, **329–330**
criteria for goals, **57–66**, *59–61*, *65*
CSV files for email lists, 132–135

Customer Relationship Management (CRM) tools, 20–21
    for comments, 261–262
    Connected HQ, **298–299**, *299*
    JibberJobber, 299
    Rapportive, **299**
Customer Service link, 287
customers in Signal, **262**
Customize The Updates You See On Your Home Page option, 52
Customize Your Public Profile link, 47–48, *49*
customizing
    awards, **89–90**
    education, **85–88**, *86*
    groups and associations, **88–89**, *89*
    profiles, 47–48, *49*
    websites, **84–85**, *85*

D

daily checklists, **272–278**
Daily Digest email, 184
Daily Practices Master worksheet, 264
Daniels, David, 266, 285, 287
dates attended in schooling, 87
Decline template, **213**
Decline And Block template, **213**
degrees, 87
Demographics tab, **216–217**
Description section, **79–80**
descriptions
    company profiles, **104–108**, *105–108*, **110–111**, *110–111*
    events, **228–229**
    groups, 204–205, 211
    in Title fields, **79–80**
Diamond, Ava, 327, 337
Dictionary.com for keywords, **72**
disclaimers
    company profiles, **112–113**, *113*
    ethical considerations, **325**
discovering keywords, **70–71**, *71*
discussions for groups, **187–188**, *188*
Doran, George, 55
Download As A PDF link, 72
DropIn game, 291

E

E-Bookshelf app, **246–247**, *247*
Ecademy site, 8
edit function in browsers, 98
Edit Profile section, 38
Edit Your Public Profile link, 47
editing
    company profiles, **109**
    events, 230, *230*
education, customizing, **85–88**, *86*
elevator pitches, 310
email
    company addresses, 104
    connecting with, **134–136**, *134–135*
    groups, 184, **205**
    hacks, **319**
    individual invitations, **136–138**, *136–137*
    new accounts, **29–31**, *31*
    preferences, **49–51**, *50*
    for reports, **168–170**, *169–170*
    signatures, **294–295**, *295*
Email And Password option, 54
email lists
    cleaning up, **132–134**
    importing, **133–134**, *133*
Email Marketing: An Hour a Day, 266, 285, 287
eMarketing group, 318
employees
    hiring, 268
    promotion, **112–113**, *113*
employers, researching, **307**
end-user agreement (EUA), 11
Endless Referrals, 144
Enter Email Addresses option, 136
entrepreneurs, **310**
    Amazon reading list, **312–313**
    keywords, **310–311**, *311*
    paid accounts, **314**
    SlideShare, **313–314**
    subgroups, **312**
ethical considerations, **324–326**
etiquette, InMail, **153–154**
EUA (end-user agreement), 11
Evans, Dale, 7

events
    checklists, **275–276**
    messages for, **231–233**, *232*
    from others, **234–235**, *235*
    profile sharing for, **233–234**, *234*
    setting up, **227–231**, *228–230*
    sharing, **231–232**
    status updates, 258
Excel spreadsheets for email lists, 132
Executive LinkedIn Profile Questionnaire, **28**, 70, 73
Executive Suite group, 318
experience in profiles, **95**, *96*
expert designation in Answers, **64**
Expertise Request option, 319
experts
    Best Answers, **267**, *268*
    identifying, **226–227**, *227*

F

face to face (F2F) meetings, 252
Facebook
    business use of, 8
    for events, 229–231
Facebook Marketing: All-in-One for Dummies, 123, 284
Fairall, Brett, 304, **307–310**
favors, 223
feedback
    groups, 214
    polls, 249–250
feeds, RSS, **213–214**, *214*
Field Of Study field, 87
fill-in-the-blank updates, 121
Fill the Funnel blog, 310
Find Jobs link, 41
finding. *See* searches
first-level contacts, **39**
    CRM systems for, 20
    employees, 123
    hiding, 46
    industries and locations, 66
    messages, 43, **143–144**
    statistics, 60, 164
flagging spammers, 196, *197*
folders for profiles, 159–160

Follow Company tool, 125
follower statistics, 119–120, *120*
following
    companies, **125–126**, *125*
    group members, **200**
free accounts, 9
Fricke, Victoria, 329
Friday tasks, **281–282**
FT Press, E-Bookshelf app by, **246–247**, *247*
Function tab for Group Statistics, **217**
future of LinkedIn, **19–23**

G

Garner, Rob, 68
geographic region, searching by, 165
Get Introduced Through A Connection
        link, 147
Get LinkedIn Content In An RSS Feed link,
        54
Get More Applications option, **235–237**,
        236
ghost posting, **325**
Gill, Libby, 333
GitHub app, **244**
goals
    defining and creating, **55–58**
    metrics, **57–66**, *59–61*, *65*
    status updates, **256–257**, *257*
Google Alerts, 171
Google keyword tools
    AdWords, **70–71**, *71*
    entrepreneurs, **310–311**, *311*
Google searches
    search engine optimization, **64**, *65*
    for yourself, **27–28**
Google toolbar, **296**
grading tools, **301**, *301*
grammar issues, 28, 82
Group Join Link, 210
Group Profile page, 191
Group Rules link, 193, 208
Group Statistics section, 191
groups
    access, **205**, *205*
    announcements, **214–215**, *215*
    big, **191–192**, *317–318*

checklists, **274**
customizing, **88–89**, *89*
descriptions, **204–205**, 211
discussions, **187–188**, *188*
email, 205
finding, **182–185**, *183–184*
growth and interaction, **64**
importance, **180–182**, *180*
inviting members, **210–211**
job seekers, 305
jobs, **190**
joining, **186–187**
languages, **206–208**
limits, 185
management teams, **206–208**, *207*
Members and Search links, **190**
messages, **144**
moderating submissions, **209–210**, *209*
More tab, **190–191**
names and setup, **202–203**
nonprofits, 333, **335–336**
open and members-only, **181–182**
order, **197–198**, *198*
polls, **188–189**, *189*, 208
promotions, 189, 196, 208
real estate professionals, 331
recruiters, **317–318**
reverse engineering, **201–202**, *201*
RSS feeds, **213–214**, *214*
rules, 193, *194*, **206–208**, *207*, *209*
skills-related, 254
spam management, **196–197**, *197*
statistics, 191, **216–218**, *216*
strategic contacts, **198–200**, *199–200*
templates, **211–213**, *212*
types, **204**
websites, 205
Groups, Companies, And Applications link,
        51
Groups directory listing, 206
Groups tab, **39–41**, *41*, 184, 202
Groups You May Like feature, 37, 41, 180
growth
    groups, **64**, **217–218**
    LinkedIn, 5, **9–10**
Growth tab, **217–218**
Guericke, Konstantin, 5

H

Hachi app, **299–300**
Halligan, Brian, 3
Halpert, Marc W., 335
Hanks, Brad, 331–333
Helpful Links section, **47–49**, *48–49*
Here on Biz app, **297–298**, *298*
Hero Connect Veterans feature, 290
Hide RSS With No Activity option, 188
high-traffic keywords, **310–311**, *311*
hiring managers, **316–321**
Hoffman, Reid, 5–6
home page
    features, **33–37**, *34, 36–37*
    menu bar, **38–44**, *38, 40–43*
    monitoring networks, **165–167**, *166*
    People You May Know feature, **148–151**,
        149–150
Home tab for Answers, 220
honors in profiles, **91**
Hootsuite.com tool, *257–258*, **300**
HubSpot company profile, 106–108, *107*

I

I Don't Know (IDK) response, 130, 148,
    150
I Recommend This Book link, 248
iContacts, importing, **133–134**, *133*
IDK (I Don't Know) response, 130, 148,
    150
I'll Accept Introductions And InMail
    option, 93
I'm On LinkedIn, Now What???, 163, 221,
    304
Import Your Desktop Email Contacts
    option, 133
Import Your Resume tool, 75
Imported Contacts option, 39
importing email lists, **133–134**, *133*
Inbound Marketers for Marketing
    Professionals group, 193
inbound marketing, **3–4**
    connections strategy, **263–267**, *266*
    updates, **256–258**, *257, 259*

*Inbound Marketing: Get Found Using
    Google, Social Media, and Blogs*, 3
Inbound Marketing Certified Professionals
    group, 182
Inbound Marketing University program,
    182
inbox
    activity and sentiment, **63**
    People You May Know feature, **151**
Inbox tab, **42–43**, *43*
incomplete profiles, 26
individual invitations, **136–138**, *136–137*
industries
    groups, **186**
    networks, 66
    in Title fields, **77**
industry-based apps, **244**
    Amazon Reading List, **248–249**, *249*
    Creative Portfolio Display, **248**
    E-Bookshelf, **246–247**, *247*
    JD Supra Legal Updates, **245–246**, *246*
    Lawyer Ratings, **246**
    My Travel, **251–253**, *252*
    polls, **249–251**, *251*
    Real Estate Pro, **247**
    Skills feature, **253–254**
Infinity visualization, 292
Influencers
    connecting to, 123
    events, 233
    and groups, 180, 195
    keywords, 72
    names, 84
    searching for, 71–72
    Signal, **261–262**
initial settings
    account management, **52–54**, *53*
    appropriate, **54–55**
    email preferences, **49–51**, *50*
    Helpful Links, **47–49**, *48–49*
    privacy controls, **46–47**
    profile, **44–45**, *45*
InMail
    company profiles, 126
    etiquette, **153–154**
    LinkedIn Analytics, 291
    strategic contacts, **145–146**

Insights tab, 126–128, *127*
interaction in groups, 64
interests, optimizing, 83
introductions
 asking for, **145**
 obtaining, **146–148**, *147*
Introrocket.com tool, **315**
invitations
 colleagues and classmates, **151–152**, *152*
 group members, **210–211**
 home page suggestions, **148–151**, *149–150*
 Inbox suggestions, **151**
 individual, **136–138**, *136–137*
 job seeking, **306**
 pending, 42, *43*
 strategic members, **198–199**
Invitations tab, 42, *43*
iPad app, **292–294**, *293*
iPhone apps
 CardMunch, 20, 137, *137*, **297**
 Here on Biz, **297–298**, *298*
 LinkedIn access, 294
IRS 990 Form, **334**

J

JD Supra Legal Updates app, **245–246**, *246*, 322–324
JibberJobber tool, 304, 307
 description, **162–163**
 obtaining, **299**
Job Discussions, 190
Job Seeker Premium account, **41–42**
jobs and job seekers, **304**
 Alba tips, **304–307**
 Fairall tips, **307–310**
 groups, **190**
 job board, 305
 Linked HR group, 192
 postings, **123–124**, *123*, 126, 190
Jobs group, 318
Jobs tab, **41**, *42*, 123
Jobs You Might Be Interested In section, 37
joining groups, **186–187**
Just Joined LinkedIn section, 35

K

Kanter, Beth, 333–334
key people, sharing events with, **231–233**, *232*
keyword lists, **68**
 making, **72–73**
 related skills, **68–70**, *69*
 searches, 171
Keyword Tool link, 70
keywords
 Advanced People Search, 140
 company profiles, 105
 Dictionary.com and Thesaurus.com, 72
 discovering, **70–71**, *71*
 entrepreneurs, **310–311**, *311*
 events, 228–229
 goals, 257
 names as, 84
 paid accounts, 314
 People search, **71–72**
 Signal mentions, 63
 Specialties field, 81
 Title fields, 80
Khare, Phyllis, 123, 284
Klout grading tool, 301, *301*
Kred grading tool, 301

L

labs, **289–292**, *291*
LamB networks, **130–131**
languages, 16
 company profiles, 107–108, *108*
 groups, **206–208**
 profiles, *54*, **91**
 search by, 41, 71, 139
large corporations, **18**
Latest Discussions view, 187
Latka, Nathan, 121
Law And Legal link, 226
Lawyer Ratings app, **246**
leads, 61, 221
Learning Center, 44
legal professionals, **321–326**
Legal Updates app, **245–246**, *246*, 322–324

lighting
    photos, 327–328
    videos, 329
likes on updates, **64**
Linked HR group, 192, 318
Linked into Law, 321
LinkedIn ads. *See* ads
LinkedIn All Updates section, 35
LinkedIn Answers. *See* Answers
LinkedIn for Good tool, 333
LinkedIn Home tab, **38**
LinkedIn overview, **4–5**
    businesses, **17–19**
    future, **19–23**
    growth and visibility, **9–10**
    history, 5–7
    network and advanced search, **11**
    profile types, **11–17**, *13*, *15*
    rise of, **8–10**
    as social network, **7–8**
    uses, **11**
LinkedIn Signal. *See* Signal tool
LinkedIn Today, 294
    articles, 43, **62**
    home page, 35
LinkedInLabs.com, **289–292**, *291*
LinkedStrategies groups, 208
LION networks, **130–131**
lists for Signal, **260**
Little Ol' Me syndrome, **326–327**
local groups
    joining, **186**
    recruiters, **317–318**
location
    networks, 66
    new accounts, **30–31**, *31*
    in Title fields, 77–78
location-based groups, 206
logos
    groups, **202**
    LinkedIn, 33
Lotus Notes widget, **296**, *297*
low-competition keywords, **310–311**, *311*
Lurssen, Adrian, 326
Ly, Eric, *5*

M

Mac search widget, **296**
Macomber, Laurie, 2–3, 131
Make A Recommendation box, 174
Manage Advertising Preferences section, **52**
Manage Security Settings link, 54
Manage Settings For LinkedIn Plugins On
    Third Party Sites option, 52
Manage tab for groups, 211
Manage your ads link, 285
Manage Your Recommendations link, 49
management teams and rules for groups,
    206–208, *207*
managers
    group, **193–194**
    promoting, **207**
Manymoon company, 242
marketing
    assets and materials
        compiling, **27**
        identifying, **225**
    inbound, **3–4**
    LinkedIn. *See* LinkedIn overview
Marketing Solutions, 225, 284–285
Martin, Alan, 253
Martindale-Hubbell Lawyer Ratings app,
    246
Mayaud, Christian, 130
McMeekin, Gail, 327
measurable criteria for goals, 57
Members links for groups, 190
members-only groups, **181–182**
Members Only page, 184
mentions on Signal, **262–263**
mentors, searching for, **142**
menu bar, 38, *38*
    Companies tab, **43**
    Contacts tab, **39**, *40*
    Groups tab, **39–41**, *41*
    Inbox tab, **42–43**, *43*
    Jobs tab, **41**, *42*
    LinkedIn Home tab, **38–39**
    More tab, **44**
    News tab, **43–44**
messages
    for events, **231–233**, *232*

first-level contacts, **143–144**
group members, **144**
inbound marketing
  crafting, **264–265**
  sending, **265–267**, *266*
  worksheets, **264**
InMail, **145–146**
strategic members, **198–199**
metrics for goals, 57
MLT Creative profile, 106, 111, *111*, 117, *118*
Mobbios tool, **309–310**
mobile biographies, **309–310**
mobile devices, **292–294**, *293*
MOCHA Veterans tool, 290
moderating groups, 194, **209–210**, *209*
Moderation Queue option, 207, 210
Monday tasks, **278–279**
monitoring lists, **260**
monitoring networks
  competition, **170–171**
  connections, **167–168**, *167*
  home page, **165–167**, *166*
  Network Statistics link, **164–165**, *164*
  reports, **168–170**, *169–170*
monthly checklists, **272–278**
More tab
  Answers, 220, 267
  events, 227
  groups, 184, **190–191**
  options, **44**
  polls, 250
  Reading List, 248
  skills, 68, 70
  travel tips, 253
Moss, Dennis, 330
moving sections, **96–98**, *97*
Mullen, Jeanniey, 266, 285, 287
multifield search engine, **10**
My Q&A tab, 222
My Travel app, **251–253**, *252*

N

names
  companies, **103–104**, *104*
  groups, **202–203**

home page, 33
as keywords, 84
new accounts, **30–31**, *31*
school, 87
Network Statistics feature
  contacts, 39
  total connections, **59–60**, *59*
  working with, **164–165**, *164*
networks, **129**
  checklists, **273**
  connections, tagging, **155–158**, *156–157*
  email
    connecting with, **134–136**, *134–135*
    individual invitations, **136–138**, *136–137*
  email lists
    cleanup, **132–133**
    importing, **133–134**, *133*
  groups. *See* groups
  JibberJobber tool, **162–163**
  job seeking, 308
  LION vs. LamB, **130–131**
  monitoring. *See* monitoring networks
  organizing by PDFs, **160–161**, *160*
  Outlook Social Connector, **161–162**
  People You May Know. *See* People You May Know feature
  Profile Organizer, **158–160**, *159*
  recommendations, **172–177**, *172, 175, 177*
  Salesforce app, **163**
  search, **11**
  strategic contacts. *See* strategic contacts
  Xobni, **162**
new connection statistics, **60–61**, *60*
New People link, 60
NewIn Pure Energy app, 292
News tab, **43–44**
newsfeeds for groups, 213
non-LinkedIn testimonials, **177**
Nonprofit Solutions, 333
nonprofits, **333–336**
NOT operator
  Advanced People Search, **140**
  competition searches, 171

O

offers in company profiles, **111–112**, *112*
offsite privacy option, 52
Only Share This Question With
    Connections I Select option, 222
open groups, **181–182**
open networkers, 130–131
OpenLink paid accounts, 314
opportunities, **262**
Opportunity Preferences section, 93
optimizing time, checklists for, 272
    every day actions, **278–282**
    monthly, daily, and weekly actions,
      272–278
OR operator
    Advanced People Search, **140**
    competition searches, 171
order of groups, **197–198**, *198*
organization profiles, **91**, **160–161**, *160*
Outlook email, importing, **133–134**, *133*
Outlook Social Connector, **161–162**, **296**
Overview page for company profiles, 105,
    108, 118
owners of groups, **193–194**

P

page statistics, 121–122, *122*
paid accounts, **314**, **316–317**, **336**
paid management tools, **162–163**
Palm apps, 294
parentheses () in searches, 140
Partner InMails, 49
passwords
    best practices, **29–30**
    changing, 54
patents, **91–92**
PDFs
    downloading profiles, 72
    organizing by, **160–161**, *160*
    strategic contacts, 142–143
PeerIndex grading tool, 301
People search, **71–72**
People You May Know feature
    colleagues and classmates, **151–152**, *152*
    contacting, **146**

home page, **35–36**, *36*, **148–151**, *149–150*
    Inbox suggestions, **151**
    InMail etiquette, **153–154**
people you should know, **154–155**, *154*
personal branding, **306**
personal notes in invitations, 149
Personal Relationship Manager (PRM), 307
personalizing public profiles, **84–85**, *85*
photos
    profiles, 46, **110–111**, *110–111*
    women, **327–328**
physical events, 228
planning status updates
    campaign-specific, **257–258**, *259*
    goal-related, **256–257**, *257*
polls
    checklists, **276**
    groups, **188–189**, *189*, 208
    industry-based, **249–251**, *251*
Porterfield, Amy, 123, 284
Portfolio Widget, 242
positions in Title fields, 76
Post A Job button, 123
Post A Promotion link, 189
posts
    ghost, **325**
    jobs, **123–124**, *123*, 126, 190
potential employers, researching, **307**
potential strategic contacts, **142–143**
preparation, 26
    business documents, **26–27**
    Executive LinkedIn Profile
      Questionnaire, **28**
    marketing materials, **27**
    résumé, **26**
    web references, **27–28**
privacy control settings, **46–47**
private profiles, 14
PRM (Personal Relationship Manager), 307
proactively job seeking, **304–305**
Prodromou, Ted, 289
product mentions in Signal, **262**
Products & Services tab, **110–112**, *111*,
    115, *116*
Professional Experience and Goals, **81–82**
Professional Headline section, **73–75**, *74*
professional profiles, **13–14**, *13*

Profile And Recommendation settings, 53
Profile Organizer tool, 21
   accessing, 38–39
   paid accounts, 314
   working with, **158–160**, *159*
Profile tab, 38–39
profiles, **11–13**
   awards, **89–91**
   backing up, **98**, *99*
   business, **16**
   checklists, **273**
   company. *See* company profiles
   Contact Me section, **92–94**, *93*
   education, **85–88**, *86*
   groups and associations, **88–89**, *89*
   incomplete, 26
   interests, **83**
   job seeking, 304
   personalizing, **84–85**, *85*
   professional, **13–14**, *13*
   Professional Experience and Goals, 81–82
   Professional Headline, **73–75**, *74*
   public, **14**, *15*
   rules of engagement, **94**, *95*
   saving, **160**, *160*
   sections
     adding, **90–92**, *90*
     moving, **96–98**, *97*
   settings, **44–45**, *45*
   sharing, **233–234**, *234*
   sharing contact information on, 316
   skills and experience, **95**, *96*
   specialties, **81**
   Summary elements, **82**
   Title fields, **75–80**
   views, **61**, *61*
Projects and Teamspaces application, **242–243**, *243*
Projects section in profiles, **91**
promoting managers, 207
promotions
   company profiles, **112–113**, *113*
   groups, 189, 196, 208
public profiles
   personalizing, **84–85**, *85*
   working with, **14**, *15*

publications in profiles, **92**

Q

qualitative goal measurements, **62–66**, *65*
quantitative goal measurements, **59–62**, *59–61*
questionnaires, **28**, 70, 73
Questions & Answers option, 53
Questions tab, 224
quick response (QR) codes, 309
quotation marks (") in searches, 140

R

Rapportive app, **299**
Reading List app, **248–249**, *249*, 312–313
Real Estate Pro app, **247**
real estate professionals, 247, **331–333**
realistic goals, 58
recommendations, 172
   asking for, **173–174**
   company profiles, **113–115**, *115*
   evaluating, **66**
   finding, **172**, *172*
   giving, **174–716**, *175*
   job seeking, **308–309**
   managing, **176–177**, *177*
   template, **173**
   testimonials, **177**
   women, 330
Recommendations link, 38
Recruiter accounts, 9
recruiter tips, **316–321**
related skills
   keyword lists, **68–70**, *69*
   profiles, **95**
relationships
   Answers for, **222–224**, *223*
   traditional marketing, 4
Remove Connections link, 39
reordering groups, **197–198**, *198*
replying privately to questions, **223**, *223*
reports, **168–170**, *169–170*
repurposing SME materials, **224**
Request A Replacement option, 176
Request Recommendations tab, 173

Request To Join option, 205, 207
Request To Join template, 211
requests for business, **63**
researching potential employers, **307**
responding to searches, **260–261**, *261*
Resume Builder tool, 292
résumés, **26**
reverse engineering groups, **201–202**, *201*
RoboForm tool, 30
Rofo's Real Estate Pro app, 247
RSS feeds, **213–214**, *214*
rules for groups, **193–196**, *194*, **206–208**, *207*, *209*
rules of engagement in profiles, **94**, *95*

S

Salesforce app, **163**
samples for polls, 250
Save As Text Only option, 70
Saved Articles option, 43
saved searches, 170–171
saving profiles, 160, *160*
Schaffer, Neal, 130
scheduling
    blogs, **268**
    posts, **300–301**
    updates, *257–258*
Schmoozing Calendar, 187
school names, **87**
Search and Social: The Complete Guide to Real-Time Marketing, 68
search box on home page, **33**
search engines
    multifield, **10**
    SEO, **64**, *65*
searches
    Advanced People Search, **138–141**, *138–139*
    for events, 235, *235*
    by geographic region, 165
    groups, **182–185**, *183–184*, **190**
    Mac, **296**
    paid accounts, 314
    recommendations, **172**, *172*
    responding to, **260–261**, *261*
    results, **61–62**

saved, 170–171
strategic contacts, **198–200**, *199–200*
second-level contacts, 39, 60, 164
sections in profiles
    adding, **90–92**, *90*
    moving, **96–98**, *97*
See All Activity link, 227
See All My Answers link, 226, 267
See More link, 149
See Q&A link, 267
See Who You Already Know On LinkedIn option, 151
Select All option for messages, 266
Select From Your Connections List link, 174
Select What Others See When You View Their Profile link, 46
Select Who Can See Your Connections link, 46
Select Your Language link, 54
self-employed people, profiles for, 106
self-promotion by women, 327
self-service ads, 285, 289
Send An Announcement tool, 214–215
Send Invitations link, 210
Send Message option, 266
Send To Individuals option, 206
Sent Recommendations page, 174, 176
sentiment of interactions, **63**
SEO (search engine optimization), **64**, *65*
Sequoia Capital, 5
service mentions in Signal, **262**
service pages, **115–117**, *116–118*
Set The Frequency Of Emails setting, 50
Set The Frequency Of Group Digest Emails setting, 51
setup
    events, **227–231**, *228–230*
    groups, **202–203**
    reports, **168–170**, *169=170*
Share an Update status, 35
Share Group link, 193, 210
Share On LinkedIn link, 206
sharing
    connections for introductions, 147
    contact information, **316**
    events, **231**
    profiles, **233–234**, *234*

questions, 224
by real estate professionals, **332**
Sharing bookmarklet, 231, 251, **296**
Shaw, Dharmesh, 3
Show All RSS Discussions option, 188
Show Profile Photos Of Other Members
option, 52
Show Updates option, 53
Signal tool, 22, 259, 292
clients and customers, **262**
company mentions, **262**
Influencers, **261–262**
keyword mentions, **63**
lists for, **260**
responding to searches, **260–261**, *261*
searches, 171
signatures
email, **294–295**, *295*
messages, 265
Sitecore ads, **289**
skills
keyword lists, **68–70**, *69*
profiles, 95, *96*, **253–254**
Skills & Experience link, 68
Skills feature, **253–254**
Skills option, 44
SlideShare application, 22
entrepreneurs, **313–314**
working with, **240–242**, *241*
small corporations, 18
SMART (specific, measurable, attainable,
realistic, and timely) acronym, 55
smart phones, **294**
SME materials, repurposing, **224**
social marketing, 2–3
inbound, 3–4
connections strategy, **263–267**, *266*
updates, **256–258**, *257*, *259*
LinkedIn. *See* LinkedIn overview
Social Media for Nonprofit Organizations
group, 336
Social Media Marketing: An Hour a Day, 7
societies, **88**
solicitation considerations, **324–325**
spam in groups, **196–197**, *197*
special offers in company profiles, **112**, *112*
specialization by legal professionals, **322**

specialties in profiles, **81**, 106, **110–111**,
110–111
specificity of goals, **56–57**
SpeechIn feature, 290
spelling issues, 28, 82, 84
spreadsheets for email lists, 132
staff changes, tracking, **125–126**
Start A Discussion link, 213
state ethics rules, **325**
statistics
connections and contacts, **59–61**, *59–60*,
164
follower, **119–120**, *120*
groups, 191, **216–218**, *216*
LinkedIn membership, **6–7**
travel, 253
status updates
campaign-specific, **257–258**, *259*
company profiles, **118–121**, *119–120*,
126
goal-related, **256–257**, *257*
Stengel, Geri, **334–335**
Stengel Solutions, 334
Stevens Institute of Technology display ads,
288–289
stories in job seeking, **308**
strategic contacts, **138–141**, *138–139*
first-level. *See* first-level contacts
groups, **144**, **198–200**, *199–200*
InMail, **145–146**
introductions
asking for, **145**
obtaining, **146–148**, *147*
listing, **141–142**
people you don't know, **146**
potential, **142–143**
strategic networkers, **130–131**
style sheets, 27
subgroups, 190
creating, 208
description, 182
entrepreneurs, **312**
Subgroups tab, 208
subject lines in messages, 266
submissions, moderating, **209–210**, *209*
Submissions Queue link, 209
Success Stories, 284

Summary section
  elements, **82**
  Group Statistics, 216, *216*
  groups, *203*, **204**
  Professional Experience and Goals,
    81–82
  Specialties field, 81
Swarm visualization, 291

T

tagging connections, **155–158**, *156–157*
targeted products, **115–117**, *116–118*
targeted updates, **118–121**, *119–120*
templates
  contacts, **145**
  groups, **211–213**, *212*
  introductions, **148**
  invitations, 151
  recommendations, **173**
  recruiters, **318–319**
  thank-you letters, 170
test scores in profiles, **92**
testimonials
  ethical considerations, **325**
  non-LinkedIn, **177**
TextIn feature, 290
thank-you letter template, 170
Thesaurus.com for keywords, **72**
third-level contacts, 60, 164
third-party applications, **21**
  BufferApp, **300–301**
  CardMunch, 137, *137*, **297**
  Cloze, **300**
  Connected HQ, **298–299**, *299*
  grading tools, **301**, *301*
  Hachi, **299–300**
  Here on Biz, **297–298**
  Hootsuite, **300**
  industry-based. *See* industry-based apps
  JibberJobber, **299**
  Rapportive, **299**
This Is a Virtual Event option, 228
This Week's Top Experts feature, 220
3 and 3 technique, **268–270**
Thursday tasks, **281**

time optimization, checklists for, **272**
  every day actions, **278–282**
  monthly, daily, and weekly actions,
    272–278
TimeDriver.com, 112
timeliness of goals, **58**
TimeTrade account, **315**
titles
  events, 228
  job postings, 124
  Title fields, **75–80**
Tools And Analysis page, 70
Top Experts, 267
top searched keywords in paid accounts,
  314
Top Supporters list, 154–155, *154*
TopLinked.com site, 154–155, *154*
TopLinked group, 191
total connections statistics, **59–60**, *59*
traditional marketing, **3–4**
travel plans, **251–253**, *252*
TripIt.com, 251–253
Tuesday tasks, **279–280**
Turn On/Off Your Activity Broadcasts
  link, 46
Tweets application, 22
12 Secrets of Highly Successful Women, 327
Twitter, 8, 229–230

U

umbrella goals, 55
unfollowing
  companies, 125
  people, **191**, 200–201
updates
  campaign-specific status, **257–258**, *259*
  checklists, **273–274**
  company profiles, **118–121**, *119–120*,
    126
  for events, 231
  goal-related status, **256–257**, *257*
  groups, 190
  inbound marketing, **256–258**, *257*, *259*
  likes and comments on, **64**
Upgrade Your Account link, 54
URL shorteners, 118, 210

V

VA (virtual assistant), 243, 272
Vahl, Andrea, 123, 284
Vaillant, Jean-Luc, 5
Vaughan, Pamela, 107
vendors, searching for, **142**
Ventureneer, 334
Veterans feature, 290
videos, 22
    company profiles, **113–115**, *114*
    SlideShare, **240–242**, *241*
    by women, **328–329**
View Companies You're Following link, 52
View More Related Words link, 72
View Profile section, 38
View Your Groups option, 51
Viewers Of This Profile Also Viewed box, 47
virtual assistant (VA), 243, 272
virtual events, 228
visibility, **9**
Volunteer Experience & Causes section, 92
von Rosen, Viveka, 321

W

Web 2.0, **3**
web addresses, 294
web references, listing, **27–28**
Webb, Susan Somerset, 327
websites
    click-throughs, **62**
    customizing, **84–85**, *85*
    groups, **205**
    Title fields, 77
Wednesday tasks, **280**
weekly checklists, **272–278**
Weekly Digest email, 184
Weiner, Jeff, 6
Welcome Message template, 212, *212*
Wells, Greig, 31
"What" issue in goals, 56
What's Happening view, 187–188
"Where" issue in goals, 57
whitepapers, 287, 289

whitespace in profiles, 82
"Who" issue in goals, 56
Who's Viewed Your Profile feature, 36, 61, 165, *166*, 314
"Why" issue in goals, 56
widget for Lotus Notes, **296**, *297*
WIIFM (What's in It for Me)
    Description section, 79
    events, 228
    groups, 195
    tagging connections, 158
women, **326**
    guidelines, **330–331**
    Little Ol' Me syndrome, **326–327**
    photos, **327–328**
    recommendations, 330
    self-credit, **329–330**
    videos, **328–329**
WordPress app, **243–244**
Worldwide Membership Statistics, **6–7**
WOWsume tool, **309–310**

X

Xobni company, **162**

Y

Year in Review feature, 291
You Unstuck: Mastering the New Rules of Risk-taking in Work and Life, 333
Your Activity for groups, 190
Your Groups link, 40, 198
Your LinkedIn Network box, 36–37
Your Messages tab, 43
Your Settings for groups, 190

Z

Zapar, Stacy Donovan
    competitors, 47
    email addresses, 153, **319**
    groups, 213
    proactivity, 273
    recruiter guidelines, **316–321**
Zoble, Adrienne, 187